VIOLENCE
OF
ACTION

Untold Stories of the
75th Ranger Regiment in the
War on Terror

MARTY SKOVLUND, JR.

with Charles Faint and Leo Jenkins

Foreword by Mat Best

A15 Publishing
PO Box 66054
Hampton, VA 23665
www.A15publishing.com

ISBN 978-0-9989005-0-6

Cover and Page Design - Lorie DeWorken, MINDtheMARGINS LLC

Second Edition

DEDICATION

To the Rangers who made the ultimate sacrifice.
To the wives who will now walk alone.
To the children who will grow up fatherless.
To the parents who will never see their son grow old.
To the families that have an empty seat at the dinner table.
To the nation that lost one of her best.
To the men who must court demons every time they close their eyes.
To the Regiment–past, present and future.
One for the Airborne Ranger in the Sky

"*Violence of Action* is the book about the 75th Ranger Regiment that we've been waiting decades for. While Rangers hit targets night after night throughout the War on Terror, they did it largely in silence and behind the veil of strict Operational Security. While many have written about Special Forces, SEALs, Delta Force and others, almost nothing is out there about the Regiment's unmatched contribution to the fight in Afghanistan and Iraq, until now. *Violence of Action* pulls back the curtain and allows the reader to finally catch a glimpse of the Rangers in bloody combat."

—Jack Murphy
New York Times Best Seller and author of the *Deckard Series*

"As I alternated between chuckling at the humor of the Rangers and gripping the pages with anxiety as I placed myself in their shoes while they fought door to door and leapt rooftop to rooftop, I was blown away by the raw honesty of the book. *Violence of Action* isn't a work about individual accomplishment or chest bumping. Instead, whether in training, in the calm moments before the storm, or in the heat of battle itself, Violence shows us that the driving force behind the excellence of the Regiment is every Ranger's biggest fear - to fail the man next to him."

—Nick Palmisciano
President, Ranger Up

"*Violence of Action* is a book like no other. It is a compilation of incredibly impactful stories from individual accounts among some of America's best and brightest—US Army Rangers. While saturated with gripping stories of brave men fighting America's battles abroad, this book is about love, passion, grief, sorrow and most of all, a brotherhood."

—Kerry Patton
Author of *Contracted: America's Secret Warriors*

"I salute Ranger Marty Skovlund, Jr. for having produced a book that vividly portrays for us the poignant details and ethos of America's finest Warriors

iv

combating the GWoT. This book is a must read for any young man who thinks he may have the desire and ability to become an elite Ranger. It is even more so for any non-commissioned or commissioned officer who aspires to lead Rangers. The matter-of-fact presentations by the Rangers in this book of actual combat leadership situations are lessons that cannot be taught in any school. These stories underscore their incredible heroism, their uncanny super-human feats under fire borne of intense and continuous training and their ultimate dedication to their Ranger Brotherhood to the degree that they offer their lives willingly to protect their Ranger buddies. This magnificent book accurately captures significant historical data and contributes to the developing legend of the elite 75th Ranger Regiment."

— **Gary Dolan**
2011 Ranger Hall of Fame Inductee and author of *Of Their Own Accord*

TABLE OF CONTENTS

Dedication iii

Foreword 1

Preface 4

Introduction 8

Chapter One—2001 14

Chapter Two—2002 23

Chapter Three—2003 29

Chapter Four—2004 97

Chapter Five—2005 122

Chapter Six—2006 155

Photos 184

Chapter Seven—2007 195

Chapter Eight—2008 213

Chapter Nine—2009 226

Chapter Ten—2010 252

Chapter Eleven—2011 326

Epilogue 374

A Word On Transition 376

Acknowledgements 380

Glossary 383

The Ranger Creed 396

About the Author 397

FOREWORD

T he Global War on Terrorism (GWoT) forever changed the way the world views Special Operations Forces (SOF). The 75th Ranger Regiment is a small but essential part of the elite fraternity of quiet professionals in the Special Operations community who selflessly dedicate their lives to protecting our freedoms through service in the profession of arms.

Throughout their history, Rangers' reputation as one of the world's most elite light infantry units is well-earned. In the wars in Afghanistan and Iraq following 9/11, Rangers stepped out of the shadows and took on the role as leader in direct action raids, killing or capturing more high value targets than any other unit, SOF or conventional. With meticulous planning and small teams, the 75th Ranger Regiment has proven effective at removing the enemy with prejudice, whether by land, sea or air.

Although the accomplishments of the 75th Ranger Regiment have rarely been publicly recognized, their exploits deserve to be known. Reader, please know the men recounting their stories in these pages do so not for social or professional recognition (most names have been changed), but rather to honor fellow Ranger brethren and to enlighten the world to the sacrifices required to maintain liberty and democracy across the globe.

In typically assertive Ranger manner, I reach my conclusion quickly: thank you Brothers for your selflessness, your humility and for boldness in telling your stories. While I am thankful for many things in my life, utmost on the list is having served with the men of the 75th Ranger Regiment. I am deeply honored and humbled to write the foreword to this seminal piece of Ranger history.

Godspeed and Rangers Lead The Way.

—Mat Best, Former 2/75 Ranger

In memory of:
Staff Sergeant Ricardo Barraza and Sergeant Dale Brehm

PREFACE

"The more you lose yourself in something bigger than yourself,
the more energy you will have"
NORMAN PEALE

U nlike many who contributed to this book, I was not a great Ranger. From the time I arrived at the 75th Ranger Regiment's 1st Ranger Battalion in the spring of 2006, I did anything but thrive in the intense environment of Ranger life. In fact, it was a daily struggle to simply survive. I scraped and clawed my way through nearly five years and five combat deployments, hoping each day the warriors with whom I shared a Scroll would see fit to let me continue standing in their ranks. The privilege to walk and fight amongst these giants was the highest honor bestowable on any man worthy of the title. I am forever indebted to them for that privilege.

History is lost if it is not recorded. Here I have done my best to prevent that fate from befalling the GWoT Rangers. This book is homage to these men, the history they made and the impact they had. The 75th Ranger Regiment contributed more to the Global War on Terror (GWoT) than most will ever know; this book is only a small glimpse into its contributions. I had three goals in creating this work:

1. Record the impact of the 75th Ranger Regiment in the GWoT
2. Recognize sacrifices made by Rangers over a decade of sustained war
3. Inspire future generations of Rangers

Now, nearly three years after the book's initial release, I believe these goals are realized. I have received reviews both online and in person from people who previously had no idea of the Regiment's crucial involvement and efficacy in the fight against terrorism.

The book has also inspired new Rangers. One soldier wrote me, saying, "Several of my buddies and I are about to go through Ranger selection and have been passing your book around the bay and it's been our favorite read. There aren't many books about Ranger history and hearing stories of the great men before us gives us something to aspire to." In addition, I've heard from current Rangers who were assigned it as mandatory reading as a newly enlisted Private. There are few things more humbling than to know you've made a positive impact on the legend of the unit you once served.

Writing about true events can be a sinister act, as true events involve real people. People that feel real feelings, bleed real blood and weep real tears. I spent hours on the phone discussing the events described; events many have no desire to remember, much less describe in detail. This book does not consist of mere paper and ink; but innumerable sleepless nights, hard liquor and tears. So, in the pursuit of writing *Violence of Action*, I said to these Rangers, "Tell me your story." I might as well have said, "Here, take this dull knife, carve your heart out of your chest and lay it on a plate. Oh, and try not to be too messy about it." But what was the alternative? Let the story fester within the soul forever? Let it die, never to be told; never to be remembered? Which is the worse fate? I'm not sure, but hope I did right by these men and our Regiment. Those whose words you read in these pages poured their hearts and souls into this work.

Now, I want to describe exactly what this book *is* and *is not*. This book is a collection of real stories written by Rangers and men and women supporting those Rangers who were actually there. I collected firsthand information of as many of these events as possible to most accurately record factual accounts of this period of Ranger history.

As with any firsthand account, it is in the eye of the beholder. Anyone who has seen combat knows all involved remembers the same event differently. Although we strive for accuracy, these stories *are not* official After Action Reports (AARs). The Regiment and Pentagon reviewed this book before its release, but neither the 75th Ranger Regiment, the U.S. Army, nor the Department of Defense officially endorses what is written.

This is the work of an entire generation of an elite group within the warrior caste. It is presented in chronological order, covering the period from September 11, 2001 to September 11, 2011. Events happening before or after those dates, while important, are outside its scope. Within this time frame, we did our best to portray both major and minor events and transformations within the Regiment.

These accounts *are not* sugarcoated; they are raw, told without regard for political correctness, romantic notions of combat, or anyone's feelings on what war *should be*. To paint a complete picture, we include vignettes from some who are not Rangers but are very much a part of the Ranger story.

This book is not a political commentary. We do not have an ax to grind and have no intention of expressing our personal feelings on anything outside the scope of the Ranger mission. This book *is not* a description of the selection process to get into the Ranger Regiment. This book *does not* cover the long and storied history of the Ranger lineage. There are great books which go into detail about each.

Finally, this book *is not* a tell-all, an exposé, or "the book the 75th Ranger Regiment does not want you to read." This book is written with paramount attention paid to operational and personnel security. Many who contributed are still out doing the job. With this in mind, all names in all stories are changed with the exception of public figures and those who explicitly granted permission. I include real names of the fallen, to ensure their names live on and their heroic actions are known to history.

This book contains stories told countless times in the barracks room, on the battlefield and at the backyard barbecue, but unknown to the public before its release. As true accounts, they're sometimes critical of both Rangers and members of other units. These accounts *do not* reflect the relationship between the Regiment and these units and men; but are rather simply a recollection of frustrations on particular missions by those who lived through them. It is not my intent to degrade, embarrass or take away from the accomplishments or contributions of anyone. Everyone plays his part and everyone has bad days – I know I certainly have! Still, I keep these critical stories; without them the work is incomplete. Including these deeply personal, controversial vignettes shows that these men are just that – men. Men who volunteered to do extraordinary things.

I knew when starting this book in the fall of 2013 it was a major undertaking, but not until I was months into the project did its gravity hit me. The responsibility to write, collect, organize and portray previously unwritten history is a staggering yet worthwhile burden. When it's the history of men who have sacrificed life, limb and emotion to accomplish great feats, the burden is that much more.

On the night of this book's first release, I and many other Rangers gathered at a local restaurant in Denver to celebrate the launch and do a book signing. Something very special happened though. It wasn't only the contributors to the book that were signing each copy. It was every Ranger present; a testament to this book being bigger than any single one of us. It's the story of every Ranger who has ever served. These sacred stories are chronicles for generations of future warriors; testaments of courage, leadership and sacrifice. I suggest, quite boldly, that you have never read anything like this work and are not likely to ever again.

RLTW,
Marty Skovlund, Jr.

INTRODUCTION

"Wherever the Ranger Battalion goes,

it is apparent that it is the best"

GENERAL CREIGHTON ABRAMS

You can't put your finger on it and you can't quite identify what it is. It is a certain presence that resides permanently around him. He stands straight, the type of posture rarely seen in men today. The posture silently screams self-confidence. The kind of confidence that comes from going out night after night to hunt other men. Men that hunt back. His back is rounded, his shoulders wide. The arms are like leather. The neck thick. A man doesn't get this way by accident. It comes from hours under a ruck, climbing ropes, lifting heavy things, climbing walls and carrying other full-grown men. Running for miles, endless miles. Miles that make feet bleed, soaking white socks red. Miles over road, on gravel, on sand, on dirt, up hills, down hills, upstairs, down stairs…miles that crush a man's soul at the mere thought.

He wears a watch on one wrist, a simple Timex. It is well worn from the hundreds of missions it has seen. The other wrist has a black metal bracelet. It is scratched and beat up, but never leaves the wrist. It bears the name of a fallen brother. The name of a man who left behind a daughter, a wife, parents. The name of a man who he shared a room with, played Halo with after the mission, drank beer with. The name of a man who received nothing but silence in response to the Sergeant Major beckoning him during that final roll call.

His arms are tattooed. They bear the images of skulls, Spartans, a tattered American flag and flames. There is a strange way in which the ink compliments the blank stare on his face. Almost a slight frown, yet a look of deep thought. His hair is longer than the average soldier, but not too long. He's particular when he explains what he wants at the barber, but then again, he is particular about everything in his life.

He pulls his kit out from its cubby in the ready room. It falls over his shoulders in a familiar way. It's weird how easily the distinctive sound of the Velcro on the cummerbund evokes the looming prospect of combat. The Peltor headset goes on, plugged into the radio on his side. He turns them on and turns them up. It just got real loud. The MICH goes on; the NODs are flipped down and tested. He's paranoid, he knows he put fresh batteries in last night, but changes them out again anyway. The amber lenses are dusty, so he takes a red rag and rubs them clear. The helmet is heavy and weighs on a man's neck, but he is used to it—he's spent hours under the weight of Kevlar, night vision, strobes, Velcro and flashlights. He snaps the safety line around his waist pulls his gloves on and slips his Oakleys over his ears. He sighs, then does a few squats to make sure everything is on just right. Finally, he grabs his wrist Garmin and his quarterback forearm pad; one goes on each forearm.

He turns the knob on his MBITR and asks for a radio check. He gets a response and is satisfied. Someone yells out that FMC will be in five minutes. The others start shuffling away from their cubbies. He grabs his rifle, pulls the charging handle back, checking to make sure it is clear, and then releases the bolt. He slides a plastic magazine in and routes the adjustable sling over his shoulder and starts walking for the door. As he walks away, all that heavy gear looks kind of small on his V-shaped torso. He walks with a gait that is swift but quiet.

He floats into the dark, his playground. The air is thin, the moon barely visible. The only sound is the crunch of pea gravel under his hiking boots as he walks away toward the flight line. Half a world away, men of a similar age are drinking, playing beer pong and setting new high scores on video games. But he is boarding a rotary wing aircraft in the hopes of taking a few more souls off this planet during this period of darkness. Few have seen or done what he has and fewer still do it with his ferocity.

He is a Ranger. He is the hammer some nights, the scalpel others. His work is carried out with unprecedented speed, surprise and violence. He does not seek glory, nor recognition of any kind. He lives by a creed, but for his brothers. He is satisfied knowing that he is doing exactly what needs to be done.

The dirt whipped up from the farm field and pelted the back of the Ranger as the twin rotor helicopter which inserted him and his platoon took off. The night was dark, no moon to give their position away. The ground was slightly damp from the rain that fell earlier in the day, which would make for a silent foot movement. It would be a short walk, only 1.6 kilometers to the target building tonight. Another day, another dollar, thought the Ranger to himself.

As he walked, he moved his rifle methodically back and forth while using the weapon's infrared laser to illuminate any dark areas. No talking, just the occasional radio chatter to keep the platoon updated on the progress of the movement. He listened to the packs of dogs that barked far off in the distance, always wondering if they could sense what danger crept through the darkness. The Ranger's squad was on primary assault tonight, meaning they would be the first to initiate the breach into the target building. The platoon settled into a quiet, brisk pace and it didn't take long to cover the distance. Soon, the target building was in sight. The platoon started to break down and move to their predetermined areas, almost as if they had been to this very building a hundred times before. A tall courtyard wall surrounded the target building, which was typical of most of the houses they *hit*. They knew this before even leaving for the mission and were prepared.

Having carried out this same type of mission hundreds of times before, his squad methodically moved forward and quietly placed a ladder against the outer wall and slowly but surely gained entry to the courtyard. The trick to scaling a wall in full kit was remaining silent and undetected. It always surprised the Ranger how much junk was just laying around these courtyards, haphazardly strewn about for what must have been years. For that reason, each step was carefully planted, ensuring no noise before entry. Green IR lasers flooded the front of the house, checking every crevice to make sure they would not be compromised. The building's inhabitants appeared to be asleep, and the squad intended to keep it that way for as long as possible. This was his favorite part, the Ranger thought to himself. The mix of adrenaline and anticipation was intoxicating!

The Ranger moved up to the primary entrance while simultaneously assessing it to determine the appropriate method of breaching. The plan was to explosively breach, but as he took a knee and checked the door, he discovered it was unlocked. *Perfect.* He made the appropriate radio call while he and his team flipped up their night vision devices and prepared to flow into the building. Because the primary breach was unlocked, there was no need to make any noise upon entrance.

3...2...1...the Ranger opened the door and immediately took aggressive steps into the building, wanting to move out of the *fatal funnel* as soon as possible. The lights were all off inside and he made his way through the first room which appeared to be a living area with his team behind. His veins were coursing with adrenaline and his right thumb was firmly planted on the selector switch. *Just give me a reason to flick it down*, he thought. He cut aggressively into the first bedroom while maintaining silence. Two adults, one of which the Ranger assumed was the target, were lying completely asleep in a bed. *They don't even know we're here*, he thought to himself. As the Ranger who flowed into the room with him pulled security on the female, he nudged the sleeping male lightly with his suppressed rifle. *This guy is about to have a bad night*. The male awoke, groggy and not yet realizing the predicament he was in. Then, with eyes suddenly flashing wide he saw the hulking man towering over him with a rifle in his face. Just that quick the Ranger grabbed him by the shirt and violently yanked him out of bed and onto the floor.

By this point the rest of the house had been successfully cleared, only about twenty seconds from initial breach, no sound made and not a single round fired. It was just another night on the job. Not unlike the hundreds of

11

other direct action raids this Ranger had executed in pursuit of high value targets all over Iraq and Afghanistan. This was the *new normal*, and he knew Rangers were becoming frighteningly good at the art of surgically applied violence.

Not every night was a sexy Hollywood firefight. On most Ranger missions, not a shot was fired. Although this book details major operations with furious battles, the raid just described is typical of Ranger missions, especially in Iraq. According to the Regimental website, the 75th Ranger Regiment is a direct-action special operations raid force that conducts forcible entry operations and special operations raids across the entire spectrum of combat. Their official mission is to plan and conduct special missions in support of U.S. policy and objectives.

No other unit in the Department of Defense, whether it be a conventional or special operations force has the range of capabilities that the 75th Ranger Regiment brings to the table. The Regiment's four battalions, geographically dispersed throughout the U.S., can deploy anywhere in the world for no-notice missions in high-risk, uncertain, and politically sensitive areas via land, air or sea. Although the direct action raid is the most commonly utilized capability, the unit is also proficient in and capable of airfield seizures, special reconnaissance, counter-terrorism, personnel and equipment recovery, combat search and rescue and foreign internal defense—and more. The platoon is the most common operating size, but the 75th is unique in its capability of working in elements in size from four-man teams to Regimental operations. This provides the combatant commander a scalable force not found in any other special operations unit; one reason the Regiment has been so gainfully employed since the onset of combat operations after 9/11.

The 75th Ranger Regiment became the workhorse of the Command in the years following 9/11, executing thousands of raids against high value targets every year. Commanders soon found that a Ranger platoon was one of the most effective and efficient tools to use against the most important targets. Because of that newfound confidence from commanders, the Regiment was executing missions that only a few years prior were considered outside their capabilities. It is a common misconception that the Regiment is used primarily to support Special Missions Units by pulling security for them.

Anyone in the know will tell you that is rarely the case. In most instances, Ranger elements work independently, or in some cases side by side in harmony with other Special Mission Units.

Many find it hard to believe that Rangers are working at that level because of their relatively short pipeline to get into the unit compared to other SOF entities. It is hard to explain, but there is something very special about the Regiment. *The Ranger Standard* is a very proud tradition and possibly the best explanation of why the Regiment has come so far. The standard is excellence in any assigned mission and because that is the standard, the Regiment *WILL BE* excellent—they don't know another way. It doesn't matter if the mission is to move to contact through the mountains of Afghanistan or clandestine special reconnaissance in a denied area. If a Ranger is given a mission, then he will not only do it, he will do it better than anyone else would or could.

If a Ranger does not uphold *The Standard,* he is quickly removed from his position. A seasoned Ranger team leader must fight for a squad leader position, a squad leader must fight for a platoon and so on. Rangers are the only special operations unit that will make its leaders go back through selection before moving up to ensure *The Standard* is maintained at all levels. Rangers do not have their own branch like many of our SOF brethren; if a Ranger of any rank is not among the best when performing their job or moving to the next level of responsibility, they are re-assigned to *the big Army* instead of being shuffled to a different position within the organization. It is an extremely competitive environment day in and day out. That competitiveness and pursuit of excellence drives *The Ranger Standard,* which has in turn propelled the Regiment to heights never before seen.

As you read this book, you will have an in-depth look at what the modern Ranger has been up to in the decade following 9/11. This is just a glimpse though, as much remains veiled in secrecy. Nonetheless, I think you will find that the tip of the iceberg that we've exposed in this book is quite amazing.

CHAPTER ONE

"Cry 'Havoc' and let slip the dogs of War."

WILLIAM SHAKESPEARE

On September 11, 2001, radical jihadists fundamentally changed our country. They brought war to America's front door via commercial aircraft rammed into icons of our wealth and power, marking the beginning of a new era for the 75th Ranger Regiment. When the towers fell, it threw the United States military into more than a decade of sustained combat. Rangers didn't know it at the time, but the Regiment would not miss a single day of the coming long War on Terror.

For the 75th Ranger Regiment, the war started immediately. The Regiment took its first casualties on the night of October 19, 2001. Specialist Jonn Edmunds and Private First Class Kristofor Stonesifer of 3rd Ranger Battalion (3/75) were killed when the Black Hawk helicopter they were riding in crashed. On the night of Oct. 19, 2001, A and C Companies of 3/75 conducted a combat parachute jump into Objective Rhino, located southwest of Kandahar, Afghanistan. This marked the official transition from a largely garrison unit that trained for combat to a force to be reckoned with that was now at war. Four MC-130s dropped 199 Rangers from the unusually low elevation of 800 feet above ground level with zero illumination to seize a

14

landing strip for follow-on forces, provide an aerial refueling point and destroy any Taliban forces present. The mission was also planned for a psychological effect on the enemy, proclaiming, "You wanted a fight? Well, here we are!" to those responsible for the terror attack just five weeks prior.

Eleven enemy combatants were reported killed by ordnance dropped from strike aircraft ahead of the combat jump and another nine were reported as fleeing the objective. By the time Rangers landed and assaulted the objective there was only one enemy fighter remaining, whom they handily eliminated. The mission was a success, completed in less than six hours, with no American personnel killed and just two wounded in the initial jump.

Although this was the first combat jump of the war, it would not be the last. Not even a month later on November 10, the Regimental Reconnaissance Detachment (RRD) Team Three performed a combat military free fall jump onto Wrath Drop Zone in southeastern Afghanistan. The mission was to establish a combat landing strip for follow-on forces. The mission was yet another early success for the Regiment.

The next combat jump would come days later on November 13 when two squads of Rangers from B Company, 3/75 with attached U.S. Air Force Special Tactics personnel, performed another combat parachute jump onto a drop zone near Alimarden Kan-E-Bagat, Afghanistan. This small element again jumped with zero illumination, in even colder temperatures (which makes parachutes descend faster) exiting the aircraft from only 500 feet above ground level. This is considered dangerously low, as a parachute malfunction from this height does not allow enough time for activation of the reserve parachute.

Upon hitting the ground, almost everyone in the small Ranger assault element sustained injuries. Despite the hard landing, the Rangers were unfazed and continued the mission. After successful completion of their objective, they moved out at a run to make it to the extraction point on time— again using mind over matter to operate while injured.

A week later, RRD Team Three conducted a combat static line jump onto Shiloh Drop Zone in southeastern Afghanistan to establish another landing strip for follow-on forces. Establishing these hubs for aircraft to land on were vitally important to the war effort as Afghanistan is a landlocked country inaccessible to naval landings and rotary wing aircraft without established fueling points in country.

Although the tempo of operations had not yet increased to a sprint, Rangers were involved in the fight early and often as the War on Terror picked up steam. No one really knew at that point how long the deployments would last, how many there would be and what the next decade would have in store. At this point, they were taking it one mission at a time.

SEPTEMBER 2001

"9/11"

It was evening, and we sat quietly; alone, yet together. I was torn between the two worlds that had become my immediate reality; my head processing the images unfolding in front of me on the small, corner-mounted television and my heart reaching for the quiet figure in the hospital bed. Judy sat breathing, watching. The rain was soft, as usual, and we were alone together for a rare moment. Years later, I would know it was by design. I looked at her eyes; they were tired and sad, but still somehow beautiful. She was visibly weary, but I still saw the same beauty in her that I fell in love with in her daughter, Kelly, who I was set to marry in December. I looked back at the television: fire, death, rubble, fears. Inside of me, rage cranks like a turbine.

"I can't believe I'm fighting to stay alive in a world like this." Her words snatched me back into the room. It wasn't what she said that shocked me; it was the matter-of-fact delivery. I was back in the present, and in a rare moment, unsure of my words, so I said nothing. It is a miserable day, and for Judy, her last and worst birthday.

She was completely coherent for this one moment and said, "Are you going to get involved in this?" "Yes." I replied. She again inquired, "With the guys with the beards, and the big butts?" as she started slipping away again. I laughed. Judy always made me laugh. Her laugh, like that of her daughter, is infectious and captivating. It can light up a room, even one inescapably consumed by death. I knew to whom she was referring. And although I wasn't quite sure about the *big butts* part, I gave her a pass in consideration of the chemotherapy and high doses of painkillers running through her body. I managed to reply with a simple, "Yes."

The next day she announced that she was ready to go home and she did. She and her husband, Lou, had spent over thirty years working in medicine. They knew the end of this story, and so did we. It was, unfortunately, one of only two certainties the post-9/11 world now brought for our *family*—the second was that I would be involved in its aftermath.

I was a squad leader at the time in 2nd Platoon, A Company, 2/75, otherwise known as The Blacksheep. They were my family; I grew up in my four years there. We trained together, fought together, drank together and lived together. We had waited for our time to close with and destroy the enemies of our country—anytime, anywhere—but not like this. We never imagined an America where thousands of our people would be murdered in our homeland. I felt a pain of responsibility for this and vowed to avenge that day.

As Rangers, we found ourselves in an odd circumstance, already set to deploy for a routine exercise in Jordan called *Early Victor/Bright Star*, where we would train Jordanian Rangers, even though we were certainly on the brink of a real-world deployment. Bags were packed and pallets loaded, so we waited, not knowing if we would still push out to the Middle East or have our training deployment canceled or CNX, (pronounced *kanked*). We spent our time as we always did, conducting dry fire drills in the house, battle drills on Noble Hill, tape drills in the Quad and PTing at a pace that would make most people vomit. Just another week—only it wasn't.

SEPTEMBER 17, 2001

The week at my fiancé's childhood home proved equally uneventful. Family came in from all over the country as best they could. We went about life as normally as possible considering the circumstances. While I went through the motions at Battalion, Kel spent as much time with her mother lying absently present in her bed; half in this world, halfway home with the Lord. Then it happened, a day of clarity.

Her boy had arrived and Judy sat in her living room and talked to her son Tony and Lou's parents. She laughed and they reminisced. It was fun. I made two important phone calls: the first to a bishop who I pulled out of the phone book, the second to my Ranger Buddy, "Mike." Now, there are certain things you can always count on with a Ranger. A Ranger is a man of action. A Ranger does not hesitate and he knows when it's time to execute, and a Ranger completes the mission. Another fact about a Ranger is that he never operates alone, so when he gets a random call from another Ranger, you can rest easy knowing that one will become two, two will become a team, a team will become a squad, and so on, in short order. It is ingrained into the fabric of our beings from Day One. It is who we are.

When Mike arrived, the scene was set: a bishop we had never met (and would never see again), a humble altar set up in front of the wall of family photos and memories (one final memory), and Judy sitting in her chair with Lou at her arm. Amongst the sadness of the week's events, Kelly was a singular point of beauty—brown hair and deep eyes to match, standing small with rosy cheeks in a pair of jeans and a t-shirt. We said, *"I do,"* and kissed. I knelt beside Judy and asked her if she understood what had happened, she was fading, but a response of, "Yes," escaped from her. She looked down at me and smiled. I promised I would take care of her little girl for the rest of my life, and she was taken back to bed.

That night, Mike and his wife Janice, with baby in tow, took us for a humble honeymoon celebration at the Puyallup Fair. I ate hot dogs, the girls chatted, Mike and I talked about our impending trip. *Was all of this really happening?* It was. Two days later, Judy went home to be with the Lord, and less than a week after that we deployed.

It was a blur. More training. *Why are we training? There is a war on!* Locked down in a camp outside of the city of Amman working with the Jordanians, validating air missions while trying to pinpoint where our sister battalions might be. After a few weeks, we were allowed to check our e-mail. I received my turn in the tent and after what seemed like twenty minutes (it was probably more like two—Rangers are not a patient breed) of connecting to the Internet, I had a message in my inbox from Kelly. The message read, "You need to call me immediately." I rushed to my platoon sergeant and explained the situation, he fetched me the CO's iridium satellite phone that we used for such special circumstances and as I dialed in, I knew what the rush was about.

We connected and it was nice to hear my new bride's voice as she jumped right into a conversation I will never forget. Now, if you can agree that a Ranger is a unique beast, you will also understand that a *Ranger Wife* is a wondrous anomaly. She is a strong, intelligent and beautiful creature that is also uniquely gifted with fortitude and a resolve that you rarely see in anyone. These ladies are quite literally our backbone.

"You're not going to believe this..." she started.

"You're pregnant," I replied.

"Yup."

I smiled, but a pang shot across my chest. Married, mother recently dead, new husband gone and now she's pregnant, all in a world on the certain doorstep of all-out conflict. What kind of husband am I? What kind of father am I already? I vowed to never be like mine, but already; I was absent.

October arrived and we sat in a makeshift chow hall tent watching our brothers from 3/75 jump into Objective Rhino on Fox News like the rest of our homeland. We felt cheated. *Those bastards!* The war had started and we sat impotent, watching from what seemed like the closest location our Regiment was positioned. Eventually, we loaded the birds and went home, stopping briefly in Shannon, Ireland for what I would later come to know as the customary *welcome back from a dry region* one-hour alcohol binge.

We were sullen and defeated; we felt like we had missed our opportunity to deploy and that 3rd Battalion had wronged us. *How could they choose 3rd Batt?* We didn't get it back then. And we didn't know what we didn't know. We didn't understand that 3rd was no different than 2nd or 1st (*sorry, brothers, just let it go—Ranger truly is Ranger regardless of the Battalion, although it is a blast to see the personality differences per unit*). We didn't understand that the "combat dream" we were chasing wasn't real; and most importantly, we didn't understand that the days of the 18-hour hit-it and exfil-style deployments were in the wind like the parachutes over Rio Hato. We would eventually get our chance and we all would pay for it, some more than others and some with their lives.

It came and went: Objective Rhino, fixed wing training; Operation Anaconda, rotary wing training, RRF 1 and ranges…so many ranges. We rode trucks more now; they wanted us to be more rapidly accessible. (I felt like I had been saying that for years . . . "Guys, we DO have helicopters!") We watched the war from home, bitterly awaiting our chance. While it all raged overseas, Kelly waged a battle of her own: morning sickness and discomfort overshadowed by the pains of loneliness. No mother to comfort her, no husband to help her. When people ask us about our *Ranger Family,* how we could stay close for so many years and why we still, to this day, travel to be together every Thanksgiving, it just makes sense to us. All she had were the Ranger wives and all I had were my Ranger buddies. Together, yet separate.

I took a squad in 1st Platoon, C Company 2/75 the Mad-Slashers during this time, which added more chaos to my world. More family ripped from me while a new, surprising bond developed. These men would become the Rangers with whom I would go to war, hump the Hindu Kush, fast-rope into the Shegal Valley, jump and mature over three combat rotations. These men became what I think about when I remember my days in the war—the boys I would protect, challenge and genuinely care for. These were the men who huddled around me as the first, pixelated image of my child slowly downloaded on the CO's laptop in Bagram, Afghanistan.

-BRANDON YOUNG
2/75

OCTOBER 2001
"OBJECTIVE RHINO"

It was October 19, 2001 and we were all fired up to take the fight to the enemy. I didn't fully understand all my emotions at the time; but in retrospect, I was excited because we had been sent to act out the aggression that all of America felt. Most Americans had a sinking and helpless feeling in their gut and wanted to find and kill the ones responsible for the terrible actions of 9/11. I was one of the truly lucky people who could do something about it, to personally direct that aggression toward our enemy.

Just like any jump, we went to the tarmac about 17 hours too early and set up our gear. My thoughts were on the mission, making sure that my reduced team had all our gear and knew all important parts of what we would be doing. I had a reduced team due to what I assume is a normal occurrence during any combat jump: higher-ranking officers wanted in on it. The command and control element for this mission had captains and majors acting as RTOs for other captains and majors. At the time, and still a little to this day, I was pissed. I gave all these "RTOs" the same scowl that I give new Rangers right out of RIP: a look of disgust, anger and disappointment. If the shit hit the fan, all these officers would fall in with a squad and act per the squad leader's orders (or so I was told; this arrangement was never going to happen). We were going to have to Ranger up and complete the mission short-handed. My anger toward these officers trying to pad their resume with a combat jump only got worse when intelligence reports said that there were active anti-aircraft guns on the objective.

A few minutes before the Jump Master Pre-Inspection (JMPI) began, I looked down my *chalk* and saw the chaplain getting ready for the jump. I am not really a follower of the Good Book, but I did grow up in an Irish Catholic family that taught me to fear the clergy and give them the utmost respect. In the past few months, I had a few very brief encounters with the chaplain. He looked like a young captain, but had a Combat Scroll (I believe from Panama, but I'm not sure.) Because of his Combat Scroll and the fact that he was a man of God, I understood why he would be on the jump.

I was assembling my team for JMPI and glanced over at the chaplain just in time to see him put an M-4 in his case. Now, I still don't know all the rules that go into being a military chaplain, but I was sure that I'd read somewhere that they never carried weapons. The chaplain had never carried a weapon during training, at the range or any other time I'd observed him. As he walked past me, my curiosity got the best of me. I stammered something to the effect of, "Sir, I see you are carrying a rifle. Isn't that kind of against your profession?" Then the chaplain said something to me that's stuck with me to this day. "My role is to protect my flock during this mission," he said with a smile.

This quick interaction shows the intense sense of duty that makes Rangers special. I came to find out the chaplain was in 2/75 as a private, and a bit of a wild child. He separated from the Army, found God, was ordained and then came back in. I've since left the Army and so far, have not started looking for God. However, I completely understand the need to re-connect with the people that understand you the best and help them in any way possible. You can turn a Ranger into a man of God but you can't take the Ranger out of a man! The Scroll is a way of life!

-ANDREW HEGGIE
3/75

CHAPTER TWO

"He which hath no stomach to this fight, let him depart;

his passport shall be made."

WILLIAM SHAKESPEARE

As the New Year came and went, 2002 would mark the first full year that American forces and the Ranger Regiment would be deployed for combat operations in southwest Asia. It would also mark the first year that Rangers were killed in combat in the War on Terror. Operation Anaconda would prove to be one of the first major operations in pursuit of Osama bin Laden, the mastermind behind the 9/11 terrorist attacks.

The U.S. military had been monitoring enemy forces in the Shah-e-Kot Valley, located high in the mountains of Afghanistan, for well over a month. In February, the Task Force (TF) Mountain commander, Major General Hagenbeck, began planning for Operation Anaconda with the intent of eliminating a pocket of fighters in their high mountain retreat. TF Mountain formed a multi-faceted operation that would incorporate both conventional and SOF with aligned Afghan partners. U.S. and Afghan forces in Gardez would push from the west of the valley, moving the enemy to the east into the blocking positions established by soldiers from the 10th Mountain and 101st

Airborne Divisions. The operation would last for nearly three weeks and would not go without mistakes and the loss of life.

Augmenting TF Mountain would be small reconnaissance elements, Advanced Force Operations, or AFO teams, which were drawn from Army, Navy and Air Force special mission units (SMUs). These AFO teams would move to strategic locations where they would establish observation posts (OPs) in order to support the conventional Army and Afghan partner units below them. The AFO teams would prove to be extremely effective not only in providing timely intelligence, but also in calling in airstrikes on enemy positions.

On March 4, 2002, one of these AFO teams consisting of Navy SEALs from a Naval Special Warfare SMU and an Air Force Combat Controller (CCT) were flying toward a 10,000-foot mountaintop of strategic importance called Takur Ghar to establish one of those OPs. As they approached the Helicopter Landing Zone, HLZ, Al Qaeda fighters who were concealed on the mountaintop began engaging their MH-47E Chinook helicopter, callsign Razor 03. This caused some of the hydraulic and oil lines to be severed, spraying fluid all over the ramp of the helicopter. Navy SEAL Neil Roberts had prematurely unhooked the safety line that tethered him to the helicopter. He was knocked off balance by the sudden jerks of the aircraft and slipped on the fluid on the ramp, falling approximately ten feet onto the snowy ground below. The crew barely escaped the ambush and managed to perform a controlled crash seven kilometers north of the mountaintop where Roberts had fallen out. Roberts was now alone, facing the enemy force that nearly felled the Chinook he was riding in. Another MH-47, Razor 04, had earlier inserted a reconnaissance element nearby and was able to arrive at the crash site within 30 minutes to pick up the SEALs and aircrew. Too heavy to reach altitude to attempt an immediate rescue of Roberts, the second MH-47 was forced to return to base to drop off the original flight crew and refuel before finally returning to Takur Ghar.

At 0500 local time, they approached the original HLZ on Takur Ghar. Again, enemy fire ripped through the bird, but everyone was inserted. They were now in an intense firefight that resulted in two of the SEALs being seriously wounded and one CCT, John Chapman, killed in action. They were

24

outnumbered and taking heavy fire, so they began to break contact and move away.

Back at Bagram Air Field, the Ranger quick reaction force (QRF) that was on standby for the mission boarded two Chinooks, one carrying 13 personnel and the other carrying 10, and made their way to the mountaintop without a briefing on the situation on the ground. Due to communications issues en route to the target, the QRF element did not receive the instructions *not* to land on the same HLZ that previous flights had attempted, nor did they know the SEALs on the ground had moved away from their original insertion location.

Just after sunup, the first of two helicopters, Razor 01, approached from the south and was hit by effective small arms and RPG fire. One RPG round hit the right side of the helicopter. The helicopter sustained too much damage to make it off the mountaintop, and had to crash land, its nose pointing up the mountain in the direction of the main enemy bunkers. The Rangers, TACP, STT personnel and the eight-man Chinook crew began moving under intense enemy fire to get out of the helicopter while returning fire. During this exchange, Specialist Marc Anderson was killed before exiting the aircraft. Sergeant Bradley Crose and Corporal Matthew Commons survived the initial impact of the crash landing, but as they exited the rear of the aircraft, the barrage of small arms fire felled them. Pararescueman Jason Cunningham and one of the medics remained inside the helicopter to treat the wounded. Meanwhile, Rangers quickly maneuvered to cover and killed two combatants, including an RPG gunner. The Rangers, with few men remaining, worked to take the hill, but were unable to do so. The controller had worked up an airstrike and within minutes U.S. aircraft were dropping 500-pound bombs within 50 meters of the friendly position. This leveled the playing field and the Rangers were no longer in danger of being overrun.

The second Chinook, carrying the Rangers of the other half of the QRF element, moved to a safe area and awaited further instructions after Razor 01 was shot down. Before long, they received orders to insert at a location that was over 2,000 feet below the mountaintop. The QRF Rangers moved for two hours up a 45-70 degree slope, in three feet of snow, weighed down by their weapons, body armor and equipment at an elevation that made breathing difficult. To make matters even worse, they were harassed by mortar fire raining down from the top of the mountain. They never hesitated as they moved, exemplifying the fifth stanza of the Ranger Creed;

…Energetically will I meet the enemies of my country…

By the time they made it to the top, they were physically exhausted but still had a mission to accomplish. They linked up with Rangers from the crashed Chinook and prepared to assault enemy bunkers a mere 50 meters away. After one more airstrike, two machine guns laid down covering fire and seven Rangers began the assault on the enemy bunkers. They moved as quickly as they could through knee-deep snow while shooting and throwing grenades in a concert of orchestrated violence. Within minutes, the Rangers killed multiple enemy combatants and overran their entrenched positions.

The Ranger ground force commander then made the decision to move all wounded to the recently acquired hilltop as it would be easier to defend in case the enemy organized a counter attack. The work was arduous because of the steep terrain and deep snow, but well worth it as they soon began taking fire from a ridgeline that was approximately 400 meters away while still making the move. During this engagement, the medical personnel that were still at the CCP treating the wounded were mortally wounded themselves as they were completely exposed to enemy fire. Both the Rangers and helicopter crewmen maneuvered on the enemy in an attempt to eliminate the threat while simultaneously risking their lives to pull the wounded to cover behind the nearby rocks. The controller called in another airstrike and the Rangers returned machine gun fire until they finally suppressed the enemy fire. This attack did not go without consequence, as the enemy claimed the life of PJ Jason Cunningham.

The Rangers consolidated and finished moving their dead and wounded to the top of the hill, while continuing to take sporadic small arms and mortar fire. The situation at Takur Ghar did not make another daylight rescue attempt possible, forcing them to defend their position until nightfall when extraction would be possible.

Finally, at about 2015 local time, four helicopters from the 160th SOAR flew in for both the Rangers on Takur Ghar and the SEALs that were still down on the mountainside. The initial reconnaissance mission gone wrong followed by the multiple rescue attempts would end up claiming seven American lives and would mark the costliest day for the Rangers since the 1993 battle of Mogadishu.

The mission did not stop after Operation Anaconda. The infrastructure for military operations in Afghanistan was nearly nonexistent in 2002. Bagram, the largest base in Afghanistan today, consisted of about thirty tents at the time. Because of this, Rangers were one of the few units who had the flexibility to conduct missions, as the conventional Army was still getting its feet on solid ground. Individual Ranger platoons were working out of safe houses, receiving their missions via radio and resupply from the air. Their Ground Mobility Vehicles (GMVs) were not compatible with the terrain at that time, so they had to improvise by moving on foot or using local vehicles. Many units could think of reasons not to conduct operations. The Rangers received missions and figured out a way to complete them no matter the obstacles. Their tenacity, flexibility and ability to find unconventional solutions allowed coalition forces to continue the mission.

June 2002

"Away At War"

So much happens in nine little months; life is knit together, relationships are forged, love is tested and deployments turn into Operation Enduring Freedom. It was less than a year and she was back in the hospital, only this time, I am not there. The Iridium phone in my hands was my only connection to another of my major life moments unfolding without me.

I heard her crying and screaming. She felt a thousand miles away, and she was. I paced back and forth outside a mud hut that I think was the gym in

Bagram, Afghanistan. Mike checked on me every now and then, but he mainly ran interference while I burned battery on the satellite phone. I thought to myself, *If you think you're calling home right now, you are sorely mistaken, Ranger.* As I listened intently, a bystander to my own life, I heard him arrive. Jaden Jude was born into the world and I was not there.

"You should see him, babe, he's so beautiful." The elation in her voice let me know that her pain was at an end. Her tears are of joy—mission complete—and this is a relief.

I wanted to feel that joy so much, to reach through the phone and hold them both, but I could do neither. I felt nothing. I realized that I have been on the phone for a very long time. Kelly was tired. She handed me off to her father. We finished the call and I went back to my tent, stopping only to tell Mike and Justin (my roommate of four years until I got married and a man I considered my brother) that all was well.

"You ok?"

"Fine, thanks..."

I walked off. I was a father, yet I was not present for the birth of my son. I am a failure, just like my father before me. On this day of joy for our family, a rage was ignited that would consume me for many years, nearly tearing my family apart. Nearly.

-BRANDON YOUNG
2/75

CHAPTER THREE

"Some must be warriors, that others may live in peace."

MERCEDES LACKEY

The year 2003 brought another war. On March 19, the President of the United States, George W. Bush, announced the commencement of combat operations in Iraq. The opening salvo was a "Shock and Awe" air campaign quickly followed by a ground campaign led by the Army's 3rd Infantry Division pushing north toward Baghdad.

The 75th Ranger Regiment was tasked with seizing multiple high value targets for the invasion effort. Failure was not an option. On 23 March, Rangers executed a high priority raid on the Al Qadisiyah chemical weapons compound. The Rangers were to insert around the building while a SMU searched for the suspected chemical weapons. As the Rangers descended in their MH-60 Black Hawks, they came under fire and one was wounded. Once the assault force landed, they again received heavy fire from positions in the well-protected target building. While Rangers were taking contact, multiple enemy vehicles started speeding toward their positions, only to be neutralized by the hovering attack helos. Although a fierce firefight, the mission was short lived. They were airborne again within the hour, mission complete. Only two casualties were taken, one Ranger and one of the 160th Night Stalker pilots, both of which received prompt medical treatment. Exactly what was found inside the research facility is yet to be disclosed.

On March 24, Rangers from C Co. 3/75 conducted a combat parachute jump near Al Qaim, Iraq. On March 28, Rangers from A Co. 3/75 conducted a combat parachute jump onto H-1 airfield. Rangers then went on to take Haditha Dam, which according to rumor, Saddam Hussein threatened to destroy, potentially causing extreme loss of life and a blow to Iraqi infrastructure. Rangers in a different part of the country aided in the rescue of Jessica Lynch.

Rangers conducted a combat jump in Afghanistan in February of 2003 before the war in Iraq officially began. At the end of the year, elements of the 75th Ranger Regiment were alerted for an operation in Afghanistan called Winter Strike. From October until January of 2004, Winter Strike Rangers conducted classic Ranger operations in some of the most austere terrain in the world. Platoons conducted long movements through the mountains in search of Al Qaeda operatives that did not make it out of the country in time. It was one of the worst winters on record for Afghanistan, which, when combined with the rugged terrain, made for an extremely challenging hunt. Rangers were living off the land, sometimes taking refuge in Afghans' houses, purifying their own water and setting up patrol bases in the middle of blizzard conditions. Some platoons used civilian Hilux trucks, some used helicopters and others were on foot the entire time. Some platoons stayed out for over 30 days at a time. It's a testament to the flexibility that the 75th Ranger Regiment brings to the table.

The Rangers were fighting two wars simultaneously. Captain Russell Rippetoe, Specialist Ryan Long, Staff Sergeant Nino Livaudais, Corporal Andrew Chris, Sergeant Timothy Conneway and Sergeant Jay Blessing all made the ultimate sacrifice.

FEBRUARY 2003

"THE JUMP"

On February 25, 2003, a platoon from C Company, 2/75, along with attachments from A Company and HHC were streaking through the air to conduct an airborne assault near Chahar Borjak, Nimruz Province, Afghanistan. My boots were laced tight, double knotted and the excess tucked in. The tan suede had been rubbed bald in some places from hundreds of miles traversed in both training and combat. The tread on was not as fresh as it was when I first put them on, but they fit my feet like a fine glove. My legs pushed the Vibram soles into the metal floor of the cramped C-130 aircraft as I tried to stabilize myself while the bird bumped its way through the air.

I volunteered for this, I thought to myself. I took pride that we did what so few others had the stomach to do. I knew that most did not have what it took to exit an aircraft mid-flight into a foreign hostile country. I knew even fewer would do it with the threat of Iranian jets that were scrambling to intercept us. My calloused hand gripped the yellow fabric that connected me to a steel cable, my lifeline. At the moment, the yellow fabric was merely responsible for helping me keep my balance, but in less than ten minutes it would have my life in its proverbial hands. I was staring blankly ahead, quietly saying a short prayer while gazing through the customary Ranger face camouflage pattern; dark on the high features, light in the shallow. It was the first and last time we ever "camo'ed" up in Afghanistan. I always thought the pattern made us look like cats, but the enemy saw it differently; "Painted Demons" they called the Rangers in Panama. I thought on this briefly while the lumbering aircraft did evasive maneuvers. It was appropriate, maybe even romantic, since my fellow brothers in arms and I wore the paint in honor of those Operation Just Cause Rangers we had grown up worshiping.

I thought about my family back home who did not really know what I did, but told their friends that I, "Jump out of planes, or something." Yeah, something like that. I snapped back into reality as a Ranger NCO approached me. He quickly made sure my static line was safely routed over my shoulder. I always felt an adrenaline rush when the doors opened and this day was no different as the afternoon sun flooded the inside of the aircraft. The mission's intent was to scare the enemy out of their hiding spots. Once they start moving, they're easier to hunt. Hunting just happened to be a Ranger specialty.

I quickly touched all attachment points on my harness, I knew they were right but did it anyway. For men of our trade, attention to detail is the difference between life and death. "One minute!" rang from deep within the jumpmaster's chest and we all ceremoniously echoed the command. My heart started to race in anticipation. My grip tightened and as the aircraft slowed its pace the entire chalk lurched forward. One foot was in front of the other and I was doing my best to stay steadfast in my position. You could cut the anticipation with a knife. "*THIRTY SECONDS*" and the entire column shuffled forward a bit as the first man stepped into the door. I was hunched over under the weight of the ruck hanging from my harness and wanted nothing more than to slip into the sky and be released from the screaming pain in my shoulders and rounded back. *This is just the beginning*, I told myself, *the real work starts when we hit the ground.*

Right as the ominous red light flicked to green, my cracked lips broke into a smirk. The entire column seemed to be sucked forward by the gravity of the door, men disappearing one by one. The roar of the prop driven engines almost seemed to fade away as I strained for eye contact with the jumpmaster. Then it happened in one fluid motion. I handed over the yellow line, turned and then disappeared out the troop door. I gritted my teeth as I waited for the tug of the opening silk. I was now quickly descending into the open, tri-border region of Iran, Afghanistan and Pakistan. In what seemed like only seconds, I was on the ground and scrambling out of my harness. I released the charging handle on my rifle with a *clack* and moved quickly toward the assembly area. Before long, we pushed out and secured the airhead line.

It was a successful but rather uneventful day. The attached CCTs established a runway and it wasn't much longer before the rest of the platoon and I were extracted from the target in the middle of the night. Was it a successful mission? One can only speculate...

-J.M.

2/75

Only days later on March 1st, 2003, Khalid Sheikh Mohammed (KSM) or otherwise known as the "Architect of 9/11," was captured in the town of Rawalpindi, Pakistan. This was a significant leap forward in the War on Terror, as well as the pursuit of those directly responsible for the September 11 terrorist attacks. The portly, mustached terrorist is still in custody today.

MARCH 2003

"THE INVASION"

It was March of 2003 inside of a filthy GP Large tent somewhere in Saudi Arabia and we waited like anxious kids before Christmas. Our platoon was waiting for a mission, a spin-up, a purpose; we waited for anything. At this point in my first deployment, the invasion of Iraq hadn't quite turned out to be the intense bloodbath I thought it would be.

Bravo Company, 1st Platoon arrived in the Middle East ready to deal death and endure it if necessary. We hit ground and it was constant preparation and walk-through training. The first three weeks of the deployment were some of the most miserable of my life. I could handle the MREs and a shower every couple days, but what drove me crazy was the waiting. I sensed most Rangers felt this way, although you couldn't tell by looking at them. From day to day the mood was stoic, but I knew deep down they were as tense as I was.

This was my first of four deployments with Ranger Battalion, but my brothers in arms were all familiar in the way of war from a previous deployment to Afghanistan which I unfortunately missed due to Ranger School. This probably meant I was more nervous than most, but I couldn't have been the only one. The best thing about working with Rangers is the sense of levity with which tense situations are met. There was no shortage of ball busting, pranks or jokes going around as a coping mechanism for the conditions of combat. I guess compartmental-icing the things that happen in war allows one to make sense of it.

Several weeks into our deployment 1st Platoon was still preparing for our main mission. There were mission briefings, static loads, Equipment checks—the full gamut of mission preparation tasks. Amidst the surety our unit was going to execute this *special mission*, we were still shuffling back and forth to the nasty chow hall set up for the US contingent in our area. Everybody was anxious and on edge.

It must have been three weeks in when the unthinkable happened. We were going about our daily routine, heading to the chow hall for one of the two hot meals we got when we saw a small collection of soldiers from other units gathered around a tent. Several of us popped in to see what the commotion was and up on the TV we saw some American reporters filming what looked like an invasion. It appears that the invasion of Iraq started without us. 3rd Infantry Division, along with the 1st MEF was to spearhead the main offensive into the inner part of Iraq. From what I gathered on the TV reports, it looked as if the two mechanized units drove through and killed all in their way. Rangers, at least our company, were essentially taken out of the game. This led us to the realization that our several weeks of training were a waste, not to mention the several months of training prior to deployment. This was the least desirable outcome I could think of, but deep down, in a way, I was glad that we lived to fight another day. There were big things on the horizon for B Company, 1st Platoon and I was glad we were all around to see what they were.

-TRISTAN

34

In the early stages of combat in Iraq, as the Army's 3rd Infantry Division pushed north toward Baghdad, a wrong turn by the 507th Maintenance Company would result in disaster. The convoy, consisting mainly of support personnel, approached a checkpoint where they were mistakenly told to go in the wrong direction. As fate would have it, they found themselves in an intense ambush just outside of Nasiriyah, Iraq. It was a costly mistake and it resulted in eleven soldiers killed in action and seven captured. One of the captured, Private First Class Jessica Lynch, would soon be the focus of the entire nation.

After an intense search effort, the prisoners of war (POW) were determined to be held at a hospital and a special operations task force was formed for their rescue. Naturally, Rangers would play a major role in the first rescue of a POW since the Vietnam War and the first ever rescue of a female POW. What was truly remarkable about this mission was not the rescue itself; this mission would testify to the leadership in the Ranger Regiment. This mission was proof that the Ranger Creed, specifically the line "Never shall I fail my comrades," was more than mere words.

During the rescue, Rangers learned all POWs except for Lynch were dead and were recently buried in a field outside the hospital. Rangers were not expecting this and were unprepared to dig up their bodies. What happened next was truly remarkable. Ranger NCOs told their junior Rangers to pull security as they proceeded to dig up the bodies themselves—not wanting younger Rangers to be exposed to this horrifying task.

One Ranger NCO remembers it as the most gruesome experience he's had. "I was digging up a body with my First Sergeant and we picked up this girl. She was half wrapped in a bag and all the muscle and tissue came off and slid onto me. I instantly puked again…it was bad. You look to the left and right and it was all NCOs. We didn't want to expose the junior Rangers to that shit. Everyone was digging with gloves, we had no shovels or anything like that—everyone was just puking and digging."

Sergeant's stripes are not something put on haphazardly in the Regiment. They carry a heavy weight, a weight that is not always convenient or comfortable. It would have been just as easy to consider the task beneath them and to assign it to junior Rangers as they supervised. But that's not what they did. Instead, they chose to take the hard right and set the example of what *REAL* leadership is. They set the bar very high and every leader worthy of the name will have to compare themselves to that standard for generations to come.

April 2003

"JESSICA LYNCH"

As we rolled through our deployment in a period of stasis, we finally received a mission. This was the call we had been waiting for and none of us knew exactly what or where we would be going, nor did we care. We were told that a supply unit's convoy was ambushed while driving through Nasiriyah, Iraq and some of their soldiers were taken hostage. Bravo Company was nominated to attempt a POW rescue mission as a part of a joint special operations task force (JSOTF). As we received our briefing from the leadership element, I heard the birds winding up their engines in the background. From the time of the briefing to the time we packed our bags and boarded the C-130s was a blur. I barely remember having a lucid thought. Everything running through my head was scenario training playback and solemn contemplation. I was as ready as ever to put all my skills to the ultimate test, but wished it could be over as fast as possible.

It was just hours before we boarded the birds and departed our AO toward our mission staging point near Nasiriyah. I have never thrown up on an airplane in my life, but this ride was absolutely terrible. I do not remember the actual temperature, but it felt like 120 degrees. For whatever reason, we were in the standard "nut-to-butt" loading formation and I happened to draw the biggest, sweatiest, mongoloid of a human in the platoon to sit in front of

36

me. In his trying to get comfortable he made me his personal recliner. Add 260 pounds of sweaty Ranger to hot-ass weather and *nap-of-the-earth* movements on a C-130 and I never stood a chance. I don't recall how many vomit bags I filled up, but it was more than a few. During this flight from hell I still attempted to prepare mentally as much as able—quite a challenge considering my head was spinning.

When we landed at our staging area, which appeared to be an old Iraqi Republican Guard airbase, we moved equipment and gear to an abandoned aircraft hangar. This would be our planning and staging point for the mission. We met with Ranger platoons from 1st and 2nd Ranger Battalion to coordinate mission details. I felt some semblance of relief knowing that we had other Ranger brothers watching our six and embarking on this journey with us.

Daytime rolled around and as last minute planning continued, we received an update, one overpowering even to the most grizzled soldiers. The convoy members ambushed and taken prisoner had all been executed and buried somewhere in Nasiriyah. I had no idea where the information originated, but the situation immediately increased in intensity (it was later revealed the information came from a hospital employee at the facility where Jessica Lynch was being held). Before the briefing was over, one last point was mentioned. It seems that there was a lone survivor who was being kept prisoner in a hospital somewhere in town. This prisoner, who turned out to be PFC Jessica Lynch, was wounded and immobilized.

As the mission planning started to wind down, the mission gear prep began to accelerate. We checked and re-checked every piece of equipment we owned. As an M-240 Gunner, I made sure to check every link on my ammo belts and every extra barrel I had. If something was going to happen on this mission, I was going to be the most prepared Ranger out there. (This mentality is shared by every Ranger.) Leadership informed us we would not be using our normal air wing contingent, the 160th Special Operations Aviation Regiment (SOAR), to conduct the infiltration movement. We were told instead they found the "…best Marine pilots available on a Tuesday night in Iraq." I remember these words very vividly and I also distinctively remember thinking (and saying aloud) "Shit…" I have nothing but a healthy, good-hearted rivalry with my Marine brothers, but had watched a news story about several Marine pilots crashing into each other a few days earlier. I was hoping I was wrong about the Marine helicopter pilots, but unfortunately I was not.

The CH-46 Sea Knight Helicopters skimmed over the terrain flying nap-of-the-earth toward our objective. My bird consisted of my assistant gunner, the Battalion Sergeant Major and Commander and me. As we approached the LZ, my heart felt like it was going to rip out of my chest and my adrenaline was pumping in overload. At this point, I was completely unaware of the enemy status on the objective. Ba'ath party militia was reported in the area as well as Fedayeen left behind from the initial invasion. That was okay by me because I had a lot of 7.62 ammo and it was heavy. As it turned out, the hospital where we landed would be empty besides a few civilians.

Upon approaching our designated LZ I saw a flash of light and felt overpressure out the back ramp of the bird. Someone fired an RPG which exploded close to us. At that moment, the bird flared downward and directly into several telephone poles and wires. We were still a couple hundred feet above the ground and I thought that this was the end of me. My machine gun flew out of my hands and I was tossed across the bird. I swear to God my life flashed before my eyes. This was my first mission and I would die before I even got off the bird! Somehow, by the grace of God, our helicopter made a hard landing into the literal trash dump that was our LZ and we ran off jostled, but in one piece.

As the platoon was offloading and taking up hasty fighting positions behind berms of trash, one of the Rangers from 1st Platoon had tripped and immediately injured his ankle. Not quite an admirable combat injury, but enough to keep him from walking the rest of the mission. Luckily, someone found a wheelbarrow and the injured Ranger would finish out the mission riding in the wheelbarrow like a child, whining about his sprained ankle.

We started our ground movement toward the hospital down a narrow street. Since it was dark and we were under NVGs, the hospital lights gave an eerie glow making the location of the objective unmistakable. Although the patrol was only about a half a mile, it turned out to be somewhat difficult mostly because I was wearing a chemical suit and chemical protective mask

38

while carrying 800 rounds of 7.62 ammunition, along with a machine gun and side arm. For those conspiracy theorists who speculate only blanks were carried on the mission and that we knew there was no viable threat, I can assure you you're wrong. I would invite you to try and hump all that shit in and out of hot-ass Iraq while your adrenaline is forcing you to sweat like a whore in church. I was losing fluids at an unsustainable rate.

As we reached the breach point, a large concrete wall, the breach team ran up to set a charge while we pulled security along our route. It was strangely quiet in the town, like it was empty. The blast from what must have been ten pounds of C-4 blew a squad-sized hole into the hospital complex. If the sound of the breach and the helicopters didn't stir up enemy fire, I wasn't sure what would. Despite our noise, we never received a shot fired toward us while inside the hospital perimeter. As the movement preceded, my squad leader, assistant gunner and I moved to set up on our gun position, which is where we would stay for the remainder of the mission. This support by fire position turned out to be the perfect vantage point to see the POW extraction team and soccer field, where I would later observe one of the most gruesome scenes of my life.

We still had not fired a shot nor taken any enemy fire. We heard that a Marine contingent at a blocking position some distance away had exchanged fire, but I cannot confirm it. With a rooftop vantage I saw a fire team from my platoon move through an alley below us to take up another security position for the extraction team's LZ. As the team was moving through this small alley, one of my Ranger buddies knelt in what looked like a medical refuse pile. This pile of medical waste turned out to be the area where they disposed of lost appendages from surgeries or accidents…they were literally kneeling in human body parts and medical garbage. One Ranger attempted to take a stable shooting position and sat right on a used hypodermic needle. To this day I still tease him about this disgusting accident. Back at the staging point, medics would inoculate him with every vaccination known to man. Fortunately, he didn't catch anything nasty.

The POW exfiltration team came in on MH-6 'Little Birds' and made their breach point at the side of the hospital. We all watched as they flowed into the door and then back out with Jessica Lynch in what seemed like five minutes. I don't know the actual breach to extraction time, but it seemed absurdly quick. They certainly earned their money in efficiency that evening. From that point on, we knew the mission was a major success, but it wasn't quite the end for the Rangers.

During the 'infil' and extraction, the leadership element met up with the hospital employee informant who told them the remaining soldiers from Jessica Lynch's convoy were buried in a soccer field across the street from the hospital. They were all in one shallow grave, stacked on top of another. The bodies had started decomposing from a few days in the ground. As previously mentioned, this was the same soccer field over which we pulled security.

My gun team and I watched in horror as several Rangers from Bravo Company 1/75 (to include a squad from 1st Platoon) began uncovering these bodies by hand and lifting them out of the hole. Some of the arms and legs of these soldiers *de-gloved* as they were pulled up from the earth. To this day, which includes three follow-on deployments to Iraq and Afghanistan, this was the most gruesome sight I've ever witnessed. I felt bad for the soldiers treated like this on their last days on earth and bad for my fellow Rangers enduring this horrible task. The Ranger creed clearly stated that we shall "...never leave a fallen comrade..." and the Rangers on that field performed that task in its entirety.

As the last bodies were extracted from their shallow grave, we prepared for our exfil movement as if this was any other training mission. The squads received their directive and began to peel back toward the landing zone. The injured Ranger was still in a wheelbarrow and being pushed by fellow Rangers. He had turned the wheelbarrow into a personal tactical vehicle, still pulling security with his weapon. We loaded the helicopters without a single shot fired from any Ranger on the mission team. We returned with all Rangers and our more fallen brothers and sisters.

When we arrived back at the hangars, we had chaplain briefings, command briefings and OPSEC briefings all thrown at us in true military fashion. We were told it was the first successful POW rescue mission since Vietnam, but whether that was true was beyond me. Although the tragedy for the 507th Maintenance Company was abysmal, a mission with no lost brothers is a success in my book. I hardly talk about it or mention it to anybody anymore. It's too hard to explain to somebody who was not there the feelings and emotions of that day. It just so happens that this was my first real combat mission in Ranger Battalion.

-TRISTAN
1/75

APRIL 2003
"Jessica Lynch and The Dig"

It has been 11 years since 2nd Platoon, Bravo Company walked into the back of a Marine Corps CH-46 helicopter. I remember the Regimental Commander telling us Rangers, "You are about to make history, men." But the POW Jessica Lynch rescue mission would turn into something we never expected.

After the helicopter took off toward Nasiriyah, I stared out the back, laughing to myself and thinking, well, *sure looks like Christmas in the sky*, and it did as tracers and explosions could be seen everywhere.

The helicopter finally sat down in a field. I ran off the ramp and *BAM!*—fell flat on my face! We had landed in a bunch of large rocks and the fall fired me up. After we collected ourselves from the cluster-fuck of a landing, a squad leader silhouetted himself on the road while shooting an azimuth with his compass to the hospital. I remember my squad leader yelling at him, "You stupid fuck, the whole world can see you!" Our company then began moving to the hospital in road march formation. Resistance was light and besides an RPG going by way over our heads we received no contact.

As 1st Squad neared the wall of the hospital, they began moving through a field flooded with water. They sank almost waist deep and soon realized there were human body parts floating in it. 1st Squad moved back

41

and my squad, 2nd, moved around them to place an ex-plosive breaching charge on the hospital wall. The assault force was still rescuing Lynch, so we could not blow the charge yet. We were told, "Use your sledge hammers to put in the breach!" I will never forget Adam and I in our MOPP Level 5 suit going crazy on that wall with the sledgehammers. It was like an adrenaline rush from hell. It was only a matter of minutes before we had a sizable opening.

Meanwhile, the assault force had secured Jessica Lynch and moved with her to a Black Hawk helicopter to exfil from the objective. The call then came in over the radio to blow the breach, but Adam and I were like, "What the fuck? We already made one!" The squad leader wanted to blow it anyway though. Since someone didn't inform the forward observer of this, the MH-6 Little Bird helicopters in orbit above us had no idea, which resulted in one almost being blown out of the sky when the charge exploded.

The perimeter of the hospital was quickly cleared and the realization that PFC Lynch's fellow soldiers' bodies were not in the hospital morgue had our interpreters questioning the doctors. The doctors informed them, "They are out front in the soccer field; we buried them days ago." My team leader looked at me and said, "Let's go."

I remember walking out to the soccer field and one of the graves had already been opened. The smell was horrifying. It was so powerful that it seeped from our clothing and skin for days after. But the smell was nothing compared to what we did next. We began to dig using the only thing we had—our hands. Looking down into the mud and seeing your brothers' and sisters' decaying bodies (five males and three females) was infuriating. They did not look human and they did not feel human. Some were advancing in decomposition faster than others.

Recovering the bodies was an important but difficult job that was aggravated by a senior NCO who told one Ranger from 3rd Platoon to "Pick him up by his arms!" to which the Ranger replied, "He doesn't have any fucking arms!" Many of us Rangers remember one squad leader had had enough, yelling, "Shut up and go fuck yourself!" to the NCO that was providing *helpful* advice from the sidelines. I took pleasure in that because hearing "dig faster" was garbage! We continued digging and noticed the female soldiers had IVs and tourniquets, but the male soldiers were in really bad shape, and it appeared that not all of their wounds were due to combat. Some of them looked like they had been badly tortured or mutilated.

Rangers would dig, get out of the hole, puke, then get back in and keep digging. Curses and the occasional nervous laugh could be heard as Rangers used whatever means they had to adapt, overcome and keep on digging. I remember one young Ranger sitting at the edge of a grave not moving but just staring down at the dead, decaying Soldier in the ground. I told that Ranger, "Get the fuck out of the way and let this country boy dig." The good Lord blessed me with a strong stomach and it thankfully helped me move a lot of dirt that night.

I remember the different emotions I experienced; I felt anger and hatred for the Iraqis, but there was a surreal moment where I was thinking, *God, I am so glad it's not me in that hole.* The eight soldiers' remains were recovered and returned to the country for which they had died. We lived the Creed that night: "I will never leave a fallen comrade..."

The one thing that has given me peace over the last 11 years, five combat tours, 24 surgeries and 19 straight months of mental hell in the VA hospital is the story of Specialist Lori Piestewa. SPC Piestewa was a Hopi Indian, a member of PFC Lynch's unit and one of the female soldiers we recovered that night.

They say the Hopi Indians in Arizona believe that when it snows, it is their ancestors (loved ones) who have passed on returning to tell them that they love them. The day Hopi Indian SPC Lori Piestewa's body returned to Arizona...it snowed.

-CHRIS BEMISS
1/75

April 2003

"Haditha Dam"

I remember stepping on to the C-17 cargo jet headed for Iraq feeling incredibly unprepared to be invading another country. The feeling gnawed at me from my gut as I stepped foot on the bird and I knew there was no turning away. It wasn't the same feeling of excitement that I felt leaving Fort Benning, GA with an unknown destination that I assumed to be a Forward Operating Base in preparation for the upcoming war with Saddam Hussein. Now it was real. We were going to war and there was no turning back.

1ˢᵗ Platoon, Bravo Company had cross-loaded two C-17s with attachments from Headquarters Company on a desert airstrip in Saudi Arabia. We waited on the airstrip, prior to boarding the aircraft, as loadmasters secured our GMVs. Our GMVs which were originally armored HMMWVs, now *sans* armor, leaving us with stripped down HMMWVs with a stronger engine, chassis and suspension than standard. We filed on to the airplane, shuffling between vehicles. We were wearing Ranger Body Armor (RBA) over our Nuclear, Biological, and Chemical suits (JLIST), carrying our weapons, assault packs, MICH helmets and in my case, an old MOLLE aid bag. There would be no red cargo net jump seats on this flight—floor space only.

Oddly enough, spreading out on the steel floor of a C-17, especially in full kit, was a lot more comfortable than trying to cram side-by-side with your fellow Rangers onto the folding seats that come complimentary on Air Force flights. Slowly, starting nearest to the nose of the aircraft, Rangers found appropriate floor space and flopped down against their assault packs. We all eventually sat down in spaces between the GMVs and the aisle left between the vehicles and the skin of the C17. Sitting close to me were PFC Matt, PFC Bob and my Ranger buddy from Anti-Tank (AT) section, PFC Jared.

Jared and I had attended the Ranger Indoctrination Program (RIP) together in July of 2002. Because of our last names, we were alphabetically close on the rosters kept by the Ranger Cadre, and therefore stood next to each other in formations during both holdover and RIP. Since formations were everything in RIP, the pain and exhaustion that was endured throughout the time required to earn a tan beret was spent together. Jared and I became close friends during those weeks in RIP and following graduation; we were assigned to 3rd Ranger Battalion, which was deployed in Afghanistan. Assignments are made by one's last name and both of us fell into Bravo Company. Less than a year later, we were sitting next to each other on a cargo jet destined for another small desert airstrip in Western Iraq that had been earlier seized by Alpha Company.

B Company 3/75 had been the company sent to Somalia in 1993 during Operation Gothic Serpent and had been on the ground in Mogadishu during the days of Oct 3-4, in an 18-hour gunfight that would later be immortalized in the book and subsequent film, Black Hawk Down. As such, Bravo Company carried a tremendous amount of unit pride and held itself to a standard that was high even by Ranger expectations.

I looked around at the men to my left and right as the loadmasters continued their final checks before closing the ramp door. Most of the Rangers on the bird that night were veterans of Afghanistan; however, our platoon leader, 1LT Joe was a prior-enlisted Ranger who was also a Somalia veteran who had served as LTC McKnight's RTO on the *lost convoy*.

Everyone was quite calm. No one spoke unless required and even then words were kept to a minimum. We took our places on the floor of the C-17 and awaited departure in a focused silence that was drowned out by the noise of the plane. Finally, the loadmaster signaled to the forward crew and the ramp began to slowly lift off the tarmac. The whine of working hydraulics dominated the inside of the aircraft and drew everyone's attention to the world that disappeared behind the closing door. At last, the ramp closed against the tail of the giant bird with a mechanical thud.

The Air Force crew in the back settled at their stations and the jet engines fired up. The familiar pitch made by turbines overtook all other noise as they worked their way up to idle speed. The engine noise leveled off and the jet began to vibrate as it sat stationary, waiting for takeoff. A large part of me hated to fly, but as we sat there waiting for the pilots to finish their checklist of pre-flight operations, the notion of flying didn't bother me nor did the thought of dying necessarily bother me. For the most part, I hadn't even considered my mortality and when I had, I casually brushed it off as something that was uncontrollable and not worth worrying about. Nonetheless, as that C-17 bound sat waiting to depart, I was scared and felt extremely unqualified to be on the bird.

The feeling was in contradiction to all training received to that point, but regardless, it was there. It was born out of uncertainty that I had about how well I would perform my job, a job that I literally hadn't signed up for. When I joined the Army, I joined as an infantryman (11B) with an airborne contract. In Airborne School, I volunteered for the Ranger Indoctrination Program (RIP) and upon completion of RIP, I was assigned to 3rd Battalion. Since 3rd Battalion was already deployed, the new privates from our graduating class were left on rear detachment to perform administrative and maintenance duties while the battalion was away. In October, the battalion redeployed back to Fort Benning and the privates in our class were integrated into the line squads. Originally, I had been assigned to 3rd Squad, 1st Platoon, but that soon changed due to a program implemented by the Regimental Surgeon.

Anticipating high casualties during the invasion of Iraq, the Regimental Medical Officers, in conjunction with the three Battalions, formed what was called the Infantryman Medic Program. The idea revolved around the idea that individual platoon medics would be better prepared to handle multiple casualties if they were augmented with a second medically proficient Ranger. Since I was the newest Ranger and had not yet integrated into my squad, I was chosen to complete a six-week EMT crash course. Following the EMT course, I was sent to a course in Pre-Hospital Trauma Management and a Combat Trauma Management Course that was taught by the Joint Medical Augmentation Unit (JMAU), a special operations outfit comprised solely of trauma surgeons and other medical officers.

In spite of all of the training I had received, as the jet made its slow start to the end of the runway for takeoff, I did not feel prepared to treat my Ranger buddies should they sustain injuries. Fear of freezing up entered my thoughts.

46

I questioned whether I had the courage to face the adversity that combat would inevitably bring. Would I have the necessary guts to keep moving forward in the face of imminent danger? What if I froze up and my Ranger buddies paid the price? Uncertainty weighed heavily on me and I was afraid of the unknown.

The C-17 came to a stop after a turn that I assumed was to align the plane with the runway. I sat there and quietly eyed the men around me. No one said a word. Most sat staring at their weapons or equipment, expressionless. I too sat expressionless, afraid to show the fear that had crept over me. Suddenly, the jet turbines fired up from idle and inertia thrusted us toward the rear of the plane. Facing the tail of the bird, I leaned back to fight the gravitational force pushing me forward. As we accelerated, we bounced around next to the GMVs that were strapped down to the floor of the airplane, the suspension of which would rise and fall as the plane sped its way down the airstrip.

Finally, the nose lifted off the tarmac and began to gain altitude. Still facing the tail, I had to continue to lean back in order counter against the *Gs* that were trying to push me forward. Seconds later, the pilots retracted the landing gear and we continued our sharp ascent. After a minute or two we leveled off and the plane banked toward Iraqi airspace. I looked around; the expressions of those around me had changed. Eyes had opened up, the hardened scowls of professional warriors lightened and a sense of excitement filled the plane. As I watched this, I noticed a change in my own demeanor. A smile crept over my face while the sense of fear I had been holding onto began to drain away, as if it had broken free like as our plane escaped the bonds of earth.

Bob leaned closer to Matt who had found space in the front seat of a GMV. I could barely hear him shout, however my eyes clearly read his lips exclaiming, "IT'S FUCKING ON, DUDE!"

Matt, a casual yet extremely intelligent and physically fit Ranger from Wisconsin, simply smiled in response and settled a little further into the space he occupied in the GMV. As I continued to look around the plane, being in the company of the best-trained infantrymen our country had to offer eclipsed the thought of failure. Furthermore, we were armed to the teeth with the best weapons and technology available. Our guns, kit, vehicles and electronics were more sophisticated than anyone else's in the Regular Army and certainly better than anything the Iraqi Army had to offer. We had the best training, we had the best support, and we had the best men.

This realization motivated and allowed me to bury my earlier feelings of uncertainty. I made a promise to myself that no matter what lay ahead, I would give everything that I had to the guys on my left and right. We had recited the Ranger Creed many times before this moment, making that very promise every time we did, but as I acknowledged that I was a more elite soldier who would never leave a fallen comrade, an entirely new level of determination to live up to that statement solidified within me.

As we neared the border of Saudi Arabia and Iraq, the dim white lights on the plane were cut and red tactical lighting illuminated the fuselage. The red lighting instantly made the flight a radically different experience. It signaled we were in bad guy country, which instantly created an adrenaline buzz throughout the plane. Everybody on the flight showed visible signs of excitement; they all sat a little bit taller, made sure their kit was a little bit straighter, their helmets a little bit tighter. We continued at cruising altitude for another 40 minutes or so, the plane banking every so often until receiving word to enter tactical descent.

All of a sudden the engines powered off and what had moments ago been a very noisy flight had become relatively quiet. Without the noise of the engines, you could hear the suspension of the vehicles as slight turbulence caused the springs to compress and rebound. The sound of tie-down chains hitting metal as the GMVs rocked back and forth became noticeable. The lack of thrust caused the plane to slow in speed giving us the feeling that we were gently gliding until the pilots dipped the nose of the aircraft and we entered our descent.

The rate at which we dropped was alarming. The GMVs lifted up against their shackles and we all held on to our safety lines that kept us secured to the floor of the aircraft in case of an emergency. While we weren't experiencing a complete loss of gravity, the descent was as exhilarating as any roller coaster I'd ridden. Other members of the platoon apparently shared this feeling as Bob raised his arms like he was on a ride at Six Flags. One by one, others in the platoon raised their arms until we were all looking around with big grins on our face in anticipation. Without warning, the lights went black, the engines fired back on and we began to level out. The pilots used the power of the turbines to take control of the rapid descent and moments later we touched down on the bumpy tarmac of the airstrip.

As we had rehearsed many times, we all took a knee and prepared to de-link from the plane once it came to a stop. The plane quickly decelerated and we all then fought the inertia in reverse of takeoff. If it weren't for my safety line, I would have gone flying toward the front of the plane as it slammed on its brakes. Finally, the plane came to a stop. I double-checked my kit in the dark then flipped down and turned on my Night Vision Goggles (NVGs). In the pitch-black of the C-17, I couldn't see anything and had to feel blindly for the snap link on my safety line. I found it and unhooked. After triple checking that I had all my gear, I made my way to the back of SSG Branford's GMV to help unshackle it from the plane. We quickly removed the vehicle tie-downs and loaded in the back. As soon as the ramp began to drop, the drivers started their engines and awaited the green light from the loadmasters.

Once the signal was given, each driver released the hand brake and began to roll forward down the ramp out of the back of the C-17. We were finally in Iraq. It was dark with no illumination from the moon. As we drove further and further from the jets, the desert got quieter and quieter. Aside from the infrared (IR) lights on the front grill of the GMVs, it was nearly impossible to see anything surrounding us in the darkness of night. Our column came to a stop near the end of the airfield and linked up with the command element that directed us to a small group of buildings to bed down for the night. Alpha Company had our security so we immediately moved to the buildings about 500 meters away.

Upon arriving at our overnight position, we quickly dismounted the vehicles, re-cleared the buildings to ensure they were empty and began priorities of work to bed down for the evening. Immediately upon setting up inside for the night, we discovered the rooms were covered with old, petrified goat shit. The decision not to clean it out before implementing the rack plan was more than likely in consideration for the little darkness there was left to catch any sleep at all. I certainly didn't argue with anyone when told to pass out. If there was one thing I had learned about sleep in RIP, it was to sleep when told. I did the best I could to clear the goat feces from around my immediate area, laid down using my assault pack as a pillow and fell asleep.

The next morning, we awoke and began priorities of work in order to be ready to leave at nightfall to begin our *disruption of enemy forces* mission. Nobody really knew what that meant other than we were going out to close with and destroy whatever enemy we could find. As 3rd Squad began to prepare their equipment, M-203 gunner PFC Tommy fell ill with nausea and vomiting. I assumed the color was Gatorade, but nonetheless, I'd never seen puke so fluorescent green before. His vomit reminded me of antifreeze and it was immediately clear he needed medical attention. Without the availability of a hospital or any other medical care outside of what the platoon medic and I had in our aid bags, the options for PFC Tommy were few. SPC Dave was the platoon medic who I worked under. Dave quickly made the determination that he needed IV fluids and directed me to start a saline lock. After getting permission from our platoon sergeant, SFC Jack, Dave initiated an IV and intravenously gave Tommy the anti-nausea medication Phenergan to fight dehydration and ease the vomiting. The Phenergan kicked in and immediately sedated him, who was left to rest for the remainder of the day.

Shortly after, a WARNO came down to begin preparing for our first mission. Details were vague, but we were to only be gone from the airfield 24 hours. Apparently we were using what we had designated as H-1 as our new FOB. We were told to leave our rucksacks in the buildings, which would be watched by the security element left behind. In addition to our weapons and sensitive items, our packing list was simple: assault packs only. One prepackaged Meal, Ready to Eat (MRE), two power bars, six bottles of water in addition to full Camelbaks and two quart canteens, one extra pair of socks, one extra t-shirt and a stripped down shave kit that consisted of toothbrush, toothpaste and a razor. The only optional item not mentioned was Copenhagen or in my case, Marlboros.

Copenhagen has been the tobacco choice of Rangers for generations, although in every platoon there are always a couple of renegade smokers whose habit is regularly ridiculed and put under fire by the dippers who have them significantly outnumbered. Smoking however, is a commitment (nobody likes a quitter!) and when everyone else bought Copenhagen at the makeshift

PX in Saudi Arabia, I bought two cartons of *Cowboy Killers*. This temporarily became an issue when packing my assault pack as I discovered I only had room in my rucksack for one carton of cigarettes. Originally, I was only planning on taking two packs, but since my ruck was full, I had to stuff the 2nd carton in my assault pack that had considerably more free room.

Better to have and not need, than need and not have, I told myself as I zipped up my bag after double-checking that I had everything.

As we waited for word on the mission, I periodically checked on Tommy while hanging out with the members of my original squad. 3rd Squad had a lot of experience with all the privates having at least one deployment and the leaders having two. SPC Plasman, Sergeant Long and SSG Branford were all from the black beret days prior to the War on Terror and had years of Ranger experience. SPC Mike O'Neill had graduated Ranger School a few weeks prior and both PFC Panatela and Matt would probably have been on their way had it not been for this deployment. Listening to these guys talk about the possibilities that lie ahead for the platoon gave me insight on what to expect, although there was far from a unanimous consensus on what that would be.

Afghanistan had been mostly quiet for 1st Platoon aside from the helicopter crash on the night of the invasion that took the lives of SPC John Edmunds and SPC Kristofer Stonesifer. The prior deployment had been full of stories of long patrols and anticlimactic raids. Would Iraq be the same? Would all the action go to Special Mission Units and the Regiment be stuck with objectives that were dry holes? "Surely not," SPC Plasman reasoned, "We're facing a conventional army out there. The Taliban doesn't compare to the Republican Guard." Sergeant Long thought otherwise, "I bet they just lay down their guns and surrender. Desert Storm all over again. We bomb and they come out waving their underwear on a stick." "Or we pull security for the SMU's while they kill all the bad guys," Mike added. "Maybe they toss us a squirter every once in awhile."

For a moment the group seemed to consider Mike's suggestion to be the most plausible. After all, that had been B Company's role in Somalia and a good chunk of Afghanistan. I had no idea what to expect and instead of adding my two cents, I sat quietly listening in. Myself, I sided with SPC Plasman, hoping he would be right. On the other hand, we had already been in

Iraq for nearly 12 hours and I had yet to hear a gunshot or a bomb drop. I had half expected to roll off the back of the plane with guns blazing, but instead, found myself half-rested and listening in on 3rd Squad's debate leaving a question as to whether we'd even see real combat.

SSG Branford and SPC Dave finally returned from the operations order with an answer. We had a mission to seize a radio tower that was under control of the Iraqi Army and civilian workers. Details were vague, but we were going with 2nd Platoon and expecting resistance. SPC Dave informed me that I would ride on SSG Branford's vehicle and fall in with the Weapons Squad leader, SSG Shank. A North Carolina native with a thick backwoods accent, we called SSG Shank, *Gunny* due to the time he spent prior to enlistment in the Army as a Marine. While Gunny was never officially a Gunnery Sergeant in the Marines, the name fit, as he was the only prior Marine in 3rd Ranger Battalion, if not the entire Regiment.

As late afternoon came, PFC Tommy started to recover from the sedative effects of the Phenergan. To my surprise, Tommy felt fine except for a bit of wooziness. Doc concluded that he'd either had a temporary bug or might have eaten something in Saudi that hadn't sat right. Regardless, he was good to go and even if he wasn't, Tommy probably would have had to be held down for us to leave without him. I think everyone had that attitude. Despite uncertainty or skepticism about what was ahead, the platoon was primed and ready to find out.

Prior to loading our vehicles, the Platoon Sergeant walked up to me and performed a surprise inspection of my packing list and sensitive items. When he got to my assault pack, the first thing he noticed was the carton of cigarettes that had been crammed in there on top of everything else. The Platoon Sergeant was the most vocal of the smoking critics in the platoon. With a visible lump of Copenhagen in the corner of his bottom lip he asked, "Matthews, why do you have a carton of cigarettes for a mission that's only going to last 24 hours?"

I kept my reply as simple as possible, "Sarn't, I bought two cartons in Saudi and can only fit one of them in my rucksack."

"Well, if you fall out because of the extra weight, your ass is mine...I don't wanna hear any excuses."

The actual weight of the carton was a half-pound, max.
"Roger, Sarn't."

"You know those things are gonna give you lung cancer, don't ya?" He asked rhetorically as he spit tobacco juice into the sand.
"Roger, Sarn't."

He eyed my kit and me for a moment longer. Satisfied, he moved on to quiz others on their awareness of the upcoming mission. I looked at Dave, the second-most vocal antismoking advocate in the platoon who smiled, "Told ya, you should quit, dude."

Shortly before sunset, Bravo Company's 1st and 2nd Platoons loaded our vehicles and left the airfield in a convoy across the desert. An hour after nightfall, we linked up with Charlie Company and picked up 3rd Platoon, along with two sniper teams and Command Sergeant Major (CSM) Birch. CSM Birch's addition immediately boosted morale as word quickly passed that he was armed with an SR-25 sniper rifle and ready for a fight. Our CSM was already a legend amongst the lower enlisted men of 3rd Battalion. A Ranger who had grown up in 2nd Battalion, CSM Birch left battalion in the eighties to join the Army's Special Mission Unit, spending nearly 20 years there before coming to 3rd Battalion six months prior.

We departed the rendezvous point with Charlie Company, now with three line platoons plus attachments from mortars, snipers, mechanics and a control element from HHC that included the Battalion Executive Office (XO) and Air Force JTAC. Riding in the back of a GMV in full kit is extremely uncomfortable. Every vehicle had four men in the front, four men in the back and a heavy gunner in the turret, manning either a .50-caliber M2 machine gun or a MK19 automatic grenade launcher. We also had 240B machine guns mounted to swing arms in the back of each vehicle, with PFC Tommy manning ours. Across from Tommy was Matt, whose M-249 SAW was also mounted to a swing arm. Across from me, Sergeant Jonathan, a mechanic from HHC, sat with his M-4 carbine. The four of us did our best to sit outward despite the bench seats that faced inward, while scanning the darkness as our convoy moved further and further away from friendly forces. After hours of driving through what seemed like endless desert, we arrived at our remain-over-day (ROD) site as the sun broke over the horizon. Quickly we sat up security and camouflaged our vehicles in a natural depression prior to performing priorities of work and implementing a rest plan.

Although we had been up driving all night, getting sleep that day was next to impossible. Between rotating out to pull security or radio guard, word was there was a change in mission and that a FRAGO had been issued. Rumors that we'd be diverted to seize a hydroelectric dam began to go around and the persistent detail in that rumor was Saddam's Republican Guard was holding the dam. By reputation, the Republican Guard was Iraq's best-trained unit who had all taken an oath to defend their homeland to the death. As Rangers, we respected their decision to die for their country and felt happy to oblige them, but the possibility of going up against Iraq's finest stirred up enough excitement to effectively prevent anyone from getting any sleep. After four hours of planning, our company commander issued his new operations order, confirming the gossip. Intelligence suggested that Saddam intended to blow up the Haditha Dam and blame it on the Americans. The result would have been disastrous for the Iraqi people and mass flooding would prevent 3rd Infantry Division's push to Baghdad.

The plan consisted of 1st Platoon securing the western side of the dam to allow 2nd Platoon to move across, setting up a battle position on the east side and begin clearing the complex. 3rd Platoon, C Company would move to the south of the dam and secure a power station about 500 meters to the southwest of our position. Instead of assaulting from the south, the CO devised a route to the objective that took us around the western shore of the reservoir, hopefully giving us the advantage of quickly securing the high ground and dam complex with overwhelming force.

As we had the night before, the assault force loaded our vehicles and left the ROD site just before sunset on a near 20-mile journey to the Haditha Dam. A few hours after darkness fell we began to hear bombs explode in the distance. We would see a faint flash on the horizon, followed seconds later by the rumbling of distant thunder. Discomfort quickly settled in as we rode overland to the objective and like two nights before, low illumination from an absent moon made it difficult to see further than 50 yards. Less than a mile from the objective, the column of GMVs came to an abrupt halt. One of the vehicles broke all four bolts to its steering box and was immediately disabled.

The mechanics quickly identified the problem and came up with a plan to fix it on the fly. Since the steering box could be secured with only three bolts for the short distance to the target, the mechanics quickly removed one bolt from three other vehicles and secured the steering box, making the GMV operational in 20 minutes. Considering the conditions and lack of tools and spare parts, everyone in the platoon was amazed at the proficiency of the mechanics and how quickly they got us back up and running.

Before the convoy began moving again, SSG Branford reminded us we were nearing the objective and to remain alert. I went over my end of the plan again: link up with SSG Shank once we arrive at the objective. With the vehicles loaded, we once again began movement across the desert. We moved slowly but steadily across the uneven terrain until arriving at an asphalt road springing out of the sand. Once on the hardball, the vehicles raced toward the dam structure. Arriving, we screeched to a halt and immediately dismounted our vehicles. Quietly, the assault force gathered to begin clearing the western flank. I linked up at the side of the road near a guardrail with SSG Shank who told me to stay within arm's reach.

SFC Jack and 1LT Joe took 1st and 2nd Squads, along with B Team from 3rd Squad to assault a complex of buildings in our AO.

The assault began with no resistance. 2nd Platoon could cross the dam to the east side and began making their entry into the complex itself. 3rd Platoon, C Co. also made their way down to the power station. Bravo Team, 3rd Squad cleared the first building and set up an overwatch position on the rooftop with a sniper team. Shortly after clearing the first building, we heard small arms and .50-caliber gunfire to the south. Charlie Company ran into enemy personnel at the base of the dam and a quick engagement followed.

As this happened, SFC Jack set a 240B gun team on another key piece of terrain to cover the movement of 1st and 2nd Squad as the two squads began to clear the rest of the objective. Building by building, 1st and 2nd Squads began clearing the compound of 12 concrete buildings. Suddenly 1LT Joe called out that enemy soldiers were running in the low ground, about 100 meters from our position and illuminated their movement with the infrared laser on his rifle. SSG Shank immediately lifted his M-4 and took aim on the runners. I, along with Sergeant Pelt joined Gunny and took aim at the squirters alongside him. It was clear they were running to a fighting position.

SSG Shank yelled out, "I got 'em, sir!" I rotated my selector switch from safe to fire, my finger lightly on the trigger as we tracked the moving targets. Before I could finish asking myself whether we were really going to shoot, SSG Shank began firing. My finger contracted several times in rapid succession, each time, my shoulder absorbing the recoil of my M-4. All three figures dropped nearly at once. We stood there for a second, weapons at the high ready, lasers locked on our downed targets waiting for them to resume movement. None of them budged. The realization hit all three of us, at once, but I initially second guessed it. *No way, we had just killed those guys. Killing another person was supposed to be difficult.*

Everything in life taught me that taking someone's life was supposed to be something that took guts to do and what we just did was entirely too easy. There was no thinking involved. No moral reasoning as I pulled the trigger while aiming at a moving target. No different than being on a night range at Fort Benning, except that we weren't back home in Georgia. We were in Iraq and the three bodies we illuminated with our lasers weren't pop-up targets, they were people. Only now, they were dead people.

SSG Shank broke the silence in a disappointed tone, "I just lost my job." He turned as he lowered his weapon, putting it back on safe. Sergeant Pelt responded, "I thought all fighting-aged males were considered hostile?"

"They are, but did they even have weapons?"

I glanced back in the direction we'd just fired, "Looked like they were armed to me, Sarn't."

SSG Shank looked at me hard. I could see he was genuinely worried about whether the targets were armed. Behind him, one of our vehicles drove up the hill toward the compound of buildings, its IR light illuminating the concrete structure.

"Yeah, and they were definitely running toward that fighting position," Pelt added. Gunny continued to eye me for a moment and looked to the south where we had just fired. Out of the corner of my eye, the GMV moving up the hill began to turn into the center of the group of buildings. Gunny took a deep breath, which signaled me to let out the one I felt I'd been holding the entire time. As we both relaxed, a loud concussion caught our attention and what looked like a large roman candle raced out of the low ground toward the buildings 1st and 2nd Squads were clearing. Under night vision, we watched a glowing ball fly just over the rooftop of a building with a GMV outside and explode in an airburst that sent a shower of shrapnel everywhere.

Brief silence was followed by an eruption of small arms, machine gun and RPG fire from the base of the hill. In an instant, all hell broke loose. Rounds began impacting the buildings our platoon was maneuvering to take. SSG Shank, Sergeant Pelt and I quickly moved to the support by fire line that was set up along the guardrail 20 meters away.

The Rangers in the support-by-fire position returned fire on the Iraqi positions below us. I immediately took up a position next to Bob to begin helping suppress targets; however, before I began firing, SSG Branford yelled for me to take a knee back by the vehicle. I looked at SSG Branford with disappointment and he responded to it with, "We can't have the guy helping the medic get shot. Get back to the fucking vehicle!"

The entire fire team was already fully engaged in small arms fire with the enemy, making this the exact wrong time to argue my case for getting extra marksmanship training. Everybody had a job to do and mine really wasn't to be shooting people. I quickly picked up from my position and fell back to the GMV on the other side of the road. SSG Shank had already begun coordinating fires with the heavy gunners of the GMVs at our position, while SSG Branford directed the support by fire at the guardrail. PFC Panatella laid down three to five round bursts on the SAW. Sergeant Long called out targets for Bob to engage with his M-203 40mm grenade launcher and SPC O'Neill carefully suppressed a fighting position, talking Long and Bob on to a group of Iraqis. In the distance, we saw a flash followed two seconds later by a large airburst explosion over the rooftop that snipers and B-team, 3rd Squad had their positions on.

While I hated the lack of participation that I presently had in the fight, I had a perspective on everything that was going on around me. The position that I was forced to take gave me a nearly unobstructed view of the intense firefight. Bravo Team and the snipers quickly moved from the rooftop after an airburst exploded barely 30 meters away. They quickly set into a covered position on the top of the hill and were immediately engaged by a fighting position at the bottom, about 200 yards away. Matt returned overwhelming suppressive fire with his M-249 SAW as Tommy engaged with the M-240B that he had dismounted from our vehicle. The combination of automatic fires allowed for the team to gain fire superiority. The engagement was quickly over, leaving five Iraqi soldiers dead and several Rangers to quickly celebrate their first kills before identifying more targets just moments later.

As B Team's initial engagement continued, a rocket close by 1st Squad's position lifted off and began a near vertical trajectory toward the reservoir. My first thought was that we had incoming enemy aircraft, but as I watched the rocket's climb over the lake, its trajectory made a radical change and took a nose dive and impacted on an island in the distance. It dawned on me that we had just fired a Javelin anti-tank missile at something, but despite the secondary explosions, I didn't know at what. All I knew was that even my good buddy Jared was getting in on the action. Even though I had no idea what he had fired at, seeing the secondary explosions afterward let me know he had hit his mark.

Before that realization could really set in, the distinct and very loud, angry, wasp-like buzz only made by a McDonnell-Douglas MH-6 Little Bird filled the fading nighttime sky above us. I looked up and watched two momentarily hover a few hundred feet above our position before one of them accelerated forward in what can only be described as a nose dive toward an enemy bunker with their 7.62mm mini gun on full auto, showering us with spent casings that left second degree burns on exposed skin. As the pilot neared the end of his gun run, the Little Bird fired its rockets and the bird quickly gained altitude. As soon as the first Little Bird cleared the airspace, the second Little Bird repeated the same maneuver on a separate target, dropping casings on top of our heads and ending with rockets that lit up the area. This time when the second Little Bird banked, the sky lit up with anti-aircraft fire from a Russian S60 anti-aircraft (AA) gun. Evading the AA fire, the Little Bird cleared the airspace, while his wingman, already on station, zeroed in on the gun targeting his fellow Night Stalker and swooped in on a second gun run, eliminating it before they could become a factor on the battlefield.

Night was quickly into turning day and the Little Birds became more vulnerable as light spilled over the horizon from the east. They ran a couple of more fire missions and were soon called off the objective. Later we would learn that while one pilot was flying, the co-pilot was engaging enemy soldiers on the ground from the door of the helicopter with an M-4 before manually dropping hand grenades onto Iraqi positions. With day approaching, the company received close air support from Air Force F-16s. The addition of sunlight also made identifying enemy positions much easier. I flipped up my NODs and continued to watch the battle unfold. As it became brighter, the magnitude of everything became clear for the first time. Laying to the south of us for as far as the eye could see was an interconnected trench system cut out of the desert floor, interspersed with enemy fighting positions, bunkers, AA guns, several small buildings and two large main buildings.

From near the top of the dam, a GMV sped down a dirt road but missed its left turn to Charlie Company's position to the southeast, instead driving straight south. I could see that the dirt road led directly between two fighting positions that Alpha Team's support by fire was actively engaging. Bob saw this as well and shouted out, "They missed their turn!"

As the friendly vehicle sped toward enemy positions, SSG Branford called for a cease-fire. Unable to engage for fear of hitting fellow Rangers, Alpha Team lifted fire and watched helplessly as the GMV headed directly for an ambush. The Iraqis noticed the vehicle's approach and got into position on both sides of the dirt road. When the GMV entered the kill zone, small arms and RPG fire opened up from both directions. Several RPGs zipped through the air, all of them missing their target, but we could see small arms impact all over the vehicle. The driver accelerated out of the ambush and pulled a tight U-turn. With no other choice, the Rangers sped back through the kill zone, this time shooting back. The volume of fire that coming from the vehicle on the return route proved to be superior as the rate of enemy fire was far less than the first time. Even so, my gut told me it was impossible for anyone to drive through that and not get hit. There were nine Rangers on a GMV with no armor protection. As the vehicle sped back up the dirt road to the top of hill, I prepared for the inevitable.

The shout came out before the shot-up GMV was even two-thirds to the top, "MEDIC!" I grabbed my aid bag. SSG Shank yelled, "Matthews! That's you!"

"Roger, Sarn't!" I yelled, running past him. Every muscle in my body worked in conjunction to run as fast as possible down the road toward the edge of the dam. As the vehicle neared the top, I still had 100 feet to run. Immediately my brain was flooded with every scenario I had ever experienced in training: a sucking chest wound, an upper-leg femoral bleed and a gunshot wound to the head. Everything I had been taught raced through my mind nearly simultaneously. I arrived at the GMV as Rangers that had gathered at his door were pulling out the driver, Sergeant Aaron. I could immediately see he was in pain and identified him as a casualty. I took a knee next to him and on initial assessment I could see that he was conscious, talking, did not have visible hemorrhaging, but was grabbing at his foot. I ask if anyone else is hit and get a reply that the top gunner had taken several rounds to the back plate of his body armor, but was fine. I turned my attention to the driver. "Where are you hit?"

"On the foot! Left foot!" I went to the foot next to my left hand, "Other left, dude."

"Sorry."

"It's cool, man . . . It's just the one I'm holding on to feels like it's been smashed with a fucking hammer!"

I told him to hang in there and that I would square him away. I examined his foot and finally noticed what would have otherwise been a tear in the lacing and tongue of the boot, which I quickly removed. With only his black sock on, I still could not see any blood. Once I pulled the sock down around his toes, blood began to pool up in a wound to the top of his foot. Overwhelmed with adrenaline, I exclaimed the obvious, "YOU'VE BEEN SHOT!"

Aaron leans forward to look at his gunshot wound, "That's it? It feels like someone just ran over my foot!"

We both laughed. The reality that it was merely a grazing wound and not a penetrating gunshot sank in. Each of us had been expecting the worst and when we saw that it was nothing more than a flesh wound, we both knew it was going to be ok. I don't think either of us expected to find ourselves laughing in a situation like that, but there really wasn't anything else to do about it.

"Goddamn, it hurts." This time, he restated it more out of confusion than anything else. I lean forward to access the Individual Bleeder Control Kit on left side his body armor. Grabbing his Israeli Trauma Dressing and Kerlex, I respond, "Roger, Sarn't. Good news is I don't think we need to use a tourniquet."

"Thanks, dude."

The size of the actual wound was less than two inches long and about a half inch wide. He wasn't bleeding heavily and therefore only needed a small amount of gauze and an Israeli Trauma Dressing to wrap and keep pressure on the wound. I had practiced dressing an injury like this at least a hundred times in the past six months and had his foot taken care of in less than a minute. After getting his foot wrapped, the call was made to move him to the platoon casualty collection point (CCP), which had just been newly established in the building 3rd Squad had initially cleared. With help from the other Rangers in his vehicle, we picked him up and supported him under his shoulders as we helped carry him to the building where the CCP was.

Shortly after entering into the room, I began to reassess my casualty. As expected, he was doing well, aside from being in an immense amount of pain. SSG Marcus Muralles, the battalion senior medic arrived moments later. SSG Muralles had heard the call for a medic while he was nearly halfway down the dam and come running to our position. He, too, expected the worst and was relieved to enter the room and discover Aaron with only his foot wrapped. As he caught his breath, SSG Muralles joked that he'd just ran a mile for nothing, then began to inspect the dressing and assess the wound. SSG Muralles was the senior-most medic responsible for training me and when he went over my work, I got a little nervous that I'd missed something. After undressing and inspecting the injury, Doc Muralles redressed it and told me that I had done a good job.

Positive feedback in the form of *good job* comes sparingly in Regiment and SSG Muralles telling me that I had done well instantly boosted my confidence as a Ranger. But before I could reflect on the compliment, SFC Jack entered from outside followed by SPC Dave. The two of them had been clearing the compound with 1st and 2nd squads and had heard the call for medic, too. Mike had a noticeable limp as he came in and immediately was looked over by Doc Muralles. While clearing a staircase, Dave took a misstep, sprained his ankle and nearly fell down a flight of stairs. While they are often overlooked on the battlefield, sprains, muscle tears and hyperextensions are common injuries. What happened to Dave could have happened to any of us, but for now, it meant that he was stuck in the CCP, which required me to accompany the platoon Sergeant around the objective. Before I had time to think, SFC Jack alerted me it was time to go and I immediately picked up and followed him out the door and back outside.

From the top of the hill where the buildings were, I finally had my first full perspective of the fight we were in. For one, the dam itself was enormous at nearly two miles in length. The hill where the buildings were located, occupied the area of a football field. Twelve buildings made a sloppy oval, at the middle of which, a 12-foot stone mural of Saddam Hussein had been erected. Of the buildings, two were bigger administrative buildings and the rest of the smaller buildings appeared to be quarters for the Iraqi soldiers. On the edge of the hilltop, they had previously dug out positions to provide cover for fighting vehicles that were not present when we arrived. SFC Jack immediately directed us to bring our vehicles up and use the unoccupied positions to establish converging fires with the heavy guns. With .50-caliber machine guns, MK19 automatic grenade launchers and M-240B machine guns the platoon instantly utilized the vehicles' firepower to our advantage and gained the complete upper hand.

1LT Joe then began directing fire missions for our 120mm mortars with the Forward Observer, SPC Jameson, while the JTAC began calling for F-16s to bomb two main buildings about 500 meters below that, from which the Iraqis were staging counterattacks. Undeterred, the enemy continued to maneuver in groups of 10-15 through the trench system in the low ground. Meanwhile, isolated groups of Republican Guard occupied bunkers and mortar positions and continued to engage our positions. The anti-tank section led by SPC Eric Carlton engaged enemy positions using the 84mm recoilless rifle, also known as the *Carl Gustaf*, or simply "the goose." The goose is a remarkably simple weapon system designed by the Swedish military following World War II. Its design allows the weapon to serve multiple purposes and has a wide array of rounds for different targets. In this case, enemy personnel were attempting to use a heavy cargo truck as cover in order to engage one of our positions. SPC Carlton recognized this and directed his gunner, PFC Patton, to engage the truck as he loaded a round in the breach. The gunner fired, scoring a direct hit, but only partially damaging the truck. Unlike the movies we'd grown up watching, there was no massive fireball, just a black cloud of smoke and debris followed by a concussion from the explosion. With cover still in place, Iraqis began to move back and use it to their advantage. Carlton pulled out another 84mm round, an airburst this time and set the range. He loaded it into the breach and this time directed the gunner to aim slightly over the truck. The round exploded and killed a few of the Iraqis, but with an effective form of cover, the enemy continued to maneuver and utilize it to their advantage. 1LT Joe and the JTAC noticed this and called for an airstrike on the truck. Moments later, a 500-pound bomb fell from the sky, effectively neutralizing the cargo truck for the duration of the battle.

By midday, our intersecting fires became so effective that we established what began to be referred to as "No Man's Land". From the advantage of high ground and good cover, the platoon coordinated fires so well that by mid-morning, we had pushed back the enemy over a half of a kilometer from our hill. At one point, SPC Barron and PFC Cannon spotted a dirt bike in the low ground moving laterally across the battlefield. Had it been headed south, directly away from their sectors of fire, Barron and Cannon probably would not have engaged. However, the motorcycle with two Iraqis was moving to the east, into the conflict instead of away from it. The Iraqis probably thought that being on two wheels would make them harder to target and for a moment, they were correct. Barron and Cannon both engaged with the Mk-19 and a M-240B. The motorcycle evaded the initial volley of fire and looked as if it might make it to safety. Barron ordered Cannon on the M-240B to use the machine gun and give the bike a greater lead, then walk the rounds back into it. Cannon adjusted his aim and depressed the trigger of the machine gun, letting out a long burst which he raked back toward the motorcycle. It worked. 7.62mm ate through the motorcycle and dropped its two passengers. Barron then used the opportunity to walk a burst of 40mm grenades on the bike and surrounding area to make sure no one got up.

After establishing No Man's Land, most of the shooting was relegated to the heavy guns and snipers. For the hours up until midday, snipers had been helping direct small arms fire as well as engaging individuals with their long guns. By noon, their positions in the Eagle's Nest, as they referred to it, became responsible for a quarter of the platoons' fire. By utilizing the highest ground on the dam, snipers called out enemy positions for mortars and air strikes, and and used a combination of precision .308 and .50-caliber fires to suppress and prevent the enemy's movement and assembly. Because of this effective fire, the Iraqis relied more and more on their mortar positions to dislodge us. As the targets for the F-16s became smaller, and the indirect fire intensified, the risk of losing a fast-mover became greater and the call to pull them off of the objective was made to prevent collision between an aircraft and a mortar round in its airspace. Luckily for the strike force, we had another platform to provide close air support. As F-16s checked off station, A-10s replaced them.

A-10s are slow flying, single-pilot behemoths of an attack plane. The entire aircraft is designed around a 30mm Gatling-style cannon. It has numerous hard points for attaching for everything from rocket pods to JDAMs. The JTAC makes a call on the radio and the big aircraft falls from the sky in a tactic similar to the Little Birds, but with greater effect. The A-10 would drop in and fire two short bursts from its 30mm cannon at a rate of over 3000 rounds per minute. The sound that gun made was unlike anything I'd ever heard, an explosive thundercloud of gun smoke that rained death to those in a 40 foot radius. I'd never seen anything like it. For several minutes, everyone seemed to stop and take notice. It was just the snipers calling targets for the JTAC and the A-10s taking care of the rest. The pilots would circle above like a bird of prey scanning for its next victim. The call be made and they'd swoop down from the sky and engage Iraqi positions with bursts from the cannon, followed by deployment of rockets. Each time they would dive the Iraqis would return fire, but by the end of the run, their positions would fall silent.

The rest of the afternoon continued like this, snipers and heavy guns engaging long distance targets with the help of 120mm mortars and A-10s.

Eventually we began searching the buildings on our hill for intelligence as the small arms fire died out. In the center of the building in front of the Saddam mural, we found an arms room with enough AK47s to arm every Ranger in the platoon—twice. It was reassuring to find backup weapons with enough ammo and grenades to last us for a while. They even had bayonets just in case things got close. We set up the platoon command post (CP) and established it as the future CCP should we need it. Sergeant Aaron had been moved to the company CCP at the center of the dam and Doc Dave and SSG Muralles joined the command element in this building. With two real medics at the CP, SFC Jack sent me to help 3rd Squad search buildings.

I linked up with Matt, Bob, Tommy and Panatela to help search the building which was formerly the CCP. While 3rd Squad had cleared the buildings during the initial assault, a proper search for intelligence hadn't been completed. In the building, we found the Iraqis had quite a bit of intel on us. Of particular amusement was a poster of coalition military aircraft, mainly that of the United States. Several rows of photos, probably found on the Internet, showed American fighter jets, bombers, cargo planes and even refueling planes, along with their respective descriptions in Arabic below. There were more than a couple of them so I took one, folded it up and put it in my cargo pocket. In a file cabinet, someone found files with Iraqi military IDs. I grabbed one and looked at it. A black and white photo laminated on cardstock that contained Arabic that I assumed indicated name, rank and other information. I had not a clue how it translated, but suspected it was a ID of a man fighting down below us. I wondered if he'd been killed already, or was he still somehow alive? Had this been one of the guys running in the dark that SSG Shank, Jonathan and I had shot earlier?

I decided that it wasn't the guy who I'd shot. *Couldn't be.* But the thought sat with me as we continued to search for valuable information. Eventually we gathered everything that looked pertinent and stacked it in one corner of the main room. Since this building was the second largest and for the most part out of the way, it became the collection point for everything else found throughout the mission to be taken off the objective. During the search of another building, I ran into Jared, who was in one of the best moods that I'd ever seen him in...sober. I finally got to ask him about the Javelin kill from earlier in the morning, "Dude, what were you shooting at earlier?"

"Oh, with the Javelin?"

"Yeah. Out on the lake."

Jared chuckled, "It was a mortar position, dude. Sarn't Santos pointed it out to Sarn't Jack. Could barely see the heat signature with the viewfinder."

"How far was it? I could barely see where it landed..."

"Oh, I don't know. Had to be at least 2000 meters. I thought was gonna miss until I saw the secondary explosions." He chuckled again. "Yeah, you got 'em, alright."

For the first time, I realized that at one point, the enemy had surrounded us on four sides. How no one had been seriously wounded was beyond me. Aside from Sergeant Aaron and the gunner who'd been hit in the back plate of his armor, no one had been hit in over eight hours of sustained combat. As I talked to other guys throughout the afternoon, I learned that everybody had fired their weapon. Some would shrug off whether they'd actually hit anybody, but most guys knew without a doubt. We had all been baptized by fire and everyone's mood was the best it'd been since leaving Georgia. No more the question of whether we'd actually see combat. No more fear of freezing up or failing to act. We'd all performed like we'd been trained. We had excelled in the art of war and had set the enemy back more than a kilometer. Someone found Iraqi paper money and pointed out the dam on the Iraq's 500-dinar bill. I looked across to the dam structure itself. It was huge, spanning nearly 2 miles in total length and over 14 stories tall. The magnitude and importance of the mission finally sank in. The company had just done something significant and everyone knew it.

As day turned to night and darkness fell, the line squads began digging into the hill outside of the buildings facing toward the low ground. Doc Dave and I rotated on radio guard with the platoon RTO, PFC Wolf, to monitor the platoon net and alert the leadership to any pertinent info or calls from higher up. Because of being on radio guard, we were indoors for the most part and did not have to dig positions. This was about the luckiest a private could get. While the other privates dug into the night, I smoked cigarettes under the covered entry of the building and watched bombs explode in the distance while listening to the platoon radio traffic.

Around midnight, Gunny called SFC Jack over the radio. Iraqis were trying to use the cover of darkness to get closer. Using nighttime scopes with thermal imaging, SSG Shank and his gun team leaders spotted the enemy trying to walk up on to our positions.

They were literally walking in a single-file line, weapons slung over their back like they were on a casual stroll in the park. SFC Jack and SSG Shank let the column of would-be attackers get 600 meters out and opened up with intersecting fires, mowing them down. That would be the one and only time they tried to just walk up onto us like that. But for the rest of the night, Iraqis maneuvered small groups toward us, always intercepted by heavy guns once reaching the 600-meter line we'd established. Any further out made it hard to effectively engage at night and since we had been fighting all day, conservation of ammunition became a prime consideration of platoon leadership.

About an hour later, it was reported that Iraqis were trying to consolidate again at the two large buildings about 500 meters out. Earlier in the day, the buildings had been serviced by a couple of 500-pound bombs, but tonight the call came for a one-ton JDAM on each building to neutralize the enemy posting up there. A jet made its pass and moments later a flash illuminated the sky like a lightning strike, followed by the loudest thunderous boom I'd ever heard. The concussion was so great I felt it in my chest as it shook the buildings and ground beneath me. Seconds later, another jet flew by and a second lightning strike and thunderclap that shook the hill followed. Rangers celebrated amongst themselves with hushed cheers and high-fives. It wasn't quite a fireworks show, but it sure matched any Fourth of July celebration we'd ever seen.

Every four hours I would rotate to radio guard for two hours. While off radio guard, I took refuge in the buildings and attempted to sleep. Lying on a concrete floor and trying to fall asleep after the day we had was next to impossible. Despite barely sleeping at the ROD site and only getting a few hours of sleep the night before, I was wide awake. If I'd get close to dosing off, a burst of machine gun fire or an outgoing 120mm mortar would jolt me out of it. While lying there in the darkness, memories of the previous 18 hours came flooding back. The Little Birds and A-10s, the support by fire line on the side of the road, everything vivid as if it was still happening. All this time, I'd worried about how I'd handle combat and today I'd discovered war wasn't just exciting, it was fun. I found myself thinking about how different it was from the movies, how much better it was than a video game. I felt like combat was what I'd been waiting for my entire life; that this is what I was meant to do. It was with these thoughts that I was finally able to drift off to sleep.

I awoke to the sounds of a .50-caliber machine gun engaging a target in the distance. I didn't feel as if it jolted me awake, rather it slowly brought me back into the world that was the fight for Haditha Dam. It almost felt as if I hadn't been asleep, that I'd just mentally checked out for a while. I turned my head to see Doc Dave staring at me from the doorway.

"Morning, sunshine. Get a good night's sleep?"

"Was I asleep?"

Dave chuckled, "Yeah, dude, you were passed out. And now it's my turn because you're on radio guard."

"Awesome."

"Hurry up and get your shit together so you can come relieve me." Dave left the doorway. I checked my watch…0600hrs.

As I got up, I realized how tired and slow I felt. I pulled my body armor over my head, cinched it down and put on my MICH. Grabbing my weapon, I headed to the door and outside to relieve Dave on the radio. It was the morning of the second day on the dam. We had settled into our fighting positions and prepared for another day of defending the high ground. The Iraqis had attempted throughout the night to sneak closer and as the morning stretched on, heavy gunners and mortars pushed them back. Snipers continued to engage, as did our 120mm mortars and the pilots above flew coverage, dropping death whenever called.

Mid-morning the order came down that we would be holding the dam until relieved. The order didn't specify when that relief might arrive. We'd been told the mission would last 24 hours and had packed accordingly. The platoon was low on food, water and ammunition. The order went out to conserve all supplies and squad leaders provided SFC Jack with a list of needs for the resupply, growing more urgent by the hour.

Brief engagements of sniper fire and heavy guns would periodically fill the air, but for the most part the morning lacked the excitement and glory of the day before. Being physically tired was part of it, but half of me was already desensitized to the sights and sounds of war. Engagements with the enemy became routine and while big guns would occasionally talk back and forth, the adrenaline rush that came along with it had vanished.

After PFC Wolf took back over monitoring the radio for the day, I resumed accompanying SFC Jack when he left the CP. Mid-day, SSG Santos called in a report of a kayaker off an island near the shore of the reservoir. I followed SFC Jack to a GMV overlooking the reservoir and sure enough, an Iraqi was attempting to paddle away from the island in a kayak.

"I don't believe it." SFC Jack exclaimed.

SSG Santos handed SFC Jack the binoculars, but even without them it was possible to see the kayak a few hundred meters struggling to paddle into the wind.

"He's wearing OD green." SFC Jack remarked. "I don't know, looks hostile to me. Give 'em a warning burst, Carp."

SPC Carp, who was occupying the turret, put a warning burst of .50-cal into the water in front of the kayak. Instead of giving up, the kayaker paddled harder, meeting stiff resistance from the wind.

"Fuck it," SFC Jack said, as he spit tobacco juice. "Sink him, Carp."

SPC Carp shrugged and fired off another burst that tore through the plastic boat. In seconds, it disappeared beneath the surface. SFC Jack sent Bravo Team from 3rd Squad down to the reservoir to search for a survivor. Ten minutes later, Matt and Tommy returned securing a very wet but unharmed Iraqi. When they got to him to our position, he was searched and SSG Branford found a hand drawn map of our location. We looked at the Iraqi in amazement. That crazy bastard had paddled in during the night to draw out our positions. Had this gotten into the hands of an artillery crew, it would have made their job very easy. Fortunately for us, the courageous Iraqi was too impatient to wait until dark to show his artwork to his buddies, making it now ours.

Bravo Team loaded up the detainee in a GMV and quickly took the prisoner to the dam for further interrogation. As they returned from the center of the dam, their vehicle came under fire from a four-barrel ZPU AA gun that had gone overlooked. The driver of the GMV accelerated back to our position while the mortar team located the Russian ZPU, taking out its crew with a 120mm HE round. Luckily, the vehicle returned to the group of buildings without getting hit and no Rangers on board were wounded.

The rest of the day continued in the same fashion as the morning and afternoon of the day before. Ten to fifteen Iraqis would build up the gusto to begin maneuvering toward our position, only to be cut down by intersecting machine gun and 40mm grenade fire. It became target practice for the Rangers manning the heavy guns and everyone on the line would take their turn. If anyone besides Dave, Wolf, or me had any doubts about their proficiency on the heavy guns, today was the day to erase them.

As the day progressed, engagements became fewer. At this point, no one had shaved since we left Saudi and everyone who could grow facial hair had about four days of growth. Rangers are known for their high standards of neatness of dress and appearance, making a platoon of unshaven Batt boys quite a unique sight. Unfortunately, that would change before the end of the day. Around sunset, the word came down: everybody must shave. Begrudgingly, Rangers began to pull back from the line and shave. Being only 19 years old, I had a peach fuzz mustache with only a few chin hairs, which made it quite easy to dry shave. For those who had a thik shave like 1LT Joe, SSG Shank and Jared, dry shaving with a Bic razor proved painful and bloody.

Freshly shaven, the platoon was now ready for the sun to go down on our second night on the dam. Since I was the first to pull radio guard the night before, I was the last in the rotation tonight, which meant I had the chance to rack out first. This time, I had no difficulty finding sleep. As soon as I laid my head against my assault pack, I was unconscious until Dave woke me four hours later.

Barely awake, I relieved Dave at the radio. I immediately lit a cigarette to help me wake up and lowered my NODS in order to see around me. I checked my watch. *2300hrs. Two hours to go.* If anything important came across the radio, I was to wake up 1LT Joe, but for the most part, all was quiet. Occasional updates would come across the net, but the majority of my time was spent chain smoking cigarettes and listening to the sounds of the desert night.

70

Thirty minutes before my shift was due to end, a call came through.

"All elements, be advised. We have just taken casualties, standby for SITREP," a shaken but calm voice called over the radio.

I quickly woke up the PL and informed him of the report. As he awoke, the second part of the call came through, "We have three KIA, multiple wounded. Request CASEVAC at our position, immediately."

1LT Joe grabbed the radio and listened to the rest of the transmission. I asked him what was going on after the radio traffic died down a few minutes later. He told me that Alpha Company had been hit a few miles away and that was all he knew. As my guard shift ended, I went inside and woke Wolf, passing on the news as I took a knee next to him.

"What happened?" He asked after the second time of telling him there had been casualties.

"Alpha Company got hit. Three guys dead."

"You know who?"

"No, just that there were three KIA and a bunch of other guys that got hurt."

Wolf took a moment to let it set in. "Shit's getting real now."

He was right. I stood up and agreed, "Yep. I'll be outside, man."

I went back outside to where 1LT Joe was on the radio. He put the handset down and looked at me.

"A Co. stopped a vehicle at their checkpoint. A pregnant woman got out and asked for a bottle of water, they went to help her and the car blew up."

"You're kidding me, sir."

"Suicide bomber."

Wolf came outside and asked what happened. 1LT Joe repeated the story to a similar response of disbelief. No one could have imagined this. We'd prepared for almost every type of engagement while training in Georgia, but we never prepared for Iraqis to use pregnant women as decoys. We had never prepared for suicide car bombs and the news of their using a woman to initiate one shook everybody to the core.

Wolf shook his head and spit Copenhagen off to the side, "These fucking people."

I went back inside and tried to fall back asleep. Unlike earlier in the night, rest proved elusive, as all I could think about was the situation Alpha Company was dealing with. Three Rangers lost their lives and several others were wounded. I had friends in Alpha and secretly wished that they weren't the ones who'd gotten hurt or died. Reality began to set in; that we were not impervious to the risks of war. Rangers could be killed at any moment and Alpha Company had just learned that lesson firsthand.

With morning came news of the names of our fallen brothers. Killed were Captain Russell Rippetoe, SSG Nino Livaudais and SPC Ryan Long. I didn't know any of them personally, but knew of CPT Rippetoe and remembered he rode a Harley Davidson that I'd seen around the battalion area in Georgia. The news of their passing spread around the platoon and each of us paid our simple respects. There was nothing we could do but hold the dam at all costs. They had died at a roadblock that had isolated the objective from reinforcements and it was now our duty to make sure their sacrifices were not in vain.

The assault force was entering its third day of occupation. The Company CP had received a resupply of ammunition, food and water in the middle of the night, brought to our location by the First Sergeant around 0900hrs. I hadn't shot but five rounds so only needed resupply on chow and water. As a private without a Ranger tab, I got my pick from a ransacked box of MREs. I found a Bean and Rice Burrito for breakfast that was better than Beef and Mushrooms or Chicken Teriyaki.

As I ate chow, I noticed how quiet it was. I hadn't heard any of the heavy gunfire or aircraft drop bombs and began to wonder if it was all over. It seemed logical to me as I ate my cold burrito that the Iraqis had given up. It was obvious that we had the dam and weren't giving it up. We had fire superiority in every aspect and there was no way for them to dislodge us from our positions. *We'd won.* I went outside to smoke a cigarette after eating and looked out on to the battlefield. For the first time, I noticed the number of dogs in the area probably outnumbered the platoon. While, I'd seen one or two and definitely heard a lot of them bark, I hadn't realized the sheer number of feral dogs surrounding the objective. I wasn't the only one to take note. SPC Hamburg sat in the turret of a GMV, smoking a cigarette while surveying his sector.

"Look at the number of dogs out there." He said in disbelief. "Gotta be at least fifty of them running around." He looked at me while taking a drag and nodded, "Bet they're all out for the bodies lying around. Free food."

I watched a pack of several skinny looking medium-sized dogs huddled and stationary about 200 meters away. I imagined them tearing away at a body, realizing they'd do the same to me if I was lying out there dead.

"Jesus."

Hamburg took another drag, "Yeah, I think out here they call him Mohammed..."

I finished my cigarette and began walking back to the other side of the building toward the CP. As I turned the corner, I heard wind rush over my head followed by a loud concussion and an explosion at the base of the dam. That round was different than anything we received so far. The Forward Observer, SPC Jameson declared that it was an artillery round. We waited for another one, taking cover in the entrance of the CP. A call came through from the mortars that they had gotten a back azimuth on where the round came from and air support was sent to investigate. While we waited for an update, or for the next round to come in, I began to have an urge for a bowel movement. I quickly decided that now was not the time for me to take my first combat shit, but the nicotine of my last cigarette had already taken effect. I hadn't taken a dump since leaving the airfield and had only had a couple of MREs and Power Bars since, but after eating breakfast and smoking, my bowels were ready to do their job.

War, however, would not pause for me to drop my drawers. I looked at Dave. The more I thought about it, the worse the pressure in my lower abdomen became. I finally asked him where to go take a dump. He didn't believe me at first, but when he saw I was serious, he told me about the ravine where he'd taken one earlier.

"Just be careful," he said.

I grabbed my M-4 and headed toward the ravine between our hill and the dam that was covered from small arms fire but completely vulnerable to indirect fire. I found a spot a third of the way down that allowed for good footing and took off my body armor. The JLIST chemical suit that I'd been wearing was a two-piece that had to be zipped down and nearly fully taken off in order to facilitate the process of defecating. I finally removed all necessary clothing and squatted. No shit there I was: chemical-suit around my ankles, brown t-shirt blowing along with everything else in the breeze, with a war going on around me. Details are irrelevant, but eating MREs consecutively for days can lead to *disproportionate reward versus effort factor.* It was as I was experiencing this moment of dissatisfaction that the *WHOOSH!* of an artillery shell sailing overhead came in and exploded not far away. It was by no means close to hitting me, but nonetheless I instinctively flinched and attempted to crouch lower before I realized that I wasn't in immediate danger. Doing so, I lost my footing on the incline and began to slide down the hill with my pants around my ankles. I caught myself and didn't move for a second to ensure I was done sliding. I looked down and saw my own turd about an inch from my bare thigh. If I slipped any further or forward, I was sure to smear it on my leg. The thought of falling into my own shit trumped the fact that my ass was hanging out, so before pulling up my pants, I slowly rolled to my left until I was clear of danger. Satisfied that I wasn't going to come in contact, I pulled up my JLIST around my hips then awkwardly stood up to pull the suit suspender straps over my shoulders and zip it up. I then put my kit back on, grabbed my weapon and returned the CP.

As I got back up to the building, Dave asks if they'd caught me with my pants down. I chuckled and went to my aid bag to grab hand sanitizer. One of the things I hadn't planned for was receiving artillery while taking a dump and I just escaped my first dose of it relatively cleanly. I couldn't imagine someone knocking on my parents' door to explain how their son died shitting for their freedom.

A few more artillery rounds came in that day and as we sent air support to investigate their location. As they passed over the actual village of Haditha, the pilots noticed a large group of Iraqi soldiers loading vehicles to flee to the south of the dam. After this report and the destruction of another artillery piece, the rest of the day was rather quiet.

That night was uneventful, aside from another resupply that we received from H1. An MH-47 Chinook dropped off more food and water along with ammunition and other supplies at the center of the dam. The First Sergeant decided to wait until daylight to distribute it and so the platoon continued to dig and reinforce their positions with sandbags. Working in shifts, the privates in the platoon would hack away at their positions with E-tools to break up the dry, hard soil enough to fill sandbags. While the platoon dug for the third night in a row, I sat on radio guard taking in the constant *tink, tink, tink* from their shovels hitting hard-packed soil and rock. On the horizon to the southwest, lighting flashed in the distance, followed seconds later by the rumble of thunder. I knew it wasn't lightning, but that didn't stop my mind from seeing it any differently. Word began to spread that the heavy gunners could see the heat signatures of the dogs fighting over dead Iraqis through the thermal night scopes on the vehicles. Occasionally, we would hear the pack turn on one of their own. Forced to listen to the cries of the dog being savagely mauled by members of its own pack, I came to appreciate the safety of our positions on the top of the hill even more. Never in my life had I heard dogs turn on each other like that and it was a sound that no one would forget. Eventually I woke up Wolf to relieve me on radio guard. Once back in the room, the sounds of the night were muffled by the walls and rooftop over my head. Lying there in the dark room, I quickly succumbed to exhaustion and fell asleep.

Four hours later, I woke up to Dave gently tapping my boot with his foot. At first, I couldn't understand why he was waking me up.

"Dude. Radio guard." He whispered, "It's time."

"Fucking 'eh…"

"I know. Hurry up so I can go take a piss and rack out." I looked at him for a moment, nodded and he left the room. My watch read 0400hrs. It was two hours before the sun came up, so I knew there was no more sleep for the night. I slowly pulled myself together. My arms and legs felt weighted down, motor skills slightly off. At the radio, Dave informed me that nothing had happened since he took over from Wolf and immediately stood up to leave, presumably to go relieve himself. I sat down next to the radio and put the handset to my ear and began the shift of listening to dead air interrupted by brief situation reports. Fatigue made my arms and legs feel numb and useless as I sat, desperately fighting off the urge to lose consciousness. Chain-smoking cigarette after cigarette, my mind wandered freely through memories of the past. Looking out into the night, I wondered what my parents were doing. I figured it was evening at their house and they were both sitting in the living room, watching television. Were they watching news about the war, afraid for their son? I hoped not. Wishing there was a way that I could reach out and let them know that I was ok, I sat listening to a silent radio, able to do nothing but put out the Marlboro smoking between my fingers and light up another one.

Eventually the sun began to rise and the platoon slowly began their priorities of work. Shortly after being relieved by Wolf on the radio, the first artillery shell of the day struck about 100 meters from 2nd Platoon's perimeter on the other side of the dam. Within minutes, an artillery gun from the northeast and two heavy mortar positions to the south had dialed in on 2nd Platoon's position, forcing their defensive perimeter to fall back into the dam. 1LT Joe received a call from the CO that gave him the position of the mortar tubes and SFC Jack directed snipers and heavy guns to begin engaging, while the Forward Observer called in 120mm mortars on the two positions. Within minutes of engaging the positions to our south, our hill began to receive artillery with rounds impacting inside of our perimeter.

During a break from the incoming fire, a call was made to SFC Jack that our previous night's resupply was ready to be picked up at the center of the dam. SFC Jack grabbed SPC Plasman as his driver, as well as Jared, PFC Patton and I to accompany him to pick up our rations. We loaded up a cargo GMV that wasn't being used on the line and headed to the main structure of the dam. The road leading to the center of the dam was nearly a mile and as we sped down the concrete structure, I was once again amazed at how big everything was. It almost seemed as if we were driving down a long suspension bridge, yet there was no overpass. The dam was a nearly two-mile man-made barrier holding back an enormous lake. We pulled up to the building at the center of the dam and quickly off-loaded. For the first time since the fighting started, I was actually standing on the structure on which the mission was centered. It was bigger in person than as seen from the hill where our platoon was positioned.

Greeted by Sergeant Donald Buman, or Doc Buma as he was called, I had the chance to go inside and take a look around one of the biggest hydroelectric dams in the world. Inside, I was immediately greeted by cooler air. Because the dam generated electricity, the structure itself had power and therefore air conditioning. The change of temperature was refreshing and so welcome. Doc Buma led me to the makeshift Company Aid Station where he and the Battalion Physician Assistant, CPT Ray Silver and a few other Rangers had set up inside.

Located in a big room near the main entrance, the aid station was nothing more than a couple of aid bags set up, with a Ranger guarding two Iraqi soldiers that had been wounded and captured. One Iraqi sat back against the wall with the miserable expression you'd expect from a man who'd had his jaw nearly blown off. The man looked to be at least fifty, although he was probably younger. He wore the rank of colonel, but the sad look in his eyes revealed only a man in pain, no officerly pretense. His face long, he couldn't clench his jaw in order to close his mouth. His bottom mandible hung, uncontrollable from the rest of his face, as two holes, one on each side, penetrated his cheeks. Slightly balding and overweight, he was dirty with dried blood, sweat and dust. The second guy lay on the floor with a sandbag over his head. Immediately, I could see that he was dead.

"What's up with this guy?" I asked even though I already knew the answer. Doc Buma looks at him and without taking his hands out of his pocket replies, "Oh, that guy? Yeah, I wouldn't worry about him. I don't think he's going anywhere."

I stared down at the Iraqi while Buma began to dig into his aid bag. Rigor mortis had set in and gave the skin a waxy, dull look. I imagined they had put the sandbag over his face so they wouldn't have to sit there and look at his dead expression, but part of me had wished it wasn't there. A voice inside of me didn't want to believe he was dead, that he was just asleep and still alive, but after a minute of watching and never seeing his chest rise or fall, I knew that my initial suspicion was correct.

Buma walked over to the colonel, holding a small Dixie cup then motioned to the Iraqi officer with a pill in his hand, repeating the Arabic word for medicine. The man indicated that he understood and raised his hands to his cheeks to cover both of the holes in his face. The Colonel gratefully nodded and Buma put the pill on the man's tongue and slowly poured water into his mouth. The Iraqi swallowed twice, water escaping down the sides of his cheeks as he did. Sitting there, watching Doc hand-feed pain pills to another human being took me by surprise. This was the enemy, yet for the first time, I felt compassion toward someone on the other side. The humanity of providing medical aid to the same people we were trying to kill and they us, was a juxtaposition of everything I'd experienced to this point.

"So what happened?"

"This guy was riding shotgun in a cargo truck yesterday that didn't want to stop for second platoon's roadblock. Sarn't Major Birch smoked him and his battle buddy with the SR-25."

"I guess that explains the sandbag."

Buma shrugged, "Yeah, keeps everything nice and neat."

SFC Jack yelled that we were ready to go, so my time with Buma and the wounded Colonel came to an end. Before I walked out the door, Buma stopped me, "You got any Copenhagen?"

I replied that I only had cigarettes. Buma thought about it for a second, "Fuck it, give me one. I ran out of dip yesterday." I pulled out a cigarette and threw it to him as I ran out the door. Back outside, I jogged over to the GMV and jumped in the back with Jared and Patton. We had mostly been resupplied with MREs and water, but as we drove back, I also noticed a couple bags of Twizzler licorice and small cans of Fanta orange soda. I stared at the candy and Fanta with bewilderment. Surely, it must be some kind of joke. Yet, there between our feet were enough eight-ounce cans of Fanta for the entire platoon. Jared shook his head and laughed, "What are we gonna do with orange soda?"

"Drink it." Patton responded as the GMV pulled up to our building. He jumped off the back and Jared and I began handing supplies to him, Salido and Glassmock who had both come to help unload the vehicle. No sooner than we had gotten the last box of MREs to the building the sonic boom of an artillery shell, followed near-instantaneously by a loud explosion shook the hill. A cloud of black smoke and dust lifted into the air. Before anyone could react, several more rounds impacted around the hill. Unlike yesterday, there was no whistling in the air to warn us of an incoming round. Just a loud crack from the 155mm shell breaking the sound barrier, followed immediately by an explosion that would shake the ground where it landed.

All Rangers on our hill were either in fortified positions or buildings so the rounds didn't score a direct hit and no one was wounded on the initial barrage to our position. We could tell by the accuracy of the artillery the Iraqis now had a forward observer calling fire. SFC Jack quickly ordered over the radio for the snipers to begin scanning for his position. 155mm artillery shells continued to impact on and around our hill, but after nearly three days of digging, our positions were well protected. The Iraqi observer must have realized this, as rounds began impacting between our hill and the center of the dam. He must have spotted our 120mm mortar position because rounds began creeping up the hill toward their position. Just then, a round hit directly on the far side of the retaining wall the mortarmen were using for cover. One of the Rangers who was acting as a spotter was caught by surprise and did not get down in time. From our position in the covered entrance of the CP, we could see him fly up in the air as the round exploded.

Shouts for medic could immediately be heard from the mortars' position. SFC Jack immediately called for SPC Plasman to get back in the driver's seat and Dave and I ran with him to the GMV. Plasman turned the vehicle around and sped to the road leading up to the dam. SFC Jack saw a route around the retaining wall that allowed us to take the strip of dirt between it and the edge of the reservoir. SPC Plasman accelerated down the narrow dirt path. About fifty meters from the mortar's position, the vehicle came to a halt and we dismounted. Just as we did, another round landed on the other side of the road. The four of us hit the dirt for a quick second then picked up and began sprinting toward the wounded Ranger. We got about halfway and another round came in. We quickly hit the dirt again and then picked back up after the explosion. Mortar crewmembers were huddled next to an unconscious Ranger, trying to get him to wake up when we arrived. It was immediately apparent that he had penetrating head trauma at his right temple. Orbital bones broken, his eyes had instantly swollen up and turned purple, deforming his facial features. The second thing I noticed was that the Ranger was cyanotic, which meant he wasn't getting oxygen.

Dave and I pulled him off the wall, expecting the worse. I removed his helmet to assess the trauma while Dave felt for a pulse on his neck. Aside from the penetration at his temple and damage to his eyes, there was no other visible trauma. Dave found a pulse and I leaned down to listen for breathing. Faintly, I could hear gurgling in the back of this throat indicative of an obstructed airway. Dave instructed me to begin suctioning his airway while he prepared for a cricothyrotomy, a surgical procedure that opens the airway by making an incision in the throat and inserting a breathing tube. It was a bold call in any circumstance, but even bolder under the current conditions; however, if the suction failed to clear his airway, we would have had no other choice and making the call to begin preparation was the right move. Luckily, I was able to get the suction into the back of the wounded Ranger's mouth and began squeezing the rubber bulb in order to create a vacuum to remove the obstruction. As I squeezed what looked like a large turkey baster, clotted blood and flesh began to be extracted by the suction tube. After about ten seconds, I stopped pulling up fluid and tissue and removed the suction from his mouth.

Miraculously, he began breathing on his own and color immediately returned to his face.

I asked one of his Ranger buddies what his name was and they responded, *"Feldman!"* I called out his name and asked if he could hear me. No response. Dave saw that Feldman had regained breathing and abandoned the cric procedure. He instructed me to secure the casualty's airway with an oropharyngeal tube, which resembled a plastic J. While securing Feldman's airway, the mortar section leader, SFC Smith, pulled one of the mortar's cargo GMVs up on the other side of the wall ordering us to load him up so we could get him to the Company CCP. Knowing it was only a matter of time before the next artillery shell came in and afraid of taking more casualties, we hastily began to lift Feldman up without putting his helmet back on. I had him by the shoulders while a couple of others had him at the legs and waist. SFC Smith and several other Rangers on the other side of the wall waited for us to lift him over the wall. As we did, they grabbed him by the legs and waist. In the chaos, the group on the other side of the wall began to carry him to the vehicle while I still had him by the shoulders. The wall between myself and the other guys prevented me from going any further with Feldman.

I tried to call out and as I did, he fell from my grip, his head smacking the other side of the wall leaving a bloody mark where it had hit. Immediately, my heart sank into my stomach and I knew everything we had just done up until this point to get him breathing was in vain. SFC Smith and the other Rangers quickly picked him up and pulled him into the back of the cargo GMV. I stood there for a moment, shocked, watching them load him up.

"Matthews!" Someone yelled from behind, "Let's go! Get on the fucking vehicle!"

I turned to see SFC Jack yelling at me to get my aid bag and get on the cargo truck. Snapping out of it, I quickly grabbed my bag and M-4 then jumped over the wall and into the back of the GMV, followed closely behind by SPC Dave. As soon as Dave was on board, the driver shifted into drive and sped off toward the center of the dam. Feldman started to regain consciousness, muttering incoherent sentences as we pulled up to the CCP. At once, our vehicle was surrounded by Rangers ready to aid in getting our wounded out of the back. Two of those were Sergeant Buman and CPT Silver, the Battalion Physician's Assistant. Taking his shoulders once more, I was determined not to let Feldman's head so much as touch the ground. He even helped by reaching up and grabbing behind his collar to help keep his head up as we moved him out of the vehicle. The group carried him behind a large concrete wall and set him down. As we lowered him, I squatted down on to both knees so that his head and shoulders would rest elevated on my lap.

Captain Silver and Doc Buma immediately began their assessment and worked to stabilize Feldman for CASEVAC. Buma started a saline lock for an IV, while CPT Silver assessed his head trauma and airway. As they were doing this, SFC Jack and SPC Plasman brought our GMV to the center of the dam to pick up Dave and me. With Feldman's head in my lap, I had to wait for someone to relieve me before I could rejoin the vehicle. Finally, someone took over at his shoulders and after taking one last moment with the wounded Ranger, I ran over and jumped in the back of SFC Jack's GMV. As soon as I sat down, I stared down at the lap of my JLIST suit, now saturated in blood from assisting Feldman. I rotated my sleeves and saw they too were covered in blood. As the vehicle pulled off back toward our building on the hill, I looked back one last time to the group of Rangers huddled over Feldman, the thought of his head hitting the wall at the forefront of my mind.

Dave and I sat in silence on the return to buildings. While turning the

81

corner to drive up the last 25 meters to the CP, an artillery round scored a direct hit on the lip of a defilade vehicle position manned by SSG Shank, SPC Hester and SPC Jameson. The overpressure knocked all three of them from their positions and to the opposite end of the three-sided hole while moving the GMV several feet in the opposite direction. We pulled up to the building as Rangers were helping Gunny and the two others to their feet. Everybody was ok, miraculously, as I had already started going back into response mode.

We all took cover inside the CP building and no one said a word to Dave or me as we passed by covered in blood. I led the way into the center room full of AK-47s. With the lights off, the room was nearly pitch black. Images of Feldman's head smacking the concrete wall like a wet sponge flashed through my mind into the darkness on rapid repeat. A flood of emotion ranging from anger to guilt overcame me and I threw my aid bag to the floor. With nothing else in sight, I stepped forward and kicked the steel door of an AK rack.

Dave grabbed me by the shoulder, not giving much resistance when I pulled away. I knew we'd made a mistake by not putting his helmet back on. I took his helmet off; I should have put it back on before moving him. I should have taken charge of moving him over the wall to prevent him from falling. We'd compounded his injuries and I knew it. He might have regained consciousness, but I knew there was a good chance that we'd pushed shrapnel into his brain by dropping him like that, a complication he might not survive. Expressing this to Dave was impossible. I'd try to begin a sentence and only get a few words out before I'd yell out profanity and start over. My mind was racing, replaying everything over and over.

Not even knowing he was in the room, SSG Muralles let me vent for a moment and then said in a very firm yet reassuring tone, "Matthews, you did fine. You and Dave got him to the CCP alive; you guys did your job. Now, breathe and relax."

It was just the three of us in the room. Tears swelled up in my eyes, I leaned back against the wall and sat down. Doc Muralles left no room to argue, nor was there any point in trying. There was nothing more I could do and there was nothing I could say to change what had already happened. A voice inside my head reminded me that I was a Ranger and demanded that I maintain my composure. I began to breathe. As I began to calm down, Dave looked over and said, "Why don't you go smoke a cigarette?"

"You of all people are telling me to smoke?" I half-chuckled. Dave smiled, "Yeah, man. Get out of here and go smoke."

The thought of a cigarette sounded amazing. Another artillery round impacted in the distance, but I was determined to feed my nicotine habit. I stood up and left the room, heading for the covered entrance of the building. Usually during the day, leadership wouldn't allow me to smoke close to the entrance, all of them hating the habit, but today no one said a word as I lit up and took my first drag.

Back inside, SFC Jack had finished separating the water and MREs by squad, but he decided the artillery fire was still too heavy to disseminate the supplies, except for the cans of Fanta. SFC Jack thought the platoon needed a morale boost and orange soda was the way to do it. He called for 1st and 2nd squads to send guys to the CP to run sodas back to their positions. Gerhart and Hays from 1st Squad joined Salido and Ayman from second. None of the guys could believe it when SFC Jack passed out the junior-size cans of Fanta, almost in complete shock that they had just risked running over for something so trivial. I finished my cigarette as they went back to their positions and SFC Jack asked for two volunteers to run 3rd Squad their sodas. No one wanted to go out and take chances, but Jared volunteered anyway.

"Ok, that's one. Jared's gonna need a Ranger buddy. Who's going with him?" SFC Jack asked of the guys taking shelter near the entrance. Nobody spoke up. I looked at Jared standing there and decided that I wasn't going to let him go alone.

"I'll go."

SFC Jack looked at me, I half-expected him to say that I couldn't go. Instead, he nodded and extended his arm with two cans in it. I grabbed them from him and began to load my cargo pockets with as many as I could fit while Jared did the same. With about six cans each, we were ready to head out. I looked at Jared and before I could ask him if he was ready, he took off running toward 3rd Squad's building. Without hesitation, I followed him, but halfway between the buildings I felt and heard a can fall out of my hip pocket and hit the ground behind me. Part of me didn't want to stop, but I knew I couldn't leave it behind. In an instant, I knew I was going to die over an orange soda. I reached down and picked it up before pivoting and resuming my mad dash for cover. Luckily, in the 30 seconds we were exposed, no rounds came in and we both made it alive.

Most of the squad was in the back corner of the building in the same room, taking shelter from the artillery. A few guys were in a fortified position on the outside corner of the building. Everyone in the back room was in utter amazement that we just walked in with orange soda. Panatela remarked Fanta was the soda Nazis drank in World War II but took one anyway, while Bob did his version of the *Fanta-Fanta* song from the commercials. SFC Jack's plan of boosting morale had already worked. Once opened, not even artillery shells impacting outside could prevent us from enjoying our sodas. Sporadic impacts from artillery justified hanging out in 3rd Squad's building for a few minutes. While I was there, I passed out about a half pack of cigarettes, dodging questions about the blood all over me. Before we left, I watched from the window as a MH-47 hovered with its ramp over the lip of the dam. In the distance, we could see Rangers load Feldman into the helicopter, which then took off and flew him away. A radio call came from SFC Jack to SSG Branford for Jared and I to get back to the CP. As I was headed to the entrance, I saw Jared's silhouette in the doorway. I called for him to wait up.

Jared turned and exclaimed, "BET YA I CATCH A ROUND BEFORE YOU DO! WOOHOO!" With that he was off. Barely containing myself in laughter, I followed behind almost determined not to let him win the wager he'd just made. We both sprinted back to the CP, nearly knocking several people over as we stumbled back in. SFC Jack looked at us like we had lost our minds before handing us two sodas for our work. Catching my breath, I found a place out of the way and plopped down, popping the tab of my soda can, instantly smelling its orange flavor as carbonation mist escaped the top. I then put the can to my lips and went on to drink the best hot orange soda of my life.

Dave told me they'd evacuated Feldman and he was still alive. He told me the JMAU doctors were on the Chinook that picked him up. Knowing he was in the hands of some of the best trauma surgeons in the world was reassuring. Feldman was in the best care possible and I knew for the rest of the mission those doctors would have our backs. If we could get our guys the JMAU alive, there was a 99% chance they'd survive. That knowledge reinforced the notion that we were not alone out there. We might be thousands of miles away from home, but our country stood right behind us, providing our company with every asset in her military might, spending millions of her national treasure to ensure that we could fight on to the Ranger objective and complete the mission.

Pondering this while drinking my Fanta, I realized the wisdom of the decision to include orange soda in our resupply and to risk running it to 3rd Squad. When in an environment as corrosive and inhumane as a war-torn battlefield, something as simple as drink of carbonated water and artificial flavoring allows enough of a break from the reality around you to regain the intestinal fortitude needed to overcome adversity.

While most of the platoon sat under the cover of the buildings during the artillery, a few Rangers were not so fortunate. For most of the day, Matt, Tommy, SPC Barron and PFC Cannon took up an overwatch position on the southeast corner of the hill, using a large pipe exposed by erosion as cover. Without warning, a 155mm shell screamed in over their position so close they could feel the heat of the passing round. It exploded mere feet uphill from them, sending shrapnel away from their position. SPC Barron, a graduate of Ranger school, decided the impact had come too close for comfort and ordered the men to fall back to the buildings and for the next hour, the entire platoon sought refuge under cover of concrete walls and roof. The Iraqi artillery would focus on our position a while longer before shifting to 2nd Platoon's positions on the other side of the river. Up and down the dam, back and forth between the two platoons, rounds would explode around our perimeter.

The call was eventually made by the command element to find and destroy the artillery pieces to ensure success of the mission and reduce the risk of further casualties. Our forward observers would generate a back azimuth on the artillery, but by the time the aircraft would fly over the suspected area, the guns would move to another position. We got the word that the 75th Ranger Regiment's Regimental Reconnaissance Detachment (RRD) had been tasked with searching out the artillery and calling airstrikes for their destruction. While we waited for RRD to begin their search and destroy mission, the CP building took a direct hit. The overpressure of the round exploding on the rooftop shook the entire structure, kicking up dust and debris everywhere. A few guys were shaken up, but no one was wounded and amazingly, the building was mostly undamaged. Moments later, another direct hit was made on 2nd Squad's building. As with the CP, the round failed to heavily damage the building but the two impacts were entirely too close to large groups of Rangers.

Continuing to take direct hits on the buildings risked one of them eventually collapsing, jeopardizing an entire squad and dramatically reducing our combat efficiency. 1LT Joe and SFC Jack called for us to pull out of the buildings and into the ravine where I'd nearly been caught with my pants down the day earlier. Spread out in the ravine, our risk of mass casualties was significantly reduced. While we lost the cover, we also lost the risk of the cover collapsing and further complicating the mission with a mass casualty situation. Furthermore, the low ground of the ravine prevented any Iraqi forward observer from being able to pinpoint our location.

Lying there, spread out as best we could, the platoon waited for the perceived inevitable that never came. CSM Birch walked the line with his sniper rifle slung over his shoulder, passing out Twizzler licorice to the Rangers in the rocky depression, while close air support flew overhead and the sniper team pulled security from an abandoned concrete bunker near the Eagle's Nest. While we had fallen back, security was maintained and our hilltop was never in danger of being maneuvered upon by the enemy. As the sun began to set, the artillery fell silent and indirect fire stopped for the night. RRD had used the back azimuths provided by our forward observers and called airstrikes on Russian-made 155mm artillery to the northeast. Shortly after nightfall, we pulled out of the ravine and resumed our positions on the line and buildings.

Since Iraqis had hit our building once, 1LT Joe and SFC Jack made the decision to split the CP into separate positions. 1LT Joe, Wolf and I moved to 3rd Squad's building, while SFC Jack and Dave stayed in the building across from the mural. Wolf and I rotated radio guard all night, which was far from silent as the constant traffic of the search being carried out for enemy artillery continued. The occasional rumble of thunder to the northeast would follow shortly after our comrades in arms found another 155mm.

Morning came and the day reached mid-morning without incident. The CO wanted 3rd Platoon from Charlie Company to clear the power station and begin expanding our lines. 1st Platoon was also tasked with clearing *CAS 1* and *CAS 2*, the two main buildings in the front of our hill. A small contingent was left behind to maintain overwatch and security on the hilltop. For the first time, the platoon was being separated into two elements. Since I was just an 11B assisting the medic, I didn't accompany the force tasked to clear the buildings, instead I remained with SSG Shank and the overwatch.

The platoon loaded several GMVs and took the same dirt road on which Sergeant Aaron's vehicle was ambushed days earlier. By radio, I listened as the platoon entered and cleared two buildings that barely withstood multiple impacts from precision-guided bombs and were mostly rubble. Once inside, the platoon discovered why the Iraqis had been so hell-bent on consolidating there. Inside both buildings were caches of nearly every weapon in their arsenal, along with ammunition and grenades. There was only enough room in the GMVs to clear out the weapons in one of the buildings so the platoon took out what they could and returned to the top of the hill. After their return, those of us waiting at the top heard stories of rooms filled with the stench of death and the desert littered with bodies beginning to decompose.

Charlie Company elements later seized the power station and expanded our lines to the south. The day continued quietly and word came that at nightfall the remainder of Charlie Company would be en route to reinforce our positions. At daybreak, Charlie Company arrived from the southwest and began clearing the town to the south of the dam, Haditha proper. A few hours later, we began receiving indirect fire again, this time from the southeast. As we sent our air support to investigate, the pilots reported a large element of Iraqi T-55 tanks along with cargo trucks advancing on our location. The news of enemy tanks generated quite a bit of excitement from all on the hill. We began preparing our positions for battle, but word quickly came down that F-16s and A-10s had attacked the convoy and destroyed over two-dozen T-55s, a relief to all of us. While we had plenty of ammunition and the advantage of high ground, a fight of that scale would have made for a very long day.

Following the destruction of the column of armor, the battalion commander decided we would be relieved from our positions. The call came down and our platoon began to prepare for exfil. We were leaving our GMVs in place but removed our gear to take back to H1. 3rd Platoon, B Company would fly in at nightfall and we would leave on the same birds they arrived. Preparing to pull off the dam, I began to realize how exhausted I was. For over a week, I'd received only a few hours of rest a night and when awake I was consumed with the tasks of combat. Those around me had even less sleep and for some, an even more harrowing experience. Radio guard had been easy compared to the all-night digging and security that the guys in the line squads had endured. While I'd only had the chance to fire five rounds, others had expended hundreds and I felt both fortunate and honored to be in 1st Platoon, having fought alongside those men that week.

At nightfall, we picked up our positions and fell back to the center of the dam. The battalion commander gave a speech congratulating us on our achievement and assured us that we'd earned our spot in Ranger history. Shortly after his speech, Chinooks touched down on the dam and we boarded the helicopters back to H1. After six days of fighting, the assault force had killed at least 230 Iraqi soldiers and destroyed 29 tanks, 28 155mm artillery pieces, 22 82mm mortars, 14 AAA pieces, nine S-60s, six 60mm mortars, three cargo trucks, two motorcycles and one kayak. We had also captured 18 buildings, as well as eight ammo caches.

At the end of it all, the men to my left and right forged a bond that can never be broken. We fought and won the longest sustained ground fight conducted by a single unit since the Vietnam War. Every one of us had given one hundred percent and then some, proving to the world and ourselves that a Ranger truly is a specially selected and trained soldier. We arrived at the edge of battle and energetically met the enemy on the battlefield, defeating him through superior training and effort. Like generations before us and ones who will surely come after, we fought on to the Ranger objective and completed the mission. Rangers Lead The Way!

- ROY MATTHEWS
3/75

JUNE 2003

"Into The Fray"

This mission took place over the course of June 10-12, 2003. I don't remember much of what led up to the mission, but I remember being told 101st Airborne Division was assigned the mission first. Our chain of command scooped up the mission after the 101st requested more time to prepare. We were stationed at Baghdad International Airport (BIAP) in tents not too far off the tarmac. The objective was a terrorist training camp a few kilometers from Syria, located in a wadi in the middle of nowhere. We were briefed that there were approximately 70 bad guys living and training in the compound.

I was the Alpha Team leader for 2nd Squad, 1st Platoon, Bravo Company, of the 2nd Ranger Battalion. My team was light on Rangers as we had a knucklehead we refused take out; he wasn't yet ready for missions. I had McDonald as my SAW gunner and Working as my grenadier. Both were standup dudes whom I knew could take care of themselves. They'd proven themselves time and again, and I knew we could trust them with our lives. Put simply, they were the shit.

The mission was slated for a company-sized element. We took the mortars with us and anti-tank (AT) section as well. During preparation, we pored over imagery of the objective and all moving pieces' assignments. We did the usual pre-mission rehearsals and pre-combat inspections (PCIs) before the objective ended up slipping 24 hours to the right.

The next day was more of the same. We were eventually told the mission was a go. 3rd Platoon left in the afternoon by ground while 1st and 2nd Platoon with attachments took off after dark, divided among Chinook and Black Hawk helicopters.

It was a long ride in the middle of the night. We touched down at the forward aerial refueling point (FARP) and waited to fuel back up for the remainder of the infil. We weren't far from the objective and while waiting to finish refueling, fast-movers (fixed wing jets) were inbound to *soften* the objective with an aerial bombardment. Looking off in the distance I could see flashes of explosions in the direction of the objective.

Refueled, we climbed back in for the final leg to the objective. I took one of my earplugs out and placed it in my pocket. We received all the normal time hacks on our way in.

"One minute!"

"Thirty seconds!"

I was in the middle of the bird, but closer to the back. As with any mission, but especially on a Chinook, I loved to hear the engine change sounds and begin to flare for the approach. I could feel heavy vibrations on the floor as we came closer to landing. I was on my right knee with one hand on my M-4, which was seated on my left thigh, pointed down. My other hand was on my snap-link on the end of my safety line, gate open, in turn hooked to the D-ring on the floor of the aircraft. I waited to feel the thud of landing before releasing it.

The wheels hit dirt and the ramp dropped. Quickly moving off the ramp, I peeled to my right, moving to the left side of the bird, whose nose was facing the objective. As my boots hit the dirt, I could see tracer rounds coming from our support by fire positions (SBF), which had set in moments ahead of our main effort. *Fuck. This is a big one.* We hadn't been in a major firefight yet, having hit dry hole after dry hole. *Not today. These guys are rocking and rolling.* We took a knee and waited for the Chinooks and Black Hawks to take off. Once they cleared out, my platoon moved on line toward the objective.

It was flat all around us. We had SBF positions on both sides of us shooting downhill into the wadi, making it difficult to see through our NODs as we moved forward. There were exchanges of gunfire in front of us, M-240Bs, AK-47s, PKMs and RPGs all made their presence known. MH-6 Little Birds and AC-130 Spectre gunships were overhead and rippled off rockets and guns to suppress enemy gunfire.

Their strikes started large fires and despite the wadi's vastness it was so bright I could see to the other side without NODs. We kept moving forward, when suddenly there was a loud explosion. I fell straight to the ground. I had both earplugs out at this point. What I just witnessed was a bad guy RPG fired into the sky at the Little Birds. The RPG was fired from inside the wadi, which we still hadn't seen, excepting the SBF element. I got to my feet and we inched closer to the wadi as gunfire erupted all around us.

Another rocket went up in search of a Little Bird. We were now closer and it was even louder. *Fuck.* We inched closer. I switched on the infrared laser on my rifle and scoured the edge of the wadi in front of me. I could see fighting positions dug near the edge with no one in them. I could also see into some of the wadi, but wasn't about to stick my head over for better inspection, as two rockets had just come from there.

One of the squads had broken off to the left and posted up on a bend in the wadi. Their lasers were on and jumping from the recoil of their rifles as those fellas began engaging. They were shooting in front and below me; their targets still out of my line of sight. This was the main effort's spot—my spot—as it was my squad leading point for the main effort. Since I was the Alpha Team leader, that made me point man going into the biggest part of the fight, *"Fuck, fellas, light them up!"* As they continued firing, we moved down the draw to our right, to a dirt track the enemy had evidently been using as their vehicle access to the wadi. With rifles at the ready, we began clearing it.

Now I found myself in a draw about 15 feet deep with steep sidewalls. As I moved forward I saw what was left of a truck, just a burning frame. About ten feet back from the entrance to the wadi, my squad leader called for a halt. *Fuck. Now they can see us easy.* Vehicles burned bright and it lit up the entire wadi. I thought I should throw some dirt on the fire to kill it, but thought better of it. *One, that won't do shit, and two, any bad guy watching the entrance will know we're here.*

While I was talking to myself and waiting for targets to present themselves, my squad leader was on the radio confirming we were at our release point and asking—no, *telling*—to let us MOVE. Here we were, sitting, with gunfights raging just around the corner. *Violence of action! Let me go! We're giving these bastards a chance to catch a breath. Violence of action. Keep them on the ropes. Let's go!* I can hear my squad leader yelling into the mic, "We're here. We need to move!"

91

Finally, the order was given. "Watters! Go!" Up off my knee. Rifle up. Scanning. Hard left. Into the gunfight. *Where are you? Where are you?* Scanning, walking and stumbling. I remember thinking the ground was torn up from the bombs the fast-movers dropped and it made walking a little tougher. , andI was backlit by that big-ass truck on fire and it whited-out my NODs and cast weird shadows. Holy shit, I'll never have another adrenaline pump like that one. Bad guys are in here. My boys above were just tearing shit up in here. Scanning. Then from behind me I heard two quick gunshots. I've never grabbed the ground that quick! I don't even remember thinking, just reacting. Then my squad leader's yell rang out, "You motherfuckers better start double tapping these bodies as we come across 'em!" I would later learn that we hadn't been stumbling on churned up dirt from the bombs. We were actually walking on dead bodies. Our part of the objective was the enemy's living quarters, now just a mess of collapsed tents and body parts. *They dropped ordnance right here.* My squad leader later told me the two shots I heard were his; he stepped on a dead combatant's arm and the guy jerked so he fired two rounds right below his feet.

I popped back up after he yelled out to us and yelled back, "I would if I could see shit!" Being all jacked up had me breathing heavy and moving quickly. My eye protection quickly fogged up so I pulled them off and tucked them in my helmet band. I regained my footing and set out again. I could see about 20 meters ahead and I wasn't too worried about what was below me. My job was to find what was in front of us and deal with it. *Let them double tap the bodies on the ground.* I kept my weapon at the ready and scanned with both eyes; one naked and the other behind my PVS-14. I now had a sheer cliff wall to my left. I spotted what looked like a dug-out fighting position where the wall of the wadi met the floor. I could see something inside and had my infrared laser and floodlight illuminating it. I could just make out the shape of something in there but with the firelight behind me it was tough to tell out what it was, so I kept scanning to my right.

As my aim moved back to the front of me, I spotted it. Circular glass. My body tensed at spotting something unidentifiable but surely bad. I had enough time to get *"Fuck"* through my head when my world exploded. Thousands of orange sparks came from the right past my head and left shoulder. I don't remember going airborne but vaguely remember crashing back down to earth. Things get fuzzy here. I then remember the most intense pain in my life and screaming. Both my legs hurt and they hurt real fucking bad. *Ok, they're just broken. You're okay.* I landed on my back so I lifted my head up and I could see my left pant leg in some fire light. I could see that it was shredded mid-leg and there was nothing after that. Even though I was in a shitload of pain, I was just thinking, *Well, that sucks.* Then I yelled out, "That son of a bitch shot my shifting leg off! 12 o'clock! 30 meters! Kill that motherfucker!"

I was later told that after being knocked to the ground by the impact of the RPG explosion, I immediately sat back up and expended nearly an entire magazine toward the combatant who had just shot at me. My squad leader saw the entire trajectory of my flight and landing and my sitting up to shoulder my rifle and fire 29 rounds until it broke as shrapnel had pierced it. When my rifle malfunctioned, I tried a mag change but couldn't as my left elbow and right hand sustained serious wounds.

I remember none of this, which is one of the hardest parts of the ordeal. I want the satisfaction of knowing I shot at that motherfucker. I hit the ground so hard that I scalped the back of my head, pushing all my hair into the size of a fist, even though I was wearing a MICH. That could be the reason I don't remember firing back.

I'm not a badass. It was only my training which allowed me to focus on eliminating the threat. My body took care of itself by not allowing me to feel all the pain. I was able to give commands to my team to tell them where the RPG's location. *Damn it hurts.* I was scared. I remember thinking I could die right there. I also thought that there was no way that would happen, I was still too damned coherent. I started to deny that this just happened to me. *Nope. Fuck you. I'm Matt Watters. This isn't supposed to happen. Not to me. I'm Matt Watters. No!*

I heard my squad leader, who was also a good buddy of mine, yell out "Medic!" The next thing I see is Doc G, asses and elbows, coming in at a full sprint and sliding in at my side. I said, "Doc, save my life," and he went to town. Doc G came to us while we were already in Iraq and from the word *go* he was an absolute stud. He started working on me and my thoughts turned to my wife and little boy. *Fuck. I want to see them. Don't let it end here.* Doc starts talking to me and keeping me with him. "Sing me your ABCs," he would say.

"Doc. Fuck you. I don't wanna."

"Tell me about Lindsey and Owen," he continued on. I rambled on about them while he worked quickly. McDonald and Working were busy doing some serious work. I swear to God they were right next to me laying waste. Those boys were rocking.

The next thing I heard was, "GRENADE!" Without hesitating, Doc G laid over top of me. Not a scratch on him and I was lying there all fucked up. He was ready to give his life for what was left of mine. I still get misty-eyed to this day when I think about it. I'm not sure if it went off in the marshy area where the cattails were or if it was a dud. Nothing happened.

There came a lull in the fight in front of us. The Skedco was called up and my boys unrolled it, placed me inside and cinched it up. Per SOP, they put my body armor on top of me as they dragged me away. I wanted it off, as I was having a hard time breathing and felt the armor was the reason. I flung it off and my platoon sergeant placed my MICH on my chest.

I flung that off as well as I just wanted to breathe. Some poor boys had the task of lugging my heavy ass up the draw. Midway up the draw, the Skedco started to roll, which would've resulted in my getting dragged on my face. I began working my right arm free and saw that part of my right thumb was severed. *Huh...looks like Pac-Man.* I freed my arm from the Skedco and placed it on the ground to keep me from rolling onto my face. I yelled out something to the effect of, "You motherfuckers!" These guys had been and still were getting shot at. Then I realized they were helping me and called out as they lifted my ass up, "I love you guys!"

They hauled me to the CCP and dropped me off. My first sergeant was there. God, it was good to hear his voice. He had also been my platoon sergeant in a previous platoon before I took over as a team leader. "First Sergeant! I'm fucked up!" He had called me *"Agua"* at times, as a play on my name. He told me I was going to be all right; he was going to take care of me. Reaching into my pocket he retrieved my casualty feeder cards and while hunched over me using my chest as a desk, began filling them out. I heard several rounds snap right over our heads and the RTO ran up and yelled,

"First Sergeant! We're getting shot at!" Without missing a beat, he says, "Fuck it. We'll take care of it in a minute."

A MEDEVAC was called and a Chinook came in response. I'm sure they came under fire as I heard the mini-guns bark a time or two as the bird descended. I was hustled on and strapped in. There were litters on the walls and I was placed on the floor underneath one of these stacks of litters. The bird powered up and took off. I was so damned thirsty. I'd lost a bunch of blood and it felt like I had been chewing on cotton balls for a month.

I knew the flight crew always had ice water, as the lucky bastards always seemed to have a fridge or freezer allowing them to have COLD water. I yelled out to him as he passed, but he couldn't hear me. He walked by again and I reached out and grabbed his ankle. He bent down and I yelled to him that I wanted water. He walked off and returned holding a large bottle of water. He held it to my lips so I could drink. He had frozen the water bottle earlier, which now resulted in half water and half ice. It was the best water I'll ever have.

The Chinook landed at the FARP and the ramp dropped. A guy was already waiting on a four-wheeler. The aircrew hoisted me up onto it and the rider took off like a bat out of hell. *Fuck! We're gonna eat it.* He raced up to the JMAU bird, which was a C-130 decked out like a flying hospital. The quad driver and JMAU medics hauled me up the ramp, took me from the Skedco and strapped me down to a table. The white lights were on inside the bird and I took my first look at myself. My field top and brown t-shirt was ripped and had already been cut away. There was blood all over my torso and arms. I was weak and in the process of getting strapped in, so I just laid my head back. I could feel a warm sensation in my butt/crotch area and was pretty sure I shat myself. I told the medics I thought as much. They gave me an, "Ah! No big deal. That happens when this happens." I vaguely remember the bird taxiing but don't remember the takeoff. I think that I'd been sedated at this point. The next thing I remember was waking up (sort of) in Kuwait.

In the aftermath, the details of my story were pieced together. There was a merciful lull in the fighting as I was treated and evacuated. Instead of the one I saw, there were two guys in the fighting position from which the rocket came. When I sat back up and fired, one got out and ran. The remaining RPG gunner hunkered down and loaded another round. One of my best friends was on the intermediate support by fire line up on the bend in the wadi. He said that when the RPG gunner popped back up to hit us again, they unloaded on him. In his words, "We sent that motherfucker straight to hell."

-MATT WATTERS
2/75

CHAPTER FOUR

"In my dreams I hear again the crash of guns, the rattle of musketry, the strange, mournful mutter of the battlefield."

DOUGLAS MACARTHUR

As the Regiment progressed into 2004, it became apparent to all in the organization that the unit was in transition. Rangers had been on sustained rotations of combat deployments since 2001 and were coming off the invasion and first year of combat in Iraq. The mission and operational realities began to reveal the need for change within the Regiment, which raised questions about the unit's identity. Questions such as whether the Regiment identified more with the Army or with the Command arose, or were they both? Is that possible? If so, what does that mean?

CSM Gregory Birch, who spent much of his career at Fort Bragg in the Army's premiere Special Missions Unit, was now the Regimental Sergeant Major bringing a unique mindset that filtered down through the ranks. The Regiment had previously been primarily relegated to larger raids that encompassed multiple platoons or supporting the Command's SMUs with security and other tasks. Now, the Regiment had begun to move away into unknown realms formerly only under the purview of the Command's SMUs. It seemed that Regimental leadership was pushing for a bump up in the

Command's community and they more than proved they deserved a seat at that table. Rangers were now fully integrating with the Command, carrying out missions independently and of highest importance. The platoon direct action raid became the bread and butter for most of those missions, a transition from working as a company to working as an independent platoon.

There was a palpable shift in mindset from *advanced light infantry* to exclusively *special operations*. The Regimental Reconnaissance Detachment (then RRD, now RRC) became the premiere surveillance asset for the Command. Battalion reconnaissance sections were stood up and validated by the top leadership in the SOCOM community. A fourth week was added onto the Ranger Indoctrination Program that specifically focused on shooting. The training cycle between deployments moved to a close quarters combat, or *Battle Drill 6* focus and Rangers spent thousands of hours in shoot houses perfecting breaching techniques. This was the beginning of what would become the most lethal and fierce direct action raid force that the world has seen, with some platoons executing over a hundred missions in a single 90-day deployment.

To illustrate the profundity of this transition, the traditionally strict adherence to unit Standard Operating Procedures (SOPs) began to loosen. The infamous *high and tight* haircut, which had been a Ranger hallmark, was replaced with a less conspicuous normal haircut. The Regiment stood up a Force Modernization section, which resulted in a uniform makeover. Rangers ditched the Army-issued MOLLE gear for SOF-peculiar plate carriers and pouches. Rangers traded in their standard issue boots for Oakley S.I. assault boots and Merrell Sawtooths. Even Oakley ballistic sunglasses, or *eye pro,* raised eyebrows within the Regiment's NCO Corps.

This time of transition however, was not without turmoil. When the Regimental Commander issued Note #2, which repealed the high and tight as the standard haircut, there was a lot of pushback. One 3/75 First Sergeant ordered the men in his company to keep the high and tight as the standard until he was later overruled. NCOs who were raised with strict adherence to SOPs found themselves at whiteboards drawing what they deemed *the new standard* for haircuts. This may seem like a very insignificant and trivial change to those on the outside, but to those in Regiment at the time, it was just as significant as the change from black to tan berets.

A rift began to form between some senior and junior NCOs about the direction the Regiment was moving. The younger Rangers fully embraced the new SOF focus while some in more senior billets found the changes counter to the culture in which they were raised and their view of the Ranger infantry tradition. The challenge of keeping their identity as Rangers while not sacrificing mission effectiveness was a topic of debate beginning in 2004 and raged for years to come. NCOs charged with training their men for real-world combat deployments found themselves in the peculiar position of making new standards and training for a new way of fighting. It was not uncommon for a Ranger who had just freshly donned their Scroll and Tan Beret to immediately join his new platoon on deployment. Gone were the days of having months of training to prepare. Rangers often found themselves pulling triggers overseas before doing their first training mission in garrison.

Although change was in the air, deployments and missions continued at an ever-increasing pace. The GWoT was not going away. Ten bombs exploded simultaneously on trains carrying commuters in Madrid, killing 190 and injuring 2,000. Osama bin Laden released multiple videos, confirming that he was still alive and still a threat. Combat operations continued in Afghanistan, with RRD Team 3 performing yet another military free-fall combat jump in July to emplace tactical surveillance equipment. The priority had shifted to Iraq by this point, however. The majority of Rangers found themselves taking part in General McChrystal's increasingly effective head-hunting task force that scored an important victory with the capture of Saddam Hussein in December 2003.

Despite Rangers' significant advances at a staggering pace, it was still war and the year was unfortunately not without sacrifice. On April 22nd, Corporal Patrick Tillman, a former NFL football player who became a Ranger in 2/75 was accidentally killed by friendly fire in Afghanistan. In addition, three more Rangers would be killed in action in 2004. Private First Class Nathan Stahl, Corporal William Amundson and Sergeant Michael O'Neill all paid the ultimate sacrifice. The Ranger Regiment was on a roll, but it was clear they had joined a fight with no sure end and were in it for the long haul.

EARLY 2004

"TEAM BAGHDAD"

I served on active duty 2001-2005. I did three deployments: Afghanistan in the summer of 2002, Iraq from late 2003 to spring 2004, and again to Afghanistan in the fall of 2004. By far the most action-packed and intense deployment for me was Iraq. I was 21 years old and had recently been promoted to corporal. I missed the initial invasion as I was in Ranger School at the time. Knowing I was missing out on the war lit a fire under my ass to push myself and go straight through, which I did. As I pinned on my Ranger Tab, the invasion was winding down and my platoon was sent home. All my peers received a combat star on their jump wings that deployment, making it bittersweet going straight through Ranger School but still missing out.

That summer training cycle was one of the most intense times of my life. We trained hard as we knew we were going back. It was miserable, but the skills I learned and practiced would later manifest themselves quite literally as the difference between life and death.

Just days before the start of 2004, there I was, boots on the ground in Iraq. My platoon was top-heavy with experienced Rangers. We were sent to live in the special operations compound called the mission staging site (MSS) on the Tigris River, inside the Green Zone in Baghdad. We were supposed to rotate with other platoons, but as the days and weeks wore on, we established a good working relationship with C Squadron of the Army Special Mission Unit with whom were located. They requested that we stay put, so we did. We continued running missions day-in and day-out. I was shot at via rifle fire or incoming mortar rounds nearly every day. Most times we simply ignored it, since we were en route to a target and needed to carry on the mission uninterrupted. We also did some work with British SAS, U.S. Special Forces and Polish Special Forces, but mostly we were with the Brits or Army SMU.

We went out almost every night. We were doing real missions; everything I signed up to do. My element caught 14 of the most wanted men in Iraq whose faces were on the infamous playing card deck published by CENTCOM. I even spent four hours standing on top of Chemical Ali, the guy who gassed the Kurds. We didn't have any open seats and had no place better to put him when we rolled him up.

I was a turret gunner; manning the M2 .50-caliber machine gun on the top of the Humvee was my place as a gun team leader. Weapons squad was used to either man the guns or drive. All three members of my gun team were on guns and I made sure we cleaned them and kept them ready. After that, I spent the rest of the deployment as the platoon sergeant's gunner, as he took over command of the platoon when our commander returned home early due to personal issues.

Roughly halfway though the tour, an accident involving a Pandur armored vehicle at the gates of Baghdad International Airport took out most of my squad, creating an even greater manning shortage. The Pandur hit a concrete barricade at high speed. I witnessed the entire thing and think it's possible an IED was involved. The vehicle flipped through the air, end over end and I didn't think there was any way anyone could survive. When we ran over to the wreck, the squad leader was on top of the vehicle moaning, obviously concussed, but still trying to find his men and check sensitive items. Fortunately, shortly before Ranger School I attended an EMT course, making me a squad level medic and RFR qualified. But I was the only one with advanced medical training in my vehicle, something we now desperately needed.

The Pandur was on fire and insurgents were shooting at us from the overpass a few hundred meters away. The Army Reservists manning the gate rendered us zero aid and I remember wanting to shoot them. They were only a hundred meters away. I still have the boots I was wearing and they still have my squad leader's blood on them. He was really messed up.

The turret gunner was my friend Bill; we were close, having gone through Basic, Airborne and RIP together. The top piece of the vehicle landed on him; roughly a 6-foot by 12-foot by 2-inch-thick piece of steel. Somehow my driver Josh and I pushed the plate off him. I had Josh stabilize his neck while I intubated him to maintain a viable airway. His neck felt like mush as he had broken his C-1 vertebra.

The other two in the Pandur were privates, somehow flung alongside the Pandur, landing just next to it. I both administered and directed medical care as the platoon sergeant, SFC B, called in MEDEVAC birds. I climbed aboard the bird with the wounded to the hospital to assist the medical staff, as at the time the hospitals were extremely short-staffed.

Everyone survived. Bill was in a medically induced coma for months. He has since recovered well, but not fully. My squad leader required a steel plate in his face, but made a full recovery, as did the two privates, Jon and John.

We went into Fallujah on a regular basis that deployment. The 82nd had it locked down tight with the brigade-sized element. The problems didn't start until it was handed over to the Marines. They decided to hang back to *win hearts and minds,* which doesn't really work with Al Qaeda insurgents. The insurgents used the lull to emplace their men, weapons and equipment to retake the city, so at the end of March 2004, a massive storm was brewing. My platoon and others from C Co. 3/75, along with C Squadron from the Army SMU, entered Fallujah to conduct another night raid. The Al Qaeda fighters had prepared a massive ambush with RPGs, heavy machine guns and mortars on the other end of the city. They were setting up on both sides of the road in a massive Polish ambush, with crossfire and kill lanes intersecting each other, with Americans in the middle.

They were hoping to catch a convoy headed from the military base into the city with the intention of killing them all. What they received was a convoy of Rangers and operators headed from the city to the base after a mission, by way of Baghdad. I imagine they were a bit confused, but they hit us anyway.

I remember seeing green tracers everywhere at the front of the convoy. *Wow, they're really jacking them up!* Then I remembered that our side didn't have green tracers. I pulled the charging handle on my M2 and joined the fight. I kept my gun thundering as we made our way through the kill zone. There's nothing like shooting a .50-caliber machine gun into a crowd of bad guys; it's a Ranger's wet dream.

The firefight was short but extremely violent. There were targets on both sides of the road. Richard, the SAW gunner and I engaged as fast as we could acquire targets, and they were everywhere. Thankfully Michael, the line team leader in my vehicle, spent many years in Weapons Squad and knew enough to concentrate his efforts into getting more ammo out and ready to feed my gun. I cleaned my gun every day and it paid off here. My platoon sergeant made sure I stayed on target and helped direct me. I recall the sensation of him grabbing my leg to get my attention and pointing toward more targets. I remember walking my tracers into a bad guy's gun as he was doing the same to me, the rounds were so close I could feel the heat of the bullets on my neck, but I got him first. Guys who saw it thought I was hit and grabbed me, trying to dress my non-existent wounds after we made it out of the kill zone. I effectively demolished a structure and the men inside it not more than 20 feet from me. The proximity of their muzzle flashes startled me.

The ambush disabled some of our vehicles, so we hooked them up to tow out of the kill zone. My friend Jarred, who was on his vehicle's gun, took a round through the neck. The battalion surgeon was in the vehicle behind him and saved his life. An operator had his jaw blown off but survived. It was a miracle we didn't have more casualties. There were bullets pinging off my Humvee everywhere.

Video from the AC-130 above us would later reveal that we had multiple near-misses from RPG rockets, but none of them found their mark. The ambushers were caught off-guard themselves by the lethal and accurate return fire—we killed most of them. When we made it clear of the kill zone, the Little Birds began their runs, ending most remaining survivors. A handful escaped, but were promptly dispatched by the cannons of the AC-130 gunship. I had fired most of my rounds and had to get more from other vehicles to continue. I kept my gun clean and did my job.

This was but a prelude to the first battle of Fallujah. Al Qaeda elements arrived in force to retake the city, but we killed them first. The next day several Blackwater contractors were killed and hung from a bridge in retaliation. Conventional units went to retake the city and apprehend the group responsible but were forced to pull back, effectively ushering the city's fall in April 2004. For us, it was time to go home. We were now battle-hardened warriors and had paved the way for the Ranger Regiment to transition to an increased level of responsibility in the special operations community. Our actions and demeanor while working closely with C Squadron proved Rangers could hang with the best in Iraq. We were Team Baghdad.

This cauldron brewed the skillset and experiences that would create the core leaders within C-1 3/75, the elite platoon for which Leo Jenkins was medic and featured in his book *Lest We Forget*. I was given a line team leader position and promoted to Sergeant after that deployment. C-1-1 was stood back up (it was disbanded due to lack of manpower) and we became the *Dobermans,* a nickname given to us by the first sergeant because of our ferocious demeanor, as we had three of the most squared away and badass sergeants of the Regiment!

- NICK GREEN
3/75

FALL 2004

"MOSUL"

October 2004 marked my first deployment. It was seven months since I graduated the Ranger Indoctrination Program and arrived at the 3rd Ranger Battalion in Fort Benning, Georgia. I didn't know what to expect. I was just a Private First Class who spent the last seven months getting yelled at, smoked, training, jumping, getting yelled at some more, then smoked some more just because I looked like I could use it.

I got to do some really great training since arriving the unit: ATV and dirt bike operations, night-time and defensive driving, non-traditional vehicle entry classes, rotary wing and fixed wing exercises, shooting ranges and radio operator training. I really didn't know how it would play out on deployment since I wasn't assigned to an actual platoon.

Our unit was assigned to Mosul in Northern Iraq, and was part of Task Force North, one of the three components comprising Command's task force in Iraq (the other two being TF Central and TF West). TF North oversaw the operation to track down those on the United States' most wanted list, along with Al Qaeda operatives in Iraq.

In late 2004, Iraq was busy place as both the Iraqi insurgency and Al Qaeda were very active, but more so in the central areas of Iraq, around Baghdad and Fallujah. That said, Mosul had its own Al Qaeda cell that wasn't on vacation. Just the previous year, an Army SMU with 101st Airborne support tracked down and killed Saddam's sons Uday and Qusay in Mosul.

The Ranger assault package sent to Mosul consisted of a single platoon from Alpha Company and a small support element. There couldn't have been more than 50 of us in total. Once there, we joined an Army SMU element of similar size. For the next three to four months, this small force would be responsible for hunting down Al Qaeda and key members of the insurgency.

We touched down in Mosul in early October. My expectations for Iraq changed the moment the ramp came down. Mosul was freezing, it rained the whole time and the city was gigantic. I think the last time anybody fought in the deserts of Iraq was during Desert Storm. This massive urban sprawl was not what I expected.

Our small force was located on FOB Freedom, later dubbed FOB Courage, a medium-sized coalition base that rested on a hill overlooking the city. This wasn't exactly an ideal location, as insurgents didn't have a hard time pinpointing where their mortars and rockets were landing. FOB Freedom was consistently plagued by indirect fire, but the chances of a person being hit were incredibly low.

The deployment started off slow and throughout October the team went out on just eight to ten objectives. To my surprise, I went on a handful, one of which would end up being my first and last *pulling-a-blocking-position-for-an-SMU* type of objective, the type of mission many outside the Regiment think we do 99% of the time, but in reality, we rarely do.

Typically, as a junior radio operator not part of a platoon, it is rare to be allowed on objectives, as almost everybody in this position would be put in a *watch-and-learn* capacity their first deployment. However, I wrapped up that three-month deployment with close to 20 direct action raids. Nothing to brag about, but it's 20 more than I was expecting.

October came and went; time flew on deployment. It was mostly uneventful besides a couple of casualties from a single objective. A Ranger took a round to his leg that severed his femoral artery and was quickly treated and evacuated by our medics. A second Ranger had taken a round near his armpit, which he didn't notice until he was back on base. He was a hard son of a bitch.

We did have one death in mid-October. My friend Bill Amundson was a mortarman assigned to one of the platoons in Afghanistan when his vehicle rolled over during a combat patrol. We had gone out in downtown Columbus together a few days before flying out. We were a bunch of drunken dancing fools—hard to believe it's been a decade since.

Despite the low casualties, things were heating up in Iraq. The Marines were gearing up to enter Fallujah for the second time after the coalition failed to hold the city in April 2004 following the First Battle of Fallujah. Now 10,000 U.S. Marines were a week away from assaulting the city. Everyone with a television knew it; it was plastered all over the news networks. Hell, that's how I found out about it.

A couple of days later Task Force North discovered something that wasn't being shown on CNN. Scores of trucks filled with armed insurgents were spotted departing north from Fallujah. Hundreds of enemy fighters made the five-hour drive north to Mosul, a smart choice on their part, considering U.S. forces in vicinity of Mosul were fewer than 2,000 strong.

On November 7 U.S. Marines invaded Fallujah and we crowded the television to watch the news footage. The Second Battle of Fallujah had begun. On November 8, the convoy of insurgents reached Mosul, in turn touching off the Battle of Mosul.

Mosul, a city of almost two million people, had a disproportionately small U.S. presence relative to other urban areas in Iraq, largely due to our reliance on the well-funded and trained Kurdish Peshmerga forces who could reach Mosul at the drop of a hat. An entire battalion from the 25th Infantry Division drove south to join the Marines in their fight. Sometimes I wonder if the 25th ID Stryker convoy and the insurgent truck convoy from Fallujah passed each other on the highway. I laugh just thinking about it.

When I tell you insurgents almost took the entire city on November 8, please don't think I'm exaggerating. In a well-coordinated attack, they assaulted numerous police stations, killing dozens and making off with heavy weapons, RPGs and flak jackets. In the coming days, 1,500 Iraqi security forces personnel would abandon the city. Mosul would have no police force for another month.

Our small special operations task force didn't play a huge role in the first days of the assault on Mosul. We were assigned to hunt down insurgent and Al Qaeda leadership. What could 70 men do to retake a city of two million? That task was given to the 25th Infantry Division and we would play a supporting role as needed.

On the morning of November 9, I looked out into the city and saw a scene reminiscent of old Gulf War footage: dozens of burning oil fields far off in the desert. But today, the black plumes of smoke scattered over the urban sprawl were destroyed police stations, gas stations and massive truck bombs. The fires would burn all day.

Whatever, this is Iraq. I went on with my normal routine, which included a run along the perimeter wall of the base. I was a quarter mile away from our compound when the distinct sound of an incoming mortar round exploded in my ears. *No big deal.* We would get two to three a day out here on average. They never hit anybody.

Then another. And another. It was a deafening sound no matter where you were, making it difficult to ascertain how close the impacts were. They kept coming. *Okay this is different.* I ended up taking shelter in a small concrete bunker that fits four to six grown men, the only American amongst four Iraqi civilian contractors. The mortar rounds continued. The attack lasted three minutes. All told, a combined fifteen rockets and 82mm mortar rounds were fired against us.

I sprinted to the Task Force compound as our leadership would want to get accountability on all men. The first person I ran into was SFC "O", the senior Ranger medic in Mosul. "Donov, come with me!" He was carrying his aid bag. We hopped onto our ATV and made a short drive to the 25th ID's headquarters personnel living area, which was literally down the road from our own compound. Doc O pulled the ATV up to one of the *hooches,* which is what we called the small white trailers soldiers lived in. Numerous soldiers were standing outside quietly. A sickening feeling in my stomach began to form at the sight of the soldiers' apparent lack of sense of purpose and lethargic demeanor.

Doc rushed right in through the door but I hesitated. I stood there for a few seconds trying to prepare myself. It didn't work. I walked in anyway. My memory is hazy, but I remember the trailer was very dark. The mortar round exploded on the roof and not inside the trailer. Inside, we found a soldier slumped over his laptop. I would find out later he was writing an email to his wife.

When the mortar exploded, a piece of shell casing broke through the top and entered the top of his head. He was dead instantly. I resented Doc for bringing me. *What was the point?* It was obvious that the initial call confirmed that the soldier was deceased. He could have asked any one of the other soldiers from that to help load the body.

We covered the man with his own blanket and lay him in the back of the ATV's small flatbed. He was completely covered aside from the desert combat boots sticking out. His blood slowly trickled down onto the gravel where it formed into a small dark-red pool. Doc drove away with the body to the hospital and I made the short walk back to our compound.

It was the first and only time I would see a dead American soldier. It was a horrendous feeling that I can only describe by its similarity to a terrible heartbreak. This was a man I've never seen before but ten years later my heart still hurts for him. I am not a religious man, but I am thankful every single day that I never witnessed the death of my Ranger friends though many were killed in action over the years. I can't imagine the feeling of hopelessness it would bring.

I later looked him up, Horst Gerhard Moore, a Major with the 25th Infantry Division. His friends and family called him Gary and he left behind a wife and daughter. A second American died in the attack, a Master Sergeant from the Air Force. Another American contractor with Aegis was seriously wounded.

Slowly but surely, over the next few days, the small U.S. force began regaining security in parts of the city, which still had no police force. A small group from our task force was asked to defend a nearby government facility from harassment by insurgent forces. Our command agreed and shortly thereafter we took off in a Black Hawk from the FOB and landed on the rooftop of the nearby 12-story Nineveh International Hotel. The flight lasted 45 seconds.

Snipers from both the Army SMU and the Rangers immediately set up shop overlooking the besieged building and began engaging targets on the ground. The fire support specialist and I, along with a few other Rangers, provided security while the snipers engaged.

A few days more and the Battle of Mosul officially ended, but the city was completely destabilized. The Iraqi police wouldn't return until December, another full month. The mission parameters changed for TF North. The Ranger platoon and the Army SMU troop would relocate to FOB Marez, an American base about five miles away connected to a separate coalition force's airbase. The command wanted us to have easier access to helicopters. To this point we'd been heavily reliant on our GMVs and Pandur armored personnel carriers.

I hoped FOB Marez would be as nice and cozy as FOB Freedom and was getting ready to move. Then my team leader pulled me aside and told me I wouldn't be going with the group. "What? Why?" I asked my team leader. I hated the thought of not being with the unit. "The Special Mission Unit is leaving a liaison team here and they need a RTO. You're it." It took a few seconds to process before fully understanding how awesome this assignment would be. I replied, "Roger Sarn't!" and went on my merry way.

What's a liaison team, you ask? Simple, and just like the name states: a small team that is responsible for liaising with one unit on behalf of another. We would be working with the 25th Infantry Division on FOB Freedom on Task Force North's behalf. Our mission was to tag along with the 25th on their objectives and supplement their capabilities with on-site interrogations, sensitive site exploitation and anything else that might be important. Even the smallest details can lead to the next high value target. Mosul was now fraught with high-level insurgents who came from Fallujah and *mop-up* operations had to be done right.

Our little group consisted of Pup, the team leader, Trevor, Ivica, Chase, Sam and myself. Aside from Sam and I, all were operators with the SMU. Sam was a longtime operator with a special Army unit that provided intelligence to special operations forces. Ivica was the oldest operator on his team. He recently celebrated his 42nd birthday and spent a lot of his downtime either running or playing Halo on Xbox. Uniquely, he was born in Croatia where he served in the Yugoslavian military before moving to the United States in the late 1980s to join the Army as a medic and later transitioning into the Special Forces. Fast-forward almost 16 years and he was now an assistant team leader in the SMU.

The team leader, nicknamed Pup, was a veteran of the Ranger Regiment and had been with the special mission unit for quite a while. The rest of the men were relatively new to the unit. Chase was straight out of the Operator Training Course and was on his first deployment with the SMU. We got along very well, as he was also a former communications guy in the Ranger Regiment. For the next month and a half until our rotation ended, we would live and work together out of the tiny compound that was once the Task Force North headquarters.

The first week or so we were together was slow; the 25th ID didn't have the same operational tempo as we were used to and planned direct action raids days before they happened. The time in between they would go on patrol throughout Mosul in their Stryker convoys. Most of the time we spent at the compound, sitting around and chatting while playing darts.

I remember our first raid with the 25th ID vividly. We didn't have any vehicles of our own after they went with the main force to Marez, so we walked over to the staging area. The operators were looking cool with their fancy gear. They didn't wear any name insignia, branch insignia, or even rank, so of course I was trailing behind trying to rip the rank off my collar. Soldiers judge each other based on what they wear and how cool they look, and as the Regiment had not yet transitioned to sterile uniforms, this was my highest priority. Chase turned around, caught sight of what I was doing and laughed, "Too late now!"

Shit, it was. We were already there. I had one insignia off, but the other was dangling by a few remaining stitches. Luckily, I don't think anybody noticed my cherry ass. If any of my Ranger NCOs were there, I would have been smoked for hours and then made fun of for months. You could always tell the Rangers. We were the only Army unit who wore a desert camouflage uniform with BDU colored (green) rank and name patches. Sometimes it was hilarious because it was very hard to tell what rank each one of us was unless you were right up close. I can't tell you how many times *big Army* folks have mistakenly saluted me overseas.

At the staging site, as expected, we received a lot of attention in the form of stares from 25 ID. Hell, most of the time Rangers got looks from other units and questioned who we were with. Fancy equipment means money, money means importance and many times importance means special operations. I can't imagine what they must have thought when they saw operators roll up with their dual night vision goggles, fancy weapons, hiking boots and completely sterile uniforms.

My first objective as an RTO with the SMU went down perfectly, as did the rest in the remaining month and a half. I learned a lot from those guys, and a lot about the world in which they operated, including closely held secrets about previous missions. It was an opportunity not many young soldiers would normally have.

I also got a firsthand glimpse into the world of human intelligence and informant handling. Sam, the intelligence operator, consistently used me as his personal sidekick. We would change into civilian clothes and leave the FOB in his SUV in the middle of the night to drive into Mosul and pick up Iraqi informants who were selling us information. We'd roll right up to the gate guards of the FOB and the only instructions Sam would give them were, "Hey guys, we'll be back in about an hour. Look for this vehicle and don't shoot us up."

He never informed the Task Force headquarters and the rest of the liaison team never knew we were out in the middle of the city picking up informants. *Was it reckless?* In the eyes of a cherry like myself, probably. But that's what we were taught. In the world in which this guy belonged, conducting counter-intelligence and counter-terrorism operations throughout Iraq, Afghanistan and other places, it was business as usual. *Who was I to argue with somebody*

111

who's done this for years? Besides, I would sound like a scared little girl had I expressed my doubts, so I rolled with him into the middle of one of the most dangerous cities in Iraq in the back of his Toyota 4Runner in the middle of the night. Nothing but my M-4 rifle and his Glock sidearm were standing between us and an ambush, likely be followed by a beheading broadcast on the internet for all the world to see.

This was my first deployment as a Ranger. I realized the world of special operations is precise, complicated and it'll keep you on your toes. You have no choice but to keep up with its frantic pace. The imaginations I had of massive battles and multi-day engagements did not belong in that world. The men I lived and worked with for such a short period of time made a significant impression on me that still affects me now and will to the end of my days.

Eight months later, in August of 2005, I was in Jalalabad, Afghanistan on my second deployment when I noticed a press release on the U.S. Army Special Operations Command website. The headline read, *"Two Bragg Soldiers, one Benning Soldier die in Iraq."* A sickening feeling formed in my stomach when I saw the pictures of Trevor and Ivica. Their vehicle drove over an improvised explosive device in western Iraq, killing them instantly. A Ranger was also killed and a third operator succumbed to his wounds a few days later. It was a huge loss to the special operations community. For me, it's difficult to grasp how a cowardly device like an IED could take out such great warriors. Years of dedicated service and grueling training, only to be killed by a scumbag with a cell phone hiding out of sight. It was and still is a hard pill to swallow.

I will always remember trying to converse with Ivica in my native tongue of Bulgarian while he spoke back to me in Croatian, finally giving up and telling me, "Man, my Bulgarian is better than yours!" I also remember the many games of darts I played with Trevor and trying to teach him how to use the PRC-117F radio. It's been nine years and when I look back, it was these guys who made me want to be a better Ranger. They're always the first to come to mind. Rest in peace.

-IASSEN DONOV
3/75

WINTER 2004

"FIRST DEPLOYMENT"

Succotash. Again. The waxy lima beans and flavorless corn occupy the upper right corner of my Styrofoam tray. A sort of flank steak with density far greater than the plastic instruments intended to dissect it acts as the main course. I haven't gone back to the salad bar since my senior medic, Sergeant Otic, nearly died from ingesting some of the fecal matter that made its home on the brown iceberg lettuce. But it was this or an MRE and I had already gone that route several times this week.

Our dining facility was a dingy white tent illuminated by the constantly buzzing generators just outside the front entrance. The large white tent sat in the middle of a small Forward Operating Base (FOB) known as Salerno, just outside of the town of Khost, Afghanistan. It was late 2004 and just a few weeks ago I was at Fort Bragg, North Carolina graduating from the JFK Special Warfare Special Operations Medical Course (SOMC). I had been assigned as a platoon medic to 3rd Platoon, Charlie Company, 3rd Ranger Battalion. Although I had been in the Army for over a year and a half, I was the newest member of the platoon so was dubbed, *the cherry bitch*. It was a title I really didn't mind. Everyone here had carried it at some point and it was only a matter of time before I would be able to pass it on to someone else.

The boys sat around the table and told jokes for several minutes after choking down their dinner. The billowing laugh of First Sergeant Searing was enough to drown out the irritating noise coming from the generators. First Sergeant was nicknamed *The Rhino,* and for good reason. The man's arms were bigger around than my legs and he possessed a confidence that was remarkable, even amongst other Rangers.

I was still leery of the big man at this point. A dozen of us recently joined up with the existing elements of 3rd Battalion, which had been in country for several weeks prior to our arrival. Many in my group were brand-new privates just graduated from RIP. One or two guys had just graduated from Ranger School. Upon our arrival, First Sergeant Searing gathered us into one of the tents to give us a brief introduction to the area. The company commander also introduced himself, gave a short speech and opened the floor for any questions. During his introduction, the CO told us his background including his alma mater, The Citadel.

Despite the intimidation of most of the new guys, things were going well until the CO opened the floor for questions. Private Maldo had the burning desire to know some things about the CO's school. I didn't think much of it when he asked, "Sir, is it true that you have to pee in the sink at the Citadel?" With the grace and composure of a veteran Ranger, the CO explained that in many of the dorms the bathrooms were pretty far apart and sometimes you had to improvise. The CO then calmly left us in the care of *The Rhino.*

To this day I'm still not sure if he screamed "GET OUT!" or "GET DOWN!" All I know is that it was nothing but assholes and elbows. The First Sergeant didn't find the inquiry very humorous and he let us know in his own unique way. After a very shitty 20 minutes in that tent we were brought out into the cold night air and made to create a small formation. Our section leaders were brought out and informed about what had just happened. I was introduced to the taste of Afghan dirt as I low-crawled to the tent that acted as our communications room and armory. At this moment I couldn't help but think back to the school house at Fort Bragg where just a couple of weeks ago I had a barbeque with master sergeants, joking and calling them by their first names. Now I was pulling myself across the ground in a war zone because some guy I'd never met just asked a smart-ass question to another guy that I had never met. *Welcome to life as a new guy in Ranger Battalion.*

I swallowed my comments as we left the chow hall under the guidance of our red headlamps. The camp stayed blacked out at night and using white lights had the potential to draw indirect fire, so we stumbled around making due with the minimal illumination from those red-filtered lights. My home was a bunk bed in the corner of a tent shared with eight or nine other Rangers. The extent of my possessions fit into two large green duffle bags. Our tent was equipped with a 19-inch TV one of the guys purchased from the bazaar prior to my arrival. The squad leader and alpha team leader were both big poker players so the back part of our tent was set up like a miniature casino, which frequently hosted poker nights.

After dinner was down time, typically spent watching very poor quality movies that were bought at the market for a dollar. More often than not, I would make my way back to the gym for the second or third time of the day following dinner. The gym was the only place that I felt at home during my first deployment. Everywhere else, I was the newest guy in the company, but in that dirt-floored, musky old building, I was one of the strongest guys in our company. The rattling of ancient, rusted iron plates, likely left behind when the Russians were occupying this country, reminded me of the light chatter at the breakfast table of the firehouse where I used to work before joining the Army. Through each of my deployments, the gym would act as a sanctuary from both the monotony and chaos of war.

There wasn't a great deal of activity in our area at this time. It was Ramadan and most of the terrorists were on vacation. The first mission I went on was so uneventful that the best part was simply rolling out the gate. It was pitch-black and I found myself sitting in the back of a Humvee with absolutely no armor—the thing didn't even have doors. I had no idea what to expect and had no clue how to work my NVGs. The last time that I put a round in an M-4 was...actually never. We had to qualify with an M-16 in basic training a year and a half earlier but I hadn't fired a weapon since. My class was the last RIP class that didn't have a shooting week (December 2003). As I heard some of the other guys yelling in jest at the guy who opened the gate at the FOB, *"I'm scared!" "I wanna be a princess!" "It's too cold out here..."* And here I was, trying to figure out how to get the bullet from the magazine into the fucking barrel.

The jeep bounced and jarred our bones on the two-hour drive to the objective. Green beams projected every direction from the PEQ-2 infrared lasers mounted on our M-4s as we scanned for potential threats. We very quietly arrived at the base of a hill. Atop it sat a compound barely visible with the minimal moonlight. In silence, we dismounted and began to pull security. I was instructed by the platoon sergeant to accompany him. As our element began making its way up the incline into the darkness, the monocular night vision device attached to my MICH helmet banged against my cheekbone while displaying a very blurry green image. I'd never worn these things before, let alone attempted to walk on uneven terrain with them. There was no depth perception and I stumbled, letting out an audible grunt. "Quiet, Doc," was the extent of consolation I received from any members of my platoon, almost unidentifiable in the darkness of night.

The walk took about 15 minutes. I staged outside the front gate as the assault element breached the door and cleared the central courtyard. In less than a minute, I was brought into the compound. I looked around to see Rangers moving swiftly and silently from building to building, collecting fighting age males and securing the women and children in a single room. I couldn't help but think of how fucking cool the entire thing was. I finally saw what Rangers actually do. Not what I had read in books or heard stories about, but how they actually do move with grace and violence, subduing their opponents with an incredible professionalism.

I was given the task of watching the room of non-combatants after the dust had settled on the initial assault. I had put on several layers of moisture-wicking long underwear in anticipation of the frigid Humvee infil, but the movement to the objective had left me a little warm. The room where I watched over the dozen or so women and children couldn't have been hotter. I removed my helmet and hooded facemask. The older women in the room appeared startled and began chattering among themselves. I asked the interpreter what they were saying. Apparently my blonde hair and face resembled Russian soldiers' who had occupied this region during the 1980s. I found out from the interpreter that the Russians were not very kind to the women when they were here and I saw the look of concern spreading throughout the room. *What an absolutely terrifying experience for these little kids!* 20 minutes ago they were sound asleep in their beds and now they have a man in body armor standing over them with a rifle.

I remembered that I had a large bag of candy in my cargo pocket. Every eye in the room was glued attentively to my movement as I reached into my pocket and pulled out the Ziploc bag. I kneeled and offered a piece to the closest child in the room. She was adorable; a little girl maybe four or five years old. Her brown hair was matted and wild. Her expression showed great

116

curiosity. In her little nightgown, she hesitantly reached for the brightly wrapped treasure at my fingertips. Like a little mouse that had just secured the cheese from a trap, she retreated to the safety of the group.

This set off the reaction one would imagine. I instantly became the most popular person in that province. I handed out every piece of candy and couldn't help but think about my young nieces back home. Just as we got the call for exfil, the first brave little girl came back to me and tugged on my pant leg. She handed me a brown necklace that I would later give to my niece, Hailey. It's been over nine years, but to my knowledge, she still has it.

As we made our way out of the compound, I walked through the outdoor kitchen. The walls were stained with soot and it had an ancient smell. The burnt iron kettle that was suspended from a hook reminded me of something that would have been used hundreds if not thousands of years ago. I would come to find the majority of the country was caught in some sort of a time warp. Much of the technology and culture had not ever grown much beyond that of biblical times, like a sort of time capsule allowing us a look into the past.

The drive back to Salerno was just as miserable as the trip to the objective. By the time we rolled into the security of the gates, I could no longer feel my hands. We did a quick check for sensitive items and set out to dust off our equipment. One thing about Afghanistan, you can try to get clean, but you will always be covered in dirt. Little of the country is paved and riding in the back of what is essentially a pickup truck will leave every part of you filthy. It was of little concern to me.

I hadn't spoken with my family since I had arrived and I knew that there wouldn't be a wait for either of the two working phones that we had for the 75 or so Rangers that were on that outpost. The *MWR* tent was a drafty hut with a shelf in the back with books and generic items delivered for non-specific soldiers; letters from school kids and drawings, that sort of thing. There were four desks that had layers of carvings from pocketknives of Rangers who'd sat at that table previously, anxiously awaiting their chance to speak with a loved one. Each one of the four had a phone, but only two of them ever worked. I dialed the staff duty number and asked to be patched through to my father's home line. The connection was shoddy at best and I wasn't allowed to discuss anything that I was doing or where I was, but it was a relief to hear my father's voice. He told me that everything was good and that nothing had changed at all. I would later find out that this was not at all true, but his protective instincts didn't want me being distracted by any bad news from back home. The call was short. Someone outside the fence thought that now would be a good time to lob a mortar round at our compound. I'm not sure if the sirens wailed first or the phone cut out. Either way, I'm sure that was the last thing that my pops wanted to hear. I left the tent to see guys running to the shelter of several concrete bunkers. Many of them had already dressed down for the evening and found themselves in little more than Ranger panties and body armor. The standard operating procedure was to meet in these little makeshift caves until we received an *all clear* call. We sat packed in like sardines for about 30 minutes before being allowed to return to our tents.

The next morning started out just like every other for the next few months. With hygiene bag in tow, wearing faded brown undershirts and short black silky shorts, we moved like zombies to the metal box-like latrines. Every step was more painful than the one before. Our paper-thin shower shoes were no match for jagged Afghan rocks. Once inside the humid shower room, we had it down to a precise order of work. *Face shaved. Teeth brushed. Bowels cleared. Move out.* My next order of business would be to check in with the senior medic at the aid station to see if anyone showed up for sick call. PFC *Joe Snuffy* would have a sore knee. "Here's some Motrin," would be the standard response. Then it would be 90 minutes before the dingy white tent opened for breakfast. *I wonder what kind of eggs we will have today, runny or brick hard?* After sick call, I'd be off to the gym again. *What day is it? Chest day, that's what day it is!*

Following breakfast, we were informed we'd be going to the range so the new guys could sight in their weapons. Since the last range that I attended was in basic training, I had a preconceived notion on where we would be training today. To my surprise, there was no tower, no pre- dug foxholes and no gates. It was literally just a desert. We drove out to the desert and set up targets. This reminded me of the countless times we did this growing up in Arizona. In fact, the terrain was almost identical. The zeroing process was surprisingly laid-back. No one was shouting. After sighting in our weapons we worked through line drills where we walked one direction and shot, then the next direction. Walk and shoot, run and shoot, turn and shoot, shoot and shoot. We shot until our fingers were blistered. We became familiar with every weapon system we had, including weapons commonly used by our enemies, such as the AK-47.

We ate MREs for lunch and shot into the early evening, an event we'd repeat on a weekly basis for the next few months. At night, after dinner, we returned to our tents to enjoy another movie that was clearly pirated. A half-dozen of us huddled around the TV, sitting in folding camp chairs while sharing the bounty from care packages that just came in. One particular delivery brought several cases of Girl Scout cookies from the mother of my tent mate. Knowing that he couldn't possibly eat the dozens upon dozens of boxes himself, Erik shared the contents with us. One Sunday, which was for the most part a down day, we decided to have a gangster marathon. We watched all three Godfather films, Goodfellas and myriad lesser quality movies. I personally took down six full boxes of Thin Mints between lunch and dinner that day. I regret nothing!

The days and nights blurred together in a sort of *Warfighter's Groundhog Day*. The only moments that we ever spent alone were the three or four minutes secluded in a port-a-potty with a porn magazine illuminated by a red headlamp. It's sick to say, but I still get a little excited when I see red lights. *Wake up. Shave face. Lift weights. Eat breakfast. Shoot. Eat lunch. Practice CQB. Eat dinner. Lift weights. Watch a movie. Take an anti-malaria pill. Go to bed. Repeat.* With any group of highly motivated, barrel-chested freedom fighters, boredom is a very dangerous thing. Idle hands are the devil's playthings as they say and no one was more familiar than we were.

For most, a birthday is a time of celebration, a time to bring attention to yourself and the things that you have accomplished over the past year. In Ranger Battalion, it is a cause for getting tortured. For that reason, most guys will purposely let the day come and go without mention. Occasionally, you will have a friend we call a *Blue Falcon* (BF = Buddy Fucker), which will tell the rest of your platoon that it's your special day. One unfortunate soul thought that he was going to make it through the entire day without incident. We had, however, been plotting his demise for at least a few days. It was around Christmas time and we were watching movies in another squad's tent. We had a brief intermission between films for a quick bathroom break. The birthday boy donned his red headlamp and commenced the 200 or so meter walk to the outhouse.

The six-man element responsible for carrying out the birthday festivities quickly reacted without hesitation. As the target faded into the night, the squad of Rangers affixed their NVGs and removed any colorful clothing, replacing it with an all-black base layer. Mobilizing into blocking positions, we covered any potential means of egress that the enemy personnel may have thought to take. We waited silently in the freezing cold night for him to reemerge from the row of shitters. Waiting patiently for him to move right in the middle of our formation, we peered through the darkness. He was completely oblivious of our whereabouts. As he drew closer, "CONTACT, CONTACT, CONTACT!" was shouted and one of the privates rushed at him, wrapping him up. Another and another piled on. He was no match for this type of violence of action. Before he knew what was happening, he was on the ground and zip-tied. He never had a chance. One of the senior privates produced a fresh can of shaving cream and began to go to work on the detainee. Another grabbed a case of bottled water and doused him, drenching him to the bone. The man then was violently dragged to a nearby chain link fence and tied to it. We sang happy birthday as we returned to the warmth of our tent, leaving the drenched Ranger to tolerate the freezing Afghan night. About halfway through the second movie someone remembered that he was still outside. "Oh yeah! Meh...we'll get him after this is done."

The way that Thanksgiving came and went was the same as Christmas and New Year's. The days and nights blurred together with the occasional squad-on-squad brawl to break things up. When our rotation ended in early 2005, I had gained the respect of the men around me, but realized that there were hundreds more men in the Battalion I had yet to meet. I would once again be the new guy; I would have to prove myself to them as well. I would find out this was the nature of life in a Ranger Battalion. There was no place for a guy who would rest on his laurels. If you were a good team leader, you would have to prove yourself as a good squad leader, then as a good platoon sergeant and so on. Battalion is a constant proving ground where you are expected to be at your absolute best daily. Every day may not be an action-packed gunfight the way it's depicted in movies, but the highest standards are expected to be met on a daily basis, regardless of task. That consistency in expectations is what produces the highest caliber of warrior.

-LEO JENKINS

3/75

CHAPTER FIVE

"May God have mercy for my enemies because I won't."

GEORGE S. PATTON JR.

As the Regiment continued its transformation to meet operational needs, the plan to add a support company to each battalion became reality. The Echo company would allow the line companies to focus on their primary tasks while accomplishing the maintenance required of the growing fleet of vehicles each battalion had. The support companies were authorized by the *Ranger Force* XXI expansion plan, in place for a few years at that point. The companies' first volunteers were selected from other units, primarily the 528th Support Battalion out of Fort Bragg. The new volunteers did not go through RIP before assignment, much to the chagrin of the Rangers. This was because the companies needed to be operational by a certain date, a requirement imposed on Regiment from higher headquarters. Although E Company volunteers wore a Ranger Scroll and Ranger PT uniform, they were authorized to wear the maroon beret, not the tan beret Rangers wore.

The plan was to get the new companies up to a minimum operating strength, then start sending the original volunteers back through RIP. At that point, all new incoming members would go through RIP like any other

Ranger volunteer. It did not exactly work out that way, as it was not feasible to send all the original volunteers back through the selection. In 2006, each battalion held a mini-RIP where E Company support personnel performed minimum Ranger standards in a one-week course ending with their being awarded a tan beret in what many dubbed the Tan Beret Give-Away. Also, during this transition period, support personnel that volunteered for Ranger training would be as-signed to the Ranger Training Detachment (which ran RIP) with the option to undergo selection or go straight to their battalion. Some volunteers went through RIP; others took the easier route straight to battalion where they did the one-week course to earn their beret. This did not sit well with many and the support personnel who volunteered for RIP earned the respect of their fellow Rangers while the rest were scorned.

Despite the rocky transition, adding the support company made the Regiment more lethal and more agile. Rangers no longer had to rely on the availability of outside support as these skills were now organic. The Rangers of Echo Company would go on not only to support the Rangers in the line companies, but also actively participate in missions while deployed. By the end of 2006, all Ranger volunteers regardless of military occupational specialty would have to attend and pass the Ranger Indoctrination Program or the Ranger Orientation Program, making the 75th Ranger Regiment one of the few SOF units requiring their support personnel to undergo the same selection process as everyone else.

The look of Rangers again changed as well, with the adoption of the Army Combat Uniform (ACU). This new digital pattern replaced the decades old Battle Dress Uniform (BDU), as well as its desert counterpart, Desert Combat Uniform (DCU). The weapons and equipment of the individual Ranger continued to improve, enabling each Ranger the ability to shoot, move and communicate better than ever.

The war in Iraq was violent; the death toll of American service members topped 2,000. Iraqis held their first democratic election in over 50 years and the captured Saddam Hussein went on trial. The men of the 75th Ranger Regiment were hitting their stride in methodical execution of nightly counter-terror operations, providing the muscle needed for the Command's task force to make serious ground in culling the ranks of terrorist leadership.

Primary focus had shifted to the hunt for the leader of Al Qaeda in Iraq and the hunt was moving at full throttle. Every Ranger in Iraq was busy, some platoons executing a hundred missions in one three-month deployment.

The war in Afghanistan was not as hectic as Iraq. However, Rangers from 2/75 and 3/75 distinguished themselves by leading the rescue effort for four Navy SEALs lost on Operation Red Wings. The terrain was unforgiving and the heat brutal during the summertime operation. Rangers would not rest before accomplishing the mission, some rehydrating via IVs in order to keep going. All three bodies were recovered and a small element of 2/75 Rangers found Marcus Luttrell and ensured his safe evacuation.

The Regiment fought hard, continuing to distinguish itself and further proving it was a force to be reckoned with. But the year was not without loss. Private John Henderson, Jr., Private First Class Damian Garza, Corporal Timothy Shea and Private First Class Dillon Jutras were all Rangers from 3/75 and all made the ultimate and final sacrifice.

Summer 2005

"MEDCAP"

"I can't believe Marissa would treat Ryan that way, it's just cold blooded."

"It's just not right, especially after all he has done for her!"

"What a bitch…Should we watch another episode before mid-rats?"

"Does the Pope shit in the woods?"

We were a few weeks into this deployment and had already devolved into marathon sessions of the popular television show, *The O.C.* Our platoon hit the ground running and stayed busy after being assigned the search and rescue operation for the Navy SEALs compromised during Operation Red Wings, but now the op tempo came to a standstill. The summer of '05 was starting to feel like the winter of '04 when we sat idle at FOB Salerno.

We were stationed at Bagram Airfield; our primary task was as a QRF. That sounds cool, but what it really means is sitting on the airfield in full kifor hours while another platoon hit an objective. When the opportunity arose to jock up and walk in the mountains for a day or two, we jumped on it. We had just four episodes remaining before the last season finale of *The O.C.* (available in Afghanistan at least) and no one was willing to stoop so low as to watch *Desperate Housewives*...yet.

As I entered the room where the mission briefing would be held I saw a very familiar bearded face. "Teddy P?" Oh shit. I had just referred to a master sergeant by his nickname. The last time I saw Teddy, we were students together in the Special Operations Medical Course at Fort Bragg. I had just been made corporal so addressing a master sergeant this way got some unapproving looks from my superiors. Teddy worked as a medic for a Civil Affairs unit and was putting together a MEDCAP mission (Medical Civil Action Program). The idea was to put a group of Americans into a village of tactical significance and distribute medical supplies and treatment to its inhabitants.

This was an atypical mission for Rangers, but we didn't mind. Not just because of our general boredom, but because we viewed ourselves as consummate professionals. We didn't see the difference between executing this task and a hostage rescue mission, search and rescue mission, or direct action raid. It was our job and it was time to go to work.

We loaded onto two Chinook helicopters piloted by 160th SOAR. I'm not sure if there is another unit in the US military that I respect more than the Special Operations Aviation Regiment. Each night, men from every unit in the Command put their lives into the hands of the 160th crews with absolute faith they'd take them into and deliver them from harm's way. They are truly the unsung heroes of the US Special Operations community.

Tonight would do little to test their skill. We landed in a rocky riverbed, five kilometers from the village and stepped off the ramp with motivation. As the helicopters pulled away, violent vibration and dissonance of the Chinook's dual rotors contrasted starkly with the tranquility of the star-filled and silent Afghan night in a way that was nearly maddening. The stars sparkled and shone, like the eyes of the woman to whom you've long been estranged.

One-by-one we stepped off, creating a textbook Ranger file. The moon illuminated our silhouettes as we moved from the low ground to the security of the terraces ahead. Ahead is our Battalion surgeon. Colonel "O" had come to us from another unit in the Command. I spoke with him a few times at the aid station on Bagram but most had not met him. He was incredibly intelligent man and highly likable. We also had with us a SEAL corpsman and a few other medics from Regiment, including Sergeant Prokop. Prokop was just returning from graduating Ranger school when I first arrived at 3rd Ranger Battalion. He was quite accepting of me as a new medic and helped square me away before I left on my first deployment. A couple of years after leaving Battalion, I learned he was killed in a motor vehicle accident while working as a police officer in San Diego.

As we moved through the night, I could tell the surgeon was struggling, if only slightly. We took a tactical pause and I asked if he was doing all right. I'm not sure he was accustomed to moving at a Ranger pace over rough terrain like we were. He made some comment about the weight of his ruck and not realizing that we would be moving this far. I reached for his ruck, sitting at his side and nearly gave myself a hernia trying to lift it. "Damn, Sir! You win the award for packing the most shit, that's for sure!"

I offered to take his pack, an offer he gladly accepted. All I ever did during deployments was go to the gym. We were in mission brief during my scheduled PT time that day and I wasn't about to miss leg day, so I figured this was was a win-win situation. Every one of the dozen or so terraces became a weighted muscle-up, making it a fun little game. It took another hour or so to reach the village. It was still dark so we waited for first light to contact the village elder.

My platoon sergeant and I sat back to back against an old tree about 30 meters from one of the small mud houses. I slowly pulled the Velcro strip keeping my shoulder pocket shut and took from it a much-needed treat. Most Rangers would have taken the opportunity to pack their lip with chew but I never took to that habit. Instead, I poured the contents of that bright red bag into my hand. *Fuck, I love Skittles,* I thought to myself as I filled my cheek like a chipmunk preparing for winter. The sweat accumulating from our infil created quite a chill as we sat motionless in the tenebrous dawn. This is how these things went. Hurry up and wait.

Immediately prior to this deployment I switched platoons. My new platoon sergeant was formerly one of my instructors at RIP. The man was known throughout the Battalion for his creative ability in making men quit the indoctrination course. Naturally, I was terrified of him; he levied much torture upon my fellow wannabes and me. For some reason however, I was curious about the time that he spent as a destroyer of young men's dreams. So, I inquired.

I asked about certain guys who were kicked out and others that passed and how those things came to be. When I asked if he ever felt bad about anything that he did during his time as an instructor he responded, "Yeah, there was one time in a winter class we had a combination of sleet and snow during our time at Cole Range. We found a giant puddle with the top layer frozen over. We made those guys low crawl back and forth through that ice water all night long."

"Yeah...that was my class, Sergeant." I replied.

"I don't want to talk about this anymore..." he abruptly responded.

As the sun rose, it cast light on the beauty of our surroundings. The modest Afghan homes were dispersed sporadically against the backdrop of the steep mountains. Our Civil Affairs counterparts contacted the village elders as we displayed one of the skills for which Rangers have become known the world over: *take a knee, face out, pull security.* The news that there were American doctors in the village handing out medicine had people coming from every direction. This was a very uncomfortable scenario for many. We were not accustomed to being in a village during the day. We never did presence patrols, as the Regiment wasn't exactly a *'hearts and minds'* kind of unit. The times we were on target past daybreak, we'd do everything possible to keep any local far from us. Now we were forced to adapt to the nature of the mission as fighting-aged men walked up to us. We were here to create a relationship, not start a fight.

A line formed outside of one of the larger homes. Within minutes, every man, woman and child from the entire village stood ready to receive treatment for some type of ailment. When asked, many didn't know how old they were.

They would respond with, "Between 20 and 30." The Chinook that dropped us off here must have been a time machine; it took us back to the biblical age. People well into their thirties had never seen a dentist or doctor and it showed. I spent the first couple of hours cleaning out minor wounds, many of which had been festering for some time. Imagine something as simple as stubbing your toe in a grocery store parking lot. We are accustomed to cleaning it, putting some Neosporin on it, bandaging it and waiting a few days. That standard of care was unheard of in this village.

Mid-morning, things shifted. Villagers noticed we were handing out Tylenol and Pedialyte. They lost interest in getting treatment and became concerned with scoring as much free shit as they could get their hands on. Men were getting back in line for another bottle of *head medicine* or *belly medicine,* and we had to tell them no. We had a limited amount of supplies and the bigger guys used their size to their advantage in hoarding what we gave them. We would see the same thing when tossing candy to the local kids while returning from missions. The biggest kids would overpower the smallest to get a bottle of water or Tootsie Roll.

When the local men realized that we had caught on to them they too adapted by sending in wave after wave of adorable little kids. One girl had a gold flower piercing in her nose. She was maybe five years old but had the courage of a warrior. She walked right up and tugged on the guy's pant leg, looking up with eyes that had same effect on him as a microwave on a stick of butter. We were clay in her hands. By the time we left, she had more Band-Aids and topical antibiotics than aisle nine at Walgreens.

By early afternoon we ran of supplies and called for a resupply drop. A pallet of water bottles and MREs, dropped from the back of a C-130, exploded a kilometer outside the village. We dispatched a squad to recover the contents and distributed what we could before making our way out of the village. Moving down the mountain with far less weight and in daylight made it much more enjoyable than the movement up. Regardless of the benevolent nature of our time in their village, there was still a certain hyper-vigilance as we moved toward the extraction point. I do not like being exposed on uneven terrain during the day—and the uneasy feeling that we could take fire at any moment was enough to overcome the expansive beauty of our surroundings.

We were picked up without incident and made another long, cold, cramped, night time helicopter ride back home. Most of us passed out on the chilly metallic floor of that rumbling bird. We landed in Bagram with just enough time to make the last five minutes of *mid-rats*. A few of us took the opportunity to load up on boxes of cereal and paper containers of goat milk. We had four more episodes of *The O.C.* to get through before the season finale. After our Chinook power nap and fresh stockpile of fruit loops, we were up to the task.

-LEO JENKINS
3/75

Summer 2005

"BARRACKS LIFE"

I arrived at 1st Ranger Battalion in February of 2005 while the Battalion was still deployed. I sat on the rear detachment, or *Rear-D* as it was called, for the better part of two months before everybody came back and I finally met my assigned platoon. At the time I didn't drink alcohol, so volunteered to be the permanent designated driver for my squad. I didn't really mind because I liked going out with the squad and it was a way that I could contribute and start paying my dues. After a few months of training with my crew I had seemingly been accepted into my squad. This was due in no small part to my role as babysitter of full-grown men so piss-drunk that they could barely speak, who wanted more than anything to urinate in the parking lot or on a brick wall in the middle of Congress Street in downtown Savannah.

During this time, we moved out of the old barracks, which to the best of our knowledge had been condemned some 30 years prior when they were Air Force barracks. As far-fetched as this may seem, it only took one quick look at their sorry shape to confirm the story. Tiles were torn out in multiple places, there was mold everywhere, some air-conditioning vents were held up by coat hangers and many bunks were held together with *100 mile per hour tape*. The new barracks were incredibly nice. They were technically 3rd Infantry Division's barracks, but 3rd ID was deployed so we were permitted to stay in them until ours were renovated. The new rooms were suites, which you shared with one other guy. Each guy had his own separate room and shared a kitchen and a bathroom.

The greatest thing about the new setup was that the rooms were entered from the outside, which eliminated the hallway. *The Hallway* was the ultimate symbol of misery defining the life of a Ranger Private. Each platoon had its own hallway (1st floor: 1st Platoon, 2nd floor: 2nd Platoon and 3rd floor: 3rd Platoon). The platoon spent much of the duty day spread out among the various rooms doing whatever odd jobs that came down for us. It was great if you had your Tab and needed a job done because it kept all the privates consolidated in one area. As a private, it exacerbated your daily misery. You always had to sprint the hallway unless you had your Tab. God help you if a Tab or team leader ever caught you in the hallway. Such an infraction could lead to getting smoked for hours as well as roping all the other privates into the misery alongside you. Rarely did anyone get smoked alone. No dirges were ever sung by Ranger privates mourning the hallway's elimination.

A particular Friday at the start of a long weekend, I planned to spend a quiet night alone in my room. Shortly after going to bed, I heard a knock on my door. It was my roommate (for whom I have tremendous respect), so I opened it to see what he wanted. He was drunk and proceeded to give me his version of the familiar "...you're a good dude," speech. I was quite glad to hear his speech, albeit a bit slow and slurred. After saying his piece, he left to his own room and I went back to bed. Not long after, I was woken again by a knock on my door. This knock was preceded by the voice of squad mate yelling "Farnum! Wake up! Come give me a hug!" I rose, slightly irritated and begrudgingly opened the door. I delivered the requested hug and sat to receive *his* version of the "...you're a good dude," speech. Again flattered but very tired, I listened to his entire spiel and then walked him out. But my night was far from over.

I had fallen back to sleep and once again heard a knock at my door. This time, completely irritated, I jumped up and flung open my door to see who the hell was waking me. To my surprise I see a staff sergeant in full duty uniform whom I didn't know. Standing there in only Ranger winter PT bottoms, I very quickly snapped to a groggy version of parade rest. He was holding onto a guy, a senior private from my platoon. To protect the guilty, we'll call him Forde.

The staff sergeant asked me, "Do you know this guy?"

"Roger, Sergeant," I replied, "He's in my platoon."

Apparently, Ol' Forde was picked up by Military Police at the gate and dropped off at Staff Duty and it was now my job to watch him to ensure he didn't leave nor cause any trouble.

After the staff duty NCO left, Forde went to my fridge, opened it up and yelled, "Farnum, where's the booze?"

I told him, "There is no booze and quite frankly, I think you've had enough."

He then opened the freezer and yelled, "Hot Pockets! Farnum, you're a single man, where are the Hot Pockets?" Slightly amused, I explained I didn't have any.

He then turned to me, "Let's go fight somebody!"

"Yeah, let's not," I replied.

I rubbed the sleep out of my eyes and sighed. This is going to be a long night.

Then a thought occurred to me. My stepdad drank heavily when I was growing up and would pass out as soon as he sat down to watch a movie. So let's watch a movie…

I went to my TV and started rummaging through my stack of movies. It was a very old, very small TV with built-in VHS player acquired secondhand. I had a stack of VHS tapes sourced via similar process. I grabbed *The Fifth Element* and threw it in. I sat him down in a chair in front of the TV and waited. It wasn't more than 15 minutes before he passed out. I was relieved and felt slightly accomplished. He then leaned over, crawled onto the floor and passed out again. I turned off the TV and crawled back into bed after making sure that all the doors were locked.

A few hours later, though it didn't seem like that long at the time, I woke up to the sound of my bedroom door opening. My first thought was, *Oh God, he's escaping!*

I jumped up and rushed to the front door to try and catch him only to find that the front door was still closed and locked. I then heard him behind me in the bathroom pissing. My initial relief was short-lived as I heard him hit and miss, hit and miss, hit and miss. My only thought at this point was how I was going to have to scrub that entire bathroom in the morning. *Fan-damn-tastic!*

Forde then walked out of the bathroom back toward my room and me. The entire front of his pants were soaked with piss. I backed up to allow him to go back into my room, trying to not let him touch me. He walked into my room, *dropped trou* and laid down in the middle of the floor, bare ass in the air. I grabbed a bed sheet and covered him up with it. Furious, I crawled back into bed.

About 9:30 AM, I heard him rummaging through my stuff. He nudged me and said, "Farnum, I can't find my ID. Have you seen my ID?" I hadn't seen his ID nor was I in the mood to help him find it. "I'm just gonna walk home." He lived off post and I was so enraged about the night I just didn't care. "Whatever...fine...go...just go." He left and I went back to sleep.

I woke up a few hours later and decided I'd better clean, starting my room before the bathroom. We just had a layout so my room was wrecked from me digging through my bags trying to find pieces of equipment that nobody ever used but were responsible for keeping track of anyway. Clothes were strewn all over and I just started throwing clothes into my laundry bag. I then realized that all my stuff was wet. I took a whiff of what was in my hand and knew immediately why everything was wet. *Ol' dude pissed all over my stuff!*

Gagging, I continued to throw my urine-soaked clothes into the laundry bag until I came across a pair of jeans I didn't recognize. I reached into the pocket and pulled out Forde's military ID and driver's license. This guy, who was easily two sizes bigger than I was, somehow squeezed his happy ass into my jeans and walked out! Needless to say I was livid and stayed that way for most of that weekend.

I didn't hear from him until a couple of days later. He got a hold of me because he needed his military ID to get back onto post for work. He then said something along the lines of, "Hey, man. I'm pretty sure I may have pissed all over your stuff."

"Yeah dude, ya did."

"Yeah, I figured I'd give you a couple of days before I called to let you cool off."

He was right, by this point I'd cooled off, if only a bit. We met at a bar that was close to his house where we completed a pants and identification swap.

-RICHARD FARNUM
1/75

THE RANGER MEDIC

One cornerstone of Ranger effectiveness is the medical training each individual Ranger receives. Not only is the platoon medic a graduate of the prestigious Special Operations Combat Medical Course, but it is not uncommon to see Specialists and Sergeants that are Nationally Registered Emergency Medical Technicians. At the lowest level, all Rangers are annually certified in Ranger First Responder (RFR) training. Not only has this emphasis on medical proficiency saved numerous Ranger lives on the field of battle, but it has saved the lives of civilian non-combatants and enemy fighters alike.

The Ranger combat life saver training has existed since the early 1990s as a modified version of the Army's program. The course taught at 1/75 during the 1992-1995 timeframe was essentially the Ranger version of the old Basic Trauma Life Support curriculum with several Expert Field Medical Badge-like tasks such as the litter course and manual carries added. The Army-wide requirement was one Combat Life Saver qualified soldier per squad, but the Rangers had already instituted one EMT-B per squad in the late 1980s. The Regiment therefore modified the Combat Life Saver requirement to one for every fire team, doubling the Army minimum requirement. Additionally, the Ranger Combat Life Saver certification was a critical requirement for several support personnel such as cooks, finance, chaplains and radiomen as they were key members of the casualty control points.

In September 1997, the Regimental commander, then Colonel Stanley McChrystal, directed that all Rangers were to be Combat Life Saver qualified regardless of rank or position. This was a key part of the *Big-Four* that (then) Colonel McChrystal and Command Sergeant Major Mike Hall instituted. Each individual battalion continued to run and modify versions of the Ranger Combat Life Saver program for a couple of years. In conjunction with the focus on medical training was the integration of Tactical Combat Casualty Care (TCCC), which had been introduced by Captain Frank Butler. By late 1998, 3rd Ranger Battalion had modified their version of Combat Life Saver into a TCCC course. The remaining battalions then integrated portions of TCCC into their existing programs as well. Because it was so drastically different from the Army Combat Life Saver program, it took on the present name of Ranger First Responder (coined by 3/75 in 1998). By March of 2000, the Regimental Commander directed the Regiment to do a complete analysis of Combat Life Saver and RFR to determine the best training path forward. The decision was made summer of 2000, with the Regimental Commander directing that RFR would be the course taught to all Rangers using 3/75's version, known as RFR 1.0. In October of 2000, RFR was integrated into the Ranger Indoctrination Program curriculum for every incoming enlisted Ranger. By summer 2001, RFR had become a relatively common training practice conducted by Ranger platoons prior to assumption of, and sometimes during, their ready alert status.

In July of 2003, as combat operations became the norm, the Regimental Commander directed that every Ranger in a rifle platoon would receive annual RFR training. This was to ensure it was a platoon-based and focused requirement and to alleviate the lack of compliance caused by staff and support personnel. It was during this time the Regiment, in keeping with the *Abrams Charter,* began exporting versions of RFR to other units. The earliest to adopt the RFR program of instruction were 10th Mountain Division, 101st Airborne Division (renaming it Eagle First Responder) and the 82nd Airborne

Division. The Regiment and subordinate battalions sent Ranger medics to assist those units in standing up their programs.

In October of 2003, Major Jeff Cain (former 1/75 Battalion surgeon) was assigned to the U.S. Army Medical Department Center and School and began pushing that they adopt RFR. By late 2004, they had completely revised the Army Combat Lifesaver course to reflect RFR 1.0 and the tenets of TCCC Army-wide. After this, Army Combat Life Saver and RFR began relative parallel growth and change as each adopted updates to TCCC principles. Generally, RFR stayed about a year ahead as it was easier for a single unit to implement changes to the course and the Rangers had taken on roles in the Committee on Tactical Combat Casualty Care formally established in 2002.

Coupled with RFR training was the development of the Ranger Bleeder Control Kit. Similar to CLS then RFR training, each of the battalions had their own variants of first aid kits in the late 1990's. As the concepts of TCCC became more engrained in the training programs, various versions of tourniquets became a predominant component. The early common tourniquet was a pre-made cravat and wooden dowel concept based on the traditional improvised stick & rag tourniquet. Along with those involved with TCCC development, several tourniquet concepts were explored. The initial Ranger tourniquet immediately following 9/11 was the Ranger Ratchet Tourniquet, very similar to the ratchets Rangers used for lashing vehicles. This was the primary tourniquet until 2003. By 2005, the Ranger Regiment had fully adopted the early versions of the combat application tourniquet (CAT). The bleeder kit evolved over the same time frame as the Regiment's medical staff explored the best trauma dressings. Alongside the Army's adaptation of RFR, there was a parallel adaptation of the Ranger Bleeder Control Kit as the Army Individual First Aid Kit (IFAK).

Armed with RFR training and an advanced IFAK on every Ranger, even the lowest common denominators in a Ranger platoon were very capable, medically speaking. Often times, it is a non-medic Ranger who is the first to respond to the wounded—applying self-aid if the situation arises. A great example of this is Medal of Honor recipient Sergeant First Class Leroy Petry, who hails from 2nd Ranger Battalion. During the mission for which he eventually received the Congressional Medal of Honor, he picked up a live grenade which landed next to him to throw it back at the enemy. The grenade exploded, resulting in his hand being fully severed at the wrist. Instead of drawing other Rangers out of the fight to take care of him, he did as he was trained and performed self-aid by putting on his own tourniquet and stopping the bleeding so that he could get back into the fight.

The next level of care comes from the platoon medic, who is typically a sergeant who holds the health care specialist military occupational specialty. After completion of the 18-week advanced individual training (where the medic leaves as a nationally registered EMT-Basic) which all Army medics attend, the Ranger medic will then attend advanced follow-on training. The 75th Ranger Regiment's six-month pre-SOCM (Special Operations Combat Medic) course will come first, with the prospective Ranger medic attending college classes as well as receiving on the job training. They then move to Fort Bragg to attend the Joint Special Operations Medical Training Center's prestigious SOCM course, which is nine months in duration. This is where they train alongside their peers from other SOF units such as Navy SEALs and Army Special Forces. They graduate SOCM as a US SOCOM certified Advanced Tactical Practitioner; this includes certifications such as NREMT-Paramedic, Advanced Cardiac Life Support, Basic Life Support, Pre-Hospital Trauma Life Support and Pediatric Education for Pre-Hospital Professionals.

The education a Ranger medic receives before he even steps foot into one of the battalions and the experience they gain as a member of the nation's primary special operations direct action force makes them some of the most capable and professional trauma practitioners in the world. It's all well and good to tout certifications and special training, but proof of their proficiency is *in the pudding,* so to speak.

From October 1st, 2001 to March 31st, 2010, 75th Ranger Regiment suffered 419 casualties, to include 32 deaths. Based on the data collected in the Ranger Pre-Hospital Trauma Registry (PHTR), the Joint Trauma Registry (maintained by the Joint Trauma System) and autopsies performed by AFIP, none of the Rangers who were killed in action died from injuries that could have been prevented in the tactical pre-hospital environment; proof that the lengths to which the Regiment went were extremely effective. Data received since the end of the study indicates this metric has not changed, representing a remarkable accomplishment. Over the course of a decade of sustained combat, the 75th Ranger Regiment is the only unit in the armed forces, SOF or conventional, that can claim such a metric.

SEPTEMBER 2005
"TAL AFAR"

The speed at which the plane descended to the airfield in Mosul was indicative of the increased threat level. The C-17 went into a nosedive, circled the airfield twice and then made a hard landing on a short runway. The ramp of the aircraft lowered with an incredible force. Air Force loadmasters screamed in on their forklifts to unload pallets loaded with the gear we would need for the three-month rotation. Once on the ground, it started to sink in…some of us might die here. *Fuck it.* My will was squared away and my father had a power of attorney to pay my bills while I was gone. I could focus on the task at hand.

In the spring and summer of 2005, Mosul suffered over three hundred attacks on coalition forces each month. This statistic does not include the random slaughtering of civilians and Iraqi forces occurring on a daily basis. IED, mortar, small unit and sniper attacks were the order of the day; suicide bombings became normal. Al Qaeda in Iraq had a penchant for executing and beheading civilians to enforce their rule. Our platoon had been going after their death squads all summer. These death squads would execute innocent men, women and children, using them prior as human shields if necessary. The enemy defended their territory to the death, armed with machine guns, car bombs, explosive vests, grenades and AK-47 rifles. Al Qaeda fighters do not negotiate or surrender. The territory they chose to die for was not an open field, or a piece of rocky, mountainous terrain. We fought our enemy in tiny rooms, rooftops and alleys. The enemy did not cower to surprise or superior firepower and technology. Al Qaeda in Iraq's best-trained and most lethal fighters had traveled thousands of miles to *get their jihad on;* killing coalition soldiers and Iraqi civilians *en masse* was the name of the game.

Our platoon took contact nearly everywhere we went. Anytime we ventured into Mosul or the surrounding area, somebody was always trying to kill us. Insurgents attacked the airfield on an almost nightly basis. The night of September 4, 2005, described shortly, was just one out of 110 straight days and nights of constant close combat. By the time our two platoons of Rangers left after the short rotation, the amount of attacks on coalition forces fell from three hundred per month to three.

Tal Afar, Iraq is a small city located between Mosul and the border of Syria. In late October 2004, media announced the Battle for Fallujah was imminent. Rather than face a large force of battle-hardened Marines, most experienced foreign fighters and leadership fled to Tal Afar, turning it into an Al Qaeda stronghold. Military intelligence estimated their number to be in the thousands. Tal Afar was so dangerous that most units surrounding the city would rarely venture into it. They were quick to learn that Al Qaeda controlled that city.

On the night of September 4, 2005, my platoon was tasked with striking three separate houses in Tal Afar. The mission had been in the works for days. There was a large military offensive planned for the town shortly. This mission was a dangerous one. To us Rangers, it was another night to hunt the enemy and we welcomed the chance to pick a fight. In mid-afternoon, we met in the briefing room to rehash details and finalize the assault plan. We were to capture or kill the Al Qaeda Emir of Tal Afar, his spiritual leader and capture alive anyone else we could.

A hit could go a couple of ways. Either the objective would surrender to the main assault element after their front door blew apart, or they could die trying to fight. It does no good to kill someone you need to talk to, but if we saw something menacing in hand, we usually opted for violence of action without hesitation. It wasn't always so dramatic. We were sometimes able to silently enter a house and blindfold and flex-cuff the objectives before they even knew we were there.

Going into a house with an assault force full of Rangers fills one with a confidence I doubt anyone except those with experience could understand. We were the best, surrounded by the best. We had the best equipment, training, leadership and tactics, shit…we had the best everything. On paper, we were the best platoon in the Regiment and we knew it.

As our country reeled from the devastation of Hurricane Katrina a week earlier, on the night of September 4, 2005, a small group of Rangers moved, under cover of darkness, into a fortified city controlled by hundreds of reckless and desperate men.

Before loading up in the Stryker, I found the bronze cross my mom gave me a couple of days before I deployed. I had made it for her in my high school art class. I knelt by the back of the open ramp, rubbed the cross and sent her good thoughts. I took a knee with some Ranger buddies and said a prayer before we got switched on for the evening. After our prayers, a Ranger buddy came up to me and asked, "Will you go to war with me brother?!" I answered him silently, with a bump from the Kevlar knuckles on my Oakley gloves. The ride was smooth en route to our objectives. I had no idea, riding inside that same Stryker a few hours later, the vehicle would be all but empty.

The first target building was on the outskirts of the city. Before we set up to breach the objective, our sniper element saw two men with weapons on the rooftop of the objective building. Two rounds later, the threat was no more. The sound from their rifles—unsuppressed .308 caliber bolt actions—was loud as hell. I wondered how many insurgents those shots woke. But everything stayed quiet for the moment.

The silence ended with a hasty breach of the front door. The lead assault team used a short-barreled shotgun to defeat the lock, finishing it with a swift kick. The first man rode the door in and the team followed. My team flowed in after some, establishing a strongpoint at the bottom of the staircase while others cleared. First floor clear, we flowed upstairs to secure the second floor and the rooftop. To access the rooftop we had to navigate a small staircase, lined with sacks of grain. My team leader posted to the left of the door to the roof. I stood offset to its right. You can get shot through a door if you stand in front of it. The barrel of my M-4 was pointed directly at the door, ready to lay waste to any insurgent stupid enough to dance in front of it.

I waited for a squeeze from the Ranger buddy I knew was behind me.

When I felt it, I nodded with my barrel letting JD know I was set. He gave me a silent countdown and then opened the door. *We've done this thousands of times.* I flowed out to the roof with a deadly grace. The Ranger, who gave me the go-ahead cleared the roof while I located the insurgents snipers had killed. I kicked their weapons out of reach and checked their hands visually for detonators. Once I was confident they were dead and would not trigger an IED, I moved in and searched the bodies. One insurgent had a suicide vest on, wore a chest rack and had an AK-47. The other dude had an ammo rack, Dragunov sniper rifle and was armed with grenades, one still clutched firmly, pin unpulled, in his dead hand.

The thought of entering that house and being the first to go up the stairs against two armed men immediately made me grateful that we had the best snipers in the world. Our snipers wrought serious havoc that deployment, saving us from dangerous work several times.

I was tasked with conducting a detailed search of the house, called sensitive site exploitation (SSE). It's like a small-scale crime scene effort, but completed in less than ten minutes. Sometimes, you must do this under fire or while the house is engulfed in flames. This process provides valuable information used to prosecute those we detained to lead us to the next high value target (HVT). Important people took this information and with it made important decisions. It had to be accurate and detailed. Ten minutes after breach, I completed my assigned tasks and after the leadership gained full accountability we moved out to the next target building. *Well, that went way too easy,* I thought to myself.

The second target building was about 800 meters away. It was snugly nestled smack dab in the middle of the city. This was the HVT hideout; their lair. Riding in the back of the Stryker, I conducted a hasty check of my equipment, being sure to recheck the status of my night vision. *Good to go.* I made sure my tac-light and laser were ready. My team leader put his thumb up. This was his way of asking, *"Hey asshole, got your shit ready?"* I squeezed his thumb. That provided him with confirmation through both touch and sight. It was me saying, *"Roger, Sergeant…up, up."*

We had to dismount our Stryker as fast as possible at this next target. The word via radio was, "Four personnel on the rooftop, sleeping, over."

Once we start movement to the objective, security had to be locked on again.

Due to the narrow streets and alleyways of Tal Afar, we had to infil by foot from two hundred meters from the target building. We were told to ride with our troop hatches up in Tal Afar because an officer from a conventional Army unit had been shot in the throat the previous night. Our enemy was skilled; for a sniper to make that shot on a moving target is downright impressive. We usually rode around Mosul with our hatches open. With such a large vehicle, it helps to have extra eyes to navigate the power lines and obstacles in our way.

I glanced down at my forearm pad to see the description and identifying marks of our target. The picture we had of him was that of a black silhouette. Most times we had no clear picture to go from, just a silhouette. The paper described scars, what weapons he was known to carry and what he liked to wear. It detailed whether he was known to wear a suicide vest and questions to ask him should you find him. The forearm pad also contained a small map of the surrounding buildings. My team leader gave me the 30-second hand signal. I acknowledged.

Being 30 seconds out from a house defended by armed terrorists is always a little nerve-wracking. But you settle your mind, breathe, focus on the task at hand and remember everyone comes home, no matter what. To do that, I was ready to cheat a little.

Seconds count in a gunfight. Speed typically equals success in close-quarters combat. The victor lives, the one who loses is buried, hopefully. I was taught the importance of shaving seconds. My weapon was on semi-auto immediately upon exiting the vehicle, my index finger my only safety. Not standard operating procedure, but in this environment, I'd take any advantage available. Other equipment that I had with me was turned on or checked and waiting. Pouches were unbuttoned, ready for a tactical reload. Since we didn't have sidearms at this point, we practiced reloading and failure drills thousands of times until we could do it in a couple seconds, in the dark. Some of us could reload faster than we could transition to a secondary firearm. I knew where every ordnance was on my teammates' kits in case I needed it.

The amount of training, skill, planning and knowledge that goes into a single hit is just plain surgical. Fuck, sometimes it is just downright inspiring to know you're among the best, with the best officers and non-commissioned officers in the world.

The ramp dropped. We exited in a matter of seconds and grabbed our ladders from the back of our Stryker. We waited for the lead element to begin their order of movement then we headed out. *Hunting again.*

We immediately began to scan every door and crouch under every window. Security en route to the second house was tight. We didn't talk, just used hand signals. We knew everyone by their gait. We'd been doing this for years, on the same team. We didn't have to communicate verbally. We used rates of fire to talk to each other. If somebody's rate of fire increased, then you knew that you were covered and could bound forward or break contact. We talked with our weapons and gave commands with our lasers. We kept radio traffic to a minimum. We did not want to alert anyone of the small force of deadly Americans that were now creeping through a city controlled by Al Qaeda in Iraq.

The alley that we walked through was only a few feet across and uneven. It felt a thousand years old. A feeling of uneasiness gripped me like a vice. I felt squeezed in this fatal funnel, alert to possible threats from rooftops, upper windows and doors. Over the radio, everything remained silent. All you could hear was the occasional silent whisper of someone talking to an asset overhead and the sound of gravel and pebbles crunching underneath our Merrell boots.

The uneven, cobblestoned alley played hell on my ankle. I suffered a Class-3 ankle sprain on my first deployment to Southwest Asia but continued going on missions instead of letting it heal. It always rolled, so I had to wear mountain boots and an ankle brace to give it enough stability. We sprinted, ran and walked with 65 pounds or more of body armor and equipment. I had a constant fear of it rolling, turning me from an asset into a burden for my comrades. *No way.* If I rolled it, I was just going to eat the pain and focus on the task at hand.

We crept through the narrow alley, the only light in that dark space came from our *green eyes;* light emitted by our night vision devices. There was little to no illumination that night, which would work to our advantage.

We set up for the assault. On the way to the objective we received word there were multiple armed personnel on the roof, one now moving. *Okay, the bad guys are awake.* My acuity climbed. I expected to be ambushed in the alley. I started to look for doors I could kick down so we could flow into them for cover. I was prepared to kill anything in my way.

It was all was quiet. The night was hot. My team leader turned his head and whispered softly, "JT, snipers set." This let me know the main assault team had started their part of the mission. As the breach was set, an asset, which at the time I assumed to be tasked to us, burned the target building without warning. Later we found out it wasn't ours, but a Kiowa scout helicopter tasked to another Army unit which was surrounding the city. Our element of surprise vanished. Without warning, a head poked out the front door. With the breach compromised, the assault team instinctively entered the house.

At the time, I was in the trail assault element taking a knee around the corner. I heard somebody from the lead assault team yell, "BREACH COMPROMISED!" So, I waited for the slightest movement to be made by my fellow teammates. A few seconds seemingly lasting an eternity passed. No one panicked. We waited for our brothers to do their job.

BOOM!................BOOM! Two loud explosions followed by screams. Blood curdling screams. This was not just one guy screaming. Holy shit, multiple guys were hurt, or worse. Everything we trained for was now reality.

Surprise gripped most. Fear gripped a few. The severity of the situation we faced crept over all of us as cries of, "Oh my GOD!" mixed with moans. Close friends, number unknown, cried for help in this damned alley. I sprinted past others to gain entry to the house. Simultaneously, I made peace with the fact I may get killed in the act. I was the first one in and had trouble squeezing through the door with all my gear. I forced my way through and was instantly hit with a terrible sight. In that small hallway we'd suffered five serious casualties. Wounded Rangers were grabbing at their legs. Some were screaming and writhing in pain, others just crying for help. The smell of blood, flesh and gunpowder mixed together in such a tight space filled my nostrils. I will never forget the smell.

I glanced into four small rooms as I flowed past my downed brothers to establish security in the courtyard. Making my way to the corner of the hallway to pull security first, I knew there were 30 Rangers behind me. As I arrived at the corner of the hallway opening into a small courtyard, I saw my dear friend Joe lying on his back reaching out toward his legs. I thought his legs were gone and prepared myself for the task ahead. As I knelt next to Joe, I noticed another seriously wounded Ranger in my peripheral vision within feet of us. Another good friend of mine, JB, slid in on his kneepads and immediately began work, conducting RFR. Training immediately kicked in. This moment would try all of us as men.

Rangers flowed past into the courtyard, firing, looking to establish a hard point on the rooftop to provide security as we tended to the wounded. I was going to work on Joe regardless, even if it meant being shot in the back. I knew where my teammates were and I was confident they were taking care of business. We entrusted our lives to each other.

Joe's and my girlfriends were friends. We spent lots of time together back home. Here he is, on his back...it's surreal. Joe was one of the strongest and most resilient people I've ever met. To see him screaming in agony was something which training for which could never fully prepare you. Similarly, no training could prepare you to hold down his writhing 230 pound frame. *Don't panic, conduct a head to toe assessment.* I reassured him that he was okay; I was there now, and would keep his spirits up.

He made reference to his girlfriend Michelle. "Tell Michelle that I love her," he strained to say.

"Fuck you, Joe, you tell her yourself. You're okay, bro," I knew with his screams that he had an open airway and it did not sound labored. As I conducted my head to toe assessment I scraped his back with a gloved hand, looking for blood and holes to attend to. I then heard a distinct metal sound close behind me.

Tink...tink...tink......

I glanced over to my friend JB, working on another casualty and we both looked down at our ankles. There was a blue grenade. I jumped on Joe to shield him from the blast and JB did the same for his patient.

When you are waiting on a grenade to go off at your feet, the seconds you count last forever. *Nothing.* I waited for a few more seconds before realizing it was a dud. I looked over to JB and all he could do was just shake his head. He was incredulous; the longest ten seconds of our lives were past. We went back to work as gunfire screamed from every direction. There was a huge fight going on in the house, but yet we remained unscathed.

I continued my head to toe assessment where I left off and started to take off Joe's heavy equipment. I placed his MICH to the side and undid the straps to his body armor. I lifted the front of the plate carrier over his head, being careful I didn't hit him in the head with the heavy plates. Blood was coming out of his ears, nose and mouth. I undid the buttons of his field top to get him some fresh air. I put his rifle over the back of my ankle just as if I was in an RFR training lane. I grabbed my Gerber knife out and with three swift cuts opened up his tan shirt as well as each pant leg, careful not to cut him.

Blood squirted all over my face. It got in my mouth, up my nose and in my eyes. It was all over my clothes and gloves making them extremely slippery. I reached for his tourniquet, secured with retaining bands, so it could easily be ripped away for this very situation.

His lifeblood was spilling out over this dirty floor. I had to stop it. He was peppered with small holes, the majority of his injuries to the lower half of both legs. He had one of the new CAT (tourniquets), a plastic one, with a plastic windlass to tighten the tourniquet around the wounded appendage. Trying to get the CAT's Velcro unstuck and the tourniquet's band around Joe's massive tree trunk thighs proved to be an issue. Still, he spurted blood with each heartbeat.

I finally got the Velcro unstuck and pulled the tourniquet around his leg. Getting a solid purchase on the plastic windlass with bloody gloves is really hard to do. I couldn't get a firm enough hold of it. It slipped. "Fuck this shit," I said out loud, frustrated that they gave us these stupid CATs in the first place. I carried an extra ratchet tourniquet on my kit, so I ripped it from its retaining bands and slipped it easily over his leg.
I pulled the strap as tight as I could, cranked on the lever and his blood loss stopped instantly. I took some of his blood and with my finger, made a "T" on his forehead, informing follow-on medics immediately as to what they were working with. Moving smoothly and quickly, I fought the urge to panic. I was not dead…yet. Although it seemed like an eternity, the time that had elapsed from the compromised breach to this point was less than a minute and half.

BOOM! A large explosion threw me off balance and I landed on Joe's bad leg. He immediately passed out from the pain. I made a fist with my knuckles and performed a sternum rub to his chest, trying to bring him back to consciousness. No effect. I slapped him as hard as I could, also to no avail. *This is my dear friend.* I did not want to hurt him further; I had just been the cause of him losing consciousness. But I had no choice. Checking his pulse and breathing, everything seemed fine.

We had two medics with us as well as the battalion PA, but they were busy working on the others. Help was coming. Joe was unconscious and he felt cold and clammy. He looked pale white so I began to treat him for shock. At this point, my team leader JD made his way over. He was an EMT-Paramedic and tapping my shoulder, told me he would take over. His first order of business was to give Joe a much-needed IV. Joe was in excellent hands now, so I linked up with my squad leader and teammate to get back in the hunt.

I heard yelling and screaming coming from everywhere; rooms, hallways and rooftop. To the left of me was a small hallway leading downstairs to another room. A Ranger was being engaged with grenades and small arms. Later we found out the insurgents were rolling grenades into the room from a small shaft in the wall running from an adjacent house. On the roof, we were taking constant fire. You could hear the enemy on the rooftop yelling in Arabic, throwing frags down on the courtyard and open hallway. This house needed to get cleared *STAT!*

The three of us started to clear the right side of the courtyard. The first room we cleared was a small bathroom; it just took a quick glance to see that there were no bad guys to shoot and we moved to the next room. We made our way underneath the staircase leading to the rooftop. We had Rangers on the roof playing tennis with bullets, engaging enemy directly over our heads on the opposite roof. My team flowed into another short room, cleared it and then we headed to the last room on the right. We cleared that room and as the last man coming out of the room, I picked up rear security on the roof and across the courtyard. Scanning for threats, I stopped, frozen with fear. Through a window, three enemy fighters set up a PKM machine gun less than five meters from us. They didn't fire.

Holy shit, I'm not dead yet!

I came back from my split-second daydream and yelled that I had a threat in front of me. "Sergeant! Machine gun, 12 o'clock!" I waited an eternity for fellow Rangers to start firing with me. I was met with an eerie silence. The insurgents still held their fire. *Holy fuck, I can see them but they can't see me because it's so dark.* They were scanning for targets to shoot but with so much going on I figured they did not want to reveal their presence either.

I thought about all the Rangers behind me working on wounded comrades. I felt utterly helpless and alone in that courtyard, staring at that machine gun, even though so many bad-ass Rangers surrounded me.

One of the fighters locked and loaded the machine gun. I had to think of something soon or I was going to end up riddled with 7.62mm rounds.

I was starting to hate this fucking house. I decided that since I had friendlies to my six o'clock, I was going to blind the enemy with the tac-light on my weapon. A second earlier, the thought of taking cover and throwing a grenade in their window did cross my mind. But if I missed the window, there was a chance the grenade could blow up friendlies.

The light on my weapon blinded the shit out of them. They covered their eyes and I hauled balls to the room we had just cleared seconds before to take cover before engaging. Getting into a shootout with a machine gun position only feet away with no cover seemed kind of foolish at the time. There was a window directly across from theirs. We must have been just ten to fifteen meters apart. I broke the window glass so they would focus in my direction and not aim at my friends. I knelt and right then was when I became a believer in God. I thanked him for a wonderful life, for wonderful parents who had adopted me and gave me a chance to become something great. I asked him to protect them and my girlfriend. I then asked him to guide my shots. Saying a quick amen I pressed the button on the pistol grip of my M-4 powering my infrared laser. I took a deep breath, relaxed and pointed my weapon at the machine gunner's throat. For once in the last couple of minutes, there seemed to be utter silence. I noticed the firing and explosions had stopped. The IR laser was locked on my target and I pulled the trigger. I fired and my shot found its mark, hitting the gunner in the throat. His head lurched back and his friend to his right jumped on the gun and started firing.

Bullets were flying at me and in the direction of the Rangers on the staircase, on the roof and the wounded in the hallway. Another insurgent started to throw frags at my window, so I took a knee and ate it. The explosions, coupled with shattering glass were deafening. My ears have been ringing since. A grenade rolled in through the door and all I could do was chuckle and say, "Four," marking how many times I had almost been killed in the last three minutes. It didn't go off. I decided to wait for a lull in firing and then pop up and kill them.

Waiting for a machine gun to go through two hundred rounds of ammo while glass, grenades and mayhem are exploding around you is nothing short of surreal. Finally, the lull came and I went to the door. I switched firing hands to my left so I could remain behind cover. The two insurgents ran for a piece of wall to climb up to the roof. I unloaded a full magazine on them, wounding them both. After my magazine ran dry I dropped it and reloaded. Our snipers who were set up on the roof of a nearby building finished them off with headshots. Posted in the doorway I started to take more fire from the rooftop. *Fuck, how many terrorists are there?*

I looked to my left expecting to have friendlies cover me, but there were none to be seen. They had taken cover in four small rooms where the bullets and grenades would not be able to touch them. Some sought cover outside the house. I was still by myself, nearest to the enemy. I looked again to my left as bullets whizzed by my head. *Five.* Just then the Sergeant Major and a dog handler shooting his 9mm pistol covered me while I ran to the front door.. I wanted to make it to the safety of the armored Strykers, even though they were stuck in the narrow alley in attempting to come to our aid. The drivers heard the chaos over the radio. They took a tremendous amount of fire trying to get to those of us inside that house.

I made it outside. My squad leader was directing the Strykers so we could evacuate the wounded and exfil, passing the baton to JTACs for airstrikes. I checked the Strykers for my assault team since we had been separated since the beginning of the engagement. Squad leader: directing vehicles. Team leader: wounded, but rendering aid. I had two out of three. Where the fuck was my other teammate? I rechecked all vehicles, which to my astonishment held more wounded than I knew we had. I went to the front door where my buddy Steve was taking a tactical pause. I was scared shitless to go back in to that house.

I explained to him how I could not find my teammate and how scared I was to go back in there. He responded with, "We have to. Follow me!" And I did.

We ended up finding my other teammate. He was making his way up the stairs when the machine gun started firing, shooting him in the back. The bullet passed through his back and out his chest, missing his heart by millimeters. He was now our most critical casualty. We had to get him airlifted immediately or he would die. I felt guilty; like I had just gotten my friend shot and now he may die. But I was able to put it out of my mind.

There were weapons strewn about, left on the ground by wounded Rangers. Sensitive items must be collected to keep them out of the hands of the enemy. There were live grenades and demo charges that if kicked or stepped on could make our night even worse. Without having to be told, training kicked in, again. My platoon sergeant, though wounded, was busy as hell. I started to drop red chemlights to mark the unexploded grenades that had their pins pulled. Thank God they were old Russian relics. Under sporadic fire, I made a couple of trips back and forth to vehicles to recover sensitive items. I made my way back into the house and fell in behind the battalion PA. Out of nowhere, I picked up an insurgent that had made his way from a hidden tunnel, lifting his weapon to the back of the PA's head. *Slow motion.* I saw the weapon lift. I turned, fired and kept firing until there was nothing left of his face. Turning around, I headed out of the house.

I remained outside, pulling security to ensure the city didn't collapse on top of us. Our PL carried a serious casualty, a squad leader, on his back to the waiting Stryker. Our Medical vehicle was filled to capacity, so we loaded wounded into other vehicles. The Rangers who had initially cleared the roof captured the HVTs we were there to grab. After we loaded the last of the wounded and detainees, the rest loaded into the last two vehicles. Three of my squad were wounded, one critically, clinging to life. One assault team had all their Rangers seriously wounded in the initial ambush. My adrenaline was still kicking even sitting in the back of our Stryker. There was one Ranger there with me. The severity of what we had just been through started to sink in. We checked each other for wounds since our adrenaline was still flowing. We were both untouched except for a hole in my sleeve and a long burn mark like my arm had been burned with a metal rod. I had been grazed but was otherwise, quite amazingly, no worse for the wear.

We moved the critically wounded Ranger to an awaiting helicopter which evacuated him to the nearest combat support hospital and took the remaining seriously wounded casualties to the hospital at the Mosul Airfield. How all Rangers injured that night survived is testimony to the courage and skill displayed by the best medics in the world, and to God who watched over us.

As I said at the beginning, this was just one night out of many we looked death in the face. We went on a rampage after that night. We ran hard and fought even harder. After losing so many, we were able to fill our vacant slots with Rangers from another company--guys we'd never worked with, yet who didn't skip a beat. We performed exceptionally well and made lasting friendships with the Rangers from C Company. Privates and gunners from our Stryker crews were now in the assault teams and I was made an un-tabbed fire team leader in combat; unheard of in Battalion. It was an honor to have served with these remarkable heroes.

As we flew back to Fort Benning to conclude our deployment, half of us expected to get killed upon landing. We thought it would be a fitting end. Two days before we landed at Benning, our sister platoon from A Company, 1st Platoon, slated to go home in two days as well, suffered casualties of their own. A grenade fell through the hatch of one of their Strykers with grievous results. Such is life as a Ranger; such is war. TSAF!

- JT
3/75
Dedicated to my son and the men of A Co. 3/75

WINTER 2005
"THE PHANTOM SHITTER"

As many a Ranger story begins, so does this one: *No shit, there I was...* However, only half of this statement would be accurate for this story. There was shit and to be more specific, a particular shit. Now before I get into the dirty details of this little deployment drama, let me explain something I feel has gone missing from the public's eye concerning Rangers. We are obsessed with poop and sadly, I don't even think most of us realize it. I guess I first realized it when I would head back to my hometown to hang out with old college buddies. Things I did in my new life in Battalion, were considered...how should I put it? *Off.* Pooping with the door open while engaging in conversation, asking friends to come admire my greater bowel accomplishments and describing the *Lincoln Log* I'd produced that day in such detail that a police sketch artist could draw it with his eyes closed were considered strange by the uninitiated.

With that said, pooping is a big part of Ranger life. I don't think I can say why exactly, but my guess is that from infancy in the Army, you learn that everyone poops, there's never enough toilets and the ones provided are a lot different than the ones you've experienced previously in life. Also, remember growing up? If you had a brother, remember how it was sharing a toilet and bathroom with him? Now multiply that by 40, minimum! So, long story short, if you were poop shy, you'd better get over it quickly and cope. Cope. Just like Rangers cope with day-long smoke sessions, jumping out of airplanes with 250 extra pounds strapped to them, ridiculously long ruck marches and of course the ever-elusive enemy trying to take your life...we laugh about it.

Through the course of my military training, all the way up to getting into Battalion and through Ranger School, I've experienced a wide variety of pooping styles. There is the E-tool seat poop, the sitting-on-a-downed-branch poop (hands down the best, if available, for outdoor drops) and the big-open-room-with-nothing-but-toilets-and-grunting-men-after-downing-blueberry-pancakes poop. I'd be remiss to forget the buddy-assist poop, where there is nothing to sit or balance on and your legs are so smoked you can hardly squat, so your buddy kindly holds your hand to support you while whispering words of encouragement as you try to push out the two MREs you ate for breakfast while getting your feet inspected by the Doc. And last, but certainly not least, the landmine poop. I'm sure you can tell from the name, but it is when you no longer give a solitary fuck so you quickly evade the eye of the Drill Sergeant or RI, slip off into the night, deploy your landmine and sneak back inside the wire before anyone knows you were missing.

Now that I've covered our obsession with defecation, here's my tale. It's my epic poop story, my Iliad, the one that will stick with me for the rest of my life. To those of us in A-3-3 in the know during that cold, early winter in Jalalabad (J-Bad), we refer to it as, "The Phantom Shitter." Now, there are many phantom shitter stories out there, but this one is mine. It was a day just like any other day, hotdogs and hamburgers for lunch, a check of all the vehicles, some classes by the team leaders, a little P.T. All in all, a good day to be a Private in 1st Ranger Battalion. And then it happened.

"Everyone get the FUCK in the bathroom!"

To fill you in real quick, we were staying at the airport in J-Bad, down at the end of the runway by ourselves in what used to be an Afghan police station. It was one building divided into two parts: one side living quarters, the other showers and toilets. The bathroom was pretty big, big enough to hold the whole platoon in the shower section. Now this bathroom was unique, as the toilets were only for *number two.* If you had to piss, you went around back and aimed your *.50-cal.* into the PVC pipes sticking out of the ground at angles. But inside, when you discharged a submarine, you wiped and threw the paper into the trash can next to each station as opposed to flushing it.

With that said, all the privates rapidly scrambled like cockroaches into the bathroom, as the tabbed specialists, team leaders and squad leaders moseyed in behind them, per Ranger SOP. However, on this specific occasion we were in for a surprise. This wasn't just going to be a fun time for the privates, everyone was invited to this party—group punishment! We all stood at the position of attention in the shower section and as a group we were addressed with, "Who did it?" from the platoon sergeant. I guess the puzzled looks and silence led him to elaborate. "Which one of you fucks left that gigantic defecation in stall three?" As everyone started to think this is a joke and crack smiles, the whole platoon was dropped.

Now to the average civilian reading this, it may seem like an every-day occurrence, but let me tell you, when you are getting smoked right alongside your leadership it is a bad day. Nothing good can come of it, they get mad that they're getting smoked and guess who they take it out on? Yep, you guessed it. Sticking with the theme of this story, shit rolls downhill. So, there we are, in the front-leaning rest, cranking out four-count pushups, mountain climbers, flutter kicks and various other sadistic tasks to get one of us to talk. The whole time everyone must still be thinking the situation is kind of comical and will be over momentarily. *No way the whole platoon is getting smoked over someone's larger than life stool sample.* We were wrong.

After a while, with still no confession to be had, we were put to parade rest and one by one, escorted back to stall three by a team leader, while the platoon leader and platoon sergeant stood by the door. Ordered to step into the stall, stand at parade rest, examine the excrement, we were then required to state if the offending excrement was ours, to which I replied, "Negative, Sergeant!" One platoon member worthy of mention during the interrogation was our platoon's smallest guy. He was escorted back for his personal viewing and we could hear the platoon sergeant order him to look at it. After a few seconds they ask him if it was his. His response echoed throughout the entire bathroom in a strong Mississippi accent, "Sarn't, that turd's bigger den me!" This prompted from the platoon sergeant the quietest and most diligently stifled laughs I've ever seen.

After everyone staff sergeant and below had filed through to have a good look at this extraordinary feat of human achievement, the smoking continued. I wish I could tell you for how long, but anyone who has endured a solid smoker knows that just like *Happy Gilmore,* you go to your happy place, you fake motivation and try not to be the first one to give out. After a good amount of time, certain individuals start to laugh and enjoy the suck, while others get pissed, yelling at others to confess while swearing profanities randomly. The most common phrases yelled are, "Come on guys," or the ever so popular, "What the fuck!"

I guess it finally became clear to the leadership that no one was going to confess to that brown, protein-packed monster, so with threats of breaking gravel into smaller pieces for the rest of the deployment, we were dismissed. The next day I believe we all pulled nails out of beat up pieces of lumber and maybe caught some residual smokings throughout the day. For the most part, the phantom shitter escaped unscathed and was never to be heard from again.

Unfortunately, this is the end of my story. There is no closure to be found here and one is left to his or her own imagination of what man could be capable of this level of *violence of action*. Two things always left me curious, the first being the obvious *who done it?* I always thought that during someone's going away speech, in front of our company formation, their last line would go something like, "And for all those in A-3-3 in J-Bad...it was me, I'm out!" But it never happened, at least not during my time. The other thing you may ask yourself, which I ponder in my bed late on those cold nights...who, and furthermore how, did they get that turd to flush? Clearly someone had to remove it, chop it up, or as an old squad leader of mine used to say, "Just blow it in place!" The one thing take from this story and my pooping career in the Battalion is this: in the final stanza of the Ranger Creed, when they mention *intestinal fortitude,* I always took it to mean guts, courage and heroism. After J-Bad, I realized it also literally means *gastrointestinal* fortitude and by God that Ranger had it! RLTW!

- J

1/75

CHAPTER SIX

"The art of war is simple enough.
Find out where your enemy is. Get at him as soon as you can.
Strike him as hard as you can, and keep moving on."

GENERAL ULYSSES S. GRANT

2006 brought a major change to the structure of the Regiment with the addition of a battalion, the first since 1984. The Regimental Special Troops Battalion was provisionally activated on July 17, 2006 and would be officially activated on October 16, 2007 in response to the rapidly changing nature of Ranger operations. The RSTB consists of four companies with four mission sets, enabling the Regiment and other special operations forces through increased flexibility.

The Ranger Reconnaissance Company (RRC), formerly the Ranger Reconnaissance Detachment (RRD), is a Special Mission Unit (SMU) with its own selection and training course. It is considered the premiere special operations reconnaissance asset to both the Regiment and to other special operations units. Their known missions generically include finding the enemy, penetrating enemy networks and safe havens and facilitating the defeat and destruction of the enemy.

The Ranger Communications Company (RCC) specializes in command

and control and communications support of the Regiment and other SOF. They are experts in both conventional and non-conventional forms of communication, staying proficient in myriad equipment used in the operating environment.

The Ranger Military Intelligence Company (RMIC) conducts human intelligence, signal intelligence, imagery intelligence and all source analysis operations in support of the Regiment and other special operations units. RMIC Rangers are experts at their craft, attending premier intelligence training courses setting them apart from their peers. Many become proficient in foreign languages and are among the most often deployed Rangers in the Regiment.

The Ranger Selection and Training Company (RS&TC), formerly Ranger Training Detachment (RTD) and Ranger Operations Company (ROC), is considered the "Gateway into the Regiment." RS&TC conducts Ranger Assessment and Selection Program (RASP) 1 and 2. Formerly known as Ranger Indoctrination Program (RIP) and Ranger Orientation Program (ROP), RASP 1 and 2 are the selection courses all prospective Rangers must attend and graduate to gain assignment to the 75th Ranger Regiment. The RS&TC also conducts Small Unit Ranger Tactics (SURT) and Pre-Special Operations Combat Medical Course (PSOCM).

The Regiment also ditched the traditional black cotton t-shirt and short *Ranger panties* for the more modest yet upgraded black physical fitness uniform in use today, but not without significant protest from the lower ranks. Ranger panties don't leave much to the imagination, but are extremely comfortable and don't retain odor like the new shorts. Although not authorized as an official uniform anymore, Rangers still sport them to this day both on the beach and in the gym.

The violence in Iraq continued and remained the focus of the 75th Ranger Regiment in 2006. Gains, however slow, were made. The number one target in the War on Terror, Abu Musab Al Zarqawi was killed in an airstrike and recovered by special operations soldiers, ending a nearly two-year manhunt by the Task Force. Saddam Hussein was put to death, hanged by his countrymen after being tried in Iraqi court. Changes also came to the war's leadership, with Donald Rumsfeld, the Secretary of Defense, resigning his position. The death toll continued to rise, reaching the sobering mark of 3,000 American servicemembers killed in action. Among the fallen in 2006 were Staff Sergeant Ricardo Barraza and Sergeant Dale Brehm, both from 2nd Ranger Battalion.

By this point in the war, Rangers were a cornerstone of the national counter-terror strategy. They worked primarily as individual platoons, conducting missions autonomously on targets throughout Iraq and Afghanistan. Rangers' tactics and SOPs were in constant flux in this new environment, but by 2006 the Regiment had hit its stride and was comfortable in their newfound role. They were taking the fight to the enemy every single night, arriving at the cutting edge of battle in helicopters, Strykers and even special warfare boats.

The Regiment perfected the small unit raid and used it on an industrial scale. In August 2004, the Command's Task Force under which Rangers operated conducted 18 raids. By August 2006, they averaged over 300 a month! This change was primarily due to Task Force commanders no longer using Rangers as security for special mission units; they discovered that they were just as effective in counter terror operations as the SMUs, which they previously supported. This allowed commanders to use fewer men but on more targets, which worked perfectly in concert with the Task Force's newly developed targeting methodology: Find, Fix, Finish, Exploit, Analyze, Disseminate, or F3EAD (pronounced *feed*). Gone were the days of planning for objectives days in advance. Rangers and their Task Force brethren now received missions so rapidly that Time Sensitive Targets, or TST, became the norm. On TSTs, the platoon executed a shortened version of mission planning, sometimes launching within minutes and receiving the details on the way to the objective. This strategy proved highly effective, some Ranger platoons dismantling entire enemy networks within a single three-month deployment.

June 2006
"BREACHING IN IRAQ"

In the beginning of my time in 3/75, I was a machine gunner, and I was not a fan. By my second deployment I moved to be a squad breacher. I excelled at this. I understood the operation of doors, gates and the construction of buildings due to working with my father since I was a small boy. My dad taught me the ins and outs of construction to include framing, foundations, electrical, plumbing and fine carpentry. Getting into a house or building silently was easy for me, especially in Iraq. Most of our target buildings had fortified doors because the occupants inside were up to no good. They were still no match for a 22-year-old Ranger who could easily assess the door's composition and the quickest way to breach it.

I also learned to build my own charges and demolitions. We were taught at our internal breacher's course how to make various explosives and charges that would blow through steel gates, doors, walls and implode buildings. All of this came naturally and everyone knew I was the go-to guy when it came to breaching. When we hit targets, I was almost always the number one man to enter a compound or move to the building. The teams would flow right in after I breached the door or gate. I then moved behind them, opening any doors or removing any debris that blocked their path. My primary method of breaching was with the shotgun.

One mission, the platoon sergeant called me over the radio to come breach a steel door the others could not get into. I gained entry to that door in about five seconds. Unfortunately, I had shrapnel from the door and ricochet from the shotgun covering my arm. Later that night I had doc pull the shotgun pellets and metal splinters from my arm. To be honest, I was rather used to it and the adrenaline ensured I felt nothing.

On mission, I wanted my brothers to have the best chance to overwhelm the enemy with violence of action. With that in mind, I may or may not have

158

put some extra C4 and detonation cord in some of my charges to give my brothers the upper hand when entering a building. Eventually, I was questioned on my charge building techniques. This came after the ground turned to Jell-O as the mud flap charge I built blew straight into the target house, giving my team an alternate, unplanned entrance into the target building. My squad didn't even have to use a door or secondary charge. The original plan was to blow the main gate, then have me run up and then breach the door to the target building, allowing us to flow in. Well, now I didn't have to. The charge had blown a hole straight through the gate and into the house, shattering every window of the three-story, 4,500 square foot building in the process. Maybe next time they won't put their front gate so close to their house.

Earlier in my deployment to Iraq, I was assigned directly to a SMU as a vehicle gunner. Running missions day and night, it was the best experience and group of guys I ever worked with. Eventually I was recalled from the SMU and re-assigned to my team. We hopped from one city to another and we were sometimes the first SOF direct action unit in the city. Within the Task Force, our area of operations was the entire northeast region of Iraq.

Some of the other units in the Task Force were pissed off because it was an active area, full of work to be done and we were getting the prime cuts. We were on call 24/7 with a long high value target capture/kill hit list which didn't include the ancillary insurgents we'd roll up in the company of our HVTs. We had our own area of the airfield and were supported by 160th SOAR, as always. They had no other task but to fly us to and from our objectives and to provide air support while we were on a raid site. We had only Conex boxes with no power to use as our ready room, which meant our kit and equipment was always blazing hot when we launched for a mission. We had the support guys start construction immediately for a ready room, as well as overhead cover for our Strykers. They built what is now called *The Sergeant James Regan Ready Room.*

Our SOF compound was a base inside of a base, guarded by regular Army soldiers. I felt so bad for those guys. We walked around in Ranger panties and T-Shirts while they guarded our compound dressed in full kit in the blistering Iraqi heat that would reach 130 degrees at times. Even so, those dudes always had a smile on their face when we walked by. I respect them; everybody has a job to do in the military. But I'm happy I busted my ass at the beginning of my military career so I didn't have to endure such duties.

The story I'll tell is one of the most firmly planted in my memory. One evening, my squad was hanging out in our room, playing Halo, while a few guys were in the gym. It was about midnight when our pagers went off with the code to spin up for a mission. We ran to the ready room (which was still in the Conex at this time), donned our kit and linked up at the airfield. Once there, we assigned chalks/birds and loaded, taking off within minutes of receiving the notification. It was a capture/kill mission with an offset infil, which meant we were to land about seven kilometers away and hump it in, which would suck, a lot. There were no special orders, just roll this dude up and collect intelligence on the target...the usual. We had other special attachments from a government agency with us to help with interrogations and such. Just another day on deployment.

There was no better way to get to work than sitting in the door of an MH-60 or MH-6, feet dangling and the wind blasting you, praying a bird wouldn't smoke you in the face. That was pretty much our biggest concern after seeing what a bird could do to the windshield of a helicopter.

This particular mission, it was about a 30-minute flight. We received our ten-minute warning, five-minute warning and finally our 30-second warning. The birds flared, landing right through a brownout, kicking up dust, dirt and rock. Landing the helo was unusual for the TSTs we were hitting at the time. We usually fast-roped onto almost every target, by necessity in urban environments. I was thankful for landing this night, recalling a previous ill-fated fast rope a few nights before.

On that terrible night, my team was supposed to provide security for our snipers, fast-roping directly on to the target building. I was the first off the bird. Under NVGs, the rooftop looked clear. Not so much. The rooftop was crisscrossed with electrical wires, which neither the pilots nor we could see. Unaware, we gave pilots the thumbs up and threw the ropes. The rooftop was only 12 feet away, so I didn't even bother putting my feet on the rope. I slid down, legs out, ready to absorb the impact of the landing until a thin wire found its way between my legs and right into my man-junk. Needless to say, it sucked. I dangled there, most of my bodyweight plus my full kit, bouncing up and down on what must have been the world's tiniest and strongest wire. I eventually continued the descent after getting myself clear. I signaled to the pilot to move the birds a couple feet left after I hit the rooftop, so my other buddy wouldn't have to endure the same lovely experience. Suffice it to say, I was more than happy to not be fast roping this night.

The brownout subsided after the helos departed. We moved across open farmland and shit-ditches toward mud villages, villages dimly lit by dirty bulbs sucking sporadic electricity from an insufficient power grid. We reached the main street and moved down it for four kilometers, dogs barking and people looking out to see what the commotion was about. We moved in the shadows with NVGs, so I wondered how much those people could see. Our movement was a laser light show—beams emanating from our group towards every possible threat, illuminating rooms of buildings we passed. Our security was tight and there was little time to think about how much the movement sucked. We finally came to a trail in a palm grove leading up the hill to our target building.

When we got close, each squad moved to their designated side of the building, typically forming an L-shape so all four sides of the building were covered in case of squirters. Still about 100 meters from the objective building, my squad moved on line through an open farm field. Another building stood separate from the target building and was not on our imagery. It was unexpected, but must be cleared, so three of us went to check it out. I moved through a thin woodline of about five meters depth, leading me to a drainage ditch four feet deep filled with water, also about four feet in width. I found a good place and jumped across. I was tired of having my feet soaking wet and muddy and they had just dried out.

After we crossed, we moved up the side of the target building slowly and quietly, using hand and arm signals to let each other know of our movement. We could hear voices and people moving inside. I came to the corner of the target building and *pied off* the corner to gain a better look at what we were dealing with. As I cleared the corner, my buddy behind me threw me to the left. I heard his suppressed M-4 discharge two rounds. Looking to my right I saw those rounds impact an insurgent's forehead, his AK-47 still pointed at me. The insurgent had come down a set of stairs, intent on taking me out. It all happened in a matter of seconds, but time seemed to slow at this point. *My buddy just saved my life…*

This was only the beginning. We had stumbled into a hornet's nest of Al Qaeda fighters intermingled with women and children. As soon as my buddy took those shots, a barrage of small arms, machine gun fire and hand grenades rained down on us. With our IR lasers illuminating the targets above, all three of us returned fire, quickly dispatching several fighters on the rooftop. It was a target-rich environment. We maneuvered through fire to the open field 50 meters to the right of our squad's position to obtain a better angle to engage.

Once there, I repositioned myself for a better vantage of the rooftop. The rest of my squad was in the prone, becoming one with the earth but unable to move, returning fire when possible. I maneuvered to where I had the best vantage point and started working. Very quickly the enemy homed in on my location, concentrating their fire in my direction. At this point I had nowhere to go. I was so close that if I had dropped into the prone I felt I would actually make a larger target. If I stood up and ran, it would be the same result. I threw as much accurate M-4 fire as possible. I still don't know how I wasn't hit. These thoughts were racing through my mind, all while continuing the firefight. God must have been with me that day, because at this point I was less than 50 meters from the building and in the wide open. No cover or concealment, just dirt on the flat farmland.

My squad eventually maneuvered out of harm's way and I followed in a hurry. When I heard the AC-130 gunship firing danger close, I knew it was my chance to move 75 meters to the right where the other three guys were in a muddy pasture with all kinds of farm animals. We were now 100 meters from the building from which we took fire. The AC-130 rained down ordnance, turning the ground into Jell-O. I had never felt anything like it. Minutes later, all rounds were expended.

I linked up with my squad and would be the first to move across the target. My squad followed as I moved to the ruins of the target building. All buildings on the objective were on fire. Once I returned to that thin woodline I saw one of the men I shot. Littered with bullet holes, he fell from the rooftop and into the drainage ditch along with a young boy, not more than five, under his arm. Miraculously, the boy was still alive though knocked out, presumably from the overpressure from the gunship's rounds. He looked rather dead as well, lying in a stream of his father's red blood.

We pressed on to the objective when I came along the same wall where my buddy saved my life when my foot became stuck. I could not shake it off. It was like my foot was stuck in sucking quicksand which wouldn't let me go. My buddy and I quickly hit our tac lights. I was standing in the torso of a person. It was all but unidentifiable; it had no head, arms, legs or clothes. It no longer had skin. I put my foot into the intestines and got it caught in the rib cage. I struggled free to continue to the objective. We ended up detaining several women. No one else was left. The men were now piles of mush; just random body parts and hair scattered on the rooftops.

Objective secure. We gathered whatever intelligence we could and called in regular Army to clean up the mess. We gave them credit for the mission— we didn't want to deal with it. That night we crossed off one of our top ten HVTs along with a few other less valuable targets. We never publicly received credit for the success for our missions. If it were a big time HVT, we would typically give the credit to the Army or Marine infantry unit which covered that area. When the Army unit arrived this particular night, I remember their commander rolling up and saying, "Holy shit! You guys blew the shit out of this place, are you ok!?" I stared at him with a fat dip of Grizzly in my mouth and said, "Yup."

It turned out that the guy with eight bullet holes in his body, lying face down in the ditch was still alive. Everyone said to me, "Why the hell didn't you put two in his head?" In accordance with Geneva Conventions, we are trained that the first man who comes across a body can ensure they are dead with a double-tap, but once you pass them you can no longer shoot them. So, he was now our problem. We left the mess to the regular Army to take care of and we exfilled. We ended up guarding his fat, shot-up body for a week until he died...I learned my lesson.

For my actions that night I received the Army Commendation Medal for Valor, citing me for saving the lives of my squad members. Honestly, I only did what any other Ranger would have done if they'd been in the same situation. I saw my brothers pinned down, so I lit those insurgents up as fast and accurately as possible without thinking of my own safety. As any Ranger will tell you, I was just doing my job.

- DAN
3/75

JUNE 2006
"THE TASK FORCE"

It was June 2006 and I was assigned to the Command's task force in central Iraq. This period was undoubtedly the worst and most dangerous time of the seven-year war. Service members from all coalition countries were slaughtered by hundreds of IEDs as the Sunni and Shiite civil war was in full swing. The man primarily responsible was the leader, or *emir* of Al Qaeda in Iraq. From 2004 to 2006 he was a higher priority target for the U.S. intelligence community than Osama bin Laden himself.

This was my third deployment with 3rd Ranger Battalion. My first was to Mosul in late 2004 and second was to Afghanistan in 2005. On my third I performed two roles: as the Ground Force Commander's radio operator and 2nd Platoon, Charlie Company's radio operator. These responsibilities may seem interchangeable, but they meant I was responsible for all radio systems internal to the platoon, to include five Stryker vehicles. The previous platoon radio operator was fired and being a senior communications guy in 2006, I was somehow stuck with this stressful assignment - which I excelled at in spades, I might add.

Our first month of the deployment we were based out of Baghdad's Green Zone, within an area specifically called the mission staging site, (MSS). Alpha Company's 2nd Platoon was the night platoon and Charlie Company's 2nd Platoon (2C) was the day platoon. The operational tempo was so busy we would often hit two targets a day. It was an awesome tempo for the individual platoons, but for me, being a part of the GFC's team meant I would go on every single objective, both day and night. Later, 2C was moved to Balad Air Base to conduct direct action missions against targets in nearby Baqubah. The command element included myself, SSG Ball, who was the fire support NCO and the commander. I would stay with them for the rest of the deployment.

During the daytime on June 7, one of our ISR assets spotted what was undoubtedly the target at one of the newly revealed locations. The Task Force commander at that time, Lieutenant Colonel Tom DiTomasso (now retired), immediately began initial planning to launch a strike package. If the name sounds familiar, it's because he was one of the Ranger platoon leaders on the ground in Mogadishu in 1993, where he was awarded the Silver Star and Purple Heart for his actions. He was also included in Ridley Scott's movie *Black Hawk Down.* At this time, DiTomasso was serving as the Deputy Commander of an Army Special Mission Unit.

SMU Operators along with a handful of Rangers from the 3rd Ranger Battalion boarded 160th Black Hawks to assault the safe house. As he pored over the images of the target building, DiTomasso realized the best HLZ was a clearing a short distance from the location. Fearing his men would be compromised well before they touched down, DiTomasso relayed his hesitations up the chain of command to his boss, then Lieutenant General Stanley McChrystal. He was concerned the target could slip out once the helicopters began their approach, so he recommended an airstrike against the target. LTG McChrystal agreed and at 6:12 PM local time, an F-16 fighter jet dropped two 500-pound bombs on the compound. The pilot, retasked to this mission, had no idea the importance of the target he prosecuted. The Task Force team and a small contingent of Rangers from our platoon (2nd Platoon, Charlie Company) arrived on scene shortly after and recovered the dying high value target from the Iraqi police, snatching him out of the ambulance into which he was being loaded. Shortly after the team recovered the wounded terrorist, he succumbed to his injuries and passed away.

Rangers, like with most special operations forces, are nocturnal creatures. We slept during the day and operated at night. So around 6:12 PM, most of the platoon, myself included, was ether still fast asleep or getting ready for the workday as the summer sun sets came around 8:00 in the evening. At that same time, a small team from our platoon was currently helping to recover the body of the most wanted terrorist on America's radar.

Then something big came up. "Multiple direct action raids; get your gear and vehicles ready." It was probably 8:00 PM and none of us knew the target had been killed. The Task Force was given the locations of 17 safe houses. The high value target was killed in one of them. That meant there were 16 other Al Qaeda safe houses in Baqubah just waiting to be hit. The intelligence in each location would be invaluable and would set Al Qaeda in Iraq back drastically.

Objective Avalanche was the name of the operation. *Avalanche I* was the airstrike against the high value target and Task Force commanders wanted the rest to be assaulted simultaneously. The Task Force strike package consisted of both 1st and 2nd Platoon (mine) of Charlie Company 3/75, a Special Forces team, a British SAS assault team and two troops from the Army SMU. 2nd Platoon had two objectives to hit and were officially named Avalanche 15 and the follow-on as Avalanche 15A. Unfortunately, we had to drive, as the Army SMU had first dibs on the 160th birds.

We thought we were going to get into some real shit that night! Lay the hate on some terrorist bad guys and make off with their computers! I don't remember exactly, but I think the first objectives that were hit by the assault forces were either dry holes or peaceful arrests, including ours. The most eventful thing to happen on our first objective happened while I was taking a knee on the backside of the building. I was looking up at the second story and noticed a door. It didn't lead anywhere. Not a balcony, not a walkway— nothing. It was literally a door on the side of a two-story building. It was baffling. Well, the darndest thing happened next. I saw shadows moving around on the other side, which I assumed was the platoon clearing the house. I clearly remember thinking to myself, *Shit I hope nobody opens it up and runs right through!*

I wasn't far off in my sense of foreboding. The Ranger on the other side pulled out his breaching shotgun and fired off a round right into the lock. I wasn't more than 15 feet away when I took the hundreds of wooden shards to the face. I sustained no real damage, as I was being a good Ranger and wearing my eye protection, but it could have turned out much worse.

At this time most of us thought we were on a mission to find the high value target the whole task force was focused on. We still didn't know he was killed just a few hours earlier. I'm sure the recovery team had to take the body back to Balad so the forensics people could officially identify it.

As we wrapped up our first objective, I received a call on the satellite radio from a voice I assumed to be LTC DiTomasso's relaying that the target was killed. I passed the word to the commander and he passed it down to the platoon leader. Shortly thereafter all of us had heard the good news. We were ecstatic to say the least, assuming he was killed on one of the other objectives, preferably not by 1st Platoon and definitely not by the SF guys! We loaded back onto the Strykers and made our way to the second objective, Avalanche 15A. *We better get into some shit this time.*

Wrong.

We hit the building and found a guy and his family, not interested in putting up any kind of a fight. *This is lame.* I pulled security from an adjacent rooftop. The sniper next to me expressed a similar sentiment. In hindsight, it makes sense that these safe houses weren't teeming with bad guys. It's not much of safe house if it sticks out like a sore thumb because of heavy traffic from military-aged males.

We were about four or five hours into the night. After five hours of continuously looking through your night vision goggles, they start to play tricks on you. For some it would really mess up their depth perception or would render their non-night vision eye (we were still using PVS-14 monocles in 2006) completely useless. For me, it just made me incredibly sleepy. The elation of the HVT's death having worn off, most of us wanted to leave these uneventful objectives and return to Balad.

That's when the call came over the radio, "Hey guys, get ready to load up. We've got a follow-on objective."

Fuck! Two, and soon to be three lame-ass objectives was just too much for one night. Apparently, the man they found claimed that his brother is the owner of the home we just raided and he will gladly take us to him. *What a shithead of a brother.* So, we loaded up in our Strykers. I think it was probably around 5:00 AM at this point and the sunrise was only an hour away. The drive didn't take longer than ten minutes; we ended up parking our vehicles under a highway overpass. Iraq had a strict curfew at night so no civilian vehicles were on the roads.

We split the platoon down the middle; one half would stay and man the vehicles, the rest would walk a half-mile to the brother's location. Since I was the guy who listened in on the SATCOM channel, I already knew that the rest of the assault forces were back home either sleeping or wrapping up their after-action reports. There was no chatter from the operations center on the channel other than with our element.

Roughly 18 of us went on foot to the new objective. Was it Avalanche 15A1 or 15AB? I don't know, I don't remember and frankly, I don't care. We left the vehicles behind because they were too loud and could easily give us away. We crept on foot to what appeared to be a large office building construction site. *What the hell is this place?* It looked nothing like a neighborhood. It was literally just a complex of large unfinished office buildings. Yet another dead end I assumed.

That's about the time all hell broke loose. At once, we began to take automatic fire from what seemed like three different directions. That first 20-30 seconds of contact was the most intense incoming fire I had ever received. We ran for cover to a small wall, maybe a foundation for a future building and returned fire. I don't think anybody knew where the incoming rounds were coming from. It sounded like a dozen guys were engaging us from multiple spots.

I looked up and noticed a giant halogen light attached to the top floor of an unfinished eight-story building. It was shining directly above us and nobody seemed to notice. One of the snipers was next to me, so I pointed up and said, "You should take that out." He agreed and without saying a word raised his rifle. One missed shot. A second missed shot. And finally, a third missed shot. I brought my own M-4 up and caught sight of the light through my ACOG. One shot was all it took…to both knock out the light and give me bragging rights. We were now engulfed in darkness and the bad guys couldn't see us, but the relentless fire never broke.

At this point, we were only a minute into the engagement. On this occasion, we didn't have any air support from either the 160th's attack helicopters or Air Force AC-130 gunships; they checked off after we wrapped up the second objective. Rangers began to identify where the insurgents were holed up and returned accurate fire. Under night vision we could see their muzzle flashes magnified no matter the distance. There was no point in keeping the Strykers away at this point; everybody in a two-mile radius knew we were there, so we called them in for support. We needed their turret-mounted .50-caliber machine guns equipped with thermal scopes and they arrived with guns blazing.

What a sweet sound it was. They were engaging enemy targets as they found them but we continued to receive intense fire from multiple directions. This clown—no—this genius, who we thought was fucking over his brother, legitimately led us right into an ambush. *You've got balls, sir. I hope you enjoy Guantanamo.*

We began to move away from our positions toward a small cluster of buildings where we believed the closest insurgents were holed up. We definitely did not own the battle at this point. As we moved through the rubble, I heard the distinct call "FRAG OUT!" from one of the squad leaders. I took a knee beside the wall I was hugging and didn't move. It's best to not run around when a grenade has been released, especially if you don't know its intended destination.

The explosive blast was on the other side of the wall of which our element was taking a knee. It didn't collapse the wall, nor did I feel any overpressure. My Sordins—a combination ear protection and communications headset—completely shut off. I thought they broke! Being a radio operator, my communications equipment ran through my headset. If I can't use my headset, then I can't use my radios, which renders me just about worthless. In today's day and age, having working radio communications is paramount. Then I remembered how they were designed. It's a rare occurrence that only happens when the decibel level is so high that the headset automatically shuts off to save the user's hearing. They soften or cancel high decibel noises (as in this case) but amplify lower decibel sounds such as conversations and footfall in gravel.

We hustled through the opening in the wall into the adjacent area. Two Iraqis lie dead from the explosion, one younger, one older...much older. I couldn't believe how close they were to us. We weren't more than 20 meters from the spot where we first took contact.

Our small ground element, comprised of two squads—not exactly the most ideal maneuvering element—began gaining momentum as we cleared building after building. Strykers engaged targets from a distance and enemy fire began to subside. Daylight crept over the horizon as the summer sky showed the first signs of a purple haze. I took a position on a rooftop with the ground force commander. Nearby, our fire support NCO, who had no fire support to call, engaged targets as he saw them. It was just 30 minutes after we first took contact. Either we killed them all—doubtful—or they bugged out once the Strykers unleashed their machine guns.

It was now broad daylight. Curious Iraqis living nearby tried to get close enough to see what happened. Air support finally came in the form of two Apaches, but the fight was already over. We were still grateful for their presence. I have no idea what unit they were with, but they stayed with us over the area until we exfilled.

The squads searching the buildings where there were confirmed insurgent sightings reported back massive amounts of blood and spent ammunition but few bodies. However, they did find a dead insurgent rolled inside a rug. Whoever was trying to recover the body must have left in a hurry as Rangers were closing in. The .50-cal gunners reported killing six to eight insurgents, the squad leader's grenade took out two and then there were several unconfirmed kills from numerous Rangers in the squads. *That's it?*

The platoon sergeant, likely a present on all 3rd Ranger Battalion's deployments since 9/11, expressed to us that it was, "...the most intense firefight I've ever been in." A squad leader would later express his disbelief that not a single Ranger suffered so much as a single scratch. That was indeed unbelievable. We loaded into our Strykers and were ordered back to the MSS in Baghdad, rather than Balad. After what we went through, I figured I could get away with a quick nap during the 45-minute drive back.

"Donov! Wake the fuck up!" the Major barked at me not more than thirty seconds later.

Goddammit...

When we arrived at the MSS, our humble abode from the previous month, our platoon was ordered to a small airfield where the 160th birds were staged. What looked like the entire SMU squadron was formed up (sort of) next to a small element of 160th personnel. We formed up (not sort of) next to them. The SAS and Special Forces elements must have gone their separate ways. Even our sister platoon must have made its way back to Tikrit.

Lieutenant Colonel DiTomasso stood in front of the gaggle, this *sort of* formation. I don't remember his speech word for word, but it went something along the lines of,

"We killed him, but don't think this is over. There is still a lot of work to be done. Bin Laden is still out there, Zawahiri is still out there and Al Qaeda in Iraq is far from beaten. Our job is unfinished and we are going to keep getting after it; here, in Afghanistan and in Africa. But for today, great job!"

Hey, I want to go to Africa too. I felt proud to be part of this operation and to stand in front of this warrior who commanded these titans. Although the glory went to the pilot of the F-16, previously on a routine mission, we all felt a huge sense of pride and accomplishment. At the end of the day, it was the efforts of the Task Force's relentless raids against Al Qaeda that led us to the most highly valued target in the world.

- IASSEN DONOV
3/75

July 2006

"SKITTLES"

In the military, many orders are yelled at you. The lower your rank, the more you are yelled at. Being yelled at in that environment doesn't necessarily mean you did anything wrong, it may just mean what is being said is a matter of life and death, literally. Many of these yelling orders came during training exercises inside the safe confines of a US military base. All these orders were very specific and simple such as, "GET OUT OF THE FUCKING DOORWAY!" or "HURRY THE FUCK UP!" There was one particular order that always made me laugh inside because of the irony. When my superiors would yell, "BE FUCKING TACTICAL!" my subconscious would always respond to that remark with a very snobbish, *Well, screaming for us to be tactical isn't very tactical at all.* All joking aside, that order was burned into my mind as the difference between life and death. That order would echo whenever I would put on my equipment. I knew I could be tactical and move with stealth that would make a ninja proud. Yet, the equipment I carried had to be tightly controlled in order to do so.

In Tim O'Brien's book, *The Things They Carried,* O'Brien writes, *"There was at least the single abiding certainty that they would never be at a loss for things to carry."* Timmy identifies that no matter the conflict or time in history, soldiers will be forever loaded down with the burden of both heavy equipment and emotional cares. I was no exception to this single abiding certainty. Putting on my mission equipment, or *kitting up,* as we referred to it, was a lengthy process. I would start with my body armor and everything on it: seven full magazines of 5.56mm ammo (210 rounds), two concussion grenades, two fragmentation grenades, one smoke grenade, an exploitation kit, an explosive breeching kit, a detainee kit, a bleeder kit, one tourniquet, fast rope gloves, compass, knife, watch, headlamp, strobe, team radio, eye protection, eight anti-structure rockets and water. Once I was kitted up, I could don my helmet, gloves and sling my rifle.

Now that I was fully kitted up, I would find a quiet room and jump up and down frantically. Any piece of equipment that made a noise or shook loose I would silence or tighten down. I'd then pace back and forth in front of a mirror looking for anything that would shine. Anything shiny would be subdued. Once I was satisfied with my adjustments, I would store my kit with the same care a mother would take placing her infant to bed. We were taught that our equipment could take our life as easily as it could save it, especially if we weren't *tactical.*

My first year in the Army was all training time with the intent of preparing for war. Every day we'd wake up before the sun and start our morning exercises. Physical training would begin with a five to ten mile run to warm up. Once the team was nice and exhausted the real pain began. We'd do strength and team building exercises, relying on our teammates to complete the drill. We'd all be smoked to muscle failure, yet we'd get through it together. The physical pain would make our bodies tremble as our minds tried to make sense of it all. Whenever a team member would cry out or whimper, the squad leader would remind us to *suffer in silence*. This was the squad leader's way of saying, "SHUT THE FUCK UP AND BE FUCKING TACTICAL!"

To suffer in silence is not just reserved for morning PT alone, it's instilled in the very fiber of military and special operations training. While conducting airborne operations, strict noise discipline was enforced. Although every time I jumped out of an airplane I wanted to scream in fear, I had to find a way to make that leap in silence. During hand-to-hand fighting I wanted to yelp in pain when I got my eye gouged, but I ignored the pain and fought back. Whether in pain, excitement, or fear, we learned to ignore our natural response and stay silent and tactical.

In the summer of 2006, our platoon was in the fields of Afghanistan raiding an enemy training camp. The raid did not go as planned, partly because we underestimated the number of enemy combatants we'd encounter. In the first hour on the ground we realized we were heavily outnumbered and out-gunned. An extraction was called to retrieve us. Once half the platoon loaded the aircraft, it slowly took off to return to a FOB. Suddenly, the training camp we thought we'd subdued came back to life. A barrage of small arms and machine gun fire roared in the direction of the helicopter. As the aircraft rotated clockwise, two rocket propelled grenades slammed into the fuel ballast, forcing the pilots to make a crash-landing. I watched this from my fighting position 200 meters away. *How many of my friends just died?*

There was no time for emotion, no time to think about the blood of my comrades, it was time to suffer in silence, remain tactical and secure the crash site.

Again I'll cite the book, *The Things They Carried*. "*...Made stupid promises to themselves and to God and to their mothers and fathers, hoping not to die.*" When we Soldiers face the dire end, we make deals with our creator in hopes to survive. It's along the lines of the old Army saying, "There are no atheists in foxholes." O'Brien also mentions that this act is *"stupid."* While this may seem an insult to religious folks, I agree, that this act is

173

somewhat stupid. I never put much thought into how I would act once facing the end. I guess, I just assumed if it were to happen in combat it would be a quick, painless bullet to the face, or if I were wounded badly enough, Doc would give me morphine and I would just fade away. Either way, I never envisioned myself as the type of man pissing his pants and praying for someone to save him. It's just not the way I act. At least, it's not the way I *hope* I would act.

The platoon set up a 360-degree perimeter around the dead helicopter. The firefight ended as abruptly as it had begun. An eerie calm settled and stalks of corn swayed back and forth with the breeze. In the distance, I could hear sounds of cattle lowing and chickens clucking away. The sun was slowly rising across the valley as the morning prayer songs played on loudspeakers. In this muddy cornfield, we were all in the prone and paired up. I was lucky to be paired up with my friend Ron, a sniper from Philadelphia. The platoon radios were crackling from tactical operations headquarters trying to figure out how to get us off this mountain. Ron and I made small talk while the command staff discussed. The sun was now fully up and we knew we were in trouble; we never work in the light, the darkness is a key advantage. I suddenly heard someone breaking brush toward my right, the very excited Air Force JTAC. He squatted between Ron and I and said, "Dig in, it's coming in danger close." And with that, he hopped up and was off to the next fighting position to pass the news.

It turned out while my bosses were screwing around on their radios and I was admiring the scenery, we were about to be overrun, big time. We would find out later the morning prayer was actually a reinforcement call to the surrounding villages. Within a couple of hours, over 300 enemy fighters surrounded the 30 of us. The CCT called in 500-pound bombs to be dropped just outside our perimeter. Because the enemy was closing in fast, he had to call the bombs to be dropped at *danger close* range, meaning there was a higher likelihood of us getting hit.

My friend Ron and I accepted the fact that this may be the day we die. I reached into my pocket and pulled out a pack of Skittles I'd been saving for the flight back. I had prepped the Skittles the night before by opening the pack, releasing all the air, rerolling it and tightening it together with tape. I did this because I knew the enemy could hear the Skittles moving in my pocket and I had to remain tactical. I opened the candy and placed it on the muddy ground between the two of us. I presented it as if it was our last meal. We took our time savoring each little Skittle, appreciating this token of normalcy in the midst of a war. I thought of my family; the pride in my father's eyes, my mother hugging him, my sisters all smiling with their hair flowing in the wind and finally my nephew and his laugh that always said, "You're funny, Uncle Billy!" When the bombs hit, the entire world shook. The explosion was so loud it just turned to white noise. The corn above us leaned back against the concussion. Trees shattered and turned to splinters. Shrapnel flew over my head, splitting foliage with ease. And just like that…it was over.

-VILHELM RED
1/75

July 2006
"SKITTLES: A SNIPER'S PERSPECTIVE"

This happened at the beginning of our deployment for yet another rotation in the continuous cycle that all Ranger Battalions lived and accepted as the new norm. We planned to grab an HVT in the Helmand Province, one of the most heavily reinforced and unabashedly anti-American territories in Afghanistan. At this point in time, all of Helmand was a stronghold for Al Qaeda. The area is mainly flat with poppy and marijuana fields comprising its majority. These cash crops make plenty of money for Afghanistan's growing radical Islamic forces.

It was pitch black and I opened my eyes to screaming. "One minute!" *Funny, I thought we had a few more.* The last time I closed my eyes after looking at the light board, it had said *"…ten minutes out, enemy on target,"* with the addition of a smiley face drawn on it. A light board is nothing more than a piece of Plexiglas with illumination tape stuck to it so you can write on it with a china marker and everyone can see what it says in the dark. I felt the bird pitch, the engines growing louder as the rotors fought the air, lowering us into the blackness of the Helmand. My heart rate increased as I felt humidity and smelled the dank air. We were about to land, so I prepared to exit explosively and encounter anything that might be waiting for us. Everyone moved up on a knee while trying to stay upright, fighting the aircraft's violent motions. We reached for our safety lines while checking each other and ourselves; a good pat on the back or thumbs up meant all was good.

I pulled down my PVS-15 dual night vision goggles and re-entered the familiar green world of war. I quickly dialed in the focus as a final check and went through my PCIs (Pre-Combat Inspections) once more. I patted down my kit and pounded a bottle of water, a sequence I've done so many times before. I pulled back the charging handle of my rifle, just far enough to see that shiny new round in my SR-25's chamber.

As the bird flared, I tried to maintain my balance in preparation to run out the back of the helo's fatal funnel. No imagery ever tells you the condition of the LZ; you may step onto solid ground or mud. I felt the bump from the landing gear hitting the ground and began a speedy exit from one of the loudest aerial platforms in the world. Yup, fucking mud and mud for a speedy exit is not ideal for 40-plus Ranger assaulters, all in the ballpark of 250 pounds or more.

As I ran out the back of the aircraft, moving as fast and quietly as possible in the black of night, my head was on a swivel, taking in everything I could. *Where will I move if I take contact right now?* It's what we've rehearsed time and time again, but these are very real thoughts and there is not always ideal cover. On some occasions actions come almost subconsciously. I saw my friend Austin pause quickly and reach down toward his foot. He had lost a shoe running through the muddy field. He just picked it up, stuffed it and drove on to the release point. Not ideal, but funny.

We moved out of the field and down to a low-lying area. We did a quick route recon and decided to use a creek that smelled like shit but was the best way to get where we had to go and provided some cover if we took contact. Off in the distance, I could hear the sounds of breaching charges, *bangers* (flash-bangs) and gunfire as the main assault force breached and cleared their target compound.

For this target, I was a sniper team leader attached to Reconnaissance Team Two, led by Tim, their team leader. We were to observe and isolate the lower eastern part of the objective, consisting of a few fields and smaller structures, which Wade and I had cleared prior to setting in to our positions. They were small and seemed to be where the harvested poppy and marijuana were stored. They were piled high. We walked out of the structure and heard the familiar sound of gunfire. Looking up we saw tracers streak the night sky. The radio sprang to life, relaying that an element was in contact, so we moved back into the ditches we were lying in previously.

Now back in our defensive positions, I jumped back and forth between radio channels, trying to stay up to speed on all the events happening on target. After what seemed a short time, but in reality was probably an hour or so, I heard the call to prepare for exfil. Time flies when you are moving, adrenaline pumping.

A few moments later, one of the blocking positions reported more contact and began to engage. It's times like this where I'd instantly react and get the job done, regardless of the other things happening around me. We took a smoother route back to the insertion point as we found another irrigation ditch. It was slightly drier at least.

Still moving, I saw the first bird come in to extract the first element. As the MH-47 made its approach the insurgents within the area, previously hidden and awaiting our extraction, opened up with a large ambush. A fury of fire erupted; insurgents engaged with everything they had, to include RPGs and belt-fed automatic weapons. As the Chinook lifted back off into the night, it attracted plenty of fire but hauled ass away, unscathed. At this point, I was still following my teammates up to the bridge, which consisted of nothing more than a few logs. Almost all of us were across the bridge when all hell broke loose again.

The next bird came in to extract the main assault force (1B). As they powered up for takeoff, gunfire erupted from outlying positions in the field and from the rooftops in the compound. The assault force rushed into the vulnerable aircraft, by now a huge bullet magnet. but I was distracted with jumping back into the creek. I rested my SR-25 on the bridge and began to engage targets, yelling, "Contact on my laser!" while firing into bursts of

177

enemy muzzle flashes across the fields we just crossed.

To my right, Danny, a Mk-46 gunner for our team, along with Wade suppressed the small woodline 200 meters away where I marked the contact. I was firing too and amazingly there was no lull in the return fire. All other parts of our element were also engaging the initial area of contact at this point.

As I was changing a mag, I saw Wade crouch back into the ditch, which was now filled with Rangers firing away. Almost immediately we were back up and reengaging like we had rehearsed a thousand times. The enemy fire would stop briefly, then continue again a few moments later. They must have had their *dead gunner* drills down, as this happened about three times and the amount of gunfire we were raining down on them was extraordinary.

As this was going on, one of our *goose* teams maneuvered to our right and prepared to fire their Carl Gustaf 84mm recoilless rifle. They hit them twice. Once is usually good and twice is awesome, yet the goose team didn't hesitate for a second. They loaded up another HEDP (High Explosive Dual Purpose) round with an air-burst option for delivering an explosion directly above an enemy position. They set it to airburst and prepared to engage the bastards still shooting at as and the helo lifting off behind us. It was so loud. Dan was yelling "Fire!" We were yelling "Fire!" and then it went *BOOM!* Someone behind me screamed to reload and re-engage, but the goose team was already rocking through the reload uncommanded. They beautifully performed the critically-important crew drill, and just like that another round was loosed in the direction of our enemy. They prepared to send more death down on the enemy and I could somewhat make out a muffled, "Back-blast area clear," call followed by another thunderous boom from the tube.

We had been in contact for several minutes, though the concept of time in a gunfight gets hugely distorted. It all seems to run together as the events play out. We didn't hear anything from that woodline anymore, hopefully because we killed every last one of those savages. As all this was going down, the fully loaded Chinook with 1st Platoon, B Company was getting shot to shit as they lifted off. We found out a very short time later that they sustained critical damage to the aircraft and had no choice but to put her down. The pilot did the best thing possible by staying near the Ranger elements still on the ground. This allowed us to rapidly move to support the downed bird and her passengers.

On top of the downed bird and heavy fire, we were rapidly losing the cover of darkness. We often talk of how we own the night, but we can also own the day, although our advantage is less. As professionals, we stack the deck in our favor whenever possible. Our enemy was a formidable opponent and it'd be a huge risk to attempt flying another bird in for exfil. We heard a rumor of a contingency plan to take down a compound and fight through the day until extraction at the next period of darkness.

In Ranger Regiment, shit will go wrong, but we are the best at adapting to shit going wrong. It's why we're so good at what we do in combat. We have leadership who assess the situation, set the right conditions and execute from the hip. They act without hesitation and succeed, precisely because the men they led trust their plan will not fail.

Fire slowed to sporadic bursts. The AC-130 overhead was *Winchester*, meaning the platform was completely out of ammo. To put into perspective the level of contact and number of enemy, this was the second AC-130 we ran dry during this mission. We configured in a hasty defensive position consisting of Battalion Reconnaissance Teams Two and Three, a 60mm mortar team and a Gustaf team. We were all generally in the same area, near the creek with a small wall running along the upper area of the creek we'd been fighting from, somewhat close to where we first got inserted. I looked through a crack in that wall. Sitting there, I re-configured my kit with one hand; moving mags around, double checking all my shit, readjusting pretty much everything and eating some wet Skittles out of my pocket.

Because I had opened the Skittles bag prior to the mission for easier access, they got soaked when I jumped into the creek to avoid gunfire. I probably contracted some fucked-up disease from eating them. Suspecting this, I probably shouldn't have shared them with the other guys, but if one of your brothers asks for some Skittles, you give him some. I was later given a healthy dose of Cipro from John, our team Doc.

It's the little things that are a bizarre comfort. I drank some water from my Nalgene bottle, waiting on our next move. I was soaked and covered in mud, but hey, it is what it is. Other guys checked their kit. As one watched for the enemy, another reset his kit and prepared for the next fight. We were far from done. A new magazine is a must. Never go from one gunfight to another without putting a fresh magazine in your weapon. It is a sin not to, and a known thirty is always better than, *I think I've got twenty-five.*

Set in my new position, staring through a crack in a wall just big enough for my barrel and a decent sight picture, I took it all in through my scope. We had a diverse set of weapon systems, arranged along this wall in one of the worst places in Afghanistan. We were a force to be reckoned with. *Bring it.*

Radio chatter was going crazy. We just heard the bird went down a short distance from our current position after taking an RPG and heavy gunfire. The first call over the radio identified several casualties. My heart sank. Then a few very long minutes later, we received a second call stating there were no casualties with the exception of the platoon leader, who had received a superficial gunshot wound.

Relief rushed over me. Having grown up in B Co., I knew pretty much everyone. Mike, the other recce team leader, confirmed we were the closest element to the crash site and we'd be moving there to assist. We picked up and started along foot trails winding through irrigation ditches. I could hear gunshots: some close, some far away. Another AC-130 checked on-station and quickly started working. We were in a target-rich environment, and an AC-130 is the equivalent to an invisible angel of death. I could hear it wheeled up overhead, raining hell.

After a few hundred meters we arrived at the crash site. The Chinook was in the middle of a poppy field with ditches running through it like a grid. We set into the ditches in order to strengthen the hasty perimeter already set by the platoon and crew from the downed bird. Once in our new positions, our visibility was blocked due to the high poppy crop and sun that was slowly coming up which washed out our NVGs. We were in one of the wildest places in the country. Without the cover of night, we were quite exposed.

The enemy began to mass in outlying areas. The AC-130 engaged again, with quick and deadly force. In a few instances our forward observer, Mike, would come by to let us know to stay low as he called in danger close fire missions on our side of the perimeter. It echoed through our headsets. You better have your head down when rounds start raining down, shaking the ground. It made me smile a bit when I considered the big picture; the crazy situation we were in at this point. The next stage of the plan would be coming shortly: the craziest and fastest exfil I've ever had the privilege to be a part of.

The plan to get us out was coming to fruition. Chinooks were back on station doing mini-gun runs on all tree lines, irrigation ditches and the walled compounds. They took fire again from enemy positions as hostile forces continued gathering. Leaving this shithole without being shot down (for most of us) might just become a reality.

The plan for extraction was simple. The AC-130 would suppress the enemy as the exfil birds came in one after another to pick us up. Groups of us would rush into the aircraft and take off immediately. Sounds easy, but coordination between air and ground assets had to go smoothly, or smooth enough at least, to make it all work. Rangers would have to move quickly along the ditches. Even up on a high knee, the crops were still too high for us to see and if you were too high above them, you exposed yourself, a potentially fatal mistake. With heavy suppressive fire the teams running to the aircraft should have a chance to get to the bird and off the deck. We'd have to get this right three different times.

As the first bird came in, everyone moved up on a knee and began laying down the most ferocious fire they were able. *We are no-shit laying down suppressive fire just to exfil. Are we in fucking 'Nam?* It was a wall of hot lead. The amount of destruction going downrange was mind blowing. The pounding and the ground shaking from the explosions was one of the most unbelievable experiences I've ever been a part of. Just like that, the first chalk ran and loaded the bird. As they tore out of the HLZ, rocks and dirt blasted us from behind.

Time came for the next group to get out, and this all happened in rapid succession to reduce the chance of the enemy hitting another aircraft. I will also add they landed, literally, as close to us as they could, which was the beauty of the 160th SOAR - they are the best in the world and I've seen them do unreal acts on so many targets with their aircraft. They are the Jedis of rotary wing flight; they will get it done. *Night Stalkers Don't Quit!*

So, with the second lift up and away, we were next. We received warning that we were next and in seconds we heard the loud *whomp, whomp, whomp* of rotors pummeling sky as the bird came in fast and flared behind us.

Half of us were still firing as the bird touched down.

I was up and running behind Ben, our recce section platoon sergeant. As we ran, I had the stupidest thought ever. *Get to da choppa!* I was literally grinning ear-to-ear as I ran through the hot exhaust from the engines and hauled ass up the ramp to the front near the cockpit where the two forward gunners sat. I glanced out the window briefly. One of the crew was down on his mini-gun surveying the area for any threat within range. I leaned up against the airframe, grabbed my safety line and searched for a quick hook-up so that as soon as the last few Rangers boarded I could snap in.

Again, I went through my kit, magazines first, from right to left. The ones on the right were spent, as I pull mags from right to left. I always move toward the left side of my kit and also my non-firing side, being a righty. I pulled the mag from my SR-25 and put in a fresh one. My mag count was down to three 20-round mags out of the original seven. As an assault sniper, you don't carry a ton of ammo, never anticipating expending that much. 140 rounds, for most cases, enough, but sometimes you have these unforeseen days.

The bonus of running a 7.62mm weapon system is that if you absolutely must, you can use machine gun ammo. It is a last resort though, as you pull ammo from a dominating weapon system meant for suppressive fire and one of the highest casualty-producing systems we carry at the platoon level. Not to mention, it is horrible for a match-grade sniper barrel. As I checked my gear, I looked over at Major Hammer and just smiled and nodded. Guys are running on the bird, being counted by the crew chief and another Ranger. Sergeant Major Harlem ran on and immediately manned the empty M-240 on the right side of the aircraft where the crew chief, currently outside, would normally be. Decisive actions like these made me so proud of the men and the organization that I was a part of.

As the last man ran aboard, I reached down to snap in, and I was pressed to the floor, ramp closing as we gained altitude. The mini-gun next to me opened up as we left the beautiful shithole that is the Sangin Valley. I've never been in an exfil where the bird lifted off as fast. The Chinook is the fastest helicopter in the Army and when they open her up, it is awesome.

The ride back was the same as any other; guys were doing the usual:

slamming water and leaning on each other to doze off. There was the occasional loud laugh over the constant loud whir of the engines, followed by a knuckle bump or pat on the back. Everyone was covered in mud and sweat, the usual stink of tearing it up all night as if the madness earlier was just another day. *But the thing is ... it was.* You never knew what you would encounter on a target, or how it would play out. We were extremely lucky to suffer no casualties besides the platoon leader's tiny nick. That in and of itself is mind blowing; you just don't get many divine intervention cards, but we seemed to have pulled one that night.

We flew back to Kandahar and piled into the giant tent where we lived temporarily. It was a total dump with a hundred or more guys from our Task Force living on top of each other in bunk beds. The downed Chinook was destroyed by an AC-130 with a couple 105mm rounds. The bird was beyond any means of recovery and was destroyed so that insurgents couldn't remove anything useful from it. Looking back on it all, I am amazed at how seamlessly it went. We studied our unfortunate situation and we adapted. Ranger leadership trains to make quick decisions, act and overcome every obstacle that confronts them. Using these principles, success is the usual outcome. This is why the 75th Ranger Regiment is the best in the world.

- R.J.S. 1/7

Marc Anderson, A Co. 1/75, receives his birthday "pink belly", Afghanistan, 2002.

Unidentified Ranger, 1/75, scans for targets on Takur Ghar, Afghanistan, 2002

Photo by 75th Ranger Regiment

Unidentified Ranger clears a building during the initial invasion of Iraq, 2003

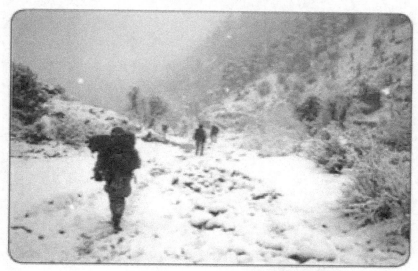

Photo by Brandon Young

2/75 Rangers on a combat mission through the Kantiwa Valley, Afghanistan 2003

185

Photo by Roy Matthews

1-B 3/75 Rangers on H-1 Airfield, Iraq, 2003

Photo by Leo Jenkins

A 3/75 Ranger is "balled up" on his birthday, Afghanistan, 2004.

3/75 Rangers on a mission, Afghanistan, 2004

Two 3/75 snipers before a training mission, 2005

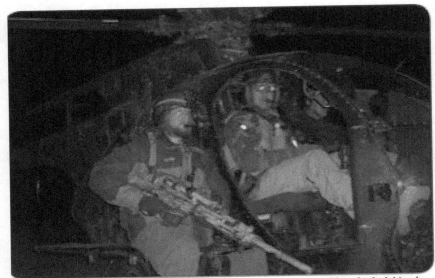

Photo by Jack Murphy

A 3/75 sniper preparing to take off on an MH-6 "Little Bird" in support of a successful HVT raid, Afghanistan, 2005

Photo by RJS

1/75 Rangers pose for a group photo, Afghanistan, 2005

Photo by RJS

1/75 Rangers on a reconnaissance mission, Afghanistan, 2005

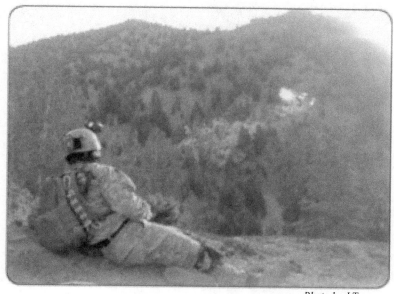

Photo by J.T.

3/75 Rangers call for fire on enemy positions, Afghanistan, 2006

Photo by RJS

A 1/75 sniper scans for targets on a mission, Afghanistan, 2006

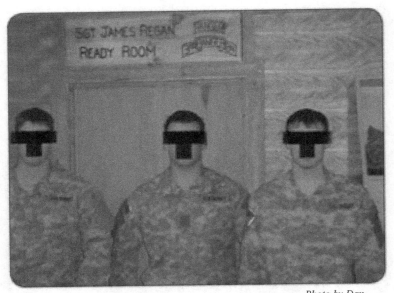

Photo by Dan

Rangers from 3/75 stand in front of the new James Regan Ready Room, Iraq, 2007

Jason Dahlke on a reconnaissance patrol in the mountains, Afghanistan, 2008

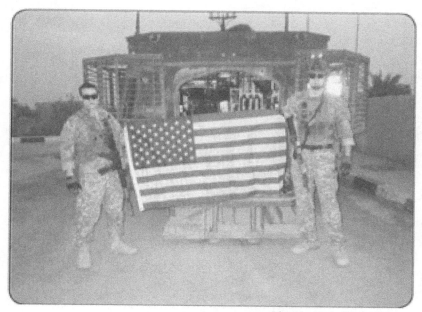

C Co. 1/75 Rangers after a combat mission in Iraq, 2008.

A Ranger from C Co. 3/75 scans for enemy insurgents during a combat operation in Helmand Province, Afghanistan, 2009

Photo by Grant McGarry

A squad of Rangers from 2-C, 1/75, Afghanistan, 2009

Photo by 75th Ranger Regiment

A Ranger scans for targets while on a mission, Afghanistan, 2010

Photo by Logan Lewis

Kevin Pape's squad from 3-C, 1/75 before a combat mission, Afghanistan, 2010

1/75 Ranger dog handler with his multi-purpose canine after a mission, Afghanistan, 2011

Photo by Sergeant Brian Kohl

A Ranger from 3/75 on patrol, Afghanistan, 2011

CHAPTER SEVEN

"It is foolish and wrong to mourn the men who died.

Rather, we should thank God that such men lived."

GEORGE S. PATTON JR.

I have always been patriotic. I was raised to respect the flag, respect my elders and to love my country. But growing up, I never felt a chill crawl up my back when I heard the national anthem. I did not stop mid-stride to stare at a flag waving on a pole. I did not tear up when I watched 4th of July fireworks explode while God Bless America played on the radio. All that changed in a C-17 on the return from my second deployment.

We woke from an Ambien-induced slumber on the final approach into Savannah, Georgia. We returned the night of the 4th of July…just in time to miss all the festivities. Everyone was excited to be back home after a long trip to Afghanistan. As we started to circle Savannah, someone pointed out that you could see fireworks going off below through the small porthole in the aircraft's door. A few of us took turns looking, much to the dismay of the crew who wanted us to stay seated and buckled. After we returned to our seats and as we were about 90 seconds out, Staff Sergeant "Joe" started belting out the *Star Spangled Banner*. What ensued was moving to say the least; every barrel-chested freedom fighter on that aircraft started singing it with him. I don't know if words can accurately describe the sound and energy of 60 of the most patriotic men on earth, battle-proven, singing their country's anthem in unison. No concert, no musician, no performance will ever compare to the sound of camaraderie and pride which filled that aircraft. As we sang our hearts out, I looked at the black and white infrared flags attached to our shoulders. *There is no place on earth I would rather be, with this group of men and this flag on my shoulder.*

Patriotism can't be taught. Patriotism can't be forced down your throat as something you *should* feel as an American. I firmly believe it is learned and maybe it even needs to be *experienced*. That night I learned what patriotism truly felt like. That night I was a *born again American.* I didn't care if we missed the Independence Day festivities, the last few minutes of that flight was a better celebration of America than any cookout or day at the beach. It was like the first time I realized I loved the girl I was dating. I fell in love with America and remain deeply in love with her to this day. No amount of politics, economic woe or reality TV shows will ever make me fall out of love.

In 2007, the Regiment continued their full engagement in operations both in Iraq and Afghanistan. This year was the costliest to this point in the war for the 75th Ranger Regiment. Sergeant James Regan, Private First Class Kristofer Thomas, Private First Class Ryan Garbs, Corporal Jason Kessler, Specialist George Libby, Corporal Benjamin Dillon and Sergeant Steven Ganczewski all made the ultimate sacrifice.

FEBRUARY 2007

"JIMMY"

Prior to my Iraq deployment, Sergeant Regan was my team leader in Weapons Squad. I met him as Corporal Regan during my first deployment to Afghanistan; he shipped over right after graduating Ranger School. He was very smart, older and mature. I would talk with him about college and what I should do with my career and so on. He was a no-nonsense team leader and would help me with anything I needed. When you're a new private, you spend the first six months proving yourself. Well, I was only in 3/75 for three months prior to deployment, so yeah, I was still proving myself. Corporal Regan proved to be different. He mentored and taught instead of using other methods of correction typically utilized on new guys.

I went through two more training cycles/deployments with Corporal-turned-Sergeant Regan before this trip to Iraq. We came to know each other very well. Everybody was close in our platoon. At the time, I was a breacher and team leader for my squad. This was my third deployment to Iraq and we had returned to the same place we'd stayed before. This time everything was complete; we had a ready room as well as an overhang for our Strykers. It was a drastic improvement since our last rotation only months prior. This deployment was a mix of HAF (Helicopter Assault Force) and GAF (Ground Assault Force) missions.

Early in the deployment, we were on a GAF night mission and I sat in the rear left position of the Stryker closest to the ramp. En route to the target, our Stryker hit an IED. All I remember was a bright flash; I was knocked unconscious from the overpressure. I came to with everyone in the Stryker yelling my name and hitting me and Doc performing blood sweeps. I told them to get off of me, I was fine. I was definitely out of it. That specific seat must have been special, as I was the only one in the Stryker was affected by the overpressure.

Several missions later, the code for a capture/kill GAF op came across our pagers and in a very shitty area. We conducted mission planning and then loaded up in Strykers. My squad was the number two Stryker in the order of movement as we departed for the long ride to the objective. We sat in the back of the cramped, dark Stryker for a couple hours, falling in and out of sleep with nothing to do but stare at each other, drink Rip-Its and spit dip. Out of nowhere, we heard a large explosion. *Holy shit, we just hit an IED!* But our Stryker was not the target. The IED hit the third vehicle back but was so big; the explosion felt like it was on top of us.

The radio chatter began, confirming that it was the third Stryker. We moved the disabled Stryker out of the blast area as quickly as possible, emptying out of our Stryker to begin loading it with the other squad, which included the platoon sergeant and a medic. They were all ok, just dizzy and shaken up. The only person that was not removed was Sergeant Regan. He was still in the Stryker. Coincidentally, Sergeant Regan was sitting in the exact spot I was when I was the only one affected by a blast, just missions prior.

I grabbed the hooligan tool off the back of one of my other teammates who was carrying it, as breaching equipment was spread amongst the lower ranking guys. While running behind the rolling Stryker, which was being towed toward out of the impact zone we were frantically trying to pry open the damaged back ramp. The medic was still inside the Stryker doing whatever he could to stop the bleeding and tend to other injuries Jimmy (Regan) sustained. Finally, they told another medic and me to jump on top of the Stryker to pull Regan through the top hatch. I was so pissed off. I hopped on top of the Stryker as soon as I knew the plan, while the medic took off his belt and wrapped it around Regan. He handed me one end of the belt and the other medic the opposite end. We pulled him up like it was nothing. My adrenaline was pumping.

Somehow, I ended up with both sides of the belt and pulled him the rest of the way through the hatch and into my lap. We were being towed toward the MEDEVAC HLZ. Other members of my squad were busy preparing the litter to transport Regan from the Stryker to the bird once we hit the HLZ.

I sat with Regan on my lap while they were doing this, as he lay there going in and out of consciousness. I gave him sternum rubs to keep his attention, calling his name, *"Jimmy"* as we all referred to him. I told him he was going to be ok and urged him to talk to me. I monitored his vital signs and breathing, which were not good at all. Once we arrived at the MEDEVAC HLZ, we loaded him onto the litter. I handed him carefully down to my guys and saw them run into the brownout, Jimmy disappearing into the dust. I didn't know it at the time, but that was the last time I would see Sergeant James J. Regan.

We continued our mission. Unfortunately, we were en route to the target building when we took the IED so the mission continued as usual, even while dragging a downed Stryker with us. We were so pissed that we vowed to shoot every person on that target. But in the end, we are not merciless killers, no matter how good the vengeance might have felt. We hit our target silently, meeting no resistance that night. We captured the objective we were looking for and began our exfil with a handful of detainees. We received updates during the mission of Regan's status, reporting that he was doing well and was going to make it, but still in critical condition.

When we arrived back at the SOF compound, the chaplain was there to tell us he passed. We mourned as if losing a blood brother. And I was still covered in his blood, which I did not want to wash off. I don't know why—I guess I felt like it was a part of him or something. I can't explain it. The new ready room we had built was renamed the *Sergeant James J. Regan Ready Room* that day.

Sergeant Regan was killed in action on February 9, 2007 and I remember it like it was yesterday. It will be forever burned into my mind. I can never do anything but serve my country for the rest of my life. I crushed through my bachelor's degree in just two years and seven months, thinking of Jimmy when he attended Duke University. He was my role model and motivation to get my degree, and fast. He is my motivation for many other things I have done. Every day, men fall protecting our country. What makes me better than them? Nothing. I regret leaving the Ranger Regiment, but continue to serve our country in the private sector and as a sniper in the Army National Guard and an instructor for the US Air Force. My heart truly lies in the pursuit of closing with and destroying enemies of our nation. Since my six-month window closed to return to the Ranger Regiment many years ago, I seek to get back in the fight any way possible, just to fight alongside brothers who are like-minded, ridding this world of terrorism.

- DAN

3/75

"OF MOTTOES AND MEN"

I never was a Ranger, and frankly, I never wanted to be. That's probably fortunate for me, because I'm not sure I would have made the cut.

After completing a branch detail to the Infantry with the 101st Airborne Division and transitioning to Military Intelligence (MI), I served in the 2nd Infantry Division in the Republic of Korea. It seems silly now, but pre-9/11, Korea is where you went if you wanted to do something *hard* OCONUS. I got my first company-level command in Korea and after two years my wife and I returned CONUS for the MI Officers' Advanced Course. While in the Advanced Course, my branch manager paid our class a visit. She had a list of available duty positions, but there was only one I wanted: the 5th Special Forces Group in Fort Campbell, Kentucky. She had a requirement for my grade and specialty and just like that I was on orders. It was that easy.

The ease of getting into an SF Group as an enabler was, as I found out, a major issue. At the time, and as far as I know continuing to this day, Special Forces was the only ARSOF unit that would go pot-luck-style when it came to enablers. All enabler assignments to Group were *needs of the Army;* a soldier could go to 10th Special Forces Group just as easily as he could go to 10th Mountain. The major problem with this was, of course, quality control. *Need of the Army* attitude toward enabler functions meant that some good and some not-so-good enablers made it into support positions in Group. Over time, the screw-ups of the poor enablers overshadowed the accomplishments of the good ones and enablers as a whole were often mistrusted or un-empowered. 5th Group was great to me personally but I didn't think I could reach full potential in an organization in which the enablers as a group were not the professional equivalent of the operators we supported.

So, after commanding the Group Military Intelligence Detachment and the Group Support Company, I transferred *across the airfield* to 2nd Battalion,

160th Special Operations Aviation Regiment. In the time that I was a Night Stalker, I frequently deployed to Afghanistan in support of a joint SOF task force, where I served as the J2 for the SOF aviation element. It was there that I first worked closely with Rangers. I remember one mission in particular, in which a Chinook got shot down on an objective. Despite the massive damage to the aircraft, the pilot safely (but somewhat roughly) put it down in a field.

People said it was a miracle no Rangers or 160th members got killed, and maybe it was. But I think it was due to the skill of the pilots coupled with the excellent design of the aircraft more than anything else. I remember watching the Predator feed as the Task Force destroyed the damaged bird. That was a whole lot of money and capability up in smoke, but it had to be done to prevent the aircraft and its sensitive equipment from falling into the hands of the enemy. But it was still a good day because everyone came home from that objective. *Humans are more important than hardware.*

Prior to my time in the 160th, my only experience with Rangers was in the form of a previous battalion commander who had been an officer in a Ranger unit and a battalion XO who, before becoming an officer, had done some of his enlisted time in the Regiment. To say that I found both these men unimpressive would be an understatement. Fortunately, I had several opportunities to work closely with the Ranger Regiment and find out that there was probably a reason those two clowns were no longer in the Ranger Regiment.

It takes a special kind of man to be a Ranger. Even from the outside looking in, it's clear that being a Ranger is nothing short of a way of life. One can go to a three-month school to earn a Tab that says Ranger, but to *be* a Ranger, it takes a commitment to a punishing Spartan lifestyle of training, hardship and deprivation as well as near-constant combat deployments.

For me, the type of person who thrives in the Ranger Regiment was exemplified by a photo that hung in the entryway of the Task Force headquarters building in Afghanistan known as the Joint Operations Center (JOC), or the *plywood palace*. There were several pictures placed conspicuously on the walls of the JOC. One of the most motivating to me was that of a man hurtling headfirst down from a New York skyscraper toward certain death; one of the Twin Towers' 9/11 jumpers. *This is why we are here.*

I'd think this to myself whenever I walked past.

But there was another very powerful photo on that same wall. This one featured a young man sitting upright in a hospital bed, right hand raised at a 90-degree angle, an oxygen mask attached to his face and tubes running from his chest. Flanking him on either side are two equally grim-looking young men dressed in fatigues and holding a US flag pulled tightly between them behind the wounded man's hospital bed. Although there is no caption, it is clear what is happening: a re-enlistment.

The men in the picture look young. Because operators in all other direct-action task forces are all *much* older, there is nothing these three men can be other than Rangers. Seeing that picture gave me chills. Despite being severely wounded in combat, this young man was signing up for more. He wasn't lying in that bed feeling sorry for himself, he simply *Rangered up* for more opportunities to combat America's enemies alongside his Ranger brothers. *These are the kind of people I'm working with,* I remember thinking about this photo.

Since our unit supported all the various *customers* in the national SOF task force, I worked with just about all US SOF units that have direct action as a specified mission. I quickly learned that each unit has its own specific culture and unique way of doing business. I also learned that I liked working with Rangers best.

Rangers' mission planning was what really stood out to me. They plan meticulously, execute aggressively and conduct ruthless after action reviews (AARs). Excruciating attention to detail is in their organizational DNA. Working with Rangers in Afghanistan, it was clear that the Regiment progressed far past its legacy role of pulling security for other units and is fully capable of conducting a wide range of special operations missions, even commanding a subordinate task force.

I did several short deployments as a Night Stalker and developed working relationships with several Rangers on similar short deployment cycles.

My role in the mission planning process was limited; Rangers had their own planners and intelligence officers, and they were quite good. Nonetheless, every morning I accompanied the 160th senior pilots and planners over to the Ranger headquarters area, located on the backside of the plywood palace housing the Task Force and sat in on the morning brief. At this brief, the pilots and Rangers discussed the upcoming night's mission. At this point in the war, even relatively complex missions were routine. Although planning was thorough, it was not onerous or time-consuming due to the experience pilots and Rangers had with each other, and the standard operating procedures (SOPs) that the two units developed together.

Particularly sensitive or complicated missions necessitated additional planning meetings. I attended these briefings as often as possible and helped where and when able, which was not often. But I had good interpersonal skills and I was a pretty good intel officer, so I made some good connections within the Regiment.

The 160th pilots sometimes invited me to go along on missions. I usually turned these offers down, because it was hard for me to support the mission if I was actually on the mission. Being a prior infantryman, I figured I could probably handle myself even if the worst happened, but being a relatively inexperienced outsider meant that I would most likely only end up being in the way if things went sideways. I realized though, if I turned down missions long enough people would start to think I was scared and would reflect poorly on the S2 section, so I went on one or two per rotation.

Most of the missions I went on were completely uneventful, but I do remember specifically one trip to J-Bad. Our pilots were flying in support of a Ranger HVT mission, and the plan was to travel in either three or four MH-47s from Bagram to Jalalabad, land and refuel and wait for the trigger to conduct the mission. This was a pretty cut-and-dried operation, something Rangers and 160th pilots did almost every night.

I was along solely as an observer; I rode in the jump seat immediately behind the two pilots. This gave me a literal front-seat view of the operation and because I had a headset, I heard the radio chatter as well. I'm a big guy, even bigger all geared up for a mission and the jump seat was relatively small. I shifted my feet to get into a more comfortable position and accidently jarred loose the co-pilot's radio cable. He noticed and got it fixed right away so it wasn't a big deal, but I was more than a little embarrassed.

Before we left on the mission, my battalion commander made it clear to me that I was to get off the helo at J-Bad and the strike package would pick me up when they returned from the mission. That was what I planned on doing anyway; I had a good friend who was doing deep-cover HUMINT work out of J-Bad and he had agreed to host me for the evening while the op went down. The flight out to J-Bad was uneventful; the only action was the crew chiefs conducting the usual test firing of the machine guns shortly after takeoff.

When we landed at J-Bad, the first thing I noticed was the terrain. It was dark, of course, but through my NODs I could see that the FOB was set in a bowl, with high ground on pretty much all four sides and a small village just outside the wire. It looked like this base was just begging to be over-run. Appearances can be deceiving, however and when I linked up with my HUMINT friend he outlined the base's impressive defense system. He also explained that while there was in fact high ground around the base, much of it was a lot farther away than it looked through NODs. Apparently the local tribes were friendly too, so they rarely got more than the occasional indirect fire round shot their way.

Our mission got postponed while we were on our way to J-Bad, so I was able to get caught up with my friend at length over some cold soda and Pop Tarts in their unit's break area. The Rangers we flew in with linked up with the operational unit there at J-Bad and continued mission prep. We had a *no later than (NLT)* time to execute the mission, and if the hit didn't go down at that point, we were going to load back up and return to Bagram. About 15 minutes or so before the NLT time, I said goodbye to my friend and went back out to the landing zone. It was still dark, of course, but I could see well enough to find my way back to the airfield. On the way, however, a large laser dot suddenly appeared on the chest plate of my body armor. Thanks to the dust in the air I could tell it was coming from one of the helicopters and I wasn't being targeted by a sniper in the village or surrounding hills. I flipped down my NODs and immediately found the culprit, one of my pilot buddies sitting in the cockpit of one of the MH-47s. With my NODs I could see him holding a ground laser designator and pointing at me. He probably thought I was going to freak out seeing that big green dot on my chest, and I probably would have, had it been coming from anywhere other than a US aircraft. I made a gesture in his direction that let him know I was on to his antics and the laser switched off. I couldn't see facial expressions at this distance but I knew the pilot in question well and knew he'd be smiling.

I was smiling too as I boarded the aircraft and prepared to return to Bagram. After checking in with the pilots and the crew chief who informed me that the mission was canceled and we would soon return to Bagram, I went back into the cargo area of the aircraft, took off my helmet, and using my assault pack as a pillow, fell fast asleep. A short time later, I heard the MH-47's rotors start spinning and I groggily put my helmet on and secured my assault pack for the ride home. I was about to make my way back to the jump seat when a large group of Rangers hustled into the back of the helo. They moved with a sense of purpose of dudes mounting up for something big. These guys had the switched-on look of men about to *land on the X.*

Uh oh.

The ramp closed and the Rangers clipped in their safety lines as I began to think about how I was going to explain to my battalion commander how I ended up going on this op after he specifically instructed me not to. I decided there was nothing to be done now, so I sat back down on the floor and clipped in too. One Ranger, probably an NCO, went from soldier to soldier doing pre-flight PMIs. When he got to me, we looked at each other through NODs and I gave him a thumbs up. He looked at me without reacting and went on to the next guy. I'm sure he was thinking something along the lines of *who the hell is this guy?*

They had a dog along for this mission. The dogs were always muzzled while they were on the helos. I asked a crew chief about this once. He explained, "Oh yeah, they have GOT to be muzzled. Sometimes they get so scared or amped up, especially coming back from an op, that they'll put a bite on anyone who happens to be around. A detainee, a member of the strike force, a crew chief, yeah, they need those muzzles." I thought that was odd given the way I usually saw the dogs back on the FOB; they always seemed so calm.

The noise from the rotating twin blades reached a pitch that indicated takeoff was imminent. I watched enough Predator feeds to know what happened immediately after landing. I decided that once the ramp went down I'd run out with the Rangers and after establishing 360-degree security, I'd attach myself to the nearest tabbed Spec-4 until the platoon sergeant or platoon leader decided what to do with me on the mission. I'd be the best ammo bearer or litter carrier I could be tonight, I resolved. It didn't occur to me until after my sleep induced grogginess wore off that I could just stay on the helo and fly out with the crew after the insertion.

It turned out to be moot anyway, as the helos all suddenly powered back down. Whatever order had sent the Ranger strike force running out to the helos was now countermanded and the mission was canceled yet again. I don't remember who we were after but he must have been someone important, because we spent the whole night at J-Bad, waiting to have enough intel to go after him. We were there so long that we ended up flying back in full daylight. This was a very rare thing for our Task Force, which operated almost exclusively in total darkness, when our comparative advantage was highest. Flying home in daylight made the pucker factor a little higher, but it gave me the opportunity to see Afghanistan in the daytime, something I had only done once or twice before.

This part of Afghanistan was absolutely beautiful. We flew through low-lying valleys full of water and green trees, past fields filled with crops and over children and farmers who waved at us as we passed. We had an uneventful flight back to Bagram and I think everyone was glad to be back on base and to catch some sleep after a mostly-uneventful but nonetheless long and tiring night.

Someone once said that war is long periods of boredom punctuated by sheer terror. I think that description is accurate. Many missions were canceled, or were *dry holes* that resulted in no shots being fired. That's one of the reasons I laugh when I hear videogame producers talking about wanting to make their games *more realistic.* If you want to make a war game more realistic, have the character spend three or four hours in full kit, sitting on the tarmac in almost total darkness, waiting for an op that may not even happen because it got weathered out, the intel trigger wasn't met, or your higher headquarters called it off for some inexplicable reason and you never even find out why. *That* would be a realistic video game.

At this point I had been promoted to major and was sometimes the senior Night Stalker present at briefings with the Rangers; most of the pilots being either senior captains or chief warrant officers. While I was technically the highest-ranking unit member present, I was a non-pilot staff officer, not in charge of anything past my own PowerPoint slides. Nonetheless, because of my gold oak leaf and the fact that they had seen me around so much over the last couple of deployments, some of the Ranger officers referred their questions to me. Toward the end of my time with the 160th, after several deployments to Afghanistan working with the Rangers, our pilots briefed the acting Ranger commander, whose day job was the operations officer for one of the Ranger battalions. One time when we were briefing this particular operations officer, he made a perplexed look on his face and looked back over his shoulder in my direction. When the pilots briefed the Ranger task force commander, who was usually a lieutenant colonel, they would start off their spiel with "NSDQ, sir," which was an abbreviation of our unit motto and this particular officer didn't know what that meant. Stopping the briefing, he asked,

"Hey, what does 'NSDQ' stand for again?"

"Night Stalkers Don't Quit," I informed him.

"Well that's..." he started and then paused, struggling to find the right word. Ending his sentence with the word he felt was most appropriate (although disparaging to the unit), he turned back around and the briefing continued. I took his words in the spirit in which I thought he meant them— good-natured ribbing between men who knew each other well—but I wasn't sure how the pilots would feel. Unlike my service in 5th Group, I had to make it through assessment to get selected as a Night Stalker and had to graduate from Green Platoon like the pilots. I was a Night Stalker through and through; our motto, our creed and our unit were and still are very important to me. But I think there is often just a different level of *esprit* that operational types in SOF units possess that support guys like myself simply don't. I glanced down at the pilots to check their reaction and while one of the flight leads caught my glance and rolled his eyes in a way that I knew meant *Freakin' Rangers,* none of them seemed particularly put out. But I noticed that some of the older Ranger NCOs sitting in the front of the briefing area looking at us, with their faces positively aghast.

I didn't give the operation officer's comments or the expression on the

Ranger NCOs' faces another thought until the end of the briefing, when it was traditional for everyone to rise and salute the commander. Since this was the Ranger headquarters, we always refrained from sounding off with our unit motto and merely saluted silently. But this time, a loud cry of "Night Stalkers Don't Quit!" competed with the usual thunderous "Rangers Lead the Way!" The interesting thing was, our motto didn't come from our pilots, it came from that handful of Ranger NCOs.

As we prepared to leave, some of the Ranger NCOs approached our group of Night Stalkers. "Hey sir, we apologize for what he said," one began, "We remember what the 160th did for us in Somalia, we have nothing but respect for you guys."

I explained that it wasn't a big deal to us. "It's cool, we know he didn't mean anything by it." But it was a big deal to the Rangers and the NCOs still looked dubious. One of them said, "Yeah, well, if someone said something like that about our motto..." He didn't finish his sentence. He didn't need to. (Note to self: never insult the Rangers' motto). What the operations officer said wasn't a big deal to us. He meant it as a joke; the people it was directed toward took it as a joke. We didn't think it was funny, but it wouldn't fundamentally affect the nature of the relationship between the two units. In fact, if anything, my regard of the Rangers only increased after this experience, seeing in the reactions of the Ranger NCOs, the respect warriors show each other.

I'm not a pilot and I think I was still in high school during the Black Hawk Down incident in Somalia, but to those Rangers, it didn't matter. I represented something bigger, a concept much larger than myself. To them I was a Night Stalker, a representative of something that they respected. I left that briefing room feeling pretty good.

- Charles Faint, LTC, USA
MI

SUMMER 2007

"STARS"

It was the summer of 2007, a warm dark night. The stars were countless on nights like this. No light from the city to drown out their majesty. What a beautiful and hypnotizing sight. I forgot everything that was going on around me. When I looked up, all my cares melted away. Even the noises of the diesel engines were overwhelmed by glory. As I stared up at them I thanked God for their beauty and I prayed that, like the stars, my men and I would live through the night.

"One minute," comes the cry over the radio; after a short prayer, I turn my gaze from heaven and look into the eyes of the men who place their very lives into my hands. Six men willing to go, without question, anywhere I tell them, simply because they trust me. We have trained hard together and they have given everything I've asked of them. In return, I've done everything in my power to keep them alive. I would lay my life down for every one of them and I know they feel the same toward me.

"Thirty seconds, get ready," says the vehicle commander. "No movement on target." I look at the men about to charge into a night of unknowns, fully confident that everything will fall into place. They look at me waiting for silent commands. I cut the lights. Eyes that before showed compassion and love now show no emotion, no remorse and no fear. All six pairs of evil green eyes look at me and waiting for me to join them. A chill runs up and down my body as I think about the fear these men have bestowed on those we have hunted in the past. I reach up and flipped down my night vision goggles from atop my head and the night gives way to a clear picture in green and black. No more darkness. I am one of them. In our element, we are unstoppable. We own the night and darkness cannot hide our prey.

It is said that the time for something to go wrong is on the way to the target. The ramp drops and we rush out of the back of the metal beast, weapons pointing in all directions, looking for the slightest movement. As I watch my men establish a foothold on the street, I know that at the slightest sound, all weapons will fixate on that position, ready and eager to fire. However, not a trigger will be pulled unless an enemy hostile is identified.

I point them to the target building and the only sound is the vehicles. The vehicle commanders have their heavy machine guns pointing at the target house to cover us as we move.

I look up at the commander as we silently edge toward the two-story building.

"Door closed," the commander says, "shifting to the roof."

At once, all the heavy guns move rapidly toward the roof of the building. If somebody tries to ambush us from the roof, the guns will open up and turn the roof into Swiss cheese and the ambushers will become the ambushed.

As the guns move I send my demolition team, the Alpha Team leader and his rifleman, to the front door. A two-man team well-versed in opening doors meant to keep men like us out. They run but make no noise, even with their heavy equipment. As they approach the door, the Alpha Team rifleman stays focused on the door. If it opens he will lead the charge into the building. The Alpha Team leader pulls out an explosive charge and prepares it while simultaneously running forward. He places it between the doorknob and the door jam, right over the locking mechanism.

The team leader and the rifleman begin to back away from the door. They move to a corner of the building just three feet away and crouch into a small ball. The team leader holds the ignition system in his hand.

"Charge set," my Alpha Team leader says.

Not knowing what lays in wait for us behind the door, I command, "Burn it," into the radio.

"Burning."

Sliding his finger into the pull ring of the ignition system, he pushes the pin in, turns it a quarter turn and pulls.

The night is no longer silent as the sound of shredding timber fills the night. Windows shatter and pieces of glass fall to the ground. The walls around me shake. Where a door once stood, only smoke remains. Like water bursting forth from a dam, men flow into the unknown.

I am fifth into the building. I hear gunfire. *Bang, bang, bang, bang, bang, bang!* My team throws a diversionary grenade, commonly called a *banger* into the room to scare the enemy and keep them off balance. The sound is so real, but often it is mistaken for gunfire.

As I enter the room I look straight across a vast space to an entrance leading to a hallway. Pieces of brick and mortar fly off the wall. Flashes of light come from around the hallway corner. I look for a target across the way but am blinded by the wall.

"Contact front," I call over the radio. "Alpha left, Bravo right," I yell over the ear-piercing gunfire.

I move to a staircase to my right, coming into position to begin the assault. As I look to my left I see my Alpha Team rifleman, a man I had trained and had come to know over the last two years, bent over at the stomach and dropping to the ground. My mind races with the worst thoughts. *He's hit, abdominal wound, he won't make it.*

"Weapon down!" the unwounded rifleman yells, while transitioning to his sidearm.

As I come to the staircase I still cannot see down the hallway. With no idea how long the hallway is, I choose to use a diversionary grenade. As I pull it from my kit, concrete starts to fly all around me. The staircase, inches off my right side, becomes the impact zone for an enemy firing sporadically, pulling the trigger but not aiming at anyone. I don't think twice about the rounds grazing my head, my men are depending on me and I need to act.

I look across the way at the rifleman whose primary weapon went down, now holding a 9mm handgun. I stare at him in the eyes. He has a wife back home; she has no clue that I am about to send her husband of two years into a dark hallway and possibly to his death. He does though, and nods his head, signaling that he's ready, willing, and eager to go. I toss the grenade down the hallway. *Bang, bang, bang!* I head into the room on my right with my Bravo Team, while my Alpha Team proceeds down the hallway.

"Clear!" yells my Bravo Team leader before I even get to the door.

Bang, bang, bang, bang! Rapid gunfire breaks out behind me.
I turn around and do not see anyone. The hallway opens to the right. Bravo Team and I move rapidly down the hallway, rifles raised, unsure of the status of Alpha Team. As we approach the corner to the right, I hear more sporadic

gunfire and the sound of a door opening. I flow around the corner not knowing what to expect. There is an open door to my front, leading outside and a body, lying still on the ground.

The walls are riddled with holes. The white tile that lines the floor is now covered in blood. Eyes once filled with life and courage are now empty. There is no movement. I look at the shell of what was once a man. I walk up to the body with no emotion.

"One enemy KIA," I report over the radio.

"Is it him?" my commander calls back.

"Roger, it's him."

"All clear out here," my Alpha Team Leader says, bringing his team in from outside.

I looked up at the stars on the way back to base. The sky was beautiful and peaceful, with no violence in the heavens that night. I thought about what happened, as I lost myself in the splendor of the stars. I said a prayer and thanked God for once again delivering the enemy to us and every one of us home. There was something about the stars that gave me peace. Their warmth melts everything away.

-Tim Trask
1/75

CHAPTER EIGHT

"Let your plans be dark and impenetrable as night,

and when you move, fall like a thunderbolt. "

SUN TZU

2008 was a year of transition for the war in Iraq. On November 17, the Iraqi Parliament ratified the Status of Forces Agreement (SOFA) which fundamentally changed the relationship between Iraq and the United States. President Bush and Prime Minister Maliki signed the agreement on December 14, 2008 with an effective date of January 1, 2009. The SOFA dictated military commanders would continue to move U.S. combat forces out of major populated areas, with the movement complete by June 30, 2009. The agreement also stipulated all U.S. forces would withdraw from Iraq by December 31, 2011. The United States would, however, continue to fight Al Qaeda and other terrorist organizations in Iraq as needed.

The 75th Ranger Regiment also modified its structure with the addition of a fourth rifle company to each of the three line battalions, in concert with the expansion of all Army special operation units. The addition of "Delta Company" brought an additional 118 Rangers to each battalion, which then underwent a lengthy training and validation process much more rigorous than the typical Ranger training cycle. Each of the three rifle battalions took experienced Ranger NCOs from the original three line companies to form the core of the new leadership, which were then augmented with brand new Rangers to train for the upcoming combat deployment.

The addition of the extra rifle company completed what was a four-year Regimental transformation. The 75th Ranger Regiment was now fully staffed and trained for what would be very challenging years ahead. The Regiment was unfortunately not without loss in 2008; Sergeant First Class David McDowell, Specialist Christopher Gathercole, Specialist Thomas Duncan III and Sergeant William Rudd all made the ultimate sacrifice.

NOVEMBER 2008

"IRAQ"

If there was anything I remembered from my first deployment to Iraq in 2008, it would be the buildings we scaled. It didn't matter if they were two, three or four stories high; we were getting to the top. Most of the time the ladder didn't reach the roof. We would climb to the very top of the ladder, lean up against the wall and then reach up to grab a buddy's hand. In my case, I had to jump up to grab his hand, ensure that I had a strong grip and pull myself up. I had to do this in all my equipment, increasing my weight to roughly 240 pounds. We would even lay the ladder down as a bridge between buildings and cross from rooftop to rooftop. There were instances where there were no ladders, so we would just jump to the next roof. I remember looking down from four stories high atop a building, thinking, *this sucks*. Yet I still loved my profession. What other job in the world allows me to visit another country, climb buildings and kill or capture the worst kind of men?

One of the other things about Iraq that lingers was clearing rooms and buildings. By the end of my 2008 deployment I was a close-quarters combat expert. One particular mission I remember well. Our platoon was sent to hit a huge mansion, home to a high-level Al Qaeda accountant. The plan was for two squads to breach and clear; 1st Squad had the first floor and 2nd Squad (mine) had the second. The remaining squad, 3rd, climbed buildings to pull over watch for us. As soon as the last rays of sunset were gone and the shivering cold of Iraq in November kicked in, my platoon stepped into the Strykers and rolled out toward the target building. Sitting in the Stryker, our squad leader briefed us again on the mission, ensuring we knew every detail for the night. Not a second after he was done briefing, my team leader would also verify that I knew every step. I would respond back by telling him every detail of the mission in a practice known as *back-briefing*. Our squad leader then said, "Five km away." I racked a round in my rifle, turned on my NODs and waited in silence for the Stryker to stop. When we were two kilometers out, the Stryker came to a halt and dropped ramp. Like a hive of killer bees, we moved out toward our objective with purpose. You'd think the people of Iraq would hear the millions of street dogs barking and howling at us, but not once did any of the local inhabitants check outside. Upon reaching the target building, 3rd Squad began to climb to the roofs to pull security on the target building and surrounding buildings. We were ready to climb over the wall too. Sergeant Pape, after studying it, said, "I'm pretty sure we can get that gate open," so our squad leader said to give it a shot. My buddy gave him a tool to pry open the gate and ever so quietly the gate slowly moved open. Sergeant Pape looked at me and said quietly, "I don't feel like climbing fucking buildings today."

I feel the same way.

Once the gate was open, I could see a huge mansion with a giant courtyard with a swimming pool. This was the first time I had seen a pool in Iraq. Not long after the gate was opened, 1st Squad showed up and moved toward the breach point to inspect the door. Before taking out the explosives, they checked to ensure that the door was not locked...no need to use explosive if you can perform a silent breach. What luck, the door was unlocked. Over the radio, "Door is unlocked, 1st Squad preparing to breach," was passed.

1st Squad stacked up and slowly opened the door into the unknown. As soon as they moved in, their flashlights lit up the first room. My squad went next, looking for the stairs to the second floor. As we entered the room, guys from 1st Squad were already detaining two male suspects. We flowed through the room into the main part of the building, where the stairs were easy to find. Like wolves, we moved quickly, looking for prey to attack. One Ranger is dangerous, but if we're in a pack, you best start running. Once we cleared the stairs to the second floor, Alpha Team moved toward one end of the hallway and Bravo Team (my team) moved toward the other end. We came upon a room and I entered it, simultaneously raising my weapon. We moved swiftly, clearing the room with our flashlights…and found it completely empty.

We then moved toward an open door that led to a second room. Flowing through the room, I realized we were so quiet yet so fast. It was surreal, like something you only see in the movies. But there I was, doing it and it was very real. As we moved through the second room there was nothing but emptiness. We cleared toward the closet, full of expensive-looking clothing; before we moved out, something caught my eye. I looked at the bed and told my team leader, "There looks like there is something underneath the blanket." I moved to the opposite end of the bed and with my left (non-shooting) hand I removed the blanket violently, revealing a shocked, frightened couple looking into the barrel of my rifle. I quickly brought my left index finger to my mouth and whispered, "Shhhh." Nodding their heads, they did not move and remained quiet. My team leader told me to watch them as he helped everyone else clear the building. "Roger, Sergeant." I moved toward the male suspect, taking him off the bed and zip-tying him. I quietly said in Arabic, "Don't move, or else I'll shoot," he obliged and responded in English, "I won't move a muscle."

The mission was a huge success. We caught the accountant, found a ridiculous amount of money, some weapons, and valuable information leading to other Al Qaeda members. Once again, we landed another huge blow to the Al Qaeda network. I recall not long after this mission our hulking, super powerful yet very intelligent Weapons Squad leader approached me. He asked me, "Norcross! Do you plan on scalping anyone on this deployment?" Half-joking and half-serious I responded, "I plan on doing just that, Sergeant." With a huge smile on his face he said, "Well when you do, make sure I'm there. I want to learn the proper way to scalp someone." I laughed. "You can count on me."

I don't think he knew at the time that I was being honest. Before I left home, I had a ceremony performed on me called the *Protection Way*. During the ceremony, the medicine man told me to bring back the scalp of the enemy, so that when I'm out of the Army, another ceremony can be conducted with the scalp of the enemy, as is tradition. I come from a long line of warriors dating back to the days when Spain controlled Arizona and New Mexico. Since then my family has served in every one of America's conflicts. I'm glad to say I fought with a group of warriors of this caliber. It was a fulfilling experience to be a part of history and to have served with 75th Ranger Regiment. I never scalped anyone of course, but I will never forget those times, or the friends I made. Nor will I ever forget our fallen comrades. One for the Airborne Ranger in the Sky!

-LEOPOLD
1/75

NOVEMBER 2008
"AL QAIM"

We were about halfway through our deployment to Balad, Iraq and many changes were in the works. The SOFA had been signed and would be taking effect at the beginning of the new year and the presidential election had recently wrapped up. The military's focus was shifting from Iraq to Afghanistan, leaving fewer Rangers to take on the workload still existing in Iraq. This had our platoon gainfully employed, flying all over the country on a nightly basis.

It was the night of November 28 and it was beginning to look like we would have a night off. Usually, if we didn't have a mission by about seven in the evening, chances were we wouldn't be going out at all. That night was a little different though, as the number one HVT in Iraq at the time came up on our radar. He was the leader of the Islamic State of Iraq (ISI), which was an Al Qaeda front organization. This was one bad dude. Intelligence reported that he and many other HVTs would be meeting at a wealthy Iraqi's house in Al Qaim, just east of the Syrian border, which prompted our mission.

Since this mission came down so late, a lot more effort had to go into planning, especially since the target was a three-hour flight away. The decision was made that our platoon would fly out in three MH-60 Black Hawk helicopters. Since we wouldn't have time to walk in, we would be landing right on the X. The target building was rather large. One squad would land to the front of the building just outside the courtyard walls, one squad (primary assault) would land right on the roof of the building and the squad I was with would land to the rear of the building. This was a pretty big fish, and he reportedly always traveled with a well-armed security detail. We should expect a gunfight.

It was almost December and as we stood on the flight line in Balad it became very clear to all of us that it would be a chilly ride out there. The birds started to spin up and before long we were boarding the black special operations helicopters for the long journey west. Generally, the helicopters we take to work have the doors removed so we can get off the bird faster, and also so we can fit more people in by having guys ride with their legs dangling out. In the wintertime it is typically too cold to fly without doors, but unfortunately for us the helicopter crews had not put them back on yet. This made for one of the most miserable flights of my life. On the three-hour flight, because of my position in the aircraft, I had the cold wind blowing directly into me. My hands were numb, I couldn't move my legs and my numbed face had snot frozen all over the right side of it. I must have looked like a mess!

By the time we reached the refueling point, the last (and only) stop on the way to the target building, I was absolutely hating life. Despite the miserable flight, I was still excited to be on this mission; excited we got the chance to go after public enemy number one in Iraq. This mission was Ranger bread and butter; land on a HVT's house in the middle of the night to capture or—if he so chooses—kill him. Nowhere else in the military will you simultaneously love and hate your job as much as you do on any given day in a Ranger Battalion.

After the brief stop to top off the gas tank, we were back in the air with just a short trip to the target building. I had checked and re-checked everything I carried, making sure I was ready for what would inevitably be a shootout when we landed. Before I knew it, the *60 seconds* call came and we had the lights of Al Qaim flashing by below us. My adrenaline began to pump ferociously and I prematurely located and grabbed onto the D-ring on the end of my safety line. You don't want to be frantically trying to un-hook when the bird is landing on the *X* like we were tonight.

My right hand on the pistol grip of my rifle and my left on the D-ring, the *thirty-second* call rang out. *Here we go*--teeth grinding in anticipation. The bird began to flare and descend and the brownout that ensued was one of the worst I had ever seen. Suddenly and without warning, the helicopter jerked violently back up in the air just before landing. *Fuck, we must be taking fire!* Maybe an RPG was shot at us? We were warned to expect them during the mission briefing. Shit just got real. *Please Lord, just let us get off this bird so we can fight!*

Just as soon as we jerked back up in the air, we were coming down again what would be a block further away from the target building. I still had my left hand on the D-ring and as I felt the helicopter jolt from landing, I pressed the gate of the D-ring open, releasing it from the floor. I shoved it in my left pocket and simultaneously jumped off the aircraft. Without missing a beat, we were in a dead sprint toward the target building, trying to cover the extra block we lost as fast as possible. I still didn't know what caused our sudden relocation and was surprised we weren't already in contact. As we were running, I saw the squad on main assault already on the roof, helicopter lifting off. We made it to the courtyard wall surrounding the target building, spreading out to pull security for the squad on the front of the building, the ones conducting the callout.

I didn't hear any gunfire and as I scanned I noticed low-hanging electrical wires crisscrossing the area our helicopter was originally supposed to land.

Maybe that was why the pilots decided to reposition? No matter now, we were here. It was only a few minutes before the call out was complete and the *building secure* call came over the radio. One of my jobs within the platoon was to conduct sensitive site exploitation (SSE), specifically focusing on electronics, so I moved to the main entrance and entered the target building, ready for the task.

The house was impressive in both size and design; you could tell that it was no normal citizen who lived here. I had a fear that our guy wasn't here, based on the lack of a firefight and my suspicions were confirmed after all the detainees were searched and the radio call came that he had left the target building at some point during our three-hour flight out. After my portion of the SSE was completed, I went down to the prayer room to take over watching the women and children that were in there. That's where I became both pissed off and intrigued.

Generally, when you land on top of someone's roof in the middle of the night and ransack their house, they aren't too pleased with you. That wasn't the case with the residents of this Iraqi mansion though. As I silently stood watch over the assortment of females which consisted of small children, teenage girls and adults, they were giggling and in a generally good mood. I told them to *shut up* in Arabic and one of the teenage girls had the gall to respond, in perfect English mind you, with "Do you know who my father is? You will not be here long." To say that I was shocked would be an understatement. I kept my thoughts to myself. Little girl, do you know who the fuck we are?

I feeling of surprise and anger quickly dissolved as I realized that she spoke English and had an quite an ego. This created a prime opportunity to exploit her for intelligence on the whereabouts of our target and his men. Excited at the possibility of contributing to the mission, my demeanor switched to the smiling, cheerful South Dakotan who just happened to have found himself in their house tonight. I began to make small talk, asking them how old they were, if they went to school and how long have they been speaking English. They started chatting as if I was their long-lost friend, asking me if I had ever been to New York and what were cowboys like in real life. Before long I transitioned into asking them about their guests earlier in the night. This is when one of the adult females jumped into the conversation, rather defensively but still cheerful and said, "My husband had guests but they were not here long." I asked her who they were and what they talked about while they were visiting. She replied, explaining that when they are over the women are not allowed in the room because they were discussing *men's business.*

I prodded a bit more, finding out that whatever it was that they were discussing, the people doing the talking were important and did not come around often. Well, I am no detective but that seemed to me to indicate that the guy we were looking for was in fact here just hours before. Maybe he and his entourage were still nearby? Because of how late in the night the mission took place, the sun now crested the Iraqi horizon. The call was made that we were going to set up shop inside the target building for the day to action possible follow-on targets.

A squad was sent in the early morning to go hit a much smaller house containing a person of interest about a block away, with a few of us providing over watch from the roof of the mansion. I manned one of our platoon's sniper's rifle on the roof, rotating the crosshairs of the scope through every male in the area, just wishing for one of them to produce a weapon and give me a reason to squeeze the trigger. Kind of sadistic in retrospect, but it was a product of the mindset required to succeed in a war zone. The daylight raid went off without a hitch and a few males who were of interest to us were brought back to the mansion. While the platoon leadership started to figure out possible courses of action in light of the new detainees, the rest of us set up a rotation for security and rest.

We weren't prepared to stay very long on this target and by noon most of us were hungry and running low on water. We had already made a courtesy call to the battle space owner (BSO), a US Marine unit, before we departed Balad to let them know we were doing a hit in their backyard. We ended up having one of their commanders come over early in the morning to aid in talking to the detainees since he already knew most of them from the Iraqi version of a town hall meeting that he routinely conducted. Our platoon sergeant talked to him about our food/water situation and the Marine made a call back to their FOB to run some MREs and water over. Man, it was nice to see them roll up! The food and water was sorely needed by the time they arrived late afternoon and I thought to myself that the Marines were now even in my book; my few encounters with them earlier in the deployment were not as pleasant.

Now, remember that the women that resided in the mansion were perfectly comfortable with us being there and had even made tea for us. Because of their ego about their wealth and family prominence in western Iraq they didn't actually think we would take anyone. Well, after we finally arranged transportation to come pick us up (the 160th SOAR birds that dropped us off were no longer available), we had to round up and zip-tie the two guys we were taking with us for further questioning. The women absolutely lost their shit. They were screaming, yelling and just generally pissed off that we had the audacity (in their eyes) to take the men back with us. I found this very satisfying, personally.

We moved to an open field across the street to await the Marine helicopters that agreed to extract us. This was my third deployment to Iraq and I had never seen an actual camel before. Well, this mission finally allowed me to check that box, as there was a herd just off our designated HLZ. Finally, the Marine CH-53 Sea Stallions flew in and made a few racetracks before descending to land. Ready to get the hell out of that town, we sprinted aboard and immediately sat down, exhausted but relieved to be on our way out. Once we were in flight, a rather funny situation arose between one of our snipers and the Marine crew chief.

The chief wanted all rifles pointed down, with muzzles resting on the vibrating deck of the aircraft. Well, that was easy enough for the rest of us, as the optics on our rifles were rather durable. But the sniper previously mentioned was not about to do that, and potentially messing up the *zero* of his precision rifle or damage the suppressor on it. If you can think of what it's like when a parent is cruising down the interstate while a child in the back seat is misbehaving, this situation was very similar. I couldn't quite hear everything, but it basically amounted to: *You better knock it off! Don't make me pull this helicopter over!* The matter was only exacerbated by the sniper's very smug *fuck you* grin while he declined to follow the instructions given. Before the situation got out of hand, one of the squad leaders stood up and calmly explained to the Marine why the sniper had to keep his rifle pointed up and reassured him that everything would be fine. Needless to say, I don't think that Marine crew chief was sad to see us get off his bird!

We ended up taking a short flight back to Al Asad Air Base where we switched over to a C-130 for a ride to BIAP and eventually back to Balad. This, I thought to myself, was much more comfortable than the ride out here last night! Within minutes of boarding the plane the entire platoon passed out, asleep for the duration of the flight.

We didn't get the bad guy that night, but he could only run for so long. I was proud to find out that the information I gained during my SSE led our sister platoon to spin up for a follow-on target, which in turn led to the capture of our target's close associate. It was a win for the good guys.

Staff Sergeant Anthony "Cookie" Davis was killed in action in Iraq during that deployment. It was in the following training cycle that we held the memorial service, the first for many of us, as 1/75 had not had a Ranger killed in action since March 4, 2002. The battalion Command Sergeant Major bellowed out SSG Davis's name during the *final roll call* and standing among brothers in that formation of Rangers, it was all we could do to keep our composure. Hearing our CSM call out the name of the fallen as if they were still standing in our ranks is one of the most soul stirring things you can experience. We are brought up as young boys being told, *men don't cry* and the tempered steel that is a Ranger is as stone-faced as they come even in the direst of situations. But standing in that formation you could hear some sniffles. The emotion in the air was as palpable as the Georgia humidity. We recited the Ranger Creed and prior to that day, I had never heard the Creed recited with such fervor. They were the same words we'd recited hundreds of times before, but the feelings which accompanied them were much different this time. That day I came face to face with a set of emotions I had not yet experienced. I looked at the family sitting in the front row of the crowd, mourning their fallen Ranger. I couldn't help but picture my own parents or my fiancé sitting in their place. Realizing your own mortality at such a young age is a very powerful experience. Combat doesn't necessarily make you think about it, as you are very much in the moment as it is happening. It's not until later when you feel the tidal wave of a thousand men's hearts breaking in

223

one formation…mortality becomes very real. We do, in fact, die. We don't live forever. When we go, people will mourn. Our loved ones will feel immense hurt. In a Ranger's line of work, that may happen sooner rather than later. *Sacrifice* is not a word to be used flippantly. Facing those feelings, accepting them and deciding how you want to live your life in light of this reality is very powerful indeed. It ages you beyond your years. I have attended many memorial services since then, but that first one will stay with me forever. It will impact who I am as a man, a husband, a father and a human for the remainder of my days.

-MARTY
1/75

"A RANGER WIFE'S PERSPECTIVE"

I will never forget overhearing a young wife tell my friend that her husband was amongst those killed during a mass casualty incident in our husbands' unit. This newlywed's life had just been turned upside down; every wife's darkest nightmare. We had been notified a few hours before, yet it hadn't fully sunk in. We typically weren't told the names of the fallen at the time of general notification; we were always left oblivious initially. To put a face and name to the notification makes your stomach sink. It is too close to home. Though you always know it is a possibility, it doesn't ease the pain.

We were reminded of the possibility of loss every year when we filled out the pre-deployment information. We almost became numb to the idea of pre-planning our husbands' funerals and simply went through the motions. Then it happens and you are thankful you did write those plans down beforehand. I went home that night and bawled my eyes out. I felt relieved it wasn't my husband and guilty for my relief at same time. I woke up the next morning and all I wanted to do was talk to my husband. I wanted to hear his voice and know he was ok. That was not an option, but I decided I would not go to work that day; I was liable to hit the next person who told me a "…four-month deployment wasn't bad at all." I needed to be with people who could empathize with the situation.

My phone already had a few messages from other wives formulating a plan to meet. We gathered at the house of one of my friends and drank coffee, trying not to replay what we had just learned. Soon, more wives started to show up, all bringing food and wine. We needed this. We needed to be together. We did what we do best: we supported each other. We spent the day laughing, crying and alternating drinks between coffee and wine. We were working through the emotions the best way we knew how. Sometimes the room fell silent and that was ok, as we knew we were reflecting and digesting the horrible event in our own minds.

The next few weeks seemed like a blur. We spent the time caring for each other, aiding families of the fallen and trying to keep a positive attitude, knowing we were only halfway through the deployment. During this time, I relied heavily on my fellow Ranger wives. They understood me in a way that my other friends and family could not.

Homecoming finally came, but it was bittersweet. It was the first time they had been home for Christmas in three years. I remember hugging my husband so tight, my stomach filled with the usual butterflies, and then remembering that not everyone was coming home. Usually we spend the first night alone but this homecoming was different. Some Rangers were hosting a welcome home party and my husband was insistent on going. I didn't argue either because I knew it was important for them to be together and blow off some steam from the difficult deployment.

After all the Rangers were home from leave they had the memorial for the fallen. My husband had spent hours the previous day shining his boots and ensuring his Class A uniform was perfect out of respect for his fallen brethren. The ceremony too was perfect. When the Rangers rose and shouted the Ranger Creed, it was unforgettable. My heart filled with pride. I realized these deaths were not in vain but for their brothers to their right and left. Any one of these great men would have been willing to make the ultimate sacrifice. I was amongst so many great warriors and heroes. Never did the Ranger Creed give me so much peace as it did that day. TSAF, RLTW!

- HILLARY

3/75 RANGER WIFE

CHAPTER NINE

"Lest I keep my complacent way I must remember somewhere out there a person died for me today. As long as there must be war, I ask and I must answer – was I worth dying for?"

ELEANOR ROOSEVELT

The new status of forces agreement (SOFA) took effect on January 1, 2009 and fundamentally changed the way Rangers conducted operations in Iraq. It was now mandatory to get permission from an Iraqi judge to hit a target, which severely slowed the pace of operations. This marked the beginning of the end of the war in Iraq, as well as the beginning of the transition to Afghanistan being the main effort. General McChrystal took over as commander of all operations in Afghanistan, which brought changes to the way the counter-insurgency effort was approached, as well as the rules of engagement in combat operations.

Rangers saw changes to their uniforms and equipment come once again. They continued to wear the ACU uniform for formations and when in garrison, but for training and deployments they adopted the Crye Precision Multi-Cam camouflage pattern, which was a significant improvement welcomed by all.

The new uniform boasted built-in knee and elbow pads as well as specially designed field tops for the summer months. Rangers also expanded the selection of boots they wore to include a variety of civilian hiking boots, wearing whatever worked best for the individual Ranger and the environment in which they were operating. Rangers tested the new FN Special Operations Combat Assault Rifle (SCAR) suite of weapons, with C Co. 1/75 being the first of any unit to deploy to combat and kill the enemy with them. The individual Ranger was now better equipped than at any other point in the unit's history; every Ranger had his own customized rifle, his own sidearm, his own radio and the best night vision devices available. This allowed highly-trained Rangers to maximize their already elite level of shooting, moving and communicating on the field of battle.

At this point in the war, Rangers had embarked on over 8,000 operations, in the most austere environments and places in Afghanistan, which had never before seen American boots. RRC Team One conducted another combat military free-fall parachute jump, this time with a tandem passenger, in Afghanistan on July 11, 2009 to emplace tactical equipment. The Haqqani Network became a principle focus of Ranger operations, along with Taliban leadership and the Al Qaeda operatives that were still in the country. Combat operations did not leave the Regiment unscathed; Staff Sergeant Anthony Davis, Corporal Ryan McGhee, Corporal Benjamin Kopp, Private First Class Eric Hario, Staff Sergeant Jason Dahlke and Sergeant Roberto Sanchez all made the ultimate sacrifice. SSG Davis was the first Ranger from 1/75 to be killed in action in almost seven years and was the only 1/75 Ranger killed in Iraq.

JULY 2009

"ON KILLING"

His mouth was open, lazily. Eyes wide and bloodshot, brown and sunken deep from exhaustion or stress, or both. His hair was long, black, matted down with sand and dirt. The night had taken a toll on him. His skin was dark brown, youthful. A razor never touched his face, yet he had no facial hair. He wore what resembled black pajamas, as dirty as his hair and face. He crouched under a tree branch. He held his AK-47 by his knees as he crouched, his grubby hands loosely grasping the foregrip and pistol grip. It was pointed toward the ground and away from us. He was unprepared and more than likely poorly trained, if he was ever trained at all.

We made eye contact and he didn't move. He just stared, mouth open and eyes wide as if in awe, as if the shock of the situation alone paralyzed him. The same moment he crouched under the tree branch to look up at us, I was pointing downhill in his direction, telling my team leader I'd heard something. A few seconds passed, a seeming eternity, where nothing changed. He remained crouched, I remained pointing and we did not break eye contact. I was shocked that someone—anyone—could get so close. On top of that, he was armed. He was one of the men we were sent to this innominate valley to hunt this morning. But he was outgunned and exposed. He knew it and his body language showed. In this moment that we shared frozen still, I could have understood if he chose to speak. But he didn't. He didn't choose to run and he didn't choose to fight. He just stared at me staring at him, pointing.

Maybe several seconds passed like this, or perhaps none at all. I drew my left hand back to the foregrip of my rifle while pulling the buttstock into my right shoulder by the pistol grip. With my thumb I flicked the safety selector switch from safe to semi-automatic, yet he remained frozen. I squeezed the trigger. The crack of a round leaving my barrel was answered by a puff of dust off his black shirt. The red reticle of my optic blurred as I loosed 13 more rounds. He remained still. The red laser from my team leader's weapon bounced on the man's chest as he acquired and engaged with an equal barrage. We broke trigger rapidly, if wildly, until at last the man fell to the ground, rolling unceremoniously behind a bush.

Cameron sat upon the wreckage of a log hut amidst the wreckage of a camp no one had heard of before and wouldn't likely hear of again. On a map of Afghanistan, I couldn't have pinpointed our location within a hundred miles without significant luck. They hadn't named the camp as far as we knew. It didn't matter much being that it was all broken logs and holes now.

You don't give names to broken logs and holes.

I took a seat beside him and watched as an Apache attack helicopter circled above like a caffeinated bird dog. Cameron leaned and spat, watching it thicken in the sand. In the movies they'd have us smoking cigarettes, helmets undone and cocked sideways whilst surveying the burning ruins of a terrorist camp. We just sat there though, thinking and saying nothing. Nothing burned. Just splintered logs and holes.

I held a rifle in each hand propped on their buttstocks. One was mine, the other belonged to a guy who was sprawled out a football field away, one arm underneath his body, another reaching toward nothing. Broken ribs protruded through his stomach and shirt. His face was flattened and distorted from the concussion of a hand grenade. When the last machine gun burst ripped through him, he bounced. We all thought...*huh*?

Turning my attention to his rifle I inspected the old wood and the rusted metal of the foregrip. Dark red blood clung to it and I wiped it on my pant leg. The wood had a shine to it now and I looked away, happy with that. I turned my attention back to the helicopter and waited.

"What happened?" Cameron asked.

I told him about the young man and how he found us and how he froze. There wasn't much to it. Certainly no heroism or gallantry and if there was, it was on the end of the one who sought us out in the first place. And now he lay in mud, made of sand mixed with his blood. It told not like a war story but as an explanation as to how I came into the ownership of this Chinese-made rifle.

We sat again in silence save for the chopping of rotors overhead. I thought of the man I shot and how long he would lie there, how his friends would carry him out. I imagined him slipping from their hands onto a hastily made litter, blood on their hands and the litter and the brown mess he left. What they would do, if anything, about his broken ribs and the holes in his gut? Where would they take him and how would they talk as they did?

"How far was he?" Cameron broke the silence and my train of thought.

"15 meters."

"Damn." He leaned again and spat quietly, aiming for the brown spatter his last had left. "That's a good kill, brother."

The families of 20 young men would soon be burying their sons and brothers. They would comfort each other with the promise that our actions would not go unpunished, as news station tickers read: *US troops kill 20 in overnight raid.*

-BRYAN

3/75

2009

"THE SWAN SONG"

In the summer of 2009, I was once again in Afghanistan and once again working with Rangers. This deployment was my fourth to Afghanistan and seventh overall. Although I hadn't been back for a while, there was still a familiar feel to the Task Force compound. The beat-up plywood B-huts were the same, the noise and the smell were the same and of course the operational tempo was still sky-high. There were a few new photos on the wall of the JOC and while there were a lot of new faces on the compound, the mission and the enemy hadn't changed much.

There had however, been some major cultural and organizational shifts in the Task Force since the last time I spent time in *The Stan.* For one thing, I immediately noticed that the Regiment had evolved enormously since the last time I was here. Having transitioned out of the *outer cordon and airfield seizure* box that people kept trying to put them into earlier in the GWOT, the Rangers were now responsible for the Task Force's *main effort* theater of operations. This was a huge increase in responsibility that reflected the Regiment's new role and the trust that the Task Force had in the Regiment's abilities.

My own responsibilities in support of the Task Force had increased as well. During this deployment, which was my last combat tour in support of what was now known as OCO, (Overseas Contingency Operations) I oversaw the exploitation side of the Task Force's overall intelligence effort. In this capacity, I had duties and responsibilities greater than anything I had experienced before. It was by far the best assignment of my career.

Something else that had changed since the GWoT started was the way the Task Force prosecuted targets. One of the unique things about the way we did business by this point was the focus on the *F3EA* targeting concept. The acronym stood for *Find, Fix, Finish, Exploit and Analyze.* This later became *F3EAD* (pronounced "feed"), with the *D* for *Disseminate.* F3EA/F3EAD was a very intel-centric targeting model, chiefly used for man hunting but transferable to other kinetic and non-kinetic operations. Focusing on F3EAD created a culture throughout the Task Force in which speed, trust, accuracy and teamwork were key components. The *'network to defeat a network'* aspect of F3EAD helped foster true fusion between operations and intelligence functions, which enabled the Task Force to create an operational tempo that worked faster than the enemy could react. It took a while for F3EAD to catch on within the Task Force, but long before I arrived back in Afghanistan in 2009, the concept had made believers of us all.

On my last deployment, the Ranger Task Force commander had something very close to a photographic memory. He regularly recalled specific details about operations or enemy personalities that were first discussed weeks or even months previously. While this was a great quality to have in a commander, many staff officers found it utterly terrifying. This was because the commander had such keen attention to detail, everyone had to step up their game. *Good enough* wasn't sufficient; everything had to be completely right. More than once I saw a staff officer or junior commander get flamed for lack of attention to detail. Consequently, we all had to keep up with not only what was happening now, but also what had happened in the past. This, of course, helped us better predict what was going to happen in the future, which was much more important.

As an intelligence officer, I appreciated that the very first thing this particular commander had all subordinate task forces talk to at the Overall Evening Briefings was exploitation. Specifically, *what information was acquired and how would it drive future targets?* Exploitation is, of course, mainly an intelligence function and sometimes a gap develops between operations and intelligence sides of an organization. But because intel was important to the Task Force commander, it was of utmost importance to all Ranger leaders. In fact, the way this particular commander ran the Ranger Regiment is a textbook case of how the operations and intelligence relationship is supposed to work: operations direct intel and intel drives operations. As a major contributor to the exploitation effort, I greatly appreciated his emphasis on exploitation functions.

The best part was, it worked. The commander, his operational planners and his highly competent J2 oversaw a Task Force enabling effort that hummed along, with intelligence leads that drove operations every night and sometimes multiple times in the same period of darkness. Exploitation became such a key component of the Task Force operations that it was emphasized as the most important aspect of the entire F3EAD process and exploitation operations were cited as the *center of gravity* in support of the Task Force mission.

Part of exploitation intelligence or what became known as *EX-INT* included the handling of captured personnel. Several years prior to this deployment, this particular commander had been wounded badly in Iraq by an insurgent who had been released just days before. So, he always took a personal interest in ensuring that the right detainees went to the *'big house'* and the detainees who weren't a threat got released. Sometimes there was disagreement over releases and the commander once loudly and enthusiastically informed me that I was becoming a *Taliban enabler* and the Task Force lawyer a *Taliban facilitator* for pushing for the rapid release of detainees with no intelligence value. He meant it as a joke, of course; in the end, the commander always sided with our recommendations and we provided legal justification to put the worst of the unlawful enemy combatants into long-term lockup while returning the others to their homes as soon as possible, with a little money in their pockets for their troubles.

During this deployment, I ran the Task Force's intelligence exploitation facility and we never knew what might come in through the doors of our facility. Whether it was people or *stuff,* it was enough to ensure there was never a dull moment. Due to the sensitivity of exploitation operations, I was given complete latitude in hiring and firing. Military or civilian, permanent party or augmentee, I could turn down anyone I didn't find suitable and could shit-can anyone I felt wasn't making the grade. We were even permitted to have our own internal screening and training process. One day a new arrival reported to the facility. This arrival was expected, because an element in Iraq shut down and the excess personnel flowed in to augment Afghanistan operations. As was usual practice, my NCOIC brought the new arrival up to my office for an initial interview. What was unusual was that my senior analyst, a civilian who was prior-service Navy, followed the new arrival into the office that my NCOIC and I shared. Not only that, but he brought some of the other analysts in with him.

The reason this was unusual was because our senior analyst, a man I admired enormously and who was critical to the facility's success, usually couldn't be bothered with *officer business* and normally didn't concern himself too much with the initial arrival of new officers, especially very junior officers like the spanking-new ensign that was now standing at parade rest in my office. Why were he and a handful of the more senior folks in the facility standing there with those grins on their faces? Then it hit me. The new arrival, an augmentee, was wearing a *Secret Squirrel* patch.

I don't mean a patch from a classified unit. I mean a circle patch with a squirrel in the middle, above which rested a *SECRET* tab. Now in our Task Force, virtually no one wore unit patches of any type. This was surely the case with enablers that didn't leave the FOB, especially ones who were augmentees. No one in my facility and as far as I can recall, no one who worked on the Task Force's main base area wore any type of patch on the sleeves of our ACUs other than a US flag, but here was this female Navy ensign, who thought it would be OK to wear an unauthorized and, quite frankly, stupid patch all the way from Iraq to my office in Afghanistan, calling all kinds of unnecessary attention to herself and our Task Force. That's why everyone was there in my office—they saw the new arrival and her unauthorized patch and having worked with me for a while knew that I was pretty hard on people who made poor decisions, especially officers. They were there to watch the fireworks.

But my anger at the new arrival immediately subsided. Yes, I was mad at her because she was wearing a stupid, attention-grabbing patch as a member of a Task Force that valued secrecy and discretion. As a fellow intel officer, she was a member of a career field in which credibility is everything. Additionally, I was quite mad she made it all the way from Iraq to my office in Afghanistan and without any officers or NCOs jacking her up and telling her to get her stuff straight. To me, that was a MUCH bigger problem. I excused everyone except the ensign and my NCOIC from the office. My senior analyst and his entourage slunk away, disappointed they weren't going to get to see what they thought was going to be an epic ass-chewing. But there was no ass-chewing, not this time. I simply explained to the ensign that she could go ahead and take that patch off, as in *right freakin' now*, because she wasn't going to need it while she was part of the Task Force and then I sent her on her way. We ended up deciding she wasn't suitable to work in the facility, and a couple of days later when I informed her we were sending her to work elsewhere on the compound, I explained to her why her first impression on her new boss (me) went so horribly wrong. She ended up doing her time in the Task Force in a different support role and I heard she ultimately ended up working out OK. But she missed the opportunity to work in the most dynamic, challenging and satisfying intel function in the Task Force because of a dumb, *hey, look at m*e move.

Most of the people who worked for me were augmentees. My XO was a tall Marine Major who chain-smoked, which was an uncommon habit for officers. He worked out extremely well and we remained friends after the deployment. There was another Marine officer who worked for me, a young captain who had been some kind of mixed martial arts expert in the Corps. He was quite boisterous and popular within the facility and it was not uncommon from time to time to hear shouting and loud laughing coming from the office he shared with three or four other people. One day, the plywood wall that separated my office from his started to shake slightly and I heard the guys next door talking loudly. I had my headphones on and was trying to watch a VTC and I was greatly annoyed with what I thought was another impromptu MMA match in the office next door. It went on so long that I was on the verge of getting up to go yell at them to knock it off when the XO walked by and gave me a thumbs up, saying, "Dude! Earthquake!" That's when I realized that it wasn't just the one wall shaking, it was the whole facility. I laughed out loud as I experienced my first-ever earthquake.

A young Army First Lieutenant worked in the same office as the Marine captain. One day, I got an email from her, in which she expressed her undying love for me and suggested we run away together to some far-off tropical paradise. Or something. I don't remember exactly what it said because I stopped reading it after the first paragraph. Since I knew that her shift had ended and she had departed the facility about a half hour before the email was delivered, she couldn't have sent the message. Since I'd been in the unit for three years at that point, I knew immediately what happened: she had committed the cardinal sin of not locking her computer when she was away from her desk.

Leaving one's computer unlocked is a minor security violation, because it potentially allows unauthorized people to access your system. So, to help people be more security conscious, it was tradition that whenever an unsecure computer was discovered, an email went out from the offender's account. The content and the recipient of the email varied, but it was always something that would be sure to embarrass the person who owned the account.

In order to reinforce the teaching point, I replied to the message with, "1LT XXXX, report to my office first thing in the morning to explain this." I was at my desk when the lieutenant arrived and checked her email messages. Because I replied to the email that *"she"* sent the night before, she read the content of the original message. A short time later, she burst into my office, totally aghast. "Sir! I didn't send that message! I don't know what happened, but it wasn't me!" she began. I cut her off, "So, you're saying you don't want to run off with me?" "Um…no?" she replied, unsure how she should answer something like that. At that point I let her off the hook and told her what happened. Enormously relieved, she burst out laughing. After I dismissed her, I heard her yelling good-naturedly at her officemates for setting her up like that, but I bet she never left her computer unsecured again.

It wasn't all fun and games; we all worked our butts off at the facility. 16+ hour days were the norm, with no days off. But it was good work, meaningful work and no one complained. Our Task Force frequently captured hard drives, cell phones and other electronic devices. Sometimes those devices held material that we could use to produce intelligence to support

F3EAD, but more often, those devices contained things that were…less useful. I'd say about 2/3 of the digital media we captured contained pirated movies, propaganda videos…and porn. Lots of porn. The sheer volume and the types of pornography that were in the possession of the supposedly *pure* jihadists exposed one of the fundamental hypocrisies of their ideology: while they were supposedly fighting in part to preserve the honor of women and to resist Western decadence and corruption, they were quite happy to load themselves up with Western pornography. All the jihadists had porn. *EVERY ONE.* It was so widespread that when several years later I heard on the news that a treasure trove of digital media had been seized on the bin Laden raid, I remarked to my wife, "I guarantee that at least half of that is porn." It turned out I was right.

While the porn exposed our enemies' ideological hypocrisy, the propaganda videos revealed their true nature. Some of the propaganda included video footage of jihadists carrying out attacks against Coalition forces, but since most of these kinds of attacks tended not to end well for the insurgents, there weren't a whole lot of these videos. Many videos featured beheadings. I guess it was a lot easier for Taliban and foreign fighters to cut the head off a guy who had his hands tied behind his back than it was to win a firefight against ISAF forces. As Americans we have a hard time understanding that there really are genuinely evil people in the world; people who won't hesitate to saw the head off a guy while he's still alive and struggling, in front of his wife and kids and on film so the rest of the world can see it too. These kinds of people can't be reasoned with. There is no bargaining or room for negotiation. These kinds of people only understand violence and the only way to protect the rest of the world from them is to either kill them or lock them away forever in a place where they can't cause any harm.

After we finished exploiting captured enemy materiel, the usual practice was to take it to the engineers on base for destruction, but later we began sending useful content back to the US for use in training. I modified our briefing room to display weapons and other items that were unique or interesting. One day I happened to be walking by the materiel exploitation area of my facility when I heard some of my guys talking to some Rangers about a peculiar device that they had found on the objective of the mission they just conducted. It was clearly a piece of military equipment, but it was unlike anything we had seen before. "What is that?" I asked. "We don't know sir, we were hoping you could tell us!" a Ranger replied. My guys took a look but couldn't immediately determine what it was. When they were done I handled it too. Three things immediately jumped out at me: whatever this thing was, it was broken; the writing on the device, whatever it was, was Cyrillic, which meant it was Russian; and...it had the radiation warning symbol. "Um . . . since none of us know what this thing is and it's some kind of broken Russian radioactive device, maybe we should take this to a safe place OUTSIDE the facility until we figure it out?"

I didn't think the device was much of a threat; at least I hoped it wasn't. But given that we didn't know what it was, it was broken, and was supposedly radioactive; I thought it was prudent to have the device removed from the facility until we could figure it out. In the morning we had some of our tech experts take a look and after some research they determined it was a Russian artillery sight or compass (I don't remember exactly) and the radiation warning was due to the tritium to make it glow in the dark. Good news! We weren't going to get cancer, from that piece at least... But that prompted a new informal rule from us: *If it's radioactive, and you don't know what it is, blow it in place on the objective.* We offered it back to the Rangers after we established it wasn't a threat, but they told us to keep it and we put it in our display case.

We kept captured weapons on the wall as well. One of the most noticeable was a Russian-made AK-47. While AK-47s are quite common in Afghanistan, this one was unusual due to its age and its unusual decor. Its last owner, a member of the Afghan Taliban who perished during the mission in which it was captured, had decorated the weapon extensively. He began with an underlay of aluminum foil against the wooden stock and then wrapped all of wood, and the metal barrel, with narrow but thick translucent orange plastic tape. Under the tape on the pistol grip and buttstock, he put color pictures that looked like they were cut out of newspapers. I assumed they were pictures of parents and either a wife or girlfriend. Having one's weapon covered with aluminum foil and hunter-orange tape isn't very tactical, and given that the tape on the barrel hadn't melted, it seemed unlikely that the most recent owner gotten the chance to fire his weapon much, if at all. I wondered if his goal was to go down fighting the infidels. If so, the Rangers obliged him. I asked the Seabees to cut the receiver and fill the barrel with lead to de-militarize (de-mil) the weapon, and we put it on the wall of our conference room. It was usually the first thing that people noticed and commented on when they entered the room for briefings.

The Rangers also captured a guy who had in his possession a cleverly modified Pakistani starter pistol with the barrel block removed and home-made lead bullets added to the starter blanks, thus making into a crude but functional gun. The barrel was smoothbore and the bullets probably wouldn't travel very far, but it seemed like it would work. It looked like it was modified from starter pistol to actual pistol rather easily, and I remember wondering if this type of pistol was specifically made to allow it to be modified in this manner. We had numerous other weapons on the wall as well, but the one that I remember most was a PKM machine gun. It was unique because it had a 7.62 bullet hole in the feed tray cover from the firefight in which Rangers killed the guy firing it and captured the weapon. It was captured during what was arguably the most significant mission the Rangers carried out during my last deployment.

Rangers conducted hundreds of operations during my time in Afghanistan and I have forgotten the names and the details of most. One mission stands out though. While most Ranger missions I observed and supported were raids, this objective was more like a deliberate attack. From what I recall there was a terrorist training camp, complete with reinforced fighting positions and logistical support, in the mountains of the restive *P2K* (Paktika, Paktia and Khowst provinces) region of Afghanistan. After a great deal of planning and shaping operations, the area was pounded by air support and artillery, and Rangers went in, delivered to the cutting edge of battle by my old unit, the 160th SOAR.

I watched the fight from my usual position inside the JOC. It is almost surreal to watch a real-time battle unfold over a video feed. There is action; movement, flashes of light, a white flicker on the screen when a large explosion happens. But there is no sound, at least not from the video. Radios crackle, there are loud announcements, but there are no sounds of gunfire or explosions inside the JOC. It makes the battle seem less…real. There is also a great sense, at least for me, of utter powerlessness. We could all see what was unfolding, but were powerless to directly influence the fight. This was especially true of enablers like me, who don't have a role in coordinating and supporting the immediate fight.

Although the mission was a success, the Task Force ultimately suffered two Rangers killed and others badly wounded. A couple of days after the battle, we had a Task Force remembrance ceremony. In most units, people who feel like they have *more important things to do* blow off many *mandatory* events. But remembrance ceremonies weren't mandatory. They didn't need to be. During a remembrance ceremony, *everyone* turned out. The JOC emptied, people interrupted their sleep cycles, and planning and operations were temporarily put on hold. Only the people who absolutely could not be excused from duty (guards, radio operators, the extremely ill, etc.) remained at their posts. The remembrance ceremonies were extremely moving. They usually involved a motivating speech by the commander of the Task Force and a eulogy from a friend of the deceased. At the end, the Rangers, in unison, recited the Ranger Creed and we were dismissed to continue the mission. There were a lot of moist eyes in the ranks after the ceremony was over and it wasn't because of the dust. America lost two Rangers on that objective: SSG Dahlke, KIA on the objective and PFC Hario, who made it off the battlefield but later died of complications from his injuries. I don't know where that objective fell in the order of major battles for the Regiment, but to me it was most memorable battle of my time in Afghanistan by far.

In terms of deployments, 2009 was my swan song. It was the best and last of my seven tours in Iraq and Afghanistan, and I'm glad it was with the Rangers. The Ranger Regiment has come a long way in the short time I was with Special Operations and the Regiment has clearly come into its own and has adapted well to the changing SOF environment. I look forward to seeing the Regiment continue to shape its role in the defense of our nation and hope to one day have the chance to support the Rangers again.

- CHARLIE FAINT, LTC, USA
MI

August 2009

"A FIGHT IN THE MOUNTAINS"

The GWoT had been going on for eight years at this point. In the early years, we had a small presence in Afghanistan while in working mainly in Iraq. The draw down and retrograde of Iraq allowed us to push hard in Afghanistan. In August of 2009, the men of Alpha Company, 1st Battalion 75th Ranger Regiment, received news they would be surging ahead of the other companies for the upcoming deployment. I personally didn't know what to think, and had no idea what was to come. The time came and just like any deployment, we headed off to our pre-deployment tasks as we had done many times before. We received our shots, filled out family separation forms, ate our last meal in the States and boarded the flight just like any other rotation. But this rotation would prove to be different than any other. I have stories that will forever live with me, both good and bad. Here is how it started…

We arrived in Salerno, greeted by our brothers in 3/75. We were supporting them on this deployment. The camp was already packed and they set up two additional Alaskan Structure tents for living and three for our ready rooms. The two living tents housed the entire company to include our enablers. Without a doubt, it gave a new meaning to *nut to butt* as our cots were side-by-side with barely enough space to stand up between them to walk out of the tent. Our briefing room for targeting and daily instruction was crammed and poorly put together. Nothing was favorable and to be honest, it was so horrible all we could do is laugh about it. But it didn't stop the mission and we continued our morning updates, consisting of a lot of talk and no action. Countless times we were told *today or tomorrow* we would execute one of the targets we were watching. The only thing that seemed certain was we would eventually be assaulting a training camp in the Paktika Province. Days passed, and a few targets were executed, but we still hadn't hit this training camp. Morale dwindled every day.

Prior to one of the most mentally challenging days of my life, we built a detailed plan to action this training camp. It was about nine or ten kilometers up in the Sreh Petaw Sar Mountains in the East Paktika Province. History shows this area as some of the most dominating terrain through stories dating back to Alexander the Great, who, precisely due to the rugged terrain, failed at conquering what is now modern day Afghanistan. Every piece of imagery we viewed was a nightmare and every time a new set of eyes saw it, they too sighed. We had been watching the area for weeks at this point and had confirmed our High Value Target (HVT) was there.

We all heard rumors of what was there. We pored over tons of imagery of the area we planned to assault which showed enemy fighting positions. We watched aerial footage of the training camp where we saw fighting-aged males learning to move in tactical formations, shoot guns and so forth. We received briefing upon briefing of their activities and makeup, sometimes described as many as 350-400 terrorists. These men had come from Uzbekistan and other areas to the north to fight us. They set up training camps in the mountains because they didn't think they would be bothered there. The command planned a kinetic strike on the training camp prior to our infiltration. Sure, we've all heard of dropping a few bombs to soften the objective, but this was a request of over a 100,000 pounds of explosive ordnance prior to our infil. A request this large had to be approved by the President himself.

Time passed and finally on August 29, 2009, the warning order dropped and the request for a kinetic strike on the objective was approved. Key players headed to the Tactical Operations Center (TOC) and the rest of us sat outside to get back-briefs from our immediate leadership. After the initial brief was done, my sniper team leader came out and briefed me on the final details. At 1845 hours Zulu time, the pre-assault fires had the green light, allowing myself and others to watch it in the TOC as it went down. It was something I had never seen before and watching it on television I'm sure did it no justice. The fires included High Mobility Army Rocket Systems (HIMARS) from Bagram Airfield and Salerno and F-15, A-10 and B-1 aircraft.

Shortly after it started we suited up and headed to the flight line where

241

we boarded three helicopters. We planned our infil for as soon as we received confirmation that there had been no movement on the objective for thirty minutes and once 2nd Platoon was on the ground, the ships would return and pick up 3rd Platoon and infil them to support us.

As we approached our HLZ, we took contact. The helicopter gunners responded with a volley of mini-gun and M-240B fire while the pilots rotated to land. Because of the instant contact, the third ship was unable to land and departed the HLZ, holding at a safe distance. I sprinted off the help while looking north in the direction of the other bird. They had instantly taken contact as their bird was landing, but I wasn't sure all that was going on, as the radio net was heavy with traffic.

We had essentially landed smack dab in an L-shaped ambush. We returned fire with good fields of fire based off a best-guess forward line trace and assaulted through the enemy. The only things I could see at this point were tracers and strobes as I scanned my sectors for enemy personnel. After a short while the gunfire subsided and a cease-fire from our end of the HLZ was called.

I cannot account for what exactly happened on the other bird but one of the men monitoring the radio, Mack, stated:

"While I monitored, I could hear 2A was taking contact. *I* briefly struck my commander on the shoulder and brought his head close to me so *I* could inform him that 2A was taking contact and that they had two enemy killed in action and that we have one friendly wounded in action (WIA) with a gunshot wound to the neck. *I* will never forget the look he gave me. He immediately got on his MBITR radio to inform 3A leadership about what was going down on the HLZ. The commander had also been talking to the pilots on his headset to confirm what *I* had told him. As he was confirming, *I* heard the RTO on the ground report to the TOC that the friendly casualty was unconscious but stable."

We had heard the call for a medic over the radio and that someone was hurt but had no idea who it was. At this point, you have a feeling inside of you that's hard to describe. You're angry and sad and curious all at once; you sit there looking to your left and right into the blindness of the night or the greenness from your NODs without a clue of who might have been hurt. The mission must continue though, so we coordinated over our radios for the other element to consolidate on us with the casualty.

At this point, the group with our FWIA had begun to move toward my location. During their movement, the third bird that originally could not land was brought in to infil the remaining troops and MEDEVAC our wounded. They landed, the ramp dropped and a bunch of hard-charging barrel-chested freedom fighters ready to bring pain to those who hurt our own stormed onto the scene. Our FWIA and the medic treating him loaded on the same aircraft as calls were being made about two enemy fighters on the southern ridgeline. An AC-130 engaged both, resulting in two EKIA.

At 2226 Zulu, the ground force commander reported that there were seven confirmed EKIA in a wadi near HLZ Lloyd, along with one FKIA. I would later find out that one of the new Rangers, PFC Eric Hario, was instantly killed as he ran off the bird. This objective was his first mission.

We received reports of five enemy personnel maneuvering to the northwest of the objective so the ground force commander gave his approval to the JTAC to conduct a call for fire mission. The assets overhead eliminated the threat; five more EKIA. Shortly after, an enemy was spotted to the west and my sniper partner and I stepped up to engage. We both shot a few rounds and connected. They called in gun runs from an A-10 to ensure he was dead.

We had been on the HLZ for almost two hours in what seemed like constant contact. The ground force began clearing through the southern portion of the HLZ, when a moment I'll never forget occurred. I was walking through the wadi with the 2nd or 3rd Squad in the order of movement. I stood about ten to fifteen feet to the back left of the man to my right. It was pitch black and at the time, I didn't know or care who I was next to. Slowly taking one step after the other, over difficult terrain with tons of boulders, we continued to clear through checking our every step. Then, out of nowhere, a burst of enemy rounds came our way. Instantly someone dropped while the remaining Rangers returned fire.

The aggression and rate of fire was insane. Rounds were ricocheting in every direction. It seemed as if the rifleman went through an entire magazine and the SAW gunner an entire drum. As they suppressed the enemy, I arrived at the wounded's side and began to try to elicit a response out of him. I received nothing and soon had another Ranger buddy next to me to help rip off his body armor to examine him for wounds. I remember reaching down by his Kevlar helmet into a pool of blood, thinking he had been shot in the head, but couldn't find an entry or exit point. While we searched, our surgeon on the ground had reached us. We did what we could to help and then let the surgeon try. Nothing could be done. This all happened in a matter of seconds, but it's an event that would change many lives forever. This objective would be the last mission that Staff Sergeant Jason Dahlke would execute in his long and distinguished Ranger career.

We finished clearing through and called in for the 2nd Strike Force, which was 3rd Platoon. They infilled and we loaded our second *Angel* (FKIA) of the night on the bird and it left with our brother in arms at 2340 Zulu. We had now been on the HLZ for almost three hours and had not even begun our journey up the mountain to the main part of the training camp. The terrain was so difficult to maneuver they brought in Apache gunships to blow up the side of the mountain enough for us to climb it. After multiple runs we began our journey to the top. Enemy chatter confirmed they were consolidating and calling for reinforcements, which the gunships intercepted and killed.

This movement to the target would prove to be the most miserable and physically exhausting I'd ever done in my life. As we climbed the mountain, more like crawled, we took contact yet again. One of the squad leaders near me engaged an enemy hiding in a bush with a suicide vest and when shooting him, the vest partially detonated. He was about ten meters from the insurgent when a huge ball of flame erupted. I remember a couple of others helping me pull him out of the fireball. I thought his legs were gone. It was clear that shrapnel had gone in many different directions. We quickly realized he had both his legs, though they were peppered with countless pieces of shrapnel. Our medics and other first responders were already treating someone else for a sucking chest wound about 150 feet further up the mountain. A military working dog also had his nose partially blown off and they were both deemed urgent casualties.

At this point—it was obviously a serious moment but caught me as funny—I looked to my left I saw a half-naked man. He was half-naked because he was being searched for wounds, but regardless, I found it funny he was wearing nothing but his underwear in the middle of an all-out battle. Being 9000 feet up in the mountains after countless firefights, the last thing you expect is someone being treated in his whitey-tighties. At the same time they were passing his dog off to us below. We tried to clean off the dog's nose but he was too amped up. We couldn't really treat him and continued to pass him down to the men below us.

The moment that was once comical turned serious as I remember looking to my right to where my Ranger buddy stood. This man was really close to one of the men we had just lost, close like family. He looked at me and I at him. I saw the dirt and sweat streaks on his face and he said the simplest words, yet they held deep emotion. "When is enough, enough?" I replied, "No fucking shit..." It's hard to truly describe or make someone who wasn't there understand how we began to feel. We had finally realized two of our friends were killed. If it sounds simple, it's not.

We passed down the Ranger with a sucking chest wound and his dog with half his nose blown off to our brothers below. At our feet, we had the squad leader with shrapnel in his legs and tiny specks of blood all over his pants. The look on everyone's face was the same. We were covered in dirt and blood, with sweat streaks or tears (whatever you had the balls to admit at the time) running down our face. We were broken off from climbing hundreds of feet almost straight up. We hadn't even hit our halfway point and who knows what else was to come our way, as constant enemy chatter mentioned the enemy consolidating and preparing to attack us again.

The truth is, we all had negative thoughts and our spirits were broken and these were the strongest and most emotionally cut off people I'd ever known. After 3rd Platoon finished packaging the urgent casualties, they moved them to the HLZ where we originally landed to conduct the CASEVAC.

3rd Platoon had just finished doing post-assault operations and exploiting the HLZ while the CASEVAC element put our wounded dog handler and his dog on the bird. At this point, one of the assets observed scattered enemy personnel in the vicinity of a few tents and buildings about 500-800 meters away from us to the northeast. We called for fire, resulting in multiple JDAMs being dropped on the structures. Shortly after this, our CASEVAC element linked back up with us. The commander on the ground reported their findings, consisting of multiple AK-47s, fragmentation grenades, ammunition and chest racks. He then ordered the guys of 3rd Platoon to blow the items in place with our own demolitions. Shortly after that and prior to continuing up the mountain, we had to hold still because an asset in the air was dropping more bombs on three separate locations where enemy movement was spotted.

We dug deep physically and emotionally just to keep moving upward, and as we were about three-quarters of the way to the top, we found a place to take a rest. It was big enough to make a patrol base. We half-assed it for sure. Thankfully, we had Apache gunships covering our movement the entire time, because at this point, we all just flopped down on the ground. I remember walking through the middle of our group with my head down, morale at an all-time low. I was working my way through the patrol base to get to the highest point I could with my sniper partner and as we made it to the highest point in the patrol base, we heard random shouting from across the valley that was dividing the next mountain range and us. At this moment everything changed. The worn mental state and the physical exhaustion seemed to subside, and it was all because of one of the greatest shots ever made in Ranger Regimental history—at least many who were there think so.

The insurgent had to be a good 700-900 meters away and out of nowhere my sniper partner, standing upright, took one shot that dinged this guy right in the neck. I only know this because I saw it through my 18-power scope. The guy dropped instantly and his buddies had to try to recover his body at the crest of the mountain. I'm not sure why it happened (partner's gun may have malfunctioned or I just decided to get on it), but I began to engage the enemy using my partner's shoulder as my bipod. At this same time, two Mk-48 machine guns began to 'speak,' a term used to describe one gun shooting a burst and then being answered by the other gun shooting a burst, going back and forth until they finished firing. I'm not sure if we hit anyone else but no one crested that hill again and shortly after, our assets dropped Hellfires on the bodies lying at the top of the mountain. I think this moment kind of helped motivate everyone, because we eliminated the enemy without taking more casualties. That shot is something still talked about today by the Rangers on that objective.

After things settled down, we prepared to continue movement to the last section of our objective. It was now well into the day and we continued to climb. Finally, the assault force reached the summit and cleared through the objective. As we moved through to the end of the training camp, we secured multiple anti-aircraft weapons, bunkers, tents and other tactical equipment. After all this, the sun was beginning to set. We had finally reached the end of our mission. Our commander reported multiple EKIA, machine guns, AK-47s, ten or more chest racks and various other items which we could link to our intended high value target.

The enemy camp represented the highest point I had ever been, in terrain I had never seen before. We could see for miles in all directions from our patrol base while the sun gave off it's last light. We spread out but stayed close enough to chat with a friend or two. We talked amongst each other about what had happened and what we missed back home, we laughed and then was silence for those we lost. The feeling in that moment was surreal and something different. Only the men that walked those mountains and lost those brothers will ever understand. Time passed and the sun set and shortly after, the Night Stalkers came in and took us home, where we'd reflect on the mission and losses we sustained for the next months and years to come.

On August 29, 2009, Alpha Company 1/75 and attachments lost two amazing men. This story is dedicated to them and their brothers on that mission. I gained friends and family that night and they will live on with me forever.

Staff Sergeant Jason Sean Dahlke, 29, was born Nov. 8, 1979, in Tampa, Florida. Jason was on his sixth deployment in support of the War on Terror, with three previous deployments to Iraq and two deployments to Afghanistan.

Jason enlisted in the U.S. Army from his hometown of Jacksonville, Florida in May 2004. He completed Infantry One Station Unit Training at Fort Benning, Georgia, before moving on to and graduating from the Basic Airborne Course. He continued to the Ranger Indoctrination Program, from which he successfully graduated in December 2004. He was assigned to Company A, 1st Battalion, 75th Ranger Regiment on June 1, 2005. He served there as a rifleman, grenadier, machine gunner, fire team leader, section leader and squad leader. He also served in the battalion recce platoon for one deployment as an advisor to local national forces. Jason returned to A Company as a squad leader in February 2009 and served in that position until his death.

He was the recipient of numerous awards and decorations to include the Ranger Tab, the Purple Heart, two Army Commendation Medals, Army Achievement Medal, Army Good Conduct Medal, National Defense Service Medal, Afghanistan Campaign Medal, Iraq Campaign Medal, GWoTism Service Medal, Army Service Ribbon, Overseas Service Ribbon, Combat Infantryman Badge, Expert Infantryman Badge and the Parachutist Badge. He was posthumously awarded the Bronze Star Medal, his second Purple Heart and the Meritorious Service Medal.

Private First Class Eric W. Hario, 19, was an infantryman assigned to 1st Battalion, 75th Ranger Regiment at Hunter Army Airfield, Georgia. He was born December 9, 1989, in Monroe, Michigan. Hario was wounded by enemy fire while conducting combat operations on August 29, 2009. He was medically evacuated to a combat support hospital where he died. He was on his first deployment in support of the War on Terror.

After graduating from Monroe High School where he lettered in football and wrestling, Eric enlisted in the U.S. Army in June 2008. He completed Infantry One Station Unit Training at Fort Benning, Georgia. After also graduating from the Basic Airborne Course, he was assigned to the Ranger Indoctrination Program, which he also successfully graduated. He was assigned to Company A, 1st Battalion, 75th Ranger Regiment in January 2009 where he served as a grenadier.

His awards and decorations include the National Defense Service Medal, GWoT Service Medal, Army Service Ribbon and the Parachutist Badge. He was posthumously awarded the Bronze Star Medal and Purple Heart.

- BORGE
1/75

Fall 2009
"DRINKING FROM THE FIRE HOSE"

I vividly remember the day that I passed RASP (Ranger Assessment and Selection Program), which was then called ROP (Ranger Orientation Program) and donned my tan beret. It was easily the proudest moment of my life. I couldn't have been more excited to begin my new job and I felt especially thankful for the people who had helped me achieve my ultimate goal as a young Army officer. I'm not sure about other branches of the Army, but for an infantry officer, being a Ranger is the most fast-paced, aggressive and competitive job you can have in the Army - and it was my turn to begin.

After I finally signed in to my battalion, the first person I met was a major on battalion staff, who (unfortunately) was known throughout the Ranger Regiment for crushing junior officers' souls and basically being a total asshole. His first words to me were something along the lines of, "Get the fuck in my office and shut up. I want you to know that whatever you have accomplished prior to today doesn't mean shit. You've got a chest full of medals and one deployment under your belt, but what have you done for the Ranger Regiment? You haven't done shit and I want you to remember that. An E-4 with a Ranger Tab and a couple of deployments has earned more respect than you."

Leaving his office that day I wondered, *What the hell have I gotten myself into?* It took me about a year before I realized that he was sincerely doing me a favor by knocking my ego down a few (or more) notches and humbling me because the responsibility placed upon a Ranger platoon leader is something that truly can't be explained in a chapter or two.

Fortunately, or perhaps unfortunately, one of the first major exercises I completed with the battalion was an airfield seizure. Without dragging out the details of what an airfield seizure consists of, needless to say, I was terrified. Standing in front of an entire task force while briefing your small part of the plan is nerve-racking in and of itself, not to mention the glare of hundreds of eyes of the entire (and more experienced) task force staring down and judging you. Leading up to the first rock drill (the detailed dress rehearsal of how the mission will go down), my first major concern was to understand the multi-level, multi-mission exercise and try not to get fired for incompetence. Luckily for me, the training event went smoothly and I made it through relatively unscathed—that is, if you don't count getting dragged across the tarmac and acquiring a serious bit of road rash.

The airfield seizure exercise, as intimidating as it was, was my first true experience of what makes the Ranger Regiment special - the world class NCOs at every level. I came to the Regiment from an exceptional conventional infantry unit and I felt that I had been exposed to top notch NCOs. But truly, nothing could prepare me for the quality of NCO that I was able to work with in my platoon in Ranger Regiment. Being dropped into a platoon was truly the *eye opening shock of my life.* I only had about 30 seconds to transition with the platoon leader I was replacing, which didn't quite set me up for success. Luckily, I had a highly proficient platoon sergeant with more than ten deployments under his belt and my company had some of the most experienced platoon leaders in the battalion.

Being a Ranger platoon leader is a completely different experience than being a conventional rifle platoon leader. Unlike a conventional rifle platoon leader where the PL maneuvers the squad and leads the platoon during combat, the responsibilities of a Ranger PL are much different. As a Ranger platoon leader, I was responsible for designing from scratch and planning my own training events with guidance from my commander, determining and requesting the resources my platoon would need, working through the massive bureaucracy within range control and executing the training.

Even the responsibilities *on target* for a Ranger PL are massively different than for a conventional PL, because the model of the *fighting platoon sergeant* was born, adopted, practiced and entrenched throughout the Regiment. The platoon sergeant, with his years of experience, moves squads, fire teams and Rangers around on target, while the platoon leader deals with the *up and out fight:* controlling assets, passing information to the Ground force commander or Task Force commander at the JOC. The PL is responsible for thinking of the next step in the plan while the platoon sergeant fights the fight. On my first real combat mission as a Ranger PL, I took almost no leadership role. Rather, I sat back and tried to figure out what I could to do help, passed up information to the commander and basically just tried to stay out of the way. When my platoon arrived back at the FOB, my platoon sergeant gave me a hug and said, "Thank God I finally have a good platoon leader." I wasn't quite sure of what to make of that until I walked into the JOC and my company commander looked at me and said, "Well, don't worry. I'm glad you popped your cherry on an easy mission, but get ready to drink from the fucking fire hose because this shit is about to get real."

That first deployment with the Ranger Regiment would change my life and my leadership. I couldn't have been prouder to serve with the modern day Spartans of combat: the strongest, hardest, most courageous men that I have ever met, the Rangers and Ranger NCOs of the 75th Ranger Regiment.

-GARRISON EAST

3/75

CHAPTER TEN

"I offer neither pay, nor quarters, nor food;

I offer only hunger, thirst, forced marches, battles and death.

Let him who loves his country with his heart,

and not merely with his lips, follow me."

GIUSEPPE GARIBALDI

In 2010, a major change to the way Rangers were selected for service in the Regiment occurred with the transition from the four-week Ranger Indoctrination Program (RIP) and three-week Ranger Orientation Program, to the eight-week Ranger Assessment and Selection Program (RASP) and three-week RASP 2. Rangers would now arrive at their battalions with more training, better prepared to immediately begin conducting combat operations. The first RASP 1 class, 03-10, began January 11 with 155 volunteers, culled from hundreds of volunteers in the pre-RASP screening process. They graduated on March 5th with 56 Rangers.

The commander of all operations in Afghanistan, General Stanley McChrystal, resigned his position in June after politically embarrassing remarks made by his staff were printed in a *Rolling Stone* article. He was replaced by General David Petraeus, widely respected for his counter-insurgency strategy in Iraq. The strategy outlined the year prior for

Afghanistan did not change with leadership however, and those on the ground continued to fight in an increasingly violent environment.

2010 proved to be the costliest in the 75th Ranger Regiment's history. 16 Rangers gave their life in some of the fiercest combat operations seen in the 21st century. Rangers were taking on the hardest missions in the worst terrain and conditions. The Regiment became accustomed to short duration direct action raids, in Iraq, almost always completed in one period of darkness. Most of those raids would not see even a single shot fired. In Afghanistan, not only were they conducting direct action raids, but also conducting movement to contact in enemy safe havens, often staying out for days at a time. The Regiment's flexibility as a special operations unit was put to the test and individual Rangers were pushed to their physical and mental limits.

Fallen Rangers include:

Sergeant Joel Clarkson

Corporal Michael Jankiewicz

Staff Sergeant James Patton

Sergeant Jason Santora

Sergeant Ronald Kubik

Captain Kyle Comfort

Sergeant Jonathan Peney

Specialist Joseph Dimock II

Sergeant Justin Allen

Sergeant Anibal Santiago

Specialist Bradley Rappuhn

Sergeant Andrew Nicol

Specialist Christopher Wright

Sergeant Martin Lugo

Sergeant First Class Lance

Vogeler

Staff Sergeant Kevin Pape

APRIL 2010

"MY CIB, RITE OF PASSAGE"

That night was a very interesting night. Once again, we went after a Taliban commander. From the *eyes above* it looked like there was something huge going on. Large caches of weapons were being transported and there were a lot of people on target. We determined this type of activity could only be Taliban. Once we arrived on target, we cleared the first compound. No one was there. There were about ten rooms, all empty, and I it was then realized that they knew we were coming. The squad leaders and team leaders both received word that enemy fighters were watching us, *be careful*. As we cleared the next compound, we found people and collected intelligence. After all was complete, the sun was up and we began to prepare for exfil.

A day exfil means much easier target identification for the enemy. In fact, on our way out, we heard a gunshot from one of our snipers. He came on the radio saying he shot a man using a radio to call for reinforcements. We cleared the body, ensuring he was dead, and then searched him. The rest of us were behind a wall pulling security for the group. We began to see people milling about at a distance. We continued to move to the HLZ for pickup. We heard and saw the helicopters approaching when all of a sudden, shots were fired.

We were now in a firefight with helicopters about to land. The guns on the Chinooks began to rain down on the enemy. Without hesitation we ran onto the bird. One of our guys, coming up off a knee, saw an enemy fighter only 20 meters from him. He opened fire, hitting him in the chest. Once we were all on the bird, the guns opened up again, killing whatever was in sight. Upon returning to the FOB, we all talked it all over and waited for the other platoon who was still taking contact. It was an intense night, but thankfully all of us made it out alive.

-DAVID BOUCHARD
3/75

2010

"DOGS"

1st Ranger Battalion started its Multi-Purpose Canine (MPC) Program in the spring and summer of 2007 with just four handlers. The program expanded to 12 handlers and 12 dogs in 2009 making it so every line platoon would have a dog team attached.

I made my way to the canine section in February 2009 after passing a three-day selection process conducted by the senior handlers, trainer and the kennel master. I re-enlisted in 2007 during a deployment in the hopes of making my way to the K9 Program. Spending much of my childhood in the Midwest on a farm, I had always liked being around working dogs, so it just seemed natural to end up in the K9 Program. I served three deployments to Afghanistan as a MPC handler. Out of my ten total combat rotations while in the Regiment, those are by far my most memorable. There are no words to describe the bond between handler and dog; seeing firsthand the morale boost a dog can bring to the team is amazing to witness.

Once the Ranger platoon learns to trust you and sees firsthand what you and your dog can bring to the fight, it becomes much easier to work together. Utilized correctly, dogs are worth their weight in gold on the battlefield. Being a dog handler is a gratifying position because you truly get out of it what you put into it.

On any given night, I was utilized by the platoon in various capacities: route clearance, detection of explosives on target and most exciting of all, chasing squirters running from the target. Obviously that's the most exciting, but just a small portion of what the K9 team brings to the table every night. You learn to be ready on the fly because nothing ever really goes as planned. You must always resort to the basics and provide the team with the best K9 asset you can while learning from your experiences. The more missions you conduct with your dog, the better the team becomes.

My longest deployment was over from spring to fall of 2010 in Kandahar. My assigned platoon was one of those who surged a month or so before the rest of the battalion. We would become known as *Team Merrill* that spring. Our mission set included conducting stay-over-day missions and clearing NAIs throughout Afghanistan. Now, as a dog handler, this brought up some concerns that were later laid to rest. Taking a dog out all night on target and then throughout the day in 100-degree heat was not something we had done before. Anyone who has been around our Belgian Malinois and Dutch Shepherds knows these dogs will go until they drop dead—they love to work that much! It was my responsibility as the handler to monitor my K9. Dogs can't talk to you like another Ranger can to tell you he's hurt or tired. You have to know your dog while trusting your instincts and monitoring them closely. I am truly grateful that I never had any issues and I'll go ahead and say it: *my* Belgian Malinois was a freaking stud!

That summer turn out to be one of the worst for 1st Ranger Battalion, as we lost six Rangers and an EOD augmentee lost his legs. I can remember clear as day, after one ROD in early June 2010 we were standing on the airfield just off the tail of the CH-47. We had just returned from a 36-hour mission as the guys walked by me. Almost all of them patted my dog on the head or pet him with watering eyes. We had lost a brother that day, Doc Peney and another was severely wounded. I do not know what in my mind told me to stand out there for them, but I did and I saw firsthand the morale and comfort a dog could bring to a team in times of sorrow. For lack of a better term, it was *amazing* to witness and it felt good to be able to do that for my brothers.

Being deployed in Kandahar and living next to the airfield also allowed me the opportunity to go out with other Ranger platoons throughout Afghanistan so I stayed busy that summer. As an attachment, you never turn down a mission, even if it's with another platoon. As I said before though, it was a deployment full of hardship and loss, but we all pulled through and stuck together like any Ranger Battalion does. I will always look back on my time in Battalion with a smile because of the bonds made, the brotherhood shared and the life experience gained. As another Ranger buddy once said, "I am proud to look back and say I was blessed to WALK AMONG GIANTS!"

I still resort back to the basic K9 handler skills I learned at the very beginning and use them in my private sector job as a K9 Handler—it just stays with you.

1/75 has done an outstanding job with its K9 Program. We have one of the best trainers out there and he has molded many guys into great handlers and produced some outstanding MPC Teams for 1/75. The assistant trainer, being one of the original four handlers at 1/75, is also worth his weight in gold for his vast knowledge of MPCs and operations. I don't know what the future holds with wars dwindling, but I truly hope Battalion does not see the working dog program as something they can do without. These dogs have proven their worth over the last decade of war. Sooner or later, even if the wars completely die out, they're going to be needed again and it would be a damned shame to start all over again after all that has been gained.

-LYNE
MPC ROBBIE & MPC LUCKY
1/75

SUMMER 2010

"TEAM MERRILL"

The 1st Ranger Battalion finished off another deployment in December of 2009. Everyone was happy to be home and to see their family for Christmas. After we returned, D Company received a new first sergeant from the 3rd Ranger Battalion. During the formation in which he was introduced, our company commander also gave us a very motivational speech: "Men, you have been selected to deploy early. Your performance over the last two deployments has set the standard. We will deploy early to Afghanistan and swing the fucking mallet!"

After the CO's speech, I thought about the upcoming deployment a lot. Mostly because in my last two deployments, I didn't fire a single shot in combat. *Maybe this year was going to be different?* Probably not, since I was a *goose* gunner. Goose gunners hardly ever see any action. Nonetheless, we trained for this deployment and we trained hard, going all over the country to prepare for the rigors ahead.

Before long, it was time to get ready to leave. We packed up and headed out, going through the motions like any other deployment. Once we landed in Bagram, we set up inside the SOF compound like usual. In those little, reddish-looking wooden huts—you know, the ones that have the shitty mattresses? Not a cozy place at all. We grabbed our gear from the pallets and bedded down.

I woke up and went to the bathroom. It was early, as the sun wasn't up yet, but it was probably around 5:30 AM on May 19. As I was making my way back to my room, I heard gunfire. I turned to look behind me and saw what looked to be tracer rounds down by one of the towers. I was very confused by this, as it was almost unheard of for Bagram, the largest base in Afghanistan, to be attacked. Still, I got a strange feeling from it.

I went back to the room and I told the men in the hut, "I think we might be under attack," but no one cared. As for me, I was concerned so I headed back outside because I wanted to be aware of what was happening. I looked at the guard tower 30 feet directly in front of our hut and saw the guards watching everything that was going down at the next closest tower, which was probably 400 meters from us. *Man those guys should be watching their sector.* Not even a minute after I thought that, three RPG rounds flew overhead, barely missing their tower. I ran back inside and yelled to the men, "WE ARE UNDER ATTACK!"

Like everyone else, I was in my PT uniform consisting of short black shorts and a tan t-shirt. I began strapping up my body armor and helmet and grabbed my M-4. I took off running toward the tower and saw Sergeant B running up the stairs. *Damn, he got ready fast!* Sergeant B took the corner. As soon as I arrived at the top of the stairs he screamed, "RPG!" I saw it go sailing by us and then exploding in midair. Fired up, we scanned over the wall, looking for the men trying to kill us. The sun was coming up so our NODs were useless. The vegetation was so thick that we couldn't see anything below us. We had no clue where the fire was coming from. Other Rangers quickly met up with us on the tower. We had it locked down.

Rangers were spread out all over the wall, guns facing out into the vegetation, just hoping to see someone to shoot. I remember the tower guard saying, "Here, I'll get out of you guys' way. I'm sure you have more experience."

A half hour passed. We hadn't received any more small arms fire or seen any more RPGs flying by. Maybe they'd moved on. *Not so.* A few minutes later Apache gunships were overhead and began laying waste everywhere. At one point, I counted seven helicopters. There were also two AC-130 gunships as well. Whoever these guys were, they just woke up a damn hornet's nest.

After a half hour or so we heard an explosion. Come to find out, some *regular Army* second lieutenant thought it would be a good idea to chase after one of the enemy fighters through a minefield. The mine took off his foot and wounded his battle buddy. A Ranger medic ran to their rescue them not knowing he, too, entered a minefield. Someone yelled at him to *STOP* and he luckily did. After they alerted him to the dangers around him, he slowly retraced his footsteps and safely made it out. As for the fighter, he didn't make it that far and ended up stepping on a mine as well. He, however, did not survive.

I remember our first sergeant coming up and yelling at us that we didn't have our eye protection on. It pissed off most of us because we got up that damned tower within minutes. He came strolling in after we got it locked down and started bitching at us about eye-pro. In the heat of the moment, we grabbed everything we needed at that very moment, nothing more. Body armor, helmet and gun. We couldn't care less about digging through our rucks looking for eye-pro at that time. The hours to follow were boring, waiting for the *all clear* so we could go back to our daily lives.

After the *all clear* was announced, a brand-new Ranger went to the phones and started talking about what just happened. Well, he was released for standards (RFS) right then and there. There are some things you just don't speak about over the phones. This attack ended up making national news back home. I'm sure it scared our loved ones, knowing that we just left and this went down. A picture in the *Stars and Stripes* later showed one of the fighters with an RPG on his back tangled up in the concertina wire. He didn't make it very far before he was shot and killed.

We were less than 24 hours into being in Afghanistan and we already saw some shit go down. I guess this was a sign of how this deployment was going to go for the Rangers of Delta Company, 1/75.

May 20th, 2010

KANDAHAR, AFGHANISTAN

We arrived in Kandahar and there was no time to sit down or relax. We geared up right away and got to work, loading magazines and dressing our helmets in camouflage. Intelligence reported around 450 Taliban fighters took control of Kandahar City, ambushing vehicles and setting up IEDs everywhere. Their safe haven was in the Zari Panjway District, dubbed *the IED capital of the world*. The plan was for the 101st Airborne Division to move in to clear Kandahar, but before that, Airborne Rangers from 1st and 3rd Ranger Battalions were there to soften it up for them.

After spending the last five months with our new first sergeant, we had developed a strong bond with him. We respected him and accepted that messed up beret of his. He told us in a brief once, "Wherever we go, we WILL take the hard road." And that is exactly what we did.

17 hours after arriving in Kandahar, we loaded up on the birds and got to work. We heard helicopters were being shot at on almost every infil and we should expect the same. We should also expect a firefight as we exit the birds. To be honest, it sounded like a suicide mission.

Inbound, we took no fire. We unloaded the bird as quickly as possible, expecting a firefight. The bird departed. Everyone was pinging, scanning the area thoroughly. *Nothing.* Not a damned thing out there but the silence of the night. We moved out. We moved in a single-file line for most the time. We were definitely taking the hard road alright, walking up and down the damned grape orchard mounds. We were not used to walking in this kind of terrain. Everyone was falling and disappearing into the five-foot ruts in the field.

Rangers were laughing at each other.

We reached the target building, set up and cleared it. It was an empty, run-down building. It didn't look like anyone had lived there for quite some time. *Was this really what we all came out here for? What a waste.* Then we moved to exfil. On the way to the LZ, we received reports of seven fighters moving toward us. Then it was five, then three, then down to two. The company commander and a few others headed over to apprehend them. They captured the two insurgents, discovering they were from Pakistan. They both had their shirts off trying to hide in a field. I will try not to judge them and what they were doing out there. *At least they still had their pants on.*

We set up for exfil and waited for the birds. As the birds were two to three miles away, we saw them taking fire. Tracers flew through the air, along with an RPG. Amazingly, the birds were untouched. They landed and we ran like hell to load up and get out safely.

Strangely enough, when we returned to base, all the talk was about everyone falling, not about the birds taking fire as they came in. Either way, it was always a good day when all the boys returned to base safe and sound.

MAY 22nd, 2010

KANDAHAR

I woke up a little after sunset. We were sharing a temporary building with the regular Army. We had the upstairs and they had the downstairs. I laid there in bed thinking, *I should get up,* but everyone was still sleeping. As I lay there, a voice came over the loudspeaker. I thought to myself, *No, our luck could not be this bad. This base is not under attack.* I can't tell you if it was ten seconds or ten minutes after that thought when an explosion rocked our building from just outside. I jumped to my window to see what had happened. I saw two U.S. Soldiers walking outside. It looked like someone was lying down but I could not tell because of the dust.

Everyone was now awake. Our guys turned on the lights and I couldn't see shit because of the glare. All of a sudden a soldier ran into our bay asking for a medic. I yelled, "PENEY!" because he was the first one dressed. Doc Peney ran outside to tend to the wounded. He found a man whose ass was blown and who also had a broken femur. This was the second time I witnessed Doc Peney spring into action and save a life. The first was in 2008 when an Afghan boy was shot in the chest.

Anyway, talk about being in both the wrong and right place for that guy. Why? They said he was just outside smoking a cigarette when the rocket came in and landed next to him. Lucky for him, Rangers have the best-trained medics in the military. They got him inside and went straight to work on him, saving his life.

Reports started coming in, "Enemy fighters have breached the compound." Everyone was ordered to stay inside. Rangers took to the roof. I knew enough about our boys that I did not need to head up there. Everyone was going to be up there looking for a kill. As for me, I headed downstairs looking for a job. Rangers had one exit secure. The other exit was not, so I placed myself there.

I looked out the doors as people were running and trying to take shelter. I told the people who are near to come inside the building. When I checked my six, I saw the most fucked up thing. In the middle of the hallway, a soldier was laying in the prone position with a M-249 machine gun aimed straight at me. I walked over to him and politely said, "Come with me." He got up and walked to the door. He was a short, stout, nerdy guy who probably didn't hit the gym too often. I told him, "I want you to face that way and I am going to face this way. We will pull cross coverage since we can see more this way." He replied, "OK." I explained to him why I wanted him here with me at the door, "If you decide to open that M-249, I am going to have a really bad day along with the people directly in front of us in the other building. From where you were laying, you can't see if someone squats down and gets on the other side of the door. If they throw in a grenade through the window, we are screwed. We have to be able to see and eliminate the threat before it has a chance to get that far." I asked him what he does for the Army. He said he is a mechanic. I guess that explained it.

Another soldier walked up to us and I let him know that we had this side covered. It was dark and when he finally reached us, I saw his rank was Captain. He then asked me what unit I was with. I said what I am supposed to say, "I'm with Task Force Blah Blah Blah."

"Never heard of them."

Well, no shit. We don't tell people who we are for a reason. He walked away. Some guys from my brother's platoon showed up to relieve me. I headed upstairs and looked outside. Helicopters started shooting. I saw rockets flying through the air. I couldn't tell if it was enemy or friendly firing that was going on out there, but it was a wild sight.

It didn't last long. I looked at the ground where the rocket hit. There was a one square foot crater in the ground along with medical supplies and blood. A few hours went by and the voice came over the loud speaker, "All Clear."

MAY 25 – 26th, 2010

KANDAHAR

We received word that we would be conducting Operation Akita Push, and it would be a Remain Over Day (ROD) mission. Our task was to clear named areas of interest (NAI) and move to a pre-planned compound. We would then set up a secure 360-degree perimeter before daylight and fight the Taliban from that position all day. When darkness fell, we were to move to exfil. It was time to *swing the fucking mallet.*

To me, this was our Alamo. We were heading to set up in the Taliban's backyard and let them bring the fight to us. This kind of operation was new for me. I was used to night raids playing offense, not defense. I had no clue what to expect since this was my first time outside the wire in broad daylight. I also remember hearing a sergeant say, "Bradley, I hope you are good under pressure, 'cuz if you have to fire that thing, all eyes will be on you." I replied,

"Yeah Sarge, no pressure at all now that you say it like that." He chuckled as he walked away.

We flew out and cleared the NAI. We found weapons and IEDs still in production. Our EOD guy blew them in place. We headed to our Alamo and quickly set up our perimeter. With the explosion from destroying the weapons, the Taliban definitely knew Americans were in the area.

Morning came and we continued to wait for the Taliban to come out and play. They did not disappoint. They first started taking shots at us with small arms. They were in small groups, maybe one to five fighters at a time. The Taliban tried to set up a mortar position but they were too slow. Our mortar team shot a round that landed on them first and with their first shot! When the mortar sergeant called back to adjust fire, the reply back was, "No man, you're good. Pink mist." Later, we intercepted a message saying, "They killed the commander!"

Since I was a *Carl Gustaf* gunner, I pretty much had nowhere to set up without having someone or something in my backblast area. I moved from 2nd Platoon's area of operation and into 3rd Platoon's. It was a cozy spot with a mud wall and tree providing me shade. I couldn't complain. I pulled out my rangefinders and started writing down the distances to places where the enemy could hide. There wasn't much out there though, just a huge open field with two grape huts and a dirt field. Where the field ended was a massive woodline, but it was over 400 meters away.

More small arms fire came our way from the east. I heard our Mk-48s open up. I was pumped. Three RPGs flew overhead. At once, we took machine gun fire from our side, though nobody knew from where. We all had our heads down while quickly peeking over to try to spot where it was coming from.

It lasted just minutes. I pulled my rangefinders out to see if I could spot them. I was scanning the woodline when I saw a smoke signature! Those bastards fired so damned much they ratted themselves out! For as long as I live, I will never forget that moment. I was excited and I said, "First Sergeant! I've found them." His reply was simple, "Well, get the goose." I felt dumb from the way he said it. It's not like I can just take a shot with an M-4 or something. Everyone in the vicinity needs to know this thing is about to go boom.

This is it; don't fuck up. I found the range to the smoke signature. *418 meters.* I grabbed the HE round from my assistant gunner. I set the round to 400 meters. I set the range drum. I wanted to make sure this round exploded in their faces and not behind them. They were never going to see this coming! I handed the round back to my AG. He loaded it up. Everyone cleared the backblast area. I took aim at the top of the smoke signature. It was around five feet tall. I yelled, "GOOSE GOING HOT!" Everyone repeated it. I squeezed the trigger, *KA-BOOM*—the round ignited and I was hit with the overpressure. It sent a shock wave through my body. Dust and rocks kicked up all over the people around me. I watch the round as it screamed toward its target. As soon as it reached the smoke, it exploded. Direct hit.

First Sergeant said, "Great shot!" My little brother's platoon sergeant said, "That landed right where it needed to be!" I quickly unloaded the round and prepped another round. After that shot, everything went quiet. We picked up their radio frequency and listened in on their chatter. "Achmed! Come in Achmed. Achmed, Come in!" But ol' Achmed did not answer.

A few minutes later, our ground commander called in the birds to see if they could confirm any EKIA. The pilots responded, confirming three EKIA. Then they bombarded the woodline with rockets and machine gun fire. By then, I'm pretty sure Achmed's friends knew he didn't make it.

That shot right there was D Company, 1/75's first time firing *the goose* in Afghanistan since the company was stood up in 2008. The company commander told me to keep that round casing so we could put it in our trophy case. So I did.

It was quiet for an hour before they came back to fight. They were shooting at us from close range. Someone said, "They are in the grape hut!" I went to grab an HEDP round. Then I heard, "NOT YOU BRADLEY! Get 3rd Platoon's goose gunner over here. You've already had your shot!" That was 3rd Platoon's platoon sergeant shutting me down so his guy could shoot. I understood we weren't able to use this weapon system very often.

The only problem I had with the order was the other goose gunner was located on the other side of the compound. It made more sense for me to take the shot and end the engagement immediately, but I was not in command and

CHAPTER TEN

had nothing to say other than, *"Roger, Sergeant."* Instead, we waited for the other gun team to get over to my position.

Finally, they arrived out of breath. I sat there and watched them. They must have sprinted to us because they were breathing hard. They looked nervous. They were loaded up and ready to fire. He took aim. He yelled out, "GOOSE GOING HOT!" Everyone repeated it. *KA-BOOM!* The round came screaming out of the barrel and jetted through the air and landed about a hundred meters over and to the right of the target. The platoon sergeant screamed in anger, "LOAD ANOTHER ONE!" They did and fired again. This time the round landed short. The platoon sergeant was highly pissed off and said they were done shooting. Now I understood why that platoon sergeant did that: to give his guy a chance to shoot. To *share the love,* so to speak. I had no problem with it at all.

We picked up more of their radio chatter. The guy in the grape hut was still alive. His buddy called to him and said, "DON'T MOVE! The Americans have set up IEDs all around you!" Hearing that made the day so much better and those missed shots well worth it. We were all laughing. It was a great idea though. *Maybe we should set up IEDs? Fight fire with fire, right?*

The day wore on. It was 107 degrees outside and we were out of water now. The people who had water were sharing with others. A small resupply came in, but it didn't last long. Guys were receiving entire IV bags from the medics just to stay hydrated.

A little later the sun started setting. The snipers came off the roof. They were up there all fucking day! Their faces were sunburnt and beet-red. One of the staff sergeants looked like hell. I remember Doc saying, "I have one more IV bag left, who wants it?" Nobody said anything. I still had water, but wasn't going to pass it up. "I'll take it." Then I saw the look on that sniper's face. It wasn't a look of sadness or anything. It was a look that told me he needs that IV bag way more than I do. "Never mind, give it to him. He needs it more than I do." He opened it up and downed it right there. Like I said, I was in the shade most of the day. He was on the roof with none. When you are out there and it is just the men, you have to do whatever you can to make sure all come home. Out there, you are family. Brothers.

It was now dark. We continued to wait to make sure we could move

266

safely to the HLZ. We started moving. It was a long walk, and I was trailing the AG of one of the machine gun teams. I knew who it was. It was a private, a short guy from Tennessee. For being as small as he was, (about 5'3"), he sure could run fast.

I saw him stumbling. He kept on doing that, *bend over with a rucksack* technique to keep the weight off his back. If you've ever had a heavy ruck on your back, you know what I'm talking about. He was sucking. We were walking next to a grape field ditch full of water and he fell in. He climbed his way out. We stopped. I walked up to him and ask him if he had any water. He said no so I gave him mine.

Every time we stopped, I headed back to him to give him more water. He was sucking, like I had never seen a Ranger suck in combat before. I took his ruck that was filled with belt fed ammo of 7.62 rounds for the Mk-48. To be honest, it did not feel that heavy to me. But when a man is dehydrated that bad, his own body weight is heavy enough.

We continued walking. Suddenly, I saw him fall into the ditch again. He was waist deep. When I got to him, he saw me. He took a deep breath and blew it out while dropping his head down. He wanted to give up on life. I extended my hand to him.

He gladly took it and we continued moving. He was falling behind now. I grabbed his body armor and started guiding him forward. I felt him trying to give up. I started yelling in his ear, "Ranger, we are almost there, you better Ranger Up!" We finally got to the LZ. Everyone was on a knee. A half hour went by. Another 15 minutes passed. Rangers were starting to sit down now. I did as well. The cool night air felt good on my sweaty skin and soaked shirt. I was tired. My eyes were getting heavy. I fell asleep.

I woke up to a captain in my face telling me that the birds are coming in and to get on a knee. I must have been snoring? I can only wonder how many others fell asleep. We hadn't slept in over 36 hours! The birds came in and we ran on, snapped in and took off. We got back and continued working until our weapons were clean. We then took a fresh, cool shower to wash off two-days' sweat and I still remember how great it felt. Afterwards, we went to bed. I can't tell you how long everyone slept, but it was between 12 and 16 hours. It was well-deserved sleep; I do know that.

MAY 31ST - JUNE 1ST, 2010

KANDAHAR

It was late May, and we were off to conduct Operation Doberman in the Zari Panjway District, a movement to contact mission. 2nd and 3rd Platoon of D Company, along with a platoon of Afghan troops and their Special Forces advisors were to take control of three pre-planned compounds. The compounds were located 500 to 1000 meters from one another. 2nd Platoon would be furthest South, 3rd Platoon furthest to the north and the ODA and Afghan fighters in the middle. Each platoon was to establish a 360-degree security perimeter before daylight.

Our last mission out of Kandahar Airfield was another ROD, the second one in four days we conducted as Team Merrill. RODs are no joke. After the last, it took days to reenergize our bodies. We prepared for this mission by loading extra ammo and water for a resupply just in case we needed it. We learned from last time; no sense in sucking like that again if we could avoid it.

After the mission brief, we prepped for the manifest call. Each Ranger sounded off with, "Here, Sergeant!" after hearing their name and loaded up onto the bus. Once every name was called, the buses departed for the airfield and dropped us off at the Chinooks.

Our platoon sergeant and medic walked between our two single-file lines to get a second head count. We loaded up onto the helicopters, sat down, snapped in and waited for takeoff. Once the birds were in the air, everything became serious. We were heading into the unknown; likely a very dangerous place.

The Chinooks landed uneventfully in a dusty field. The back ramp dropped and we rushed off, assuming our security responsibilities immediately. The birds took off and we began our move to the designated compound. With so much airborne activity, the Taliban fighters knew

Americans were playing in their backyard again.

We moved quickly to the compound, occupied by a family. We told them to leave, to go somewhere safe away from here and not to return until tomorrow. We paid them and they were happy to leave. I was sure this family would spread the news that American forces kicked them out of their home, leading the Taliban fighters to our location for a fight. *Fine. We didn't come here to hide.*

We started setting up our stronghold. My fighting position was set at the southern end of the compound to enable effective fires to the south and west. I sat between a short building which I could see around and a longer building that provided cover at my back. The buildings were just ten feet apart from each other. At the end of the short building was a large mound of dirt. Even combined, these features weren't enough cover for my liking, so I moved several heavy bags of livestock feed to my position for additional protection. We reinforced then with logs and sticks found nearby, and my fighting position was complete.

It was now morning and still quiet. Nothing happened. I could feel the heat coming on. It was going to be another hot one, over 100 degrees. I decided to build some shade using my poncho liner and bungee cords. I saw my squad leader behind us, against the wall of the short building, baking in the sun with no shade. He arrived a few days later than the rest of us because he stayed back for the birth of his daughter. This was his first ROD of this deployment. I figured I would build him some shade as he pulled security.

As I was building his shade, we intercepted more chatter from the Taliban. "Drink your morning tea and then we will fight," a Taliban commander said. Not sure how long their tea-drinking would take, I hurried to finish building my squad leader's shade. The grape hut had a bunch of half foot by two foot holes through its walls. A friend of mine inside asked me to help remove the sticks from under their feet so they wouldn't trip over them during the gunfight. They gave me a poncho to help my squad leader and I gladly helped gather sticks from inside the grape hut.

I returned to the hut grab two more sticks to run through the eyeholes of the poncho liner, completing my squad leader's shade. As soon as I stepped into the grape hut, the fight kicked off. Bullets ripped through the holes in the grape hut's walls, impacting all around us. I threw my body on the ground to avoid being hit and looked around. Everyone else was lying on the ground. Some Rangers were on ladders inside the grape hut scanning from the higher holes and ducked behind the walls for cover. RPGs screamed overhead. So many bullets were coming in! I had never experienced rounds impacting this close before. It was scary close. One of our senior medics was hit, scraped along his back shoulder by a lucky round, but it was only a flesh wound. He continued to shoot and fight on to the Ranger objective.

My squad leader ran inside the grape hut and said, "Let's use the goose!" I was all for it. We ran back to our fighting position and my AG loaded up a round. I was going to fire an HE round over a wall where we believed the enemy fighting position was. I took a knee and aimed. In my mind I was thinking, I *am going to be shot.* I pulled the trigger. *KA-BOOM!* The round hit its mark and the shooting stopped.

We brought in the Apaches to locate these fuckers and kill them—we couldn't see them. But the enemy was smart. The pilots informed us the fighters set their weapons down and began walking the road with small children at their side, knowing we would not engage them with children present. They could roam wherever they pleased. Air support was now useless and the only way to kill them was for our air support to move out and fight them on the ground again.

The birds left and the fighting soon picked back up. An enemy sniper had 3rd Squad, on a rooftop, pinned down. I learned we had taken casualties, but didn't know whom. My squad leader told me to reposition on the east wall to locate and kill the sniper with the goose. So, we moved out.

We arrived at the east wall, easily eight feet high, with portholes dug through it. Our snipers were there trying to locate the enemy sniper, thinking he was positioned behind a wall. My job was to put an HE round directly over that wall and kill him.

I climbed onto a four-foot wall to my left. On the other side of the wall was a twenty-foot cliff leading into a large well. My first fear was falling into the well—there's no telling how deep the water might be and with all the gear I had, I wouldn't be able to swim. Even if I managed to swim, I couldn't climb out, so my only option was not to fall. My squad leader grabbed my belt as I peeked over the eight-foot wall listening to our snipers talk me on to the target.

The wall the snipers described looked to be a piece of an old building. There was a blue door in the center with no roof or other side walls connected to it. Just a single wall once a part of a home, but the only thing homely about it now was the random chair sitting on the concrete pad. They believed he was behind that wall.

I pulled out my rangefinders, peeked over the wall and saw the target roughly 150 meters from us. My squad leader set the round—*150 meters*. He and my AG loaded the goose and handed it to me. I peeked over the wall again, fearful that the sniper was going to shoot me in the face after already exposing myself once. Nonetheless, this was my job and what I must do. I took my time to place the round where it needed to go. A wasted shot meant I would have to pop my head over this wall again, a risk I didn't want to take.

KA-BOOM! The round jetted from the barrel and screamed through the air. The snipers were watching the round as well. "Perfect shot dude!" The shooting stopped again. Turns out, the Taliban does not like the destruction of the goose when it goes hot. They had no idea what the hell was being shot at them. The 84MM recoilless rifle is the loudest weapon system I have ever worked with. I called it my *boom-stick* for a reason.

Since the shooting stopped we had a resupply inbound hot—a Black Hawk helicopter. He came in fast in the wrong damned spot, completely out in the open. Our leadership informed him he landed too far out and that kicking the ammo and water into that area was going to endanger men's lives. They would have to move closer to us.

The pilot picked up his bird, flew toward one of our buildings and then hit the *air brakes* before spinning his tail-end around 180-degrees and setting it down beautifully. He did almost of this all while flying sideways. It was one of the most *Hollywood* things that I've ever witnessed. It was fucking awesome and I wish I had a video of it. I'm pretty sure, given a thousand chances, most pilots couldn't do what this pilot pulled off. It was the sickest thing I've ever witnessed. They kicked out the ammo and water and then got the hell out of there. Our job was done here as well so we headed back and reestablished our fighting position.

271

Once back at our fighting position, my squad leader explained the situation. Two of our Rangers were hurt pretty damned bad. They needed immediate MEDEVAC or we were going to lose them. The MEDEVAC plan was for the entire 360-degree perimeter to lay down heavy fire for 30 seconds so the birds did not get shot down on the approach. During this, I would use my M-4 and lay down suppressive fire along with the rest of the platoon.

The birds were coming in. *It's go time.* I started shooting at a building, aiming at the door way and the windows. The birds came in and landed safely. The wounded quickly got loaded up and we got the call to start shooting again. The birds safely flew out under our suppressive fire and watching them go we could only hope it was soon enough.

The Apaches were overhead during the resupply. The Taliban stood down and were probably not going to fight until they left. I asked my squad leader who the wounded Rangers were. *Kapp and Peney.* It felt strange because just the other day Kapp and I were walking to chow, talking about our dreams. Kapp said, "I'm always a badass in my dreams. I'm killing motherfuckers." I told a different story. "Not me, I'm always getting shot in mine." I guess I will never forget that conversation.

Since we were not in contact, this was our time to refit and eat. I grabbed four extra goose rounds and a couple extra magazines from the resupply. I headed into a small room about 25 feet away from my position. We took turns eating our MREs. The Apaches pulled off station.

I was sitting in the room preparing to eat my MRE when my squad leader came in and said, "Hey, the Taliban say they're going to start fighting us again in 15 minutes." I looked at my watch and said, "Roger that." I continued eating while keeping track of that 15-minute window.

11 minutes passed and I figured it was time to head back out there to get our man-dance on with these bastards. At the time, it never dawned on me how smart these fuckers were. They must have remembered where I shot my first goose round from, so they set a machine gun aimed at my fighting position.

Walking back between the two buildings, I passed the short building where my squad leader sat out of the Taliban's view from the south side. As I passed him, I walked into my position and quickly got into the prone with my

AG. Immediately after lying down, machine gun fire ripped the wall directly behind us. The rounds impacted within inches of us. The bullets passed making sounds like someone was flicking a piece of paper. It had that cracking sound to it.

I could only imagine what it was like for that bastard behind the machine gun shooting at us. *Did he see me walk into view, get excited and twitchy and try to kill me? Or was he looking somewhere else and flinched when he looked back to his target area, seeing me lying down, realizing that he just fucked up and missed his chance?* I will never know. The only thing we both know is that he had a chance and he blew it.

As we were lying there under fire, something bounced off my foot. It must have been a ricochet from one of the rounds hitting the wall. I looked over at my AG, his face buried in the dirt, eyes continuously flinching as if someone was throwing punches at him. There was so much gunfire. We were pinned down and we could not move. *Will somebody please shoot this fucker and get him off us?*

The shooting stopped and my squad leader said, "God damn Bradley! They wanted you bad!" I replied with, "Yeah, no shit Sergeant!" Our platoon leader ran over and said they were firing from over another wall. My turn. I got orders to fire the goose over that wall and kill those bastards. After what they just put us through, I had no problem doing so—payback is a son of a bitch!

I checked the range and my AG set the distance and loaded another HE round. I hoped these bastards were in the middle of reloading because I was about to expose myself. It was a pretty damned ballsy move, but these men needed to be killed.

I took a knee and fired the round to the south. *KA-BOOM!* The PL liked my shot. He left our position to check on the rest of the platoon. That man was a hell of a leader and I'd follow him into harm's way any day.

The shooting stopped once more and the Apaches returned. The Taliban were still moseying around with children, frustrating us because we could not kill them. They moved to our east side, which made sense. They hit us from the west first and then the south. I guessed we could expect to take fire from the east next.

Our squad leader, my AG and I moved inside the short grape hut since we were exposed. 1st Squad was also located inside and we took turns pulling security with them. We did our best to keep a sharp lookout, but there were many places the enemy could hide. Vegetation was everywhere and they could easily be low-crawling through it.

The Apaches pulled off station and the fighting began again. They shot small arms fire and RPGs at the platoon. We believed the fire was coming from a building 250 meters directly to the east. I heard the machine gunners returning fire with the Mk-48 from the long building next door.

Our PL ran into our grape hut trying to see exactly where they were shooting from. I was posted up on the south side wall, looking out one of the 1x2 foot holes and providing security. I didn't see a damned thing. Matter of fact, I never even saw a single Taliban fighter that day. I felt as if I was fighting a ghost.

Our PL yelled over to me, "Bradley, get the goose. We are going to shoot that damned building where they are engaging us from."

"Yes sir!" I grabbed the HEPD round and loaded it. This would be another ballsy move. 3rd Squad and the neighboring machine gun team were going to lay down suppressive fire while we ran outside to rip off a shot.

My squad leader and PL would escort me as we ran up close to our old fighting position. We counted to three, our suppressive fire opened up and we took off running between the two buildings straight east. I was worried, ok, maybe scared, but I did not show it to anyone. I was just hoping that the enemy put their heads down during the small window we were exposed.

We made it to the edge of the short wall. We did not pass it; that was where a machine gun had us pinned down earlier. My squad leader and PL positioned themselves directly on my left and right out of the back-blast area. 200 meters in front, a wall covered the first floor of the building, making the second story the only place to hit.

I aimed into the doorway on the second floor and squeezed the trigger. *KA-BOOM!* The round looked like it was on target and going to hit as it screamed through the air. It missed the building by three feet and landed directly behind it. I could see the smoke rise over the wall, from the right side of the building. I grabbed another round and loaded it up to reengage. Before I could fire my PL says, "Stand down Bradley! The Apaches are coming in." I did and we ran back into the building.

I took that miss to heart. I was angry and mad at myself. I felt as if I let everyone down. The men were shocked to hear that I missed but not angry with me. At least we were no longer being engaged. We stayed on watch for hours. There was no sign of the enemy and all was quiet. While pulling security in the grape hut, we talked about dumb shit to pass the time. We told jokes, talked about girls and food we missed from home. We tried to make the best of it because it was very boring. But it only takes a second for a calm situation to get dangerous so everyone was on guard, staying alert.

We heard gunfire again, but this time it was further away, from the platoon located between us and 3rd Platoon. I hoped they fought them off better than we did and killed them all! It was getting late in the day and the sun would set soon. We ended up catching some chatter from the Taliban, planning to shoot the helos down when they approached for our exfil. I'd say it is a good plan, but how the hell do they know where the birds are going to land? Not even I know that yet.

The exfil plan made its way down to us from higher; they wanted us to jog 870 meters west to the LZ. As soon as those words were said, everyone immediately started bitching. "We do not know if those fuckers planted IEDs out there!" one Ranger said. "Exactly. What happens if someone steps on it or they have set up an ambush? Then we are really screwed," another Ranger said. The *what ifs* continued bouncing from one Ranger to another; nonetheless, we started planning for the jog to the LZ. At one point, I was going to carry a ladder, the goose, my M-4 and a container of goose rounds from the resupply. I just did not have enough hands and hated this idea as much as everyone else. It was all bullshit. We already had a 360-degree perimeter set up and plenty of room for the birds to fly in and get us out. *Why couldn't they just land in here?*

It was dark, the bitching stopped, and it was now quiet. I believe it was quiet because the many thoughts that were running through everyone's heads about the exfil plan. *An 870 meter jog?! Do they even know how far that is?* One Ranger said, "I'm going to sprint." That isn't a sprint, it's a damned marathon when you are loaded down with this much weight in the hills of

Afghanistan.

An hour later, we were told the birds were going to land inside the compound and we would not have to make a dash to the LZ. We were excited, happy and motivated. Mostly of all, we just wanted to get out of this hellhole we'd been fighting from all day. Fortunately, there wasn't illumination from the moon, it was completely dark. We might just get out.

We received the call to pull off the perimeter and stage up. Two birds were coming in, one at a time. I would be flying out on the 2nd MH-47 that landed. The first landed and it felt like it was sitting there forever. *Hurry the hell up!* They finally left and did not receive fire. The second MH-47 made its way in, lading safely. We made a mad dash for the ramp, piling in wherever we could. We got the correct headcount and we too flew out without being fired upon.

We made it back to Kandahar and unloaded the birds. Everyone cleared their weapon and the company commander arrived with the buses. Before he let anyone on the buses he pulled us all into a circle so we could hear him. He paused, then said with the most serious face, "Men, I regret to inform you Peney did not make it."

It was the worst news D Company 1/75 had heard since standing up in 2008. Rangers' heads dropped along with their hearts. The emptiness just filled us. It was painfully bitter. It hurt like hell because for many Peney wasn't just a Ranger medic, he was a friend and a brother. For a few, Peney was their best friend. He looked after and gave a damn about the men in his platoon. He cared about his job and always tried to do it right.

Our company commander updated us about Kapp as well, "He is in stable condition. We will head out, drop our gear and go see him. He can hear you, but he can't respond back to you." Everyone loaded up the buses. It was a long, silent drive.

We arrived at the hospital and the doctor explained what our company commander already told us. We headed into Kapp's room one by one. Rangers walked by his side, telling them who they are and to get well soon. I walked to his bedside and said, "Hey Kapp, it's Bradley." When I said that, he waved his hand and motioned his head as to say, "What's up?" I wished him well and walked away. Rangers were now grouping in the hallway after they wished him well. I looked and I see Kapp's barracks roommate walking out. His eyes were filled with tears and wiped them away as they rolled down his cheeks. It was a very emotional time for 2nd Platoon.

We left the hospital and headed back to our building. We cleaned up and went to bed. The next day, we would see Peney off. It was not going to be easy saying goodbye to him, especially for the men who knew him best. Morning came and we were patiently waiting in formation at the airfield for Peney's body to arrive. A Stryker slowly moved down the airfield and then came to a stop. Rangers moved to the back of it and waited. When the ramp opened, there was a coffin with an American flag draped over it. Rangers slowly and respectfully removed the casket and carried it to the C-17. Rangers were given the order to *Present, Arms* and we held the salute until Peney's body was loaded onto the aircraft. Jon Peney was heading home and we had to find a way to brush off the pain and continue the fight for the rest of this six-month deployment.

A couple days passed and we held a memorial ceremony for Peney. The entire Task Force stood quietly in formation. The men who knew Jon the most were the ones who did the talking about him. One-by-one, those men gave great speeches about what kind of man he was. As they spoke about him, their voices would begin to break. They tried to fight through the tears. It was an awful feeling knowing there wasn't a damned thing we could do to bring him back.

The ceremony was just about over and people formed into a single-file line that snaked around the dirt driveway. Then a song started playing over the speakers. *Amazing Grace.* My emotions broke. I did my best not to cry or show emotion, but it all finally got the best of me. The line moved very slowly as one person at a time knelt to pay his respects. A good hour passed and finally the last person said his good-bye. It was the right way to say farewell to a fallen comrade. We regrouped and 2nd Platoon formed a half moon around Jon's photo and took one last picture with him.

The men who worked with Jon Peney will always remember this: he was selfless. He had graduated Ranger School and gotten married just days before deployment. He had the option to stay home, take some well-deserved rest and spend time with his new wife. After all, he earned that time off after

277

spending months in Ranger School away from civilization and his loved ones.

Jon wasn't that kind of man though. He was the kind of man that would not let his brothers head downrange without him. I don't believe he had a selfish bone in his body. The world became a little darker after losing him.

R.I.P. Brother.

June 6th, 2010

We were heading to Orgun-E, also known as OE. We had our bags packed and loaded on a C-130. It was packed tight. We all knew that this would not be a comfortable flight. Then again, Rangers rarely go through anything comfortable.

We landed in Salerno and unloaded our gear. Everyone seemed happy just to be off that cramped-ass bird. Men started checking to make sure they had all sensitive items. We finished the checks and loaded CH-47s to fly out the rest of the way to OE. The ride was a little more comfortable, but not by much. My legs fell asleep from being stuck in between the break in the seats. *Damn, I hate this.*

We finally landed and again, unloaded our gear and rechecked our sensitive items. We carried as much of our gear as possible, the rest went onto a tiny flatbed truck. We followed the truck and it parked near our rooms for the short stay. Again, everyone unloaded the equipment and gave an *up* on their sensitive items. It was late, or I should say, early. The sun was about to come up. Everyone had picked their beds and made their *whack shack*. We all racked out shortly after.

In the middle of the day, a loud explosion woke me up. My heart was pounding out of my chest. I looked around and no one was doing anything, just sleeping. So I lied there with my eyes open, wondering if this would be a repeat of the attacks at BAF and KAF. *Are we under attack again?*

I continued to hear rockets flying over our heads and exploding. They were so damned loud! I didn't know what to do. My heart raced. I could not sleep like that and I became angry because I had no clue where they were coming from. I wished I could run outside and kill the men who were launching rockets at us.

I grabbed my gun, helmet and body armor. I headed outside and there was no one out there. I stepped into the shelter right outside the door. I sat there for five minutes and realized no one else was going to come. I wondered how the hell guys were sleeping through this. I got up and returned to my room and felt stupid for even going out there.

I was back in bed and rockets continued to fly over. I could not sleep. *Fuck it. If you die, you die. It is my time. Nothing I can do about it.* Slowly my heart beat stopped pounding and I fell asleep.

We woke up and everyone went off to get chow. As we were walking I asked, "Did anyone else react to that incoming fire?" One guy said, "Fuck no, I slept right through that shit." I couldn't believe it. I told them what I did and they laughed. I joined in laughing after I told them how dumb I felt. It was kind of funny.

"Did you hear about our terp?"

"No, what?"

Turns out, a Ranger noticed on each of the attacks our interpreter was nowhere to be found. Then he would appear as if nothing happened. It started to make sense. How else could we come under attack within 24 hours of landing at a new location? Leadership was informed and they asked to see his cell phone. Every contact was deleted. Needless to say, whether or not the terp had something to do with it, we couldn't trust him and he was shipped off to Bagram.

We entered the chow hall, grabbed our food and sat down. The entire chow hall was decked out in college flags. I saw one that was from my hometown, University of Toledo. I was filled with pride and said out loud, "Hell yeah! That's my home town!" as I pointed to the flag.

A soldier walked up to me and said, "Hey man do you remember me?" I looked at him and look back at my Ranger buddies. They had blank stares but were curious to find out where this conversation was heading. He continued to speak, "I'm friends with your little brother Kyle. We went to high school together and you were a wrestling coach. Is Kyle here?"

I replied back to him, "No man, Kyle got busted up pretty bad on a 4-wheeler. He was in the hospital for a couple days. He should be coming over here sometime in July though." I could tell it saddened him a little; he would have definitely rather seen Kyle than me. At least with my little brother there, they would have had something to talk about.

He continued to speak, "Funny we are both here on this small-ass base together." I said, "Yeah, how about those rocket attacks earlier today?" He says, "Yeah, those were cool. We actually got to fire and defend the base." I asked him what he did and he says he was in artillery. We then told each other to take care and parted ways.

As we walked back to our compound, Rangers kept passing by saying we had a meeting and to head to the TOC. Both 2nd and 3rd Platoon were packed in there. All the leadership was present. First Sergeant and the company commander stood in front looking back at everyone.

Our CO began to speak,

"Men, the reason why I have gathered us here is because I've learned that some men in the company are trying to get out of their platoons. Well, men, that is not going to happen. I know the loss of Peney has made you realize that we are not Superman, no one is. Still, nothing has changed. We came here to do a job and we are going to swing the fucking mallet. We are the tip of the spear. You need to get your minds right."

This meeting was a rude awakening. I did not know men wanted to leave because they were scared to go outside the wire. I can understand being scared; you have to be crazy not to feel something in combat. You have no clue if you'll come home or not. A little thing called *courage* makes you keep moving forward to *complete the mission, though I be the lone survivor*. Not to mention, your brothers out there depend on you. *You go, we go* was my mind set.

First Sergeant began to talk and his words were straight to the point, "Men, you are the best trained soldiers in the world. You are stronger and faster. You have nothing to be afraid of. I can't even believe we are having this talk. If you honestly don't want to be here then pack your damned bags and we will send you home."

There was only silence after they were done talking. They dismissed us and sent us to have a meeting with our own platoons. Our platoon headed into the gym and our platoon sergeant began to speak. "Well, I guess we need to talk about this and get this all out of our systems. Anyone want to go first?"

I did not have anything to say so I did not raise my hand. No one else did either. "Alright, I'll go first," he said. I don't remember everything he said, but what I do remember is him talking about Peney. "I was on the bird with Peney looking into his eyes when we lost him. I can still see the dust settling down on his eyes..." I was pretty much quiet the whole time. Only a few people spoke and our meeting was over.

As we all walked back to our rooms I heard some of the 3rd Platoon guys complaining about the first meeting. Maybe they were the ones who talked about wanting out? Didn't matter, I knew I was staying. I worked with those guys for three years; I wasn't giving up on them.

Walking back to my room, I remembered a day stateside, when we were cleaning our weapons in the company area. I walked over to my little brother's cage and talked with him. 3rd Platoon was close. They all called each other by their first names. I remember Kyle asking why my platoon doesn't and I think my reply disturbed him. "I keep it professional. And to be honest, I don't want to get too close to anyone because if we do lose someone, I'm not going home all fucked up over it." I told everyone that before I left for the Army; "I am going to come back home the same guy that left." Kyle said, "That's fucked up, bro." He is right, it is fucked, but I have made myself mentally ready, something every soldier should do. Prepare yourself to see some shit and do some shit that nobody back home will understand.

Another mission brief had just taken place. We were to conduct another ROD. 3rd Platoon was going to infil first and head straight to the target compound to get their man-dance on. There were supposed to be 17 enemy fighters staying in this compound. The guy they were going after is a guy we captured once already in 2008 when we were stationed in Salerno. I remember one of the squad leaders saying, "Man, we should have just killed that fucker then." Just goes to show you, once a shit-head, always a shit-head.

2nd Platoon was to climb a mountain and secure the top. 3rd Platoon would meet up on the mountaintop next to us. We were to wait for the enemy to come out to fight. We got ready, loaded the birds and infilled into a riverbed. It was completely dark. There was no illumination and we tried not to trip over the massive rocks, walking carefully and slowly. Even with our NODs, it was still dark. We began climbing up a smaller mountain first just to get to our mountain, which was three mountains over. *This was going to take a while…*

About an hour or so later, Apaches moved in to cover 3rd Platoon. They opened up on something and we got a great show, being at the same elevation as the Apaches. I didn't even know 3rd Platoon was in contact until I heard it: *THE GOOSE!* A massive explosion echoed through the mountain range. A few minutes later, the goose created another explosion. The Apaches continued to light up the target compound and we continued to climb that damned mountain.

We were so far away from 3rd Platoon that the only noises we heard from them were the two goose rounds and the Apaches. I didn't know they used grenades, a LAW and their Mk-48s until later. They engaged the fighters, killing 17 insurgents. I was later told the bodies were shredded so badly the Afghans they were working with started puking as they lined the bodies up in rows. Two Rangers took rocks to the face from an RPG round the enemy had fired. They stayed in the fight, nothing serious.

3rd Platoon found RPGs, AK-47s, grenades, chest racks, ammunition and IED materials. These were some very bad guys. The good news is we will never have to go after that shit-head or his friends again.

2nd Platoon kept climbing and we finally started down the backside of the first mountain. My AG was struggling to keep up. I kept looking back at him while trying to maintain my eye on the man I'm following.

Along the way, I took his rifle and our platoon sergeant carried his round ruck so he could keep up. I was mad that he was unable to perform his job and that others had to pick up his slack.

The terrain was dangerous and difficult to travel. Rocks and cliffs surrounded us. I lost sight of my squad leader and started to head up the mountain. I saw a laser signaling to where they were and started moving back down to them. As I did, I saw my squad leader walking over to me. He saw something that I didn't, a four-foot drop-off.

I stepped over the dark edge and he stopped me from falling and completely eating shit. I waited for my AG to catch up and made sure he was aware of the small cliff as well. We stopped to take a small break and let everyone catch up. We offloaded the AG's round ruck and weapon back to him.

As we were climbing up the second mountain we realized it ran right into the third, so it would be a straight shot. We wouldn't have to descend the backside of the second mountain. We kept moving higher and higher. There was a cliff to the right of us and we were walking on a very narrow path. Up ahead, there was a downward-slanted rock ledge that led to a massive drop. This was scary and dangerous; Rangers had died in similar situations in years past. I stepped onto the rock ledge and began to make my way across. It was slippery and I fell. I started sliding down toward the cliff on my stomach. I was reaching and kicking trying to stop myself from going over the edge but I was loaded down with so much damned weight I couldn't stop. I was in a panic, frantic to stop. Suddenly I stopped sliding as if an invisible hand had caught me from behind. Relieved, I slowly crawled back up the rock and to the other side. I believe someone was looking out for me that night.

I waited for my AG and helped him across by stepping out on the ledge and putting my hand out for him to grab so he didn't make the same mistake I just did. Falling off a cliff was not the ideal way for a Ranger to go out.

We reached the third mountain and were closing in on the top. The Afghans turned it into a competition between them. They started racing each other to get to the top first. As they passed by me, I did not follow because I want to expend my energy when the fighting starts, not before, racing up a mountain.

About ten minutes later, they reached the top and I saw something that I have never seen before or since. They came back down the mountain to grab rucksacks from the Americans. I know they did not have to help any one of us, so it was a very friendly gesture.

Multiple times they ran up and down the mountain to grab rucks from the men who were struggling. One of them ran down to me and he says, "RPG? RPG?" while holding out his hand, asking if he could take the goose from me. Well, you know me; I wasn't going to let someone carry my weight, especially a foreign troop. I was going to show them I'm just as tough.

I pointed down to my AG who was about 20 meters from me. My AG said that he couldn't go any further because he has cramps in his legs. The Afghan soldier gladly ran down the mountain to get his round ruck. I told my AG, "MOVE YOUR ASS TO THE TOP NOW! You are carrying nothing." He tried to argue with me and said he couldn't. I got mad again and climbed the last 20 meters without him. Finally, he got off his ass and made it to the top.

It took us five hours to climb up that beast of a mountain. The view up there was the most beautiful sight of my life. We could see seven mountaintops away from us. It was an amazing sight and I wished I had had a camera with me.

We began to fill sand bags and fortify our fighting positions. 3rd Platoon was making their way up their mountain. The sun started to come up so they set up their 360-degree perimeter on the much shorter first mountain we climbed earlier.

We were scanning, looking for enemy. The only thing we could see from this high was a small village 1,400 meters below us. Those people woke up and immediately knew we were on top of the mountain. They gathered around to watch.

The closet mountaintop to us was 400 meters away, the rest were over 1,000 meters. Nobody was going to fuck with us. We had too much standoff. And I was sure that no crazy-ass fighter was going to attempt to run up this mountain to fight us. It was looking like we climbed up this bitch just for the view.

As we scanned the area, we found what looked to be a cave entrance. A dirt trail ran straight to it. Talk ran through the platoon about a team heading down there to check it out. Instead, I received the call to take a shot at it and close it up with a goose round. The range was 322 meters down and away from my position. I took aim on it and fired. The round hit the mountain three feet too high, just above the entrance. I asked for another shot but quickly got denied. "We need to conserve the rounds in case we need them later," the PL said. I completely agreed. I'd rather shoot back at men shooting at us rather than rocks.

It was around 6:00 PM and we saw a storm brewing in the distance. It continued to move closer. We could see the falling rain, the flashes of lightning and hear the rumble of thunder. We got the call to pack up. We did, and began moving down the mountain.

As we were cautiously heading down the mountain, a couple of Rangers sprained their ankles. It started to sprinkle and darkness fell. It got chilly, but we were warm because we were sweating. We got soaked as it rained harder. Our NODs were not working due to the weather. Some wouldn't even turn on. I was lucky; mine kept fogging up, but they worked.

We arrived at the bottom of the mountain near the riverbed. Our platoon circled up, waiting for it to get late before moving out to our next target, only a kilometer away. As I sat, my body started to cool off. I shivered from the wet shirt and cold air, but then remembered. I packed a rain top. I put it on, threw my body armor back on and sat there in comfort. A Ranger sitting next to me says, "Damn, I should have brought one." One thing you need to know is how your body operates. Mine works well in the heat but not so much in the cold.

After being up for 24 hours, we were put on a rest plan. Most of the guys went to sleep. When I was woken up, I was told we were would move out in ten minutes and to wake up anyone still asleep. Everyone else was already awake. I changed back into my drenched top to keep at least one dry shirt. I was cold and miserable again. We began to move, and as my body temperature started to rise, my shirt began to dry.

We moved quickly and my AG fell out again. He was tired and kept tripping and falling over rocks. He fell off a one-foot drop, hit the ground, and his weapon went flying into the darkness. He screamed in pain and I yelled, "SHUT THE HELL UP!" He said he hurt his ankle. I asked him where his weapon went. He had no clue. Well, it had to be somewhere close, so I started looking. I had no sympathy for him. Other guys were still walking after they sprained their ankles coming off the mountain.

Our platoon halted and a medic and our first sergeant came running back to his aid. The medic gave him a *lollipop*: powerful medicine to dull the pain. As I was looking for his M-4, First Sergeant asked me what I was doing. After I told him he started yelling at my AG for not having his weapon slung. This AG is just as bad if not worse than my last. I was stuck with a guy who couldn't carry his own damned weight.

I found his weapon and brought it back to him. I grabbed his round ruck and started to carry it. As we started moving again, I kept an eye on him. Every time I looked back, I got more pissed off. He was walking fine and I was sucking. The anger helped push me though.

My AG knew I was pissed off. He kept asking for his round ruck back. I was too pissed off so ignored him and kept walking. I kept going and he kept asking, but soon I was smoked from humping that weight and trying to keep up with the fast pace. I finally broke and gave it back to him.

We then took a knee, he came up to me asking for water. "WHERE DID ALL YOURS GO!?" He said, "I drank it all." I got mad at him again for not conserving it. I knew he was a bigger guy, but if he needed a lot of water to run on, he should have packed more water bottles with him than just a Camelbak. Now I was giving him mine. Never in my life have I ever been so angry with another Ranger. Finally, we picked up and continued.

As we walked, I saw the machine gunner's AG falling out. He too was out of water and said his muscles were cramping. I grabbed his assault pack, gave him and my AG more water and kept moving. I carried it until my muscles were smoked. I gave it back to him and he carried it a short way. The medic and our first sergeant came back to check on my AG. I told them about both AGs being out of water and smoked. The medic gave them a water bottle. First Sergeant told me to sit right there and watch over those two while the rest of the platoon cleared the NAI. Our forward observer walked up to us and passed over another water bottle and the two of us continued to babysit those men.

Our platoon cleared the NAI. They found RPGs, mortar rounds, AK-47s, grenades and IED-making material. We prepared to exfil. The plan was to blow up the weapons cache with a laser guided missile from Bagram, but it didn't do enough damage so they dropped two 500-pound bombs on it as well.

When we arrived back at OE, First Sergeant came up to speak with me. "Your AG is fired!" I told him, "Thank You!" It wasn't that he was a bad guy, it was that he put other platoon members' lives in danger by not being able to do his job. We were only as strong as our weakest link. The great thing about being in Regiment is that you must prove yourself every single day. Just because you made it there doesn't mean you get to kick your feet up and relax. If you don't perform, you are sent packing. My new AG, though, was a tough, scrappy kid from Boston who had arrived at the 1st Ranger Battalion just three weeks before deployment. This kid had a heart of a lion and I looked forward to working with him.

A squad leader felt my pain and came up to talk with me. "How do you keep getting stuck with these crappy privates?" he asked. "I don't know, probably because nobody else wants them. But I have 'Boston' now. He's gonna do just fine." We packed our bags and headed back to Kandahar.

We arrived back at Kandahar from OE but did not stay in the same building because other soldiers had moved in while we were gone. Instead, we stayed in a huge circus tent, sweating it out while the heat hit over 100 degrees every day. Unfortunately, we slept during the day when it was the hottest. Some lay in bed sweating because the two AC vents that ran across the tent did not blow cold air far enough to reach us. We were miserable to say the least.

A machine gun team leader came up with a great idea. He used empty water bottles to connect a tube running from his bed to a hole in the AC vent. *Brilliant.* Everyone else did the same thing and soon there was a spider web of water bottles running to each Ranger's bunk. The cool air was no longer wasted and we finally got some sleep.

Our next mission would consist of us staying out for 48 hours (June 24-26). The RODs before were difficult, well, this one was going to make those look easy. 48 or more hours is a long time to stay awake. We were going to set up in an area where U.S. forces hadn't yet been. Like the times before, we would set up and wait for the Taliban to come for us. *These 'Alamos' are crazy*, I thought, but then again, someone has to get out there and kill these fuckers—time to be brave, Ranger up and get our man-dance on with those wannabe warriors.

We were at the airfield waiting to board when a team leader walked up. He said, "Hey Bradley, do you have a grenade on you?" I didn't, so he handed me one. I felt like a real badass. I had my M-4 rifle, 9mm pistol, the M-3 Carl Gustaf, a SOG knife and now a grenade. So armed, we loaded the birds and flew out.

We infilled, cleared an NAI and took over a compound that could house 2nd and 3rd Platoon. We paid the family that lived there and told them the same thing as the other families—don't come back until tomorrow. They left and we started setting up our fighting positions. It was still dark and we hastily worked before the sun came up.

We blew portholes into the walls with demo. To connect the compound next door, we had to take down a wall by hand. The PL wanted to make sure we could get a litter through in case any men were hit. My AG and I looked for tools. We found a pickaxe and started tearing down the wall with it, taking turns until the job was done. My AG and I found a good fighting position mixed in with 1st Squad. It was going to be another hot day of 115 degrees so we started making shade. I ran around with my AG finding the distances to the buildings, the walls and anywhere else the enemy would try to fight us.

We picked up chatter from the Taliban. They said something about attacking us but they are going to wait for the *big one*. They came back to say, "The Big One's trigger does not work." Rangers laughed and made fun of them saying things like, "You should've checked your shit," and, "Watch out for incoming arrows next," and "They might throw rocks at us." It didn't matter what they use against us. Our plan was that when they started firing at us, we'd shoot back at them with the goose. I liked the idea. *Let's shut them the hell up.*

A few minutes passed by and they started shooting. Bullets flew over our heads and hit the outside of the walls. We believed they were shooting from the right side of the building 100 meters away from us. I told my AG, "Load up an HEDP round. We are going to blow that building up."

A Ranger shot off a high explosive 40mm grenade round as we were moved up to the wall. I heard it explode and his squad leader exclaimed, "Holy Shit! I think that was an arm!"

3rd Squad continued to fight back as I lined up the shot. I remembered that these rounds shoot high so I aimed lower to ensure this round wouldn't be wasted. It was my only HEDP round.

KA-BOOM! The round impacted the building with a massive explosion. We waited for the dust to settle to see the damage. One-third of the building was destroyed. The gunfire from the northeast building stopped. We called in the birds to see if they could tell us if there were any EKIA visible. They came back with three confirmed EKIA. The kills were split up between the three of us, but who really knows how they died without examining the bodies. Maybe everyone else killed them, and I killed none. That might be something God and I discuss the day we meet, but at the time, it was all about killing these men off and trying to keep each other alive. As long as they died, even in the moment it didn't matter who killed them. We kept each other safe; priority number one.

More fighting broke out and this time they hit us from the southwest portion of the compound, 3rd Platoon's side. 3rd Platoon fended them off and held their side of the compound. After that engagement, we picked up more chatter. They planned to cease fighting and collect their dead. For an hour or more, there hadn't been any shooting. It was midday and Rangers were baking in the heat. When I got relieved from pulling security, I did my best to build them some shade.

I had just cut down a small tree with small leaves that would provide some good shade when an RPG and machine gun fire started coming in. I sprinted back to the wall to grab my goose. This time, we moved to a different fighting position to avoid shooting the goose from the same spot.

We believed they were shooting from the left side of the building. My AG set the round for 90 meters so it could burst in the air, sending hundreds of ball bearings their way. I took aim and squeezed the trigger. *KA-BOOM!* The round exploded just where I meant it to. The fighting continued so I was told to shoot the building. The bad news was I only had two HE rounds remaining. These rounds were not made to destroy buildings. My AG loaded up another round and this time the HE round impacted the building. The round caused very little damage. Our mortar teams were doing their best to drop rounds on it as well.

Our PL ran over to our position and yelled out, "Hey, we have enemy fighters low crawling up to our positions from the other side this wall (the east wall). Who has grenades?" Remembering I received one from a team leader out on the airfield, I quickly said, "I DO, SIR!" Three other Rangers ran up to the wall and pulled out their grenades. The PL said, "On the count of three, pull the pins and throw your grenades over the wall." He counted to three and we did. We continued to fight and the Apaches came in after and cleaned up anything we missed.

Everything settled down for the next few hours. We figured the enemy must be out collecting their dead again. Only a few people were on guard pulling security. Others were sleeping and trying to rest up for the walk tonight and the fight tomorrow. We were taking 45-minute shifts.

Five minutes before my shift, I started getting my gear on to pull security. It looked as if we were going to be just waiting for darkness to fall so we could move out. Out of nowhere, an RPG flew in and hit one a wall somewhere to the left of us. We returned fire.

Over the radio, I heard, "Fire the goose!" I dropped my M-4 and grabbed the goose. We set another HE round to impact the right side of the building. I went to set the range drum and it was locked up. It would not budge. "My weapon is down!" I pulled out a rag and a bottle of CLP. I squirted it on the range drum and turned the knob. It turned and I pulled a rag out of my pocket and wiped off the mud that oozed out of the cracks.

Every time a goose is fired, it kicks up a massive cloud of dust. Those small pieces of dirt and dust can lock up the range drum, which is what happened to me. (I share this information with you in case any future Rangers encounter this problem. Make sure you have a rag and CLP with you!)

About a minute later, I yelled, "The goose is back up!" My squad leader pushed to the side and I moved into his place and fired. It was another direct hit on the building and the Taliban stopped firing at once. The Apaches arrived and stayed until it was dark.

After the last engagement was over, a private I worked with for the last two deployments walked over to us. He was trembling and nervous as fuck. He said with a shaky voice, "Does anyone have a cigarette?" None of us did, but were curious why he was shaken up. He explained what happened, "That RPG blasted through the building and stuck in the fucking wall. It didn't explode though; it's still in the wall. There were three of us in there."

A civilian with us took small bits of shrapnel to the head. His injuries were not life threatening. They bandaged him up and he stayed out there with us like a soldier.

It was scary thinking about it—if that RPG exploded inside that room with them in it, we would have likely lost them all. War is such a strange damned thing. You just never know when your time is going to come. A man can only have so much luck before it runs out.

We stayed for a few hours after dark, broke our fighting positions down and moved out. 3rd Platoon headed to clear an NAI. Afterwards, they would link up with 2nd Platoon, who would move to the pre-planned compound and start setting up the platoons' stronghold. The ground was flat and hard from being so damned dry, allowing us to move fast across it. It was still hot outside and I was sweating like I had been all damned day.

We arrived at the compound we planned to take over. I *set in* next to a wall that overlooked a field and a road. It was quiet outside, except for barking dogs and women and children screaming and crying off and on. Many times I have heard these sounds. It must suck for families trapped in the middle of war. It's not their fault the Taliban has brought us to their country. We can only hope that when this is all said and done, we leave this country a better place than we found it.

3rd Platoon cleared their NAI. They found a ton of IED-making material. They were about a mile from us and began heading our way. Soon they were far enough away and a 500 pound bomb was dropped on the building. I saw the explosion through my NODs. A huge flash lit up the sky and right after, I heard the boom it made. Another was dropped to ensure the material no longer existed.

Everyone outside pulling security was told to move into the compound now that it was cleared. My AG and I looked for the best spot to allow us to engage the enemy at the furthest range on 2nd Platoon's portion of the compound. There was a dry ditch running north to south. We decided to post up there and face to the east where many civilian tents were sitting. We expected the Taliban to run off the villagers and fight us from there. The people who lived in them looked to be sheep and goat herders. Everything else around 2nd Platoon's area of operation was dried up fields of dirt with woodlines far away.

As we were setting up, our PL and our interpreter talked to the man who owned the compound. The owner was mad, but we explained to him that he needed to take his family far away because the Taliban would come and we would fight. He understood, shook our PL's hand and bowed. We gave him money like we did with the other families, and they moved away from the danger that was sure to come.

The night passed uneventfully and it was quiet all day. We were just baking in the dry heat. We watched Afghans walk from their tents to a well to pump water. We then picked up some chatter from the Taliban saying, "Yes, we know where they are, but we do not have a problem with them." Hearing this made us laugh.

Almost an hour passed and still no attack from the Taliban. It was probably 2:00 PM local time. We were all relaxed except those pulling security. Some of us had kits and helmets off as we sat there trying to beat the heat. I saw a dog breaking away from the tents. He was sniffing toward the ground and was heading straight for us. *Wow, this dog doesn't even see us. I wonder how close he gets before he shits himself when he finds us here?* Suddenly I saw the dog flinch from fear and about fall on his belly. I looked left to see and hear an RPG screaming by from 3rd Platoon's area of operation. Following that was machine gun fire. I hit the deck and low-crawled about ten feet to my helmet and body armor and threw it all on in a hurry.

I was ready to fight, but the Taliban did not engage us on our front. I was hoping to get the call to move to 3rd Platoon's location, but it never came. They had it under control and it was very boring as we stood our ground. We were not in the fight but we had to keep the 360-degree perimeter. Our mortars dropped a few rounds and then got shut down.

An A-10 Warthog sings a song of beauty; music to our ears as it fires on the enemy. It came in so fast. Those Taliban fighters were killed without even knowing what the hell just hit them. That awesome machine is so quiet on approach, so fast and so deadly. I never even heard it coming in until it fired its cannon and already flew by.

We picked up more chatter and a Taliban commander saying, "Good job, that was a good attack. Come to my position so I can get a count of who is still alive." Not long after the A-10 came back. The pilot smoked four of them in a truck with RPGs. The last chatter we picked up was, "It is getting late and we are done for the day."

As we waited for darkness to set in, my only hope was that it would come fast. I killed all the damned ants I saw around me. I must have killed over 200 of the little bastards throughout the day. Hours passed and finally it was time to move to exfil and head back to base.

We got back to KAF and took showers and cleaned the dirt from our weapons caused by the brownout from the CH-47 exfil. After finishing, I stayed up to write down everything from the last 48 hours. I did this after every mission because I wanted to remember what we did before it became nothing but a blur in my mind. These stories will one day be lost to time. Time eats at everything, and I wish my Grandpa had left something behind like this back from when he fought in WWII. It would have been an honor to read.

The next day came and I must have slept for 24 hours. I was not sure what was going to come of the day so I stayed up for a few more hours. Everyone was sleeping so I went back to bed to catch up on as much sleep as I could as well.

Two days after conducting the mission, we had a meeting. We received an update on the 48-hour mission we conducted. On a Taliban website they posted, *We have killed a bunch of US forces last night in our battle. We have also shot down one of their helicopters.* Rangers started laughing and booing the news update because it was not true. No Rangers were killed in those firefights and no helicopters were shot down. To be exact, during that two-day span, we had a confirmed 21 EKIA. Between 3rd Battalion and 1st Battalion, in a little over three weeks since our arrival, 120 Taliban fighters were killed. From the 450 they started with, only 330 remain.

As dangerous as it was being out there, we were up for the challenge of taking away the battlefield from the Taliban. The *Deployment of Alamos* strategy worked, and got it done faster than we expected. We love you America. Your boys are working hard for you!

Rangers Lead The Way!

- COLBY BRADLEY
1/75

August 2010

"IN THE WATER"

In my time in Ranger Battalion, certain things have been pounded into me. First, in your Battalion, everyone hates Alpha Company. Second, everyone hates 3rd Battalion. Finally, the Army Special Mission Unit is way better than the Navy Special Mission Unit. In my experience, this was the truth for a long time, as my platoon had only worked with the Army SMU and the *Vanilla* Naval Special Warfare teams (Non-SMU), which were much different than their *Big Brothers*. My point of view changed on this deployment to Afghanistan, though. I was among a few Rangers who deployed with the Navy SMU and my experiences differed from what most others told me about working with them.

It was 2010 and we were assigned to integrate with the Naval Special Warfare SMU in Logar Province. To say we were expecting the worst is an understatement. Most of the plane ride over (when we were awake) was filled with bitching about how bad it might be. Once we arrived and conducted the normal relief in place with our sister battalion, we started to meet the *Team* guys we would be working with. During the first part of the deployment, it was like any other two different units coming to know each other. Imagine it like a special operations version of a middle school dance. We played *Call of Duty in* our hooch and they played in their hooch.

Things started to change after two weeks, as we had been on a dozen or so missions together. During one particular mission, as we were on our approach to the objective, a decent sized stream lay in our way. You would think: *SEALs…water…just walk into the stream and keep going right?* Wrong on so many levels. I learned that night that no one likes to get wet. Even a SEAL, who has been to BUD/S and has swam in everything from a submarine's torpedo tube to a whale's vagina. Everyone hates to get wet. So what do I do? Well, I had seen the movie *Navy SEALs* with Charlie Sheen about ten times, so I walk through the waist deep water. Most people would just say *fuck it* at this point, and follow that person through the water. Not the SEALs. No, they decided a bridge about 1.2 kilometers away looked like a better option.

So my squad and I sat on the other side of this river waiting on the team guys to find this bridge. I wasn't mad about getting wet or waiting for them. I was mad because my Lifesaver candies were wet with the nasty-ass water that I just waded through. Once the mission was over , and we were waiting on the helicopters to pick us up, we made fun of the SEALs for not going in the water. To this day I am convinced that me walking through that water is what broke the ice between us. The next briefing, we came with a rope bridge made of tampons for the team guys and everyone had a good laugh about that. No, I don't remember how we found the tampons, but like with anything in Battalion, shit just appears when you ask for it.

On most missions, it was 12 to 14 of us split into two teams to augment the team guys with whatever they needed. It was a symbiotic relationship with our two units working in full integration. During this time, I could feel a shift in attitude as we started to trust each other more and become a team. What transpired next was something that would cement our bond forever, as we still talk to each other about it to this day.

We had been receiving more and more intelligence about a group of Taliban setting up ambushes on Route One near our FOB. One night we had some great intelligence and some assets overhead that spotted one of these groups setting up for an ambush later in the night. We did a quick brief and everyone loaded up on the buses. Leadership went back to the JOC to watch air assets soften the target with pre-assault fires. No more than two minutes after the first missile hit, we were in the air en route to the objective. The seven-kilometer ride was short and the energy in the bird was palpable.

As the bird landed and we exited the aircraft, we took fire from the woodline. We were glad and had expected it. I told our Mk-46 gunner to place 10 to 12 round bursts into each muzzle flash until his 200-round drum ran dry. This would allow the SEALs time to get out of the wide-open farmland and move behind a building for cover. They would then be able to clear the ditch that enemy fighters were using as a trench. Everything was going to plan until we were just 35 meters away from the enemy--inside hand grenade range. That's when it becomes more a fight of will than of who has the better gear.

On our last bound forward, the far-left side was about to move when they took fire from a PKM machine gun. Right after we started taking fire, I could see tracers chewing up the ground and the Rangers on the end of our line. I could hear Doc yell "RANGER DOWN!" while sprinting over to the left side of the line. At the same time, the SEALs were also leading a charge into the trench and taking overwhelming fire. As I moved to cover over the radio I heard a SEAL was down and others were hit. I placed the Mk-46 gunner and a

Ranger team leader next to me to create a wall so that Doc and another squad leader could pull the wounded Ranger behind cover to start working on him.

As I looked over my shoulder at Doc and the squad leader calling in the CASEVAC, I could see just behind them was a small six-inch berm in an otherwise wide-open field. This at least gave the casualty some cover, even if we had to work in the open to save him. I yelled at Doc to move him and told the team leader next to me to help treat him since he was an EMT. The Mk-46 gunner and I checked each other to see we'd been hit. All either of us found was a small through and through gunshot on the outside of his arm. As I was checking him, his Mk-46 decided right now would be a great time to double-feed two rounds into the barrel. So, while the gunner was trying to fix his gun in record time, I fired at almost cyclic to keep the rate of fire up.

The Mk-46 was back up and they had packaged the wounded Ranger up for the CASEVAC. During this time, I saw some team guys had made the long movement to us in the middle of the field and were coming in line with the Mk-46 gunner and me. *Quick back-story about the movie Navy SEALs again: remember when they take fire from the enemy and peel off, turning to run by the next guy hitting him on the shoulder, until they've all repeated through to the last man and are out of contact? Yeah,* that is 100% what happened when the team guys came on line with us after the CASEVAC birds took back off. To say that I was surprised is a huge understatement; I don't even know if I registered what was happening until I got slapped and saw a guy running behind me. I won't lie, I had a huge smile on my face when my brain got smart to what was going on and I realized what I was about to do.

As I fired two more rounds, I turned off to my right and then ran to my left and broke contact, hitting the guy who was about two arm's-lengths away from me. As I approached the end of the line, I went back down to a low knee and could not help but be disappointed. As usual, the movies made it look way cooler than it truly was. We did this until we had put about 75 meters between us and the ditch. We made our way into the other ditch on the opposite side of the field and called for fire from AC-130s once everyone was there. We then moved to the exfil site about 800 meters away.

On the ride back to the FOB, I checked on the Mk-46 gunner and prepared him to move to the hospital once we touched down. He would later be awarded the Distinguished Service Cross, second only to the Congressional Medal of Honor, for his actions that night. As we left the bird, we walked up to the receiving medics and they checked us for wounds we missed in our own checks. It was then I asked about my friend we CASEVAC'd off the battlefield. I already knew in my head he was most likely already gone after I saw him being moved to cover, but one always keeps hope that your best friends will be ok. I ran into my platoon sergeant and he told me what I expected; he didn't make it. It was like a punch to the face. It was all I could do to get in a truck and ride back to the compound. Once I made it into the gate my body went on autopilot; I put my kit away and restocked my ammunition in my spent magazines.

I don't remember exactly when the other guys came back, but I remember seeing our fallen Ranger's best friend. They were as close to brothers as they could be without blood relation. He asked for an update on how everyone was doing, as he still had not heard the news. I could feel my eyes over flowing with tears as I told him he was gone. At first he didn't believe me, but I think the look on my face said it all. He broke down in a bunker maybe 20 feet from where I delivered the news to him.

The next few days were a blur of helping prepare my friend for his Angel Flight amidst uncontrolled emotions that came and went. I could not even play *Call of Duty* for a long time, as it was the last game we all played together right before the mission. We had paused the game so we could all continue together when we returned. When people would just say his name, emotion would rush out and consume me.

The relationship between Rangers and SEALs changed after we returned from the ceremony at the airfield to send our friend and the SEAL who had also been killed to be with their families again. It was a very emotional time for everyone at the camp as we dealt with what we could. We placed our emotions on the back burner when missions came. This also led to what I think was the greatest mixing of the two forces, as we now felt a part of one team. I learned more about their unit than I had ever known, and my respect grew for them every day I was there. To clear things up, we had a sister platoon who had a different experience with them at the same time. It was hard for them to wrap their heads around how much they treated us as equals as it flew in the face of many Rangers' experiences.

At the end of our deployment, it was crazy for me to think of my first experience with an SMU back in 2004, just pulling security and being a top-gunner for them. I cleared buildings right alongside them and did mission planning as an integral part of their team. It is a testament to how far Rangers have come and it makes me smile every day. At the same time, a steep cost has been paid to be where we are today - a reminder that I carry not just on my wrist but in my soul every day. It took me over two years to come to terms with seeing my friend die in front of me, and I am grateful for the help everyone has given me along the way.

-MARTIN

1/75

SEPTEMBER 2010

"LOST IN THE SAUCE"

This story takes place in Panjway District, Kandahar Province, sometime in early September 2010. I don't remember the objective name and I couldn't show anyone the place on a map, but I can remember the details of the night as clear as the day they happened. At the time of this mission I was a 19-year-old private first class and rifleman in a line squad.

On this night, our mission was to conduct a NAI clearance, then set up a ROD site with our sister platoon. Second platoon (mine) would infil about an hour ahead of first platoon, and we would attempt to clear one or two NAIs before linking up at the potential ROD site with first platoon. Basically, we'd clear a couple of houses where intelligence reported possible enemies. First Platoon would take over a house, and together we would fortify the position where we would remain until nightfall, and then exfil back to our FOB. The entire purpose of our ROD sites was to attract enemy activity so we could engage them. We were being used as a *shaping* force, so that the regular Army units could move into the area after we left, benefitting from our effects on the Taliban fighters in the area. This was as much as I understood about the types of missions we were conducting at the time.

To provide some perspective for this story, I must explain my level of awareness at this point in my career. By now, the reader should have a basic understanding of how information is disseminated in the Army. It trickles from the top down and the lowest tier of dissemination happens at the team leader level. All our team leaders carried radios to receive information from the squad leaders, who took orders from the platoon leader or platoon sergeant, who had their information and orders from the company commander, and so on and so forth. As a rifleman, all information was received from my team leader, Specialist Rose.

This was only my third mission ever and all I knew at this point were the golden rules of being a private: go where your team leader goes, shoot what your team leader shoots, and take responsibility for your actions. Or something like that. I've forgotten most of the things I used to know as a private, but those are pretty much the basics. You follow your team leader and watch his back. The team leader is always focused on his objective, which in our case was climbing. Our squad would get to the compound just ahead of the main assault squad, climb on the walls and try to get an idea of what was going on inside the compound so the assault squad wasn't going in blind.

I would carry a litter and medical equipment in case we took casualties and also the ladder for my team leader (because privates carry the heavy shit). I would usually never climb; instead I set the ladder up, sat at the bottom and simply held the ladder just in case it fell. It was a pretty lame job, but such is the life of a private. I would also provide extra security to our rear, since my team leader would be totally focused inward on the objective compound.

In summary, being a private means that when on a mission, you aren't part of the information flow going through the command nets. You only know what your team leader has time to tell you, so situations tend to be even more confusing for new Privates, who are generally *lost in the sauce* when the shit hits the fan.

It was still warm in Southern Afghanistan in September and our infil flight was fairly short and comfortable. We used two MH-47 Chinook helicopters to infil our entire platoon. I sat packed on the floor of the bird with all the other Privates. About five minutes into the flight the door gunners did their test fires. First the mini-guns tested their weapons: *BRMMMMMMPH! BRMMMMMMMMMMPH!* Their extreme rate of fire makes them not even sound like guns, but some sort of power tool. The M-240Bs went next. *DAT-DAT-DAT-DAT-DAT! DAT-DAT-DAT-DAT-DAT-DAT!* The slower, staccato burst of the M-240B is very distinct. The sulfuric smell of gunpowder hovered around the interior of the bird before being swept away by the wind flowing in the open gunner windows and out of the back ramp hatch. The barrel from one of the SAW gunners sitting in the chair above me dug into my ankle. I kept my composure until he shifted his weight onto his gun, digging the barrel deeper into my ankle. I swatted his barrel off my leg and pulled my leg up against my chest. Something like this would happen every five or ten minutes, and I'd shift my bodyweight or bend my legs. Usually, if the flight was longer than 45 minutes, I couldn't feel my legs by the time we arrived. I leaned against the heavy litterbag strapped to my back, keeping one hand on my ladder tucked under everyone's feet, constantly reminding myself not to forget it.

Finally, after what seemed like ages but was probably only 20 minutes, we hear, "TEN MINUTES!" Everyone echoed the command and held up all ten fingers, signaling that we were ten minutes from infil. I remained sitting and flipped down my single tube PVS-14 night vision goggles. Almost everyone else in the platoon had dual tube night vision goggles except for me. *Life sucks.* My PVS-14 powered on, projecting a green image onto my right eye. I left the PVS-14 on, but tilted my helmet up a bit to give my eye a rest before it was staring at a green light all night.

"SIX MINUTES!" That was the cue to get moving. On the six-minute call, everyone on the floor heaved themselves up to a knee somehow. I struggled to get up, and grabbed the hands of whoever was sitting on each side of me in the seats and they pulled me up to my knee. I bent over, putting one hand on the floor to take some strain from my knee, which ached from the weight pushing it into the hard floor, even with kneepads on. I checked my safety lanyard, which was hooked into the floor, just to make sure I knew where to unhook it from when the time came. I tilted my helmet down and made sure my NVGs were focused for viewing further out. This made everyone in the bird look blurry but distinguishable.

While looking out the small window, I could clearly see the terrain below us. It looked like an alien planet. Mud houses, farm fields and orchards seemed to be randomly placed. Fires burned in the distance. I felt butterflies in my stomach, almost the same feeling I as before a wrestling match or a race, except the fear was amplified. I was scared to make a mistake. If I fucked up, I might get someone killed, but more than likely, I'd just get put on my team leader's shit list, which nobody wanted to be on as a private. Then there's the looming question of what the night would bring. *Are we going to take contact on infil? Will it be a quiet night? Am I going to step on a pressure plate?* There were a million variables that went through my mind on infil and I didn't start functioning until I stepped foot on the ground. On the bird, I had the luxury of second-guessing and pondering. Once I left the ramp, I had to simplify my thoughts and do my job. I waited for the one-minute call.

BRMMMMMMMPH! BRMMMMMMMPH! BRMMMMMMMPH! My body jumped, like when someone pops around a corner and says, *"BOO!"*

BRMMMMMMMPH! BRMMMMMMMMMMMMMMMPH! The left side minigun started up and it wasn't a test fire this time. *BRMMMMMMPH! DAT-DAT-DAT-DAT-DAT!* The M-240B joined in, both guns trying to defend us from what I would later learn was machine gun and RPG fire. One of the most helpless feelings in the world is taking fire while in a helicopter, because all you can do is sit there and hope to God that the bad guy doesn't get a lucky shot and down your bird. "ONE MINUTE!" The call came and everyone postured themselves to be ready to get up and run off the ramp. We could feel and hear the rotor blades cutting through the air as the bird dropped. The engines and rotors on a helicopter are loud and it's almost impossible to have a conversation. It's not like the movies. Finally the bird set down, but rougher than usual. The gunners stopped firing. I stood up and waited for the crowd of Rangers in front of me to run off the bird.

It wasn't even five seconds into it when a large flash whited out everyone's NODs. I hadn't even stepped off the bird yet, but didn't think anything of the flash and accompanying sound like a gunshot. I would later learn that by some dumb Taliban luck, we had landed with our ramp right on a trip wire *Ponzi* grenade and the first man off tripped the grenade. Somehow, when the device detonated it only sprayed the right side of the bird with shrapnel and a piece traveled up between one of the pilot's legs, but no one was wounded. We all got off the bird and set up a messy half-moon shape. It looked like a Fourth of July celebration and laser light show were both going on at the same time. Off to our right, there were rapid-fire explosions, compliments of an AC-130 Spectre gunship's 40mm cannon. The explosions were only 100 meters from us. There were infrared lasers and infrared spotlights everywhere. The FOs marked our positions with powerful lasers, all types of aircraft were pointing with their lasers down onto enemies that we couldn't see while Little Birds and the AC-130 were raining hell from above.

We all just sat there. Instead of storming the building, like it goes down in the movies, everyone seemed to be bewildered by the situation. You never want to commit to a situation that you don't understand and our leadership took some time to get their bearings. I had absolutely no clue what was going on—how many Taliban there were or where—nothing. I finally found my team leader, Rose and asked him what was going on. "Spectre is engaging squirters. We're getting ready to climb on the target compound. Just stand by." He held his hand up for a second like he was listening to a voicemail and received some new information from his radio. "Ok, let's move." We started out in a spaced out single-file line, a common formation used in Panjway to battle the threat of pressure plates. Theoretically, if you walk where the guy in front of you walked and nothing blew him up, you'll be safe.

I walked with the ladder behind Rose and our medic, Douglas, trailed behind me. We were Alpha Team, so we led. Bravo Team was trailing just behind us, led by Sergeant Lee. Our squad leader, Sergeant Dale worked his way to the front and started walking in front of my team leader. We moved along the right side of the compound, walking under low hanging trees that skirted the outer wall. I held the ladder in my left hand and suitcase-style carried my gun in my right hand. While it's arguable that carrying your gun like a suitcase is a shit-bag maneuver, I always thought it was stupid to have my gun hanging around my neck and banging into my ladder making noise.

We walked under low-hanging trees for maybe 30 meters when suddenly an infrared spotlight shined down onto a low wall, no more than ten meters in front of us. The spotlight lit up the whole area we were in and flashed repeatedly, indicating suspicious activity. We all froze, took a knee and Rose and Dale brought their guns up, scanning with their own IR lights. They scanned for a minute, maybe, and couldn't see anything. I would later learn that there were six enemy fighters with weapons hiding behind the wall, which would later be seen on footage from the ISR platforms flying overhead. Whether they were scared, or didn't know we were there, I'll never know. The situation wasn't as tense for me as it probably was for Rose and Dale because I was *lost in the sauce* and didn't even know what a flashing infrared spotlight meant. I just knew it wasn't good. I thought we might be lost or something. Dale and Rose doubled back, and we slowly crept back out the way we came, then made our way to our originally intended climb spot.

I set the tall ladder against the wall, which had a ditch running alongside it. An orchard surrounded the entire compound. My team leader and squad leader climbed up, and one of our snipers followed them. The roof had a sort of wavy structure, so that they could sit in between each hump in the roof as cover. The gunship started firing again, shooting powerful 105mm artillery rounds, which rocked the earth when they exploded. I sat down at the bottom of the ladder and I heard yelling and screaming going on in the compound. I had to make myself useful somehow. *Fuck it.* I climbed up the ladder and rolled onto the roof and sat there on a knee for a second, not sitting in the low part of the roof, but silhouetting myself against the night sky, a classic mistake.

Sergeant Dale turned around, "Get off the fucking roof!" Clearly, I wasn't that useful. I lowered myself from the roof onto the ladder, and as soon as I did a burst of rounds flew over my head and impacted the roof where I had been sitting. *CRACK CRACK CRACK CRACK-CRACK! One* thing that's always been curious to me is how you almost never hear the gun, but only the supersonic *CRACK!* of the bullet as it passes near you. I was off that ladder quicker than ever before. I got on my stomach and crawled into the ditch, not sure how to feel about my recent luck. Doc Douglas was laying on my right side, and our platoon FO, Sergeant Wayans, was on my left. I heard Wayans calling in Little Birds to suppress the enemy fire. "My position marked by IR Strobe, enemy position 70 degrees, 25 meters from my position. Engage with 2.75 rockets. Danger close."

First Sergeant popped up from inside the compound. "EVERYONE GET DOWN ON YOUR FACES!" I hugged the earth and buried my head into the side of the ditch, trying to get as small as possible. *WHUMPH! WHUMPH! WHUMPH! WHUMPH! The* rockets impacted farther left than I expected, almost at the low wall we had stopped at earlier. The explosions rocked the ground with impressive force.

The ditch we were in formed an L-shape, which faced the low wall. The compound walls followed this same curvature. After the rockets hit, the three of us sat there, waiting for whatever would happen next. Suddenly, Doc Douglas jumped up, responding to a call on his radio and sprinted to the lowest point of the compound wall, near the inner corner. He threw his gun at the nearest Ranger and leapt over the wall in one bound, with only his medical bag in hand.

During the clearance of the building, one of 3rd Squad's SAW gunners had entered a room and stepped on a Russian PMN mine, severing half of his foot. At the time, I had no idea what Doc Douglas was doing. I heard screaming inside the compound and my first thought was the gunship had inadvertently caused friendly casualties. About ten minutes after Douglas went over the wall, a group of three guys from 1st Squad gathered at the low point in the wall and began taking turns with a hooligan tool, battering the wall to make a hole. I had taken my litterbag off by now and thrown it at the bottom of the ladder. Rose, Dale and the sniper remained on the roof, not sure if the rockets from the Little Birds had fully suppressed the enemy. Finally, they broke through the wall and our platoon sergeant emerged. A group came through behind him, carrying a litter with someone wrapped up in a space blanket. One of them yelled in my direction. "Hey, get over here, grab this kit bag!" I ran to the break in the wall and our company executive officer stood there with a bag that contained the casualty's body armor, NODs and other sensitive items.

He threw the bag at me without saying anything. I slung the bag over my shoulder and began following the litter bearers. I didn't know if what I was doing was the right choice since I was separating from my team leader, but sometimes you just have to say *fuck it* and do what has to be done. We hung a right after we were clear of the compound and our route took us into a swampy path that ran underneath low-hanging trees, making walking a nightmare. For me it wasn't so bad, but the litter bearers were having a hell of a time. Every 20 feet or so, one of them would slip off the narrow path and fall into the mud, dropping the litter and causing the casualty to scream loudly.

The casualty was Specialist Rod and the way he screamed was like nothing I've ever heard before. I don't know if it was the ketamine that Doc Douglas gave him or the wound, but someone who is seriously hurt screams like a wounded animal, like their mind has left them. And it was *LOUD*. "AHHHH! AHHHHHHHHHHHHHH!" Each time the litter was dropped he would scream out louder. After ten minutes of walking through the quagmire, we emerged into an open, tilled field. I stayed close to the platoon sergeant, since I wasn't sure what to do. "Do I just drop the bag in the bird when it comes in?" The platoon sergeant responded with a calmness irregular for the situation. "Yep, just throw it on there and then run back off." We waited with Rod in the middle of the field and another squad spread out around us and pulled security outward, making sure we didn't get hit when we were most vulnerable. Rod was talking incoherently, reaching for anyone close by. He seemed to be slipping in and out of consciousness. After five minutes the MEDEVAC bird came in, flying in low, throwing up a large cloud of dust with it. We did our best to cover Rod, the litter bearers ran him onto the bird. I ran onto the bird, threw the bag on the floor and ran back off.

After the MEDEVAC, the rest of the platoon followed us into the field and I linked back up with my team leader. We ended up walking to another house that, like the previous house, was completely empty and we decided not to enter. That same night about one kilometer from us, our 1st Platoon brethren hit a pressure plate IED on a narrow path and their EOD technician was seriously wounded. Pressure plates were a huge threat in Panjway at the time. Both platoons decided our best course of action was to consolidate at the ROD site. We took sporadic mortar, RPG and small arms fire for the rest of the day and ended up getting a decent amount of close air support and mortar kills.

This is one of those stories which almost every man there that night would tell differently. The events of the night I describe only took about two hours, but there was so much that happened in that short time frame. It was such a chaotic situation, especially being as new as I was. I was too focused on my job to understand how hectic the situation actually was. Everyone is *lost in the sauce* their first few times in combat, but training usually takes over enough to get us through it all. It took a few more missions to really start being aware of my surroundings.

-KINGSLEY

2/75

November 2010

"THE CAVE"

It was November 2010. We were stationed in FOB Orgun-E, way up in the mountains. The FOB was just big enough for a chow hall, a few little white trailers for barracks used by the regular army unit stationed there, a large gravel HLZ big enough to fit multiple rotary wing aircraft and a small Special Operations camp. Our camp had five long concrete barracks. Each building had about five rooms that could hold up to ten or 12 men, but because we were a single platoon up there, we would only have four to six men to one room. All times day and night, the sound of helicopters flying over was common. Keep in mind that it was the month of November so the weather in Paktika Province was bitterly cold. There were nights we were chilled to the bone because our rooms only had two Mitsubishi wall heaters that would barely heat the room.

At this point, we had only been in country for a few weeks. We ran missions almost every night. If we had a night off it was due to weather. The missions consisted of five to ten kilometers of walking through the rugged terrain of Afghanistan's mountains. We would climb a few hundred feet to a thousand feet a night. On many missions we would see Taliban fleeing the target building, known as *squirters*. Their course of action was usually to run

306

up the nearest mountain, which would result in us calling for fire with any support aircraft on-station. We would do a battle damage assessment (BDA) afterwards to gather information and take pictures. On a few occasions, the call for fire wasn't successful which resulted in pursuing and eliminating the targets ourselves. On the night of November 14, it was the ordinary routine before mission. We would go to chow, come back to the TOC to see if we had a mission for that night. As usual, we did. We'd go to our rooms to put our assault uniforms on and walk to the ready-room to do pre-combat checks (PCCs) on weapons, radios and NODs. Afterwards, we would go to a mission briefing, which went into full detail of what we were going to do on target.

Once the CONOP was complete, 1st Squad, comprised of our squad leader, Staff Sergeant Pape, Sergeant Mays, Sergeant Roberts, Sergeant Clampman, PFC Hankman and I, would go to the ready room to build porthole charges for a ROD mission that we were supposed to do that night. At that point, we were informed that the current mission had changed and we were to pack an over-night bag to go to J-Bad. In a little less than an hour, we were on our way. Once we arrived, we were put in barracks with a single, plywood hallway. There were two sets of bunk beds in each room and the entire barracks smelled of mildew.

As soon as we settled in the barracks, our platoon sergeant, SFC Falcon and our PL, Captain Nellis, along with the other squad leaders, left for the JOC to see what the situation was. Soon after, they were informed that 1-327, 101st Airborne Division ran into heavy enemy contact in the southern portion of the Wataphur Valley during *Operation Bulldog Bite II.* They requested support from our Task Force to clear their northernmost objective. We received a CONOP quickly, then rushed to the barracks about 100 meters away.

As we put our kit on we received individual briefs from our team leaders of what would happen on target. As soon as we left the barracks, we were informed that one of our helicopters was broken and the mission was pushed to the right 24. We returned to our barracks, took off our gear and went to chow for mid-rats. Once we ate, we returned to the barracks and relaxed. One of the guys managed to find a monopoly board, so we played that to pass the time.

307

Toward the end of the game, the entire barracks shook so much that the bunk beds hit the wall. I never thought my first earthquake would be like that; it was an eerie feeling. Soon after, the squad leaders and team leaders returned from additional planning and had a new and better plan. Once we were handed our imagery, I was in awe. Our mission was to disrupt Taliban operations against coalition forces, gather intelligence and provide freedom of action for further operations. The goal was to clear a very large village with a platoon from 2nd Ranger Battalion.

For the rest of the night, I spent time looking at the imagery and studying it so that once I was on the ground, I would know what part of the village we were in. I finally managed to fall asleep and slept throughout the day into the next night. Once I woke up, we put on our assault uniforms and did the usual. Shortly after, we were informed that the mission was a go, so we waited outside the barracks for the buses to take us to the airfield.

We loaded two helicopters and flew to a small COP in the middle of a bowl surrounded by mountains. Lights glowed from the mud houses on the mountainsides. Immediately the helicopters took off to pick up the platoon from 2nd Battalion. We walked along a T-barrier wall and sat down to eat MREs. We waited for our CO and first sergeant to come out of the little shack that was basically the COP's TOC. After they exited the TOC, they took the entire platoon to an even smaller concrete shack that was just big enough to fit 30 guys shoulder-to-shoulder. The shack had no light and the intelligence officer who briefed us used a headlamp to light the whiteboard. He basically said the terrain was the steepest we would ever climb and it was a very wooded area.

Afterwards, he went into the rules of engagement (ROE), which were simple and straightforward. One of the squad leaders immediately asked what the estimated enemy force was and the intelligence officer answered, "50 to 500 fighters." In pure disbelief, the squad leader asked, "Did you say fifty to five-hundred?" and a quick yet blunt "Yes" followed it. Once there were no more questions, a firm "Good luck, gentlemen!" was said and we were sent back out to our spot on the T-barrier wall.

Not long after, we loaded onto helos and flew to the HLZ cut into the side of a mountain. We rushed off the helicopter into vegetation that made it feel like Vietnam. The HLZ was a dry rice paddy, the cool air smelled of burning trash and the night sky moved with little infrared dots of our assets watching from above. All we could hear were the helicopters leaving the HLZ echoing off the mountains and a humming of a support aircraft overhead. My squad was the lead in the formation for the platoon. It didn't take long for Sergeant Mays to get his bearing and start moving out.

We headed straight up the mountain, through the thick vegetation and woods. Not long after, we ran into an abandoned fighting position made of trees cut down and stacked like a log cabin. Immediately my heart started to pound; I could hear it in my ears it pounded so hard. We reached one of the false summits of the mountain and began descending into vegetation no taller than my head. We followed a beaten path to an HLZ that we were to clear before continuing to the objective. The name of the HLZ was *Carolina*. Once we cleared the 200-meter-wide HLZ, we continued to the mountain ridge where the village was located and started clearance of two houses.

At that time, we were informed 10 – 15 military aged males ran from a compound as we advanced toward the area. They then split into several groups and moved west down the steep cliffs into the valley. After learning of the squirters, 1st Squad took the job as *squirter interdiction team* and started the pursuit of the ones that headed west of our position. We went about 500 meters before we ran into the cliff's 400-meter drop down to the valley. SSG Pape informed SFC Falcon that we'd reached the limit of advance and could not pursue the squirters any further as an entire squad. He then directed Sergeant Mays to find a way down.

Looking across the valley, another ridge parallel from us extended about 1500 feet above our current position. While Sergeant Mays and Staff Sergeant Pape were trying to find a way down, the infrared laser from the reconnaissance assets above shined down to show the location of the two squirters at the bottom of the valley through the tall trees. The rest of the platoon was trailing behind. SFC Falcon looked down the cliff. *Damn.* It was a long way down. Sergeant Mays found a way down. SSG Pape directed the rest of the squad to stay on the cliff and told SFC Falcon that he was going to take his Alpha Team leader, Sergeant Mays and the dog handler, and Sergeant Mack, down the cliff to continue pursuit of the squirters. He looked at me and said, "Guess what I'm going to go do?" My reply was, "Going to go kill some motherfuckers…" In a calm whisper, he said "Damn straight!"

SSG Pape, Sergeant Mays and Sergeant Mack began downclimbing, despite the fact the entire squad volunteered to go with them. After a few minutes of battling with Sergeant Roberts and Sergeant Clampman, who wanted to go down with him, he still refused and went down with a three-man team. With the IR sparkle still on the squirters in the valley, they disappeared into the darkness. All we could hear was the breaking of branches while they climbed down. As soon as they reached the bottom of the cliff, SSG Pape set up an overwatch position that Sergeant Mays manned on a nearby high ground at the base of the cliff.

They made contact with one enemy rifleman who managed to squeeze one shot off before SSG Pape killed him. On top of the cliff with the rest of the platoon, all I could hear was a "tsk, tsk" sound from the suppressed weapons. After hearing the first engagement, another sparkle shined about 500 meters north and to my right. SFC Falcon asked what they were sparkling and the JTAC said it was, "five to ten fighters roaming around." SFC Falcon asked for a fire mission from the air assets overhead and a few minutes later told us to take cover as they rained down 40mm and 105mm rounds on the fighters north of us. He then radioed down to SSG Pape to take cover until the fire mission was complete.

The AC-130 ripped a series of 40mm and one 105mm on the mountainside where the fighters were located. The JTAC told SFC Falcon that the fighters dispersed and were no longer a threat. During the fire mission, SSG Pape took contact from a second rifleman that emerged from the same area as the first. SSG Pape eliminated the second rifleman and then threw a grenade in the position of the two shooters to verify the kill. Once the grenade exploded, SSG Pape assaulted through the bodies to confirm the kills, unknowingly exposing himself to a cave opening. An RPK opened up on SSG Pape's silhouette.

Sitting on the edge of the cliff, I saw tracers ricochet off rocks and into the air, looking like fireworks. One of those rounds wounded SSG Pape. Sergeant Mack immediately realized what happened and without hesitation, returned fire into the cave entrance. He engaged the machine gunner before the gunner could acquire him as a target. Following this engagement, Mack was quickly joined by Sergeant Mays as six to eight fighters fled from the cave. Mack and Mays promptly engaged the enemies as they fled and killed at least two of them.

After this, Mays jumped down from a six-foot rock ledge and low-crawled to Pape's position and attempted to pull him to cover. When he was unable to pull him, Mays radioed that Pape was down, moved to cover and watched over the cave until the rest of the element made their way down. As soon as the call was received, Sergeant Roberts, Sergeant Clampman, PFC Hankman and I slid down the cliff to their position. Following us was SFC Falcon and SSG Arrow, the Senior Medic.

Once I made it down there with the rest of 1st Squad, I saw Sergeant Pape trying to sit up while pointing to his left side. Sergeant Mays at that point was already beside him working with SSG Arrow to treat his wound the best they could. It wasn't long after that Staff Sergeant Kevin Pape died from his wounds. I had no idea SSG Pape had expired because I was pulling a security while they worked on him. The rest of the platoon made their way to us and filled gaps in the security.

The sun just started to rise behind us, making it just bright enough for everyone to put their NODs up. While we switched our NODs and IR lasers off, SSG Pape was being put on a Skedco and covered with a space blanket. It was now November 16th. SSG Victor threw several thermobaric grenades and frags into the cave, hoping to either flush the remaining fighters out or kill them all together. As the rest of the platoon headed 200 meters north up a beaten path to a medical evacuation HLZ, SSG Victor's squad bounded back to a safe distance so that we could call for fire on the cave.

After arriving at the MEDEVAC HLZ, a plowed field on the side of the mountain overlooking the valley, Sergeant Clampman and I attempted to put another Skedco litter in its case near a rock wall no higher than my torso which separated the beaten path from the plowed field. I remember looking over and seeing SSG Pape in the larger hoistable Skedco covered up without movement. I still didn't think he had died from his wounds. While working on getting the Skedco in the bag, one of the guys on the western side of the HLZ saw some of the Taliban fighters climbing their way up to the HLZ.

Without hesitation, Sergeant Clampman and I ran across the HLZ, slid in on a knee and began to engage the enemy climbing up. I could see the eyes of the enemy as they were climbing and what they were wearing; they were armed with nothing but AK-47's. I eliminated two of them before Corporal Worthington slid into the prone next to me armed with a Mk-48. One long burst of the Mk-48 pelted me with hot brass and links from the gun. It felt like lava rocks being hurled into my face. Sergeant Clampman told me we should move to SSG May's and Sergeant Roberts' position about ten meters behind us. As soon as we made our way to Sergeant May's position, he noticed fighters running into a house across the valley. He proceeded to give the command to engage with our 40mm grenades, "400 meters, house in the open, 12 o'clock, two HEDP." I loaded my first round into my M-320 grenade launcher and launched the grenade.

Now remember, we were in the mountains in high elevation; thinner air means the round will fly further. Also, we were about five-hundred feet above the target. I shot the first round...silence. Sergeant Mays looked at Sergeant Roberts and said, "Do you see where that went?" No one did. The correction was given; down 100 meters. I loaded the second grenade and shot. The second fell right on the house, as did the third. At this point, Sergeant James, our FO and a former Division I football player, was 20 feet from us against the rock wall next to the beaten path. He grabbed our attention by yelling, "You're being shot at!" That same instant a round impacted between Sergeant Roberts and me. In a frantic voice, he turned around and yelled, "Get the fuck off the HLZ!"

He ran past me as I was turning to get out of the line of fire. We ran to the southern portion of the HLZ where there was another rock wall no higher than my torso, with two trees no more than eight feet apart. As I ran toward the wall, I could see the tree branches falling off the trees from the rounds shredding them. I watched Sergeant Roberts jump over the wall and disappear. I was not far behind. When I came to jump the wall I saw on the other side was a 12-foot drop into a defilade 12 feet long and six feet wide. Sergeant Roberts was lying at the bottom and looked to be in pain. By the time I realized the situation, I was already committed to the jump and fell 12 feet, landing smack on top of of him. I busted my right arm on a rock and quickly checked to see if I broke it. Sergeant Clampman was not far behind us and he made the fall as well.

Sergeant Mays was above us standing on one of the tree roots protruding over the drop asking for my M-320 to engage the enemy. As I threw him the remaining 40mm rounds, SSG Shinman, CPT Nellis, Sergeant James and PFC Ramsay made their way to the defilade away from enemy fire, finding a safer way down. When we looked to the south from where we came, it was straight down about 10 feet and then sloped down about another 100 meters. The slope was nothing but shale rock and gravel with a treeline at the base. A few minutes passed by and Sergeant Mays took cover down with us in the defilade.

Sergeant Roberts and Mays simultaneously yelled at everyone to shut up. They were attempting to make out a faint voice on the radio. During a brief break in gunfire they heard a whisper over the radio, "Help...me..." Sergeant Mays looked around and wondered out loud, "Who is that and where is it coming from?"

15 minutes went by without any more clues from the radio. A CASEVAC helo had been called, but the HLZ was too hot to have them land. To slow the fire, we would drop bombs on the ridge across the valley and on the house where we took contact. Finally, Sergeant Mays spotted Sergeant Cox, one of our Snipers. He was about 50 meters from the treeline at the base of the slope, helmet off and weaponless. Sergeant Mays looked at 1st Squad and ordered us to follow him with SSG Arrow right behind. We were still under heavy contact. I followed Sergeant Clampman down to the base and took cover behind a tree just as he did. Sergeant Mays, Sergeant Roberts and SSG Arrow took Sergeant Cox's arms and threw them over their shoulders and carried him all the way back up to the defilade. The rest of us provided bounding security to allow them to climb up when Sergeant Clampman accidentally dropped Sergeant Cox's helmet and NODs as he was engaging a target. He had to run back and recover them before bounding back up the hill to rejoin us.

From there, PFC Ramsay and PFC Philson bounded back first, then Sergeant Clampman and I until we reached the defilade. I watched round after round miss us. In some moments, if I had misplaced my footing on the rocks,

I would have been wounded. When we were closer to the defilade, I could see Sergeant Mays looking back extending his arm to pull us all in. Back at our fighting position, we were gasping for air. Sergeant Mays told us to get a drink, but I'd been out of water since infil, so he extended the hose from his Camelbak and I was able to drink for the first time in over six hours. One more person joined us in our limited space and Specialist Taylor, a SAW gunner, provided suppression on the enemy while we bounded back. Sergeant James worked Kiowa attack helicopters for a gun-run on the slope and treeline we just left.

As I looked over, I saw SSG Arrow working on Sergeant Cox's wounds. Sergeant Cox took a gunshot wound to the lower portion of his jaw. Sergeant James kept bringing the Kiowas' gun-runs closer and closer to our position—within 50 meters. Danger close, the Kiowa would not shoot unless they knew our exact location. CPT Nellis pulled out a VS-17 panel (a bright orange square) and set it on the outer portion of the defilade in hopes the Kiowa could see it. Knowing it would not work, Sergeant James stumbled over our legs to get to the VS-17 panel while exposing himself to enemy fire. It seemed as soon as he exposed himself, the rate of fire from the enemy picked up and small trees were shot down on top of us. Sergeant James held the panel extended with both arms to show the pilots where we were, completely exposing to intense enemy fire.

He then jumped down back behind cover after being notified confirmation of our position. "DANGER CLOSE! Take cover!" he yelled. I got as low as I could in hopes of gaining cover. The gun-run was close enough I could taste the dirt the rounds kicked up. Just then, 500-pound bombs impacted the ridge across the valley and on the house I initially engaged. Not long after, Sergeant Bailey was above us to receive Sergeant Cox for the CASEVAC coming to pick up any wounded.

CPT Nellis radioed a situation report to our command. We had two wounded, Sergeant Cox and an interpreter who went by *Shotgun*. After a moment's pause, it was made known that SSG Pape was *killed in action*. That was the first time I realized he was really gone. I guess it was denial or lack of understanding of the situation and the wounds he received, but it hit us hard and a wave of anger came over me. As they started to push Sergeant Cox back up the defilade, Sergeant Clampman and I switched positions to where we could look down the slope with Specialist Taylor.

While under fire, two Black Hawk helicopters landed. Sergeant Bailey laid down covering fire while running with Sergeant Cox to the helicopters. As soon as they reached the birds, Sergeant Cox pulled Sergeant Bailey in and said, "Change mags!" As Sergeant Bailey got out of the way from the birds so they could take off after they loaded the 'terp and SSG Pape's body, he looked down at the little window on the side of his P-Mag and saw he had only four rounds left and needed to change them. As that was happening, the rest of the guys and I were being helped back up to the HLZ.

Once I reached the top, I took a knee behind the trees and turned back to help the rest of the guys up. Afterward, I noticed a kneepad that I had dropped by the tree a few hours prior when we first took fire on the HLZ. I didn't even know I had dropped it, but was glad to have it back. Soon, the platoon started the grueling climb up to the original house where we started before we began chasing squirters. Sergeant Clampman and I were dehydrated, extremely tired and on the verge of slipping into a daze. Sergeant Roberts, who was now the Alpha Team leader handed me a CLIF SHOT so I could maintain enough energy to get to the top. When we finally got up, we found the 2nd Battalion guys had already established a security perimeter. The Kiowas were still doing gun-runs and Sergeant Roberts placed me in a good security position. After a few minutes, the weapons squad leader called for a Gustaf fire mission on a single man repeatedly yelling *Allahu Akbar* at them. Specialist Shale, who was our Gustaf gunner and his AG loaded up a round and shot three 84mm recoilless rounds, eliminating the threat. Each time he fired, I could feel the punch in my chest of the round exploding, forcing air out of my lungs.

I sat there, slightly dazed and noticed my socks were soaked from sweat. Sergeant Mays, who was now our squad leader, secured 1st Squad a room in the house. The house was built into a hill and had a watermill wheel on the side with an irrigation canal. The bottom floor had wooden branches holding up the stairs where we were. As soon as 1st Squad was all in the room, we realized things had settled down and a rush of emotions hit us all. Sergeant

315

Mays said, "Staff Sergeant Pape would have been proud of what we did today."

We all managed to muster up enough strength to shed our kit and helmets. We found and drank whatever water we could. Hankman and Sergeant Roberts laid down and covered up in a space blanket, falling asleep quickly from pure exhaustion. Sergeant Clampman and I were at the other end under the blanket trying to sleep. Sergeant Mays, after handing me his extra pair of black socks, went to the rooftop with the rest of the leadership. After we fell asleep, two loud explosions filled the valley and the overpressure hit the house with enough force to wake all of us. Specialist Vale peeked into the room and told us that it was two bombs dropped on the cave where SSG Pape was killed in the hopes of destroying it.

We slept all day, although I was in and out of sleep with the Kiowas flying overhead and people talking. Once fully awake, I put on my body armor and with the rest of 1st Squad, and walked outside. A very tired Sergeant Mays, who didn't sleep at all, greeted us. The rest of the platoon had found two 81mm Chinese Mortars. Inside of a giant hollow tree stump, there were more RPGs and other weapons. Our platoon sergeant took the backpack I was carrying containing 15 blocks of C-4, a satchel charge and other explosives and rigged the stump to blow. The platoon left the house as Sergeant Mays pulled the initiators to start the timed fuse and then ran to catch up with the rest of us.

Just as we reached the top of the hill the tree trunk blew, sending red fireballs into the air and destroying the house. Neither stood a chance with the amount of explosives we used, along with secondary explosions from the RPGs and mortar rounds already inside the tree trunk. As we continued, we could hear 155mm howitzer rounds scream in and slam the valley. Each time they hit, it shook the ground we stood on even though we far away. After the two-kilometer movement to reach HLZ Carolina, darkness fell again. We set up a large patrol base on top of the small hill overlooking the HLZ.

After the sun set, the cold began to seep through my clothes and into my bones. I went from being mildly cold to freezing in less than a minute. It was so painful and my feet were so cold that just standing was excruciating. PFC Hankman was right next to me and equally cold; we shivered together for hours. Overhead, the sky was alive with our assets in support. After a few hours, we heard the sound of a helicopter in the distance. *Exfil birds?* As the noise grew louder, the outline of a UH-60 Black Hawk appeared. It hovered on the other side of the hill and dropped the two body bags full of water, ammo, batteries and MREs we requested eight hours earlier.

For the rest of that night, I faded in and out of sleep. I tried to stay awake, but a few times I woke up from the pain of cold settling in my bones, the brisk wind plowing through the grass and hitting my side and once to the sound of PFC Hankman noisily chowing down on an MRE. After we restocked on food and water, we emptied the remaining unused water bottles and cut open the MREs so they could not be used, about 60 of each. We kept the batteries and ammo. I grabbed a duffle bag from the body bag the helos dropped and managed to get some hand warmers to put inside my boots to keep my feet warm and then put my legs in the duffle bag just to escape the wind. When I looked around, just about everyone was under a space blanket to stay warm.

A few more hours crawled by and Sergeant Mays came by to check on us and to inform us that an airstrike would happen soon. Shortly after, 500-pound bombs smashed into the ground all around the HLZ's treeline. I could feel the heat from each fireball; it was the best few seconds on that cold Afghanistan HLZ all night. Afterwards, the two platoons moved down to the HLZ and got in position to be picked up. Sergeant Mays and I carried the battery bag and Hankman had the ammo with Sergeant Roberts. Echoing off the mountains, you could hear the MH-47s coming to exfil us after picking up the 101st Airborne Division we were supporting. Once they landed, I ran straight to the Chinook's warm exhaust plume that shoots directly off its tail because I was so numb in the face. As we loaded up and sat down on the bird, we snap-linked in and I leaned back to take a deep breath. As I did, I broke down. I was happy to get the fuck out of there. We paid a high price on this mission.

Once we arrived back in J-Bad, we sluggishly walked off the bird to the bus taking us back to the barracks. I didn't say a word. There was dead silence. All I wanted was a bed to lie in and to fall asleep. I woke up the day we were to leave for FOB OE. Staff Sergeant Pape's belongings going back to

317

the States were getting packed up. We had just one day off before we went on our next mission.

3rd Platoon completed six more missions that deployment and returned home. We'd been gone since July. Of all my deployments and all my missions, that deployment hit the hardest. I knew becoming a Ranger would present many obstacles and situations out of my control, but I'm not sure I was prepared to witness one of the greatest men I knew and fought alongside of die so close to me. His fate was completely out of my and every other Ranger's control. I returned home to the United States a changed man, a better Ranger and a stronger individual—both mentally and emotionally. RLTW!

-LOGAN A. LEWIS

1/75

NOVEMBER 2010

"THE CAVE: WOUNDED"

On or about November 14, 2010, Team Darby out of FOB Orgun-E prepared for another mission in the KG Pass in Afghanistan. I was a sniper attached to 3rd Platoon, C Company, 1/75. Our platoon spent the majority of the deployment in Iraq, but as the war was nearly non-existent in that country, we moved to Afghanistan where they were experiencing one of its most violent years. While waiting for the final manifest call, a call canceling our mission came across the net and we got retasked on a QRF mission. The company commander called for the leadership to go report to the TOC to prepare for the mission brief. We were told 101st Airborne Division was in a serious firefight in the Kunar Valley and had a mass casualty situation. Their element was clearing a wadi system and was ambushed by a platoon-sized element of Taliban fighters. The report said they had taken 30 casualties, ten KIA and they were still taking heavy enemy fire. It wasn't clear if we were going directly in as the QRF team, or we would be put on standby, as another

QRF team was closer and could get there faster. When we arrived in J-Bad we were put on standby in case a second QRF element was needed and as a second task, we would possibly insert to hit a few targets. After a few hours had passed we stood down; the first QRF element provided enough support to help the 101st break contact and evacuate their wounded.

After standing down, our commander was still considering inserting us to execute a movement to contact and to set up a target line for us to clear. At the time it made sense because enemy combatants were on the retreat and low on firepower and manpower. The final decision was to insert the next period of darkness. During the day prior to insertion, ISR reported women and children leaving the village. This meant one thing; Taliban fighters expected an operation in that valley and they were ready to fight.

During planning, we learned it would be a ROD and to be prepared to stay out for up to four days! Not being at our home camp, we had to scrounge for supplies.

While studying mission details in the TOC, I had a conversation with my good friend Staff Sergeant Ball. His face told me something was bothering him, so I asked. He said, "We should have gone in last night. Now they've had time to regroup and resupply their ammo. We are probably going to lose a few guys tonight." Hearing that from a senior Ranger staff sergeant with ten deployments under his belt really puts things into perspective. We had no idea what we were in for.

The assault force consisted of 3rd Platoon, C Company 1/75 with attachments and a skeleton platoon from 2/75 that had just arrived in country a few weeks prior. Our mission was to enter and clear every house and compound in the valley, over a hundred structures. We left J-Bad on the night of the 15th and landed in a small outpost in the middle of nowhere to do a face-to-face with the battlespace owner. They called the valley where we were headed *The Jungle,* named for its heavily wooded and harsh terrain. Before we loaded the helicopters for infil, pre-mission assault fires were dropped on our intended HLZ.

After landing on a remote ridgeline outside of the Kunar Valley, we started our six-kilometer movement to the first target compound. One of the first messages that came across the intercept radio which the 'terp monitored

319

was, "The Americans have landed, everyone get to your positions." From that point on it was no longer *if we* would be ambushed, only *when*.

The terrain in the Kunar Valley is unlike anything I've experienced in Afghanistan. *Heavily wooded* is an understatement. The trees and shrubs were so thick we had to walk in a file most of the movement. If you fell more than a couple steps behind the man in front, you would lose sight of him. We would walk steeply up, then down, then back up again, sometimes over rock faces and cliffs. I'm not sure how long it took us to arrive at the first target, but it seemed like four hours or so and we were all sucking pretty badly. Once we finally made it to our first target and conditions were set, the main assault entered and cleared the first building. It was a dry hole. We went on to the second target building and assaulted it. Another dry hole.

As security and assault were setting in on our third target building, a group of fighters ran out of the back of the house toward the woods. The assault force cleared the building and captured one fighting-aged male inside. When the assault was over, 1st Squad went after the squirters. Our overhead assets put an IR sparkle on the squirters to help 1st Squad find them. While at the target compound, we could see the sparkle moving further and further away from the main element. One of the other squad leaders looked at the PL and noted that 1st Squad was moving too far from us and if they were compromised we wouldn't be able to help them.

At this time, I remember looking at the ridge across from us and seeing hot spots along it. I remember thinking we might be in for it. *Those are warming fires and they probably have armed guys around them.* I relayed this to the PL along with how I thought 1st Squad was about to get ambushed. The sun was starting to crest the horizon, so our NODs and lasers were growing more useless by the minute and our element of surprise was gone. The platoon sergeant came over the radio and told 1st Squad to hold on, they would just have a gunship hit the squirters. SSG Pape, the 1st Squad leader, came back over the radio and said he followed the fighters to a cave and he was going to throw a grenade in it.

A few moments, after his radio transmission, the ambush started. The burst of AK-47 fire rang through the valley and we knew right then that 1st Squad was in trouble. Everyone at the 3rd target building immediately jumped up and started running as fast as possible to the gunfire. The platoon sergeant was trying to reach SSG Pape over the radio, but only received silence. My heart sank when there wasn't a response. While running I remember my thoughts: *Please say something Kevin, please say you're ok.* The platoon sergeant again tried to contact him over the radio, still no response. He tried a third time. Still nothing. Finally, a call came over that I would never forget, "3-7 this is 3-1A. 3-1 IS DOWN! He's hurt pretty badly."

While running to the cave site, I radioed the dog handler, Sergeant Mack and asked if the threat was eliminated. His response was that there was a squad-sized element that made it out of the cave. When we made it to the fork the trail we were following, left headed down to the cave and right, took you up a hill for a good overwatch position. At the intersection, I linked up with a Naval SMU operator in charge of the small Afghan Partnering Unit (APU) attached to us. He told me we needed to take the hill in case they tried to overrun us, so I went with him. When we arrived at the top, I moved behind a tree and started scanning the ridge across from us. The first thing I saw was a cave with muzzle flashes coming from it, so I immediately started putting rounds into it. Almost immediately I came under fire and took shelter under the same tree as the operator.

He asked me what was wrong and I replied that enemy fire just hit all around me. A few seconds later, his 'terp was hit in the leg. He looked at me saying we needed to have somebody here in case we got overrun. I told him I had it covered, so he left me there and took off with his APU unit. The APU—what a joke—those assholes were crying and hiding the whole time we were in the firefight. I remember yelling at them to pull security because they were crying and praying so much. Before the operator moved out with his element, he said his radio was dead. I looked at him and told him to change his battery, but he looked at me like I was crazy and said he didn't have a spare on him. Keep in mind that we were told we would be out for at least a few days and to bring extra supplies. This guy was supposed to be an elite Navy SEAL SMU Operator, yet he didn't have a spare battery on him? *What the fuck?*

While his element was moving out, I remember looking down the hill into the valley and seeing the rest of the platoon. I told the platoon sergeant that I was on the hill and could see them and had overwatch. A few minutes went by and the gunshots started to move a little further away. Another five minutes went by and the gunshots were even further from me.

Once I realized the platoon had moved the wounded to CASEVAC without me, it hit me like a brick in the stomach. I immediately made my way down the hill I had climbed and didn't see anyone! I realized I had been left! Completely alone now, the feeling in my gut was indescribable; so overwhelming that I dropped to a knee instantly. My anxiety shot through the roof and for some reason I'll never know, I jumped up and turned. I just had a feeling that someone was watching me.

About 25 meters behind me an enemy fighter dressed in red with his weapon at the low-ready was sneaking up on me. I raised my SR-25 sniper rifle and shoulder fired a few times. I hit him once in the stomach and he went down. I then recalled the conversation with the dog handler when we were on our way to Pape's element. He said there were seven to nine guys that ran out of the cave. So, thinking I had just run across a squad-sized element, I flew down the hill. While I was running I looked to my nine o'clock and saw the same guy in red sitting against a tree with his gun.

Still running, I heard a loud explosion. My eardrums boomed and it felt like I had gotten sucker punched on the left side of my face. My neck burned and my jaw hurt and I could see blood shooting out in front of me when I ran. I pretty much ran off the side of a cliff and fell head over heels down the hill. My rifle flew out of my hands and I just kept plummeting, hitting my head and body on rocks, trees and earth. During my fall, I somehow timed it just right and landed on my feet and ran down the rest of the way, made a right and dove into a bush. I started feeling the left side of my neck, checking to see if I had been hit in the jugular and made my way across my neck to the right side where it was hurting and could feel a hole and my jawbone.

Sitting in that bush, I un-holstered my Beretta M-9 and remember thinking, *Damn, I'm fucked.* I tried to make a radio call and all that came out was a gargled mess. Someone responded with "Break, break, break on the net. Who the fuck is that?" Again I tried to say something and barely muttered, "This is Cox, I'm hit." The next call that came asked me for the distance and direction from the group to my position. I didn't have a Garmin GPS watch on, as they were all out when I went to pick mine up. The only thing I had was the wrist compass on my watch that I bought at the PX for ten bucks. I replied that I didn't have a Garmin and asked what direction they had moved. They moved north. So I held my watch up and found north.

I began moving north from tree to tree. After a few bounds I radioed the assault force to see if they could see me. They still didn't have eyes on me because they were taking fire. I began bounding north again and after a few minutes, I stopped and radioed the assault force. They still could not see me. At this point the adrenaline was wearing off and I was getting lightheaded and dizzy. *This is really it. I'm going to die.* At the time this event happened, my wife was six months pregnant with our first son. My only thought was that I was going to make it back—I had to—to be there for the birth of my son!

I was up and bounding again and could see an embankment. Along the wall of the embankment I could see helmets going across it. I tried to yell but barely got anything out because of all the blood in my mouth. Finally, I heard someone yell, "There he is!" Several of my Ranger buddies jumped down to help me. Mays, Ramsay and Arrow, our senior medic, started performing RFR. Doc Arrow put a dressing on my neck and that little bit of pressure blocked my airway and I gasped for air. Doc Arrow grabbed for one of his cric kits and was about to give me a tracheotomy right there. Before he could open it, I grabbed him and pulled him in close and said, "I can breathe fine if you don't press on my neck." He looked down at me and said, "Listen, if you start having trouble breathing you have to tell me so I can do this!" We worked our way back to the embankment and several other guys jumped down to help pull security because we were still getting shot at. Thankfully, no one else was wounded.

Once we all made it over the embankment and were under cover, we started taking much more gunfire. I remember lying on the ground, looking up at the second part of the embankment about ten feet high. Our FO came down to our level to call in gun runs. When he jumped down, he kicked a rock. This particular rock was about the size of a softball and headed straight at my face. It hit me above my left eye and gave me a nice cut and huge bruise. Once he made it down to our level, he started calling in air support. I looked at him and mouthed, "WHAT THE FUCK!!!" Looking back, we laugh about it now.

323

I could hear Sergeant Mays talking to someone and what he said is something I will never forget, "We lost Pape down at that cave and Cox got shot in the face and fell down a hill." I couldn't believe what I had just heard.

"What do you mean you lost Pape?"

"He didn't make it man, he's gone."

After hearing that I just lay there and tried to keep myself together but my emotions took over. A million things were running through my head. How could this have happened? We went to RIP together, we were both on our sixth combat deployment and had both gone on hundreds of combat missions.

The gun-runs were intense and lasted for almost an hour. I'm not sure how many fighters were in the Kunar that day, but it was a lot. The last few gun-runs were danger close with 40mm landing right over our embankment wall. We finally received confirmation that they were sending the MEDEVAC bird. The HLZ was up on the second embankment; Bailey was at the top with a machine gun team and Captain Nellis. They decided to connect a bunch of safety lines together and try to hoist me up the wall at the three-minute call.

At the three-minute call, the assault force, starting with the Mk-48 gunners, laid down cover fire as I climbed to the second embankment. No hoisting was needed because I climbed that wall so fast that I jumped into Bailey's arms at the top. Doc Arrow stayed by my side and used his body as a shield as we waited for the bird. Finally, the one-minute call was made and Captain Nellis pulled out a VS-17 reflective panel and started running around the HLZ for the pilots to see. He scared the shit out of us because we were still taking fire. The bird finally came into view and landed. Doc Arrow and Bailey made a shield around me and ran me out to the bird.

I loaded the bird first and the 'terp shot on the same hilltop was next. Out of the corner of my eye, I could see a litter being loaded onto the bird. There's no training in the military or elsewhere that can prepare you for the death of a friend. Staff Sergeant Kevin M. Pape was on the litter and was loaded directly across from me. The bird picked up and headed toward a hospital site close by. I thought for sure we would be shot down, but we took off without incident. The pilot said the flight was just over ten minutes, but sitting across from Kevin made it seem like an hour. These images are forever ingrained in my memory. We finally landed at the hospital and there were a lot of people waiting. I was rushed off the bird and immediately prepped for the operating room. That was the last time I saw Kevin, and I only miss him more as time goes on.

-ERIC COX 1/75

CHAPTER ELEVEN

"No catalogue of horrors ever kept men from war.

Before the war you always think that it's not you that dies.

But you will die, brother, if you go to it long enough."

ERNEST HEMINGWAY

Although Rangers had transitioned out of Iraq before this date, the official end of the war in Iraq came on December 15th, 2011. This was barely noticed by Rangers who were fully engaged in the most violent years of combat in Afghanistan. Strides were made in the War on Terror though. Most notable was the raid on Osama bin Laden's compound in Pakistan on May 2, 2011, resulting in the death of the man responsible for the terror attacks almost ten years prior on 9/11. Despite this milestone, the war continued to rage in Afghanistan and Rangers continued to lead the way in the special operations task force, hunting down the most dangerous men in the country.

Unfortunately, 2011 is host to one of the worst losses of life in Special Operations history. In support of a Ranger platoon, a helicopter carrying a naval special warfare element was shot down, killing all 38 on board. In addition, six Rangers were killed in action that year. Staff Sergeant Jeremy Katzenberger, Sergeant Tyler Holtz, Specialist Ricardo Cerros, Jr., Sergeant First Class Kristoffer Domeij, Private First Class Christopher Horns and Sergeant Alessandro Plutino all made the ultimate sacrifice. SFC Kris Domeij of 2nd Ranger Battalion made national headlines as the most deployed Ranger to die in the War on Terror. He was killed in action on his 14th combat deployment.

JUNE 2011

"SOMEWHERE IN AFGHANISTAN"

My platoon left the village under the cover of darkness. My squad was in charge of escorting the detainee to the HLZ. Although it was night, it felt just as hot as the day. We marched about ten kilometers to reach the village and then moved another two kilometers to our HLZ to be picked up. As I scanned the landscape through my NODs I couldn't help but think to myself that this country and these people are so similar to my homeland, Dine Bikeyah, the Navajo Reservation.

I quickly caught myself and stopped thinking of home and focused on pulling security and scanning for the enemy. I began to run scenarios in my head; *What if we take contact from the hill?* I looked for good cover, a rock, a dip in the ground, anything. I closely watched where my team leader moved, his signals and whether I had to adjust with the formation, remaining vigilant at all times, ready to pounce at a moment's notice. While walking I saw several giant holes, at least six by six and about 20 feet deep. I pointed my IR laser at them to show the trailing squad that there were enormous holes in the ground. As we reached the HLZ, the detainee began acting disgruntled, trying to break free, even yelling for help. *"Shut that guy up!"* The new guy was unsure how to handle the situation, so I ran over to the detainee, grabbed him and cupped my left hand over his mouth as he began to yell. The yelling was muffled but somehow through his facemask he grabbed hold of my pinky finger with his teeth.

With the detainee biting down on my pinky, the intense pain quickly turned into a furious rage. I raised my right hand and began to unleash fury with my hard-knuckled gloves. He stopped biting and attempted to go into the fetal position. My team leader and the senior gun team leader had to pull me away, telling me he wasn't resisting anymore and that the situation has been handled. "Roger that," I replied. This may seem harsh, but war is not for the faint or weak of heart. This was a bad man and he had just attacked me. It wasn't uncommon for detainees to attack us, even reaching for our weapons at times. We had to show that we meant business; history has shown time and again, that if the tables were flipped, they wouldn't be as kind as us.

Afterwards, we moved into position to be picked up. While waiting for the Chinook, the first rays of dawn appeared above the horizon. While in the prone position, I prayed with the dirt to the holy ones, thanking them for watching over me tonight. In the distance we heard the sound of rotors from a Chinook, a sound which still brings comfort to me. Putting my goggles on, I readied myself for the Chinook's landing. As usual, a *brownout* occurred as the Chinook landed to extract us, kicking up dirt and rocks in our faces. We moved to our feet, sprinted through the dust, barely able to see the person in front. I grabbed hold of the shoulder in front of me until we were aboard the bird. It all happened so fast: the bird touched down, Rangers ran aboard and we were off—less than a minute. I sat back with ease on the hard floor of the Chinook and watched the sun rise in the Afghan sky. Today was a good day.

Not long after returning from the mission, we were back in the ready room. I took off the five-pound helmet and removed the 80-pound body armor; it's such a great feeling of relief. While cleaning our weapons and preparing equipment for the next mission, which could happen at any minute, the Alpha and Bravo Team leaders competitively argue on whose team is better. My team leader finally said, "Norcross had to step in and bust some Navajo skills because your boy couldn't handle the detainee. Just shows Alpha Team is better." Which brought the next question, "Why did you go all out on that guy?"

"He bit my pinky,"

"What the fuck! If you would have told me that out there, I would have let you throw a few more punches in, SHIT! I may have even helped you!"

We all laughed it off and kept preparing our equipment. After an hour had passed, we were on our way back to our rooms when our squad leader told us to head back to the ready room. *Another mission.* We quickly ran back in and received the mission brief. I strapped the dusty 80-pound body armor back on, clipped on my sweaty helmet, inserted a magazine in my faded camouflage M-4, and boarded the Stryker for the mission. *This is the life for me.*

This was my third deployment with 1st Battalion, 75th Ranger Regiment. I had one deployment to Iraq and two to Afghanistan between 2008 and 2012. I am full-blooded Dine (Navajo Indian). My clans are Kinl'ichii'nii (Red house People Clan), nishh^ Kiyaa'aanii (The Towering House Clan), bashishchnn, Ashiihi (Salt People Clan), dashicheii doo Ashiihi (Salt People Clan) and dashi-nali. I don't think anyone knew I carried a Tadidnn pouch (corn pollen) with me. Nor do I think anyone ever saw me bless myself and pray; it's very sacred in Navajo Culture and used in many ceremonies. If Tadidnn is not accessible, then ash is to be used. If that is not available, then dirt is to be used. I remember on my first deployment I did not have Tadidnn, so I was praying with dirt. Someone came up to me and asked, "What are you doing with   that   dirt?"
"Praying,"
"Praying with dirt? How does that help?"
I honestly did not want to have a full-blown conversation with him so I said, "Mother Earth."
"OH! I know what you mean. That's pretty cool."

-LEOPOLD
1/75

JULY **2011**

"A MEDAL OF HONOR"

On July 12, 2011, Sergeant First Class Leroy Petry of 2nd Battalion, 75th Ranger Regiment became only the second living service member of the War on Terror to receive the Medal of Honor. SFC Petry received the nation's highest award for actions he took in Afghanistan in 2008. His Medal of Honor citation is as follows:

For conspicuous gallantry and intrepidity at the risk of his life above and beyond the call of duty: Staff Sergeant Leroy A. Petry distinguished himself by acts of gallantry and intrepidity at the risk of his life above and beyond the call of duty in action with an armed enemy in the vicinity of Paktya Province, Afghanistan, on May 26, 2008. As a Weapons Squad Leader with D Company, 2nd Battalion, 75th Ranger Regiment, Staff Sergeant Petry moved to clear the courtyard of a house that potentially contained high-value combatants. While crossing the courtyard, Staff Sergeant Petry and another Ranger were engaged and wounded by automatic weapons fire from enemy fighters. Still under enemy fire, and wounded in both legs, Staff Sergeant Petry led the other Ranger to cover. He then reported the situation and engaged the enemy with a hand grenade, providing suppression as another Ranger moved to his position. The enemy quickly responded by maneuvering closer and throwing grenades. The first grenade explosion knocked his two fellow Rangers to the ground and wounded both with shrapnel. A second grenade then landed only a few feet away from them. Instantly realizing the danger, Staff Sergeant Petry unhesitatingly and with complete disregard for his safety, deliberately and selflessly moved forward, picked up the grenade, and in an effort to clear the immediate threat, threw the grenade away from his fellow Rangers.

As he was releasing the grenade it detonated, amputating his right hand at the wrist and further injuring him with multiple shrapnel wounds. Although picking up and throwing the live grenade grievously wounded Staff Sergeant Petry, his gallant act undeniably saved his fellow Rangers from being severely wounded or killed. Despite the severity of his wounds, Staff Sergeant Petry continued to maintain the presence of mind to place a tourniquet on his right wrist before communicating the situation by radio in order to coordinate support for himself and his fellow wounded Rangers. Staff Sergeant Petry's extraordinary heroism and devotion to duty are in keeping with the highest traditions of military service, and reflect great credit upon himself, 75th Ranger Regiment, and the United States Army.

JULY 2011

"ON TOP OF THE HILL"

Sixteen hours in and the missiles were still coming in with a vengeance from the east. Perched atop the best vantage point in the valley, my head touched 10,000 feet and my lungs felt every inch of it. Most of us doubled over, some with exhaustion, some with mountain sickness and practically everyone found the ground with their asses and backs. When we started this mission, we were nocturnal creatures, sharpened by the darkness, but now the backs of our necks baked as the sun cut through the thin air. Had it not been for the artillery engulfing the valley below, we would have been completely out of our element.

To the south and west, our brothers fought and maneuvered around shanties of Taliban trainees. Their rounds cracked and whizzed over our heads, nearly demanding our concern, but we were too deep in this now, too near dehydration and exhaustion to waste precious energy putting a helmet back on and finding solid cover. Most of us had just finished working for this viewpoint and were enjoying our 1200 calories of processed astronaut food, the first we'd had in ten hours of sustained contact and miles of brutal terrain. Nothing short of a screaming mortar was moving us; we were digging in and recharging for another long night.

Nobody ever sees these days coming. I checked my watch and noted that typically my schedule dictated the next 90 minutes be spent in the gym improving my fitness and my physique, not on this goddamned hilltop almost two miles above sea level. This was too close to heaven for any Ranger to spend a day fighting. But here I was, next to the rest of them, rationing sips of water and squeezing chemically stabilized cheese directly into my mouth.

Last night was easy. There were only 20-some odd fighters camping out in a cave that was probably as old as the Bible. We would drop some munitions, search the bodies, throw some chem-lights and call it a night. Head back for chow and sleep as long as the air-conditioning held up. But last night became today and 20-some odd hours became a hundred. Last night, I didn't need to save anything. Today, I couldn't afford to.

I watched the commander, leaning against the most authoritative rock he could find, talking to the voices inside of his Peltors. *"Cleared to engage to phase line gold. Understood, fuel bingo in 15 mikes. Tracking all."* When Newton stated that every action had an equal and opposite reaction, he clearly hadn't anticipated the mind-bending speed at which war could travel. An obtuse flex of the thumb, air passing through vocal cords, reverberations captured in a microphone, invisible radio frequencies; these were the actions whose reaction would be a 500-pound bomb humming along a laser-guided track onto a hut made of sticks and mud. Afghanistan: the only place on Mother Earth where mountains worthy of postcards and ski resorts see more HIMARS rockets than beer lodges.

I leaned my head back and allowed myself to consider how abysmal the enemy's chances were of surviving the night. There were piles of dead bodies scattered throughout the valley and we were grumbling about the farmer's tan we were getting. This was more of a janitorial effort than a fight. We would push semi-automatic brooms and open-bolt mops until higher told us the place looked clean.

The time passed, albeit slowly and eventually, the fellows from 3rd Platoon heaved and gasped their way to the peak, less exasperated by the ten or so Taliban they had just butchered than the climb up that damned hill. Finally afforded *their* chance to rest: they happily claimed *their* 1200 calories and *their* asses found the hilltop beneath them. Now we were one big, happy perimeter of valiant gunmen, satiated by recent bloodshed and tearing at airtight packages of mechanically separated chicken patties. A few took naps, soothed by the melodic percussion of explosions and the softness of the dirt beneath them, while others nervously scanned the hillside for possible reinforcements. The reinforcements weren't coming, but the night sure as hell was, creeping into the valley like the brackish water in the swamps of Fort Benning.

The hill was quiet and the mood solemn. It was becoming increasingly probable that we would spend the coming night in this valley. Nobody had slept, and nobody would. Not until this was over.

Suddenly, the platoon sergeants lumbered over with new orders and the men of 1st Ranger Battalion found their feet, all undoubtedly swollen and sore. A few enemy stragglers were spotted running west, away from the valley and the attack helicopters cut them down like stalks of Bermuda grass. The empty shells fell and echoed through the valley, conjuring the pitch and ring of church bells. It was a welcoming sound, but there was no church here. This land was not of God. This land was of the camouflaged juggernauts of the infantry. Afflicted by miserable conditions but in no way discouraged by fighting, we shouldered our rifles and steadied our pace, preparing to spend the ensuing hours of darkness hunting, fixing and finishing whatever was left in this valley to kill.

-BRYAN RIPPEE
1/75

A RANGER GOLD STAR
MOTHER'S PERSPECTIVE

Dedicated to my daughter-in-love Sarah,
Kristoffer's daughters, Mikajsa, and Aalijah,
and the sacrifices of every Ranger, past, present and future.

I'll never forget my gut reaction when two planes slammed into the Twin Towers on 9/11. We're at war. Oh no, my son is going to war. Our world changed today and will never be the same.

My firstborn son, Kristoffer Bryan Domeij, joined the Army in the summer of 2000 after graduating high school. When President Bush declared War on Terror the next fall, knowing my son was still in Ranger training and would not immediately deploy brought me much relief.

The feelings from my teen years during the Vietnam War flooded back as I remembered how conflicted I was about the political wrangling, the anti-war movement and the treatment of returning heroes.

When my teenage patriot expressed interest in becoming a Navy SEAL, I interviewed an ex-SEAL at my work and reported to Kristoffer, "Lucky for you, I made you finish out that semester on the swim team when you wanted to quit. So...just how long can you hold your breath underwater these days?" In my home, I enforced only one extracurricular activity rule: *Start anything you want. If you hate it, don't whine to quit. Mom's not negotiable; you will finish your commitment.*

I researched the different branches' special operations forces and suggested Kristoffer consider the Air Force's Special Operations who rescue downed pilots. In my limited understanding of the military, which was nil, I figured the Air Force fights from a distance so my son would be less at risk.

The only branch of the military that I told Kristoffer I wasn't willing to compromise on was the Marines, but I wasn't too thrilled about the Army,

334

either. Olive green is just not one of my favorite colors. Kristoffer talked at length with his best friend's father, a former Special Forces and Vietnam veteran, only further cementing his determination to join the Army Rangers.

When Kristoffer was 17, he asked his father, a Canadian, to sign permission paperwork for him to join the Army. When his dad said no, Kristoffer turned his charm and negotiation skills on mom. His intense patriotism reminded me of myself as a young adult and of my own passion for my country, the United States. Kristoffer's willingness to sign away his dual citizenship surprised me. My response to his request?

"No. I can't do that." What I didn't share with my son?

If you're killed, I'll feel guilty.

I was also bothered that GI meant *government issue* and my son was *my* son, *not* Government Issue. I shared my preference for his next step after high school graduation, "I wish you'd attend college," and added, "If you choose to join the Army when you're 18, I'll support you 3000 percent." But in my heart I hoped he'd choose college, not the Army.

Kristoffer's response? "I'm tired of studying. I'm tired of people telling me to clean my room. I'm tired of people telling me what to do."

And you want to join the Army?

"I want to jump out of planes and blow up stuff." As the Army's first qualified Joint Terminal Attack Controller (JTAC) evaluator, he certainly accomplished those goals. After Kristoffer's first deployment, he remarked, "I never expected us to go to war, Mom."

That's exactly why I didn't want you to join the military. As long as *I* can remember, we've always been involved in a 'conflict' somewhere.

Comments from both a chaplain and a general caused me to ponder. "You raised a warrior. Not everyone can raise a warrior."

How did *I* miss my son was born a warrior?

WHO WILL PROTECT US?

When Kristoffer was three years old, I was propelled into single parenthood. We moved into an apartment infested with creepy crawlers. One evening I walked into the bathroom and terror paralyzed every muscle in my body, except for my vocal chords. Arachnophobia, coupled with emotional brokenness, produced a shriek that probably sounded as if I was being raped.

Kristoffer rushed in. "What's wrong, Mommy?" Frozen, I pointed at a huge spider. My preschooler said, "I'll kill it for you, Mommy." His protective nature and courage stirred my mother-heart with pride.

My estrogen-drenched brain tried to nurture both my sons, Kristoffer and Kyle, into gentlemen of honor. Determined that my firstborn would never eat sugar or play with toy guns, I soon realized I'd lost both battles.

Kristoffer chewed toast into hand guns, wielded plastic Lego guns created from his imagination, drew pictures of planes and tanks, brandished kitchen knives as swords and charged forward with his toilet plunger machine gun, proving my vast misunderstanding of testosterone.

Kristoffer and his brother, Kyle, loved watching *The A-Team* television series and then reenacting the ex-United States Army Special Forces characters' stunts. Their pointer fingers aimed and fired, as their undulating thumbs *pew-ow, pew-ow, pew-owed.* Their arms liberated, simulating imaginary artillery and machine guns as they shot around the war zone, my apartment, rata-tat-ing and urh-urh-urh-urh-urh-ing.

But when they began parachuting off the top of my seven-foot tall entertainment center, I enforced my first TV parental control, "No more A-Team." And if this *Downton Abbey* gal never, ever sees another *Star Wars* movie or *Star Trek* episode, I will die happy.

In elementary school, my friends suggested that perhaps Kristoffer might have ADD because of his high energy level and risk taking without seeming understanding of the physical consequences. Whether Kristoffer flew around on roller blades or his skateboard or sprinted across the roof of our home chasing bad guys, he seemed to lack any concern or fear for his safety.

One afternoon Kristoffer burst through the door. "Mom, John said he's gonna kill me with his dad's gun." My stomach flip-flopped. My knees turned to mush hearing my son's latest neighborhood bully report. Displaced from our safe, upscale neighborhood in Orange County, California to HUD housing near gang territory, I never felt safe. With no man to protect us, I let God know my fears. *Who will protect us?*

My *just-walk-away-from-a-fight* and *how-to-deal-with-a-bully* speeches suddenly sounded hollow. I did not understand the rules of this testosterone-drenched neighborhood. As a child, I was a tomboy, but Kristoffer's confrontational spirit mystified me. Talking to John's alcoholic, rough-looking father, who leered at my body, terrified me. I wanted to lock my two sons in our apartment and never *ever* let them play outside again.

After moving to a safe neighborhood in Colorado, a tough-talking military dad marched up to me and pointed to Kristoffer. "Who is this boy's dad?"

"I am!" Surprised by my strong response to such an intimidating man, I hurled back, "What do you want?" His whiner junior high son hid behind him. Everyone—except apparently his dad—knew Bully Boy tormented the little kids in the neighborhood.

"Your son..." Mr. Army Dad's gruff voice angered me.

"And your son, sir, rides around the neighborhood dispensing foul, disgusting language on the little kids via that little voice box on his bike."

Mr. Army Man swung around and marched his son home. With an air of triumph and to my embarrassment, Kristoffer said loud enough for that dad to hear, "Way to go, Mom!" I discussed with Kristoffer the importance of not further aggravating a tense situation... and humility.

WARRIOR-IN-TRAINING

In junior high, bullies accosted Kristoffer, so I enrolled him in karate.

Kristoffer's moves appeared quite impressive. His arms and legs flung and flailed, attacking make-believe aggressors. I drew fire from self-righteous, religious parents, when I gave Kristoffer permission to handle bullies. "Do not throw the first punch, but make sure you end it."

Kristoffer loved to camp out in the backyard in a tent, smear his handsome features with camouflage face paint, eat MREs and attend events at the military bases in Colorado Springs where he climbed on tanks and pretended to drive jeeps and shoot machine guns.

I frequented thrift stores and garage sales, dragging the boys along. The first thing Kristoffer bought at the first garage sale we stopped at? A Navy aircraft carrier about two feet wide, two feet tall and seven feet long. He spent hours flying his planes over and around that ship and simulating explosion noises.

I purchased Army and Air Force jackets and cut off the beautiful, expensive-looking metal buttons to sew on my designer-label blazers. Kristoffer bought Army patches, lapel pins and BDUs. He marched off to junior high wearing an elegant Gucci-styled, double-breasted, full-length genuine wool Army winter dress coat that he discovered at Goodwill along with his Doc Martin-styled black leather Army boots. He also loved wearing his military-styled volunteer shirt for the Manitou Springs fire department, where he hung out with the firefighters on Tuesday nights, worked controlled burns and walked door-to-door checking on people after a flash flood.

Besides trying to relate to my sons as males, it was important to me to pass on the same spiritual legacy my father left to me. As a single mother, I relied on God to be my husband, provider and protector. Sometimes, it seemed as if what I studied in the Bible offered little practical application to parenting my gregarious sons. How did ancient battles, blood sacrifices, circumcision and crucifixion apply to the parenting challenges I faced? I asked God, *How do I apply biblical principles to raising sons?* The story in 1 Samuel regarding Eli, a priest and the failures of his scoundrel sons hit me hard. God judged Eli because he *failed to restrain his sons.* So I asked God, "Show me how to train my sons."

One day, Kristoffer came to me. "Here, Mommy, I found your [fake] fingernail."

"Thank you, son, for finding mommy's fingernail. Please put it in my hand."

"I'll put your fingernail on the dresser."

My normal response before asking God for wisdom? "Thank you so much for being a good helper. You are such a wonderful son."

However, my study in Judges 1:1-36 came to mind regarding the first battle for the Promised Land. God's people asked God, "Who will lead us in the battle against the Canaanites?"

God's order of battle? "Judah will go. I've given the land to him." Judah disobeyed God's orders when Judah turned to Simeon and said, "Fight with me." Judah fought a good fight, but failed to trust Jehovah's battle plan and promise to win the land.

Partial obedience is disobedience.

The outcome of Judah's partial obedience by deviating from God's orders was failure to conquer the land. If Kristoffer could not obey me, he would not learn how to obey God or man. I looked Kristoffer in his charming, beautiful, blue eyes.

"Kristoffer, put the fingernail in my hand."

"I'll put it on the chest, Mommy."

"Kristoffer, put the fingernail in my hand."

He slammed the fingernail into my palm. As he stormed out of the room, I prayed, "Well, God, I could use some help on how to influence Kristoffer to adjust his attitude."

After every Bible study class, I picked Kristoffer up from childcare and asked, "Guess what I learned about God today?"

My excitement stirred Kristoffer's curiosity. "What, Mommy? Tell me." He listened as I distilled God's truths from that day's lesson down to child's language.

Kristoffer challenged me with theological questions. "Mommy, who is the Holy Spirit? What does the Holy Spirit look like?"

"The Holy Spirit is God's special helper. He's like the wind. Can you see the wind, Kristoffer?

"No. I feel it."

"That's right. When the wind blows, you can feel and hear it. The Holy

Spirit is like the wind. Sometimes you can feel Him. He also talks inside of you. When you choose to play with Mommy's TV, is there something that tells you no?"

"Yes, Mommy."

"That, Kristoffer, is the Holy Spirit."

I wanted my sons to learn that failure is success in disguise. I never allowed two sayings in my home: *I don't know how* and *I can't.* I taught the boys to say, *I'll try.* I didn't care if they failed, but I expected them to try. Soon after Kristoffer started training men, I reminded him about those banned words. With passion, he replied, "Yea, that used to make me so mad when you said that."

Ten minutes later, Kristoffer expressed frustration about his trainees. "It makes me so mad when my guys say, "I don't know how" or "I can't."

I laughed and thought, *Oh really?*

THE ALIEN NATION

From the beginning, the military seemed like their own alien nation to me. My first interaction with anyone in the military occurred when we moved from southern California to Colorado Springs. A colonel and lieutenant colonel in the Air Force invited me to a party. I apologized for being late because I couldn't find the apartment. I guessed the number 1530 printed on the invitation was the address, only to learn that 1530 is military time for 3:30 PM.

Military conventions mystified me. I purchased colorful Army, Navy and Air Force patches at an Army-Navy store to sew on a winter bomber jacket I sewed for Kristoffer.

As a veteran accepted the money for the mix-and-match military patches, Mr. Army-Navy man scolded, "You can't sew patches from every branch of the military on one coat."

"Why not? The colors match. I love the designs."

Scarlet flushed from his Adam's apple to his forehead. I turned to flit out the door with my matchy-patchys and his tongue lashed out. "You can't do that." I didn't know if that Vet was throwing a conniption or suffering from a Vietnam-related PTSD panic attack.

When I attended my first Air Force officer promotion ceremony, I observed everyone in uniform perform like marionettes on a string. I asked, "Why did everyone leap to their feet with their thumbs turned backwards?"

"A general entered the room, Ma'am."

The only thing I knew for sure about the Army and advised my son about? *Don't sign the contract unless it contains everything you want.* Kristoffer attended a recruiting event. It came time to sign the contract and Kristoffer discovered the recruiter failed to include the Ranger Indoctrination Program (RIP). He employed the garage sale negotiation skills I taught him. "Well, I guess you just wasted your time. I'm not going to sign that contract." And he didn't until the recruiter added RIP.

Boot camp transformed a pudgy high school football jock into a slimmer, better-postured, proud soldier, but RIP, well, it ripped his body. I phoned my mom. "You can't believe his body, Mom. He's a hard body."

Kristoffer recoiled at my motherly observation. "Gross. That is so gross!"

I'd researched the physical training part of RIP and the requirements sounded awful. After completing a long grueling run, Kristoffer called. "Mom, I made it!"

Of course, I was proud of him and told him so, but I also inquired, "Why did you run all the way?"

"I ran and made it with only seven seconds left, Mom."

Those seven seconds changed the trajectory of Kristoffer's military career.

When my son joined the Army, I worried about my son's relationship with God. *That's a mother's job.* In basic training, I received a letter that made me laugh. Kristoffer decided to attend church because staying in the barracks meant cleaning the latrines with a toothbrush. *Doesn't God work in miraculous ways?*

I can't say I knew one iota about the Army Rangers. In a parent orientation at Fort Benning during RIP graduation weekend, I raised my hand.

"Are there any women in the Rangers?" If looks could kill, I'd have been incinerated on the spot.

I sensed camaraderie among the men in that room, but had no clue what forged their fellowship. When I walked outside of that building, I stopped to read the names of fallen Rangers carved on a wooden slat fence.

I never want my son's name on that wall.

The day I finally received the dreaded letter informing me that my highly-trained son was being deployed for Operation Enduring Freedom, one tidbit of information surprised me. *We can't tell you where we're sending your son.*

What?! Take my firstborn son and not tell me where he is?

I will find him.

Three days after digging deep into the Internet following links on English-speaking Pakistani and Afghani websites, I emailed my son, "I think you are fighting in these mountains and you're stationed at this airbase."

Kristoffer told his commander my conclusions and his commander demanded to know how I knew these details.

My son said, "My mom's smart."

I was never quite sure what to write to Kristoffer while deployed. Compared to Kristoffer's adrenalized adventures, I figured my life seemed pretty dull. During the Cold War, I'd traveled with a missionary singing group behind the Iron Curtain. Compared to the West, the harsh living conditions, toilets and toilet paper came as a shock. I certainly didn't want to whine about frustrations about silly American extravagances.

Kristoffer said the best and funniest packet I ever sent included news articles and all the crazy comments regarding a strict vice principal at Rancho Bernardo High School accused of conducting an underwear inspection of boys and girls attending a school dance to *ensure appropriate school dress.* Female thong-wearers were sent home to change into *appropriate* underwear.

I also emailed Bible stories that occurred in Iraq. Since I love history and archeology, I wrote, "Please don't shoot at or blow up any archeological sites."—probably not on a warrior's top ten list of targets.

When U.S. tanks rolled into Baghdad and the looting began, my interest in archeology and my mothering instincts accelerated into high gear.

Frustrated by angry, looting mobs shattering cases, breaking 2000-year-old statues and stealing valuable artifacts from the National Museum, I joked with my friends. *It's time for the moms of America to take charge, smack some hands and tell looters to go to their rooms until they can behave and say they're sorry.*

Before the Iraq invasion, Kristoffer called. I'd surmised from President Bush's saber-rattling rhetoric that an invasion of Iraq was imminent. To confirm my suspicions and Kristoffer's whereabouts, I asked, "How's the weather?"

"It's 87 degrees." Then he complained about the grit in his computer.

The same temperature as Baghdad. He's supposed to be in Afghanistan.

We hung up and I Googled the weather in Afghanistan. The high? Forty-seven degrees. By this time, I'd researched online that Army Rangers capture airports before a war begins, so I imagined Kristoffer somewhere in northern Kurdish Iraq sitting on the tarmac of a Ranger-seized airport talking to me on a satellite phone.

Kristoffer also phoned his dad. "Your mom thinks you're in Iraq." I've since found out Kristoffer was waiting in Kuwait. At least, I was right about the weather, the sand and the geographic proximity.

The next time I asked Kristoffer, "So how's the weather?"

His terse, to-the-point response? "I can't tell you that," as if the weather had become a national security secret.

So I replied, "Okay, just tell me your longitude and latitude and I'll be fine."

"I can't do that." Little did I know that longitude and latitude played a huge role in my son's job as a forward observer and a JTAC. In one of my searches to track down where Kristoffer was deployed, I even punched the call back button to obtain his phone number, but received some whacky message about the number being redirected through Hawaii.

After six or seven deployments, I lost my obsession to figure out where he was. We had our code: *A* or *I*. Kristoffer also assured me that Rangers had the best equipment, best training and was the safest place to serve in the military. He kind of failed to mention how many Rangers had already been killed in action. Yet, with every deployment, from the first until his thirteenth, I lived in a heightened state of stress. I only breathed without anxiety when he returned home—*safe*.

DEPLOYMENT AND MY HARDEST BATTLE

It's one thing to say, "I trust God."

It's another to entrust the warrior-child God wove together in my womb to God's hands when my government declares wars or conflicts and repeatedly deploys soldiers to carry out dangerous missions to capture terrorists who annihilate people for whatever bizarre reasons motivate their mayhem.

Labeled a lioness single mom by friends, I instinctively yearned to protect my risk-taker cub, even though he'd grown into a full-fledged lion with impressive skills to take care of himself and others.

The hardest thing for me, the mother of a soldier, was releasing my son to God. My constant struggle was a seesaw between, *"I hope he doesn't die,"* to *"God, I entrust him to your care."* Without question, deployments ramped up my prayer life, giving new meaning to 1 Thessalonians 5:17: *"Pray without ceasing."*

I'll never forget one particular email from Kristoffer while deployed. "Had a bad night, Mom. Will call you tomorrow. Don't ask questions."

The first words out of my mouth when he called? "Are you wounded?"

"No."

But I would soon discover he was wounded—emotionally.

At the beginning of the war, I'd subscribed to the Department of Defense (DoD) email announcing every death so I could pray for the families. At a certain point, I unsubscribed. I found it too painful to read about another death of a baby-faced soldier. After Kristoffer and I hung up, I logged on to the DoD website to read the killed in action list. I found an entry about an Army Ranger. I copied and pasted the press release into an email and clicked 'send.'

Kristoffer hit reply. "You got it, Mom."

I found out Kristoffer's deployment return date and booked a flight to Seattle. I wanted to be available, in case he needed comfort or to vent. As we waited for the plane to arrive, I cornered someone in charge to address the elephant in the room, the Ranger who'd been killed in Iraq. "When a Ranger is killed, do you get counseling for these young men?"

"Death, ma'am, is just business, it's just business. They can talk to a chaplain, if they want." I wanted to slap that man's stupid face off.

I worried about PTSD. I'd witnessed the effects of PTSD on Vietnam Vets and even worked for a man who'd served in the Special Forces. I never knew which bizarre personality would show up for work each day. My heart hurt for a brilliant man who'd sacrificed and served with such courage, but for whatever reasons, could not bring himself to acknowledge or seek out help.

Extreme trauma cannot be dealt with in a couple of conversations with a chaplain. And it angered me thinking the Army refused to address the issue, especially after Vietnam. I'm no dum-dum. I wondered if processing trauma or grief with a counselor hurt a Ranger's career. When I discussed the military suicide rate with a multiple-starred general, he said, "Yes, the DoD was taken by surprise."

That night Kristoffer wanted burritos at Taco Bell. I asked Kristoffer if he wanted to talk about the night PFC Nathan E. Stahl was killed. Kristoffer told me about driving the lead Humvee and how Nathan rode in the second Humvee when the IED exploded. My son shared his response to the horror of that night. I'll never forget the pain that crossed Kristoffer's face and pierced my heart. "There was so much blood. I can't talk about it, Mom." So I respected his wishes.

Kristoffer knew the risks of his job. My son went above and beyond for his country, his family *and every American.* My son appeared tough on the outside, but harbored a tender heart on the inside.

My tender warrior loved fighting for his country, but he loved his family even more. He deliberated long and hard before buying an engagement ring and asking Sarah to marry him because he never wanted to inflict the pain of his death on her.

He called to tell me his plans to ask Sarah to marry him and then on Monday, May 28, 2007, at 8:49 AM, he sent an email to family and friends with this subject line: I popped the *"Q."* Message: "I just wanted to tell family and friends that two nights ago I dropped down on one knee and asked Sarah to marry me. She said yes."

After their wedding ceremony, everyone celebrated at a BBQ. The women discussed breastfeeding on the right side of the deck. The Rangers drank, told stories and laughed on the left side of the deck. Kristoffer never talked about his job and I'd only discovered Kristoffer received a promotion by Googling his name, so this was my chance to find out what he did while deployed. I pulled my chair to the middle of the deck, pretending like I was listening to the women, but I was really tuned into the Rangers' conversation.

Kristoffer shot me a move-back-to-the-women's-side-of-the-deck look. No way! Here was my chance. Hearing their war stories actually relieved some of my stress about his deployments because my imagination was far wilder than their stories.

During my son's 14th deployment, for the first time, I felt relaxed, confident that he'd return home safe. I found out later that my daughter-in-love told her mom, "I have a bad feeling about this deployment." Instead of going out on dangerous missions, it was my understanding that Kristoffer was to stay in the *Star Wars* room to oversee the operations.

But on that fateful night, the mission was two men short.

MY WORST FEAR REALIZED

The peace and calm of the ordinary life I enjoyed about-faced on Friday, October 21st at 11:30 PM. "Who's knocking on my door?" I spoke aloud. My surprise at the sudden banging on my front door near midnight gave way to annoyance. Probably someone with car trouble. If I ignore the knocking, they'll go away.

The insistent pounding on my door continued for 15 minutes. I finally walked down my stairs and opened the door. Two tall men in military uniforms stood on my front steps. Without asking, I knew.

"Is my son dead?"

"May we come in, ma'am?"

Dreading their confirmation, I repeated, "Is my son dead?"

"May we come in, ma'am?"

They followed me up my stairs and told me the news. My son died, killed by an IED—an improvised explosive device—in Afghanistan on October 22nd. Bizarre, because it was still October 21st in Colorado. I asked where, but quickly forgot the name of the district. I leaned against the kind chaplain and he prayed for me. Now all I wanted was for them to leave, so I could process the explosion that had just blown up inside my brain.

"You can leave."

"Do you have someone you can call?"

"I'll be fine. I'm a single mom. I've been to hell and back. You can leave, I'll be fine." They refused to depart until I called a friend. I dialed a close friend's number and cried these horrible words, "Kristoffer's dead."

Rob and Beth drove right over. My worst, heart-crushing fear had just come true: my firstborn son...dead on his 14th special operations deployment. The first decision that I had to make? Do I call Kristoffer's brother tonight? Or let Kyle get a good night's sleep? I wanted to fly to California and hold him.

Worst. Call. Of. My. Life.

After everyone left, adrenaline surged through my veins. My body shivered beneath 12 inches of two down comforters. Spasms jolted my muscles. My mind heard my heart thumping and these oddly comforting words. "God numbers our days." (Psalm 139:16). All my fears about Kristoffer's emotional wounds from the past, concerns about PTSD and my anxiety about future deployments dissipated. My son was alive, healed, whole, safe and protected in the presence of The Lord of Hosts, Jehovah Tz'vaot, The Commanding General over heaven and earth—and over every earthly and heavenly army.

Kristoffer's death in Afghanistan—however shocking to me—did not take Jehovah, Who Is, Who Was and Who Is to Come, by surprise. My daughter-in-love posted this note on Facebook on October 24, 2011:

"'The peace of God, which transcends understanding, will guard your hearts and your minds in Christ Jesus.' Philippians 4:7

There is a part of the sea known as 'the cushion of the sea.' It lies beneath the surface that is agitated by storms and churned by the wind, it is so deep that it is part of the sea that is never stirred. When the ocean floor in these deep places is dredged of the remains of plant or animal life, it reveals evidence of having remained completely undisturbed for hundreds, if not thousands of years.

'The peace of God is an eternal calm like the cushion of the sea. It lies so deeply within the human heart that no external difficulty or disturbance can reach it. Anyone who enters the presence of God becomes a partaker of that undisturbed and undisturbable calm.' - Arthur Tappan Pierson.

I find comfort knowing that Kris is now with Jesus and his dad. I am trying to take each day and each moment as it comes and there are some really hard days to come but I am so thankful to everyone for all the love and support and prayers...but mostly to have peace that passes my understanding...knowing that God is good and that he has a plan for us. I pray you all too, can have comfort in Jesus. 'The Lord gave, and the Lord has taken away, blessed be the name of the Lord.' Job 21:1"

The Army assigned me a casualty assistance officer (CAO) who showed up at my home early Saturday morning—nine hours after receiving the news. I nicknamed him Sergeant Angel, because he was my on-call guardian angel who walked me through reams of paperwork, the funeral and more paperwork. Beth came over and when my friend, Michelle, heard the news, she didn't ask, she drove over and oversaw everything in my household that day.

I flew to Dover Air Force base, the morgue Air Force base that receives America's war dead and prepares them for burial. When I read my ticket and learned I was changing planes in that maze of terminals at Chicago's O-Hell Airport, I panicked. But people from the USO met me at every point on my trip. Between flying and crying, my shocked, dehydrated body felt no hunger. Before escorting me to my next plane, they fed me and made sure I was hydrated.

I met Army Ranger Charles, who accompanied Kristoffer's body back to the States. Two of Kristoffer's buddies, Jon and Jack, raced 90 mph on back roads from the DC area to arrive in time to honor Kristoffer's return. I asked Charles two questions. "Did you get the guy?"

"Yes."

"Did you flatten the place?"

"Yes."

Charles never left my son's side, even sleeping beside Kristoffer's casket on the journey home. In that one act, he touched my mother-heart deeply. The presence of these three men who knew Kristoffer provided strength and great comfort to me.

A dull, expressionless general from Washington delivered a mechanical script expressing the country's appreciation for Kristoffer's sacrifice. He flinched at my reply. "I'd have preferred you used a drone to drop a bomb and take out the Taliban commander's compound."

As shell-shocked, grieving families left Fisher House, another load checked in. The chaplain said they'd only planned on 50 deaths in 2011 and the toll was nearing 400. It was surreal watching a refrigerated coffin bearing my son's lifeless body move from the plane to the transport vehicle. As it pulled out of my sight and into the morgue, I longed to hug my son.

I needed more details from Charles. During the mission, he was on a headset and shared what he could. I can't even imagine the horror the Rangers experienced that night because two other people also died and many others were wounded.

I agonized. Did my son suffer?

Charles' assurance that Kristoffer was spared any pain helped me from obsessing whether my son suffered or not. The explosion from the victim-activated IED was so powerful that Kristoffer felt nothing. I praised Et Shamayim, The God of The Heavens, (Psalms 136:26) who whisked my son, healed and whole, away to heaven.

The target that night was a Pakistani Taliban commander with expertise as an IED maker. His booby-trapped compound contained bomb-making supplies awaiting assembly to explode and kill more people, mostly innocent

Afghans. This particular IED-maker was very skilled. Most aren't, so capturing this guy was crucial to saving a lot of Afghan and American lives. I couldn't help thinking: How did this Pakistani Taliban commander think that 'loving your Afghan neighbor as yourself' includes blowing them up?

Off and on over the coming months I wondered about the IED-maker who I presumed was locked up in custody. Who was he? What was his name? What about his family? Every multi-starred General I met said, "If you need anything, let us know." I wanted to know the name of the man responsible for my son's death. I wished to meet Mr. Taliban Commander and tell him about Jesus, but I figured asking permission to visit Mr. IED in Afghanistan would never receive approval.

Somewhere I learned Mr. IED's code name, which my Teflon brain can't remember. But learning he'd been killed made me feel ill inside. His death was not satisfying. I wasn't pleased with Mr. IED's career choice, but did I hate him? No. I just kept thinking. Did anyone ever tell him about God's heart of love toward him?

I also wanted the longitude and latitude of the spot where my son died to look up on Google Earth. I wanted to see the spot that absorbed my son's lifeblood. It's strange that so many Afghans and military personnel know the details of that apocalyptic night, but the family, who needs as much information as possible to help us process our hearts' apocalypse, is left in the dark.

An older, mature Christian called me and read her journaling about that wicked horrible person who killed my son thinking her diatribe would comfort me. It didn't. Another person thought I'd be comforted by his email condemning the war—NO! How could that thoughtless and probably spineless idiot think I'd be comforted by political views that basically communicated—your son died in vain?

A media firestorm hit. My phone never stopped ringing. I'd answer what I thought was a business call, only to discover someone from the media wanting an interview about Kristoffer or requesting personal family pictures. As a proud mom, I felt muzzled. When a mom's child is killed, a mom needs to talk about their child. We just want everyone in the entire world to know how amazing our child is and was. Kristoffer left orders not to talk to the media. He was just doing his job and didn't want any publicity.

I Googled Kristoffer's name and created a Google email alert. Media stories from around the world poured into my inbox. I clicked on every link and saved a PDF of every news story, until my Mac's hard drive blew up, destroying every photo I owned of Kristoffer.

As a writer, I joked that my son made the Washington Post, Huffington Post, the UK's Daily Mail, Fox News and other major networks before my writing did. His friend posted on Facebook: "Kris, you made national news...because you deserve national news, just wish they spelt your name right bud."

Another comment posted on Kristoffer's Facebook wall revealed his notoriety: "They are talking about Kris in the Congress right now on CSPAN. A congressman used Kris as an example of how we need to not cut the military to retain and recruit the best in the military. Kris really is a hero in America."

Handwritten letters from generals and typical letters from congressmen and senators poured into my mailbox. My daughter-in-law received a handwritten note from George Bush before we ever received letters from a more recent President, which appeared signed by an automatic pen.

I received a thoughtful phone call from Senator Mark Udall. "How are you doing?" I was still flying high on shock and my faith in God. He hung up feeling inspired and promised to share my feedback regarding the budget crisis with President Obama to consider adding to his cabinet a single mom who doesn't have two nickels to rub together. We know how to juggle a monthly budget every month and a half or two and I can guarantee that single moms could identify where to cut government waste.

I'd never attended a military funeral. Sergeant Angel accompanied me and guided me every step of the way. My fried brain couldn't have navigated the trip without him. Having been a single mom for years, I was not used to anyone helping or serving me.

When Sergeant Angel drove me into the cemetery, the waving flags and Patriot Guards standing at attention awed me. I jumped out of the car and started snapping pictures. Three rows of Rangers stood at attention. I immediately loved every one of them.

Westboro Baptist Church created additional, unnecessary and cruel stress to our grieving family. We worried whether the Westboro Baptist Church might find out the time and place of Kristoffer's funeral. I checked their website and kept track of their press releases and calls to protest.

But to be honest, I hoped Westboro would show up. Yep, Momma Lioness was ready to rumble. Daydreams of marching first in line as the Rangers Led the Way to confront the haters made me laugh. Kristoffer didn't come by his fighting spirit without reason.

With tears in his eyes, one of Kristoffer's crusty commanders walked up to me. "Your son was the most stubborn man I've ever met." I was glad my son had given someone else a run for their money. Worried he'd offended me, he came back later. "No offense meant, ma'am." I laughed so hard, because my son inherited that stubbornness from both maternal and paternal sides of the family. I met so many wonderful Rangers that day. The moment they introduced themselves, every name slipped from my memory. Shock had Teflon-coated every shattered brain cell of my prefrontal cortex.

General Tony Thomas placed medals and a Gold Star pin in my hands. I didn't have a clue what was going on or what the pin or medals represented. My only regret was that I wish I'd stayed in the viewing room to talk to my son longer, but I felt pressured thinking that others wanted to spend time with him, too. I needed my son to be buried with a tangible expression of my love. I carried a crystal angel that hung from my chandelier and slipped it in the pocket over my angel's heart.

The speakers and Chaplain Derek Murray's sermon were funny, honest and touching. I was so thankful the Chaplain communicated a clear presentation of our family's faith. Meeting him made me so grateful that God had answered one specific prayer; to surround my son with godly influences. As a benediction, family members sang Amazing Grace.

After the service, I walked behind the hearse holding Mikajsa, Kristoffer's three-year-old daughter in my arms. She knew her father was in the box and said, "Hurry, follow Daddy." I picked up my speed and then noticed I'd charged ahead of General Thomas and Sarah. That's probably not protocol. My paced slowed to drop back in line. An Air Force plane conducted a fly over. We were handed our fallen warrior flags.

One pallbearer spoke with me at length. "Bearing your son's casket is the greatest honor of my military career. He was a great husband, a great father, a great American, a great warrior." What better tribute could a mom hear?

This Ranger didn't understand my strength. I shared my deep faith in God—in my weakness God makes me strong. Another man trained by my son was so deeply grieved he could barely share his story about my son. My heart left Seattle with a heart heavy with concern for Kristoffer's fellow Rangers.

When a soldier hurts, my heart aches. At Kristoffer's funeral, I walked past three rows of Rangers standing at attention and these words popped out of my mouth, "You are all my sons." And that's the way I feel. We're family, bonded by my son's death.

I contacted friends and asked them to please pray for the men grieving my son's death. I will never forget the pain in those Rangers' eyes. I suspected that many did not have the hope that anchors my soul or resources available to process their grief, It's just business, ma'am mourning.

Most Gold Star parents feel like I do, even though our children are dead—trust me—we're so happy for every soldier who returns alive, wounded or not and we're here to listen or offer comfort to any of our children's buddies.

Another memorial service was planned in San Diego and the organizer booked a large auditorium, invited the press, plus important government officials to speak. I honored Kristoffer's request to avoid the media. The details of planning that memorial service are simply too traumatic to recount. Even though I was very grateful for everything that was done to organize that event, I perceived that the organizer did not want me to speak at my son's memorial service.

Thank God for Beth who stayed on phone standby awaiting my speed dials that week. I'd call, screaming from agony from dealing with people triggering deep pain. Beth allowed me to vent, talked me down off the ledge and then helped me figure out how to best respond to some who wanted to silence my input at my son's memorial service and what my heart needed to share about my son with attendees. When the Chaplain and the Rangers showed up, I felt safe. They provided the rock-solid support I needed.

Kristoffer's high school also honored him that week before a football game. An honor guard marched onto the field, someone read Kristoffer's biography and everyone honored a moment of silence. I flipped the coin to decide which team got the ball, but flipped it behind my back.

A woman walked up to offer her condolences to me. I learned her husband, a Navy SEAL, was killed when a MH-47 helicopter was shot down by enemy fire, precipitating Operation Red Wings.

Kristoffer had participated in Operation Red Wings where his job as a JTAC played an integral role in that battle. He was also one of the Rangers that made it to the top of the mountain to recover the bodies of eight Navy SEALs and eight Army Night Stalkers.

Big war. Small world.

Big God. Common familial bond.

I prayed with her and wish I could remember her name.

I returned home to discover I was the neighborhood celebrity. My favorite neighbor worked to organize donations and volunteers to install a new roof and windows provided by volunteers who wanted to honor my son's sacrifice. After years of struggling as a single mom, I'd never seen or experienced this kind of generosity, care or respect. I especially loved the screens on the windows. Kristoffer and Kyle preferred exiting out of windows in their youth, not the front door and had broken or lost every screen in my home. Come summer, my new aluminum protectors would keep out unnerving wasps and bumblebees.

But dissent over a person who repeatedly obtained media attention without my consent to discuss our non-existent relationship almost propelled me over the edge. When I desperately needed solitude, my chest almost exploded as I refereed a heated neighborhood dispute, in addition to turning away the media knocking on my front door, calling my telephone or emailing me.

I was appalled when another Gold Star parent acted jealous and made stinging, hurtful comments to me because my son received so much media attention. In the midst of irrational grief wreaking havoc on my already-shredded feelings, thankfully, others stepped forward to offer support.

I felt overwhelmed by phone calls and dozens of emails from friends, family and acquaintances. Answering the same questions over and over exhausted me. I shut down, but communicated via Facebook to keep people updated so they could pray. The prayers of friends, family, even strangers, buoyed my spirit.

A month after Kristoffer's funeral, I attended my first Gold Star Mom luncheon to be embraced by the most amazing and supportive women who understood my near heart-attack emotional pain.

The Tragedy Assistance Program for Survivors (TAPS) assigned a mentor from my Gold Star chapter to walk alongside me. Love my mentor, a volunteer GI Granny who works with the wounded warriors at Fort Carson. Nancy's wisdom, plus her example to reach out to encourage fellow survivors, helped me through many rough times and decisions.

After a few months, my civilian friends moved on. What a relief to connect with people who shared in my journey. Early on, after meeting many other survivors, I decided that in remembering and honoring my son's sacrifice, I didn't want my entire identity to become Kristoffer's death.

I attended a Grief Share recovery support group at Fort Carson and a TAPS grief seminar. I connected with the amazing Fallen Hero Family Center at Fort Carson. Two months after Kristoffer's death, I attended the SOS Christmas party. I found it sobering to realize that every person packed into the SOS house had lost a husband, father, sibling, or child. I observed a young woman wearing her husband's wedding ring on a chain dangling from her neck. That said it all. Widow. The Ranger bond I felt with a former commander of 2/75, Fort Carson's General Joseph Anderson and his wife provided great comfort.

Because Joe had lost so many soldiers, I asked, "How do you cope with the death of so many men that you know?"

"Not very well."

The Rangers returned from their deployment and I flew to Fort Lewis for another memorial ceremony. No one prepared me for the final roll call. The moment someone called Kristoffer's name and someone answered, "He's gone, sir." I felt an electrical shock fritz my mind. A shot of intense pain pierced my heart.

An officer announced my son was killed in action. Mikajsa, my three-year-old granddaughter placed her hands over her ears and then asked, "Is

Daddy better now?"

How do I respond to that question? I sucked in deep breaths trying to hold myself together. I think I said, "Daddy is with Jesus," to which she replied, "I want my daddy. I want my daddy. I want my daddy."

I want your Daddy back, too.

Throughout the ceremony, I kept thinking, Be strong. Hold your- self together. My son, a Ranger, would not want me to embarrass him. Stand strong. Breath deep. Make Kristoffer proud. You are a Ranger mom. I scanned the faces of the men standing at attention in the battalions and longed to stay and talk with those who knew my son.

Later that year, Mikajsa asked, "If Jesus can take Daddy home to heaven, why can't He bring daddy back?" Speechless, I wondered how to respond to her question, when this world seems more like home than heaven and I wanted Kristoffer back too.

Heaven—I can't wait. It will be so wonderful never, ever being separated again from those we love.

PROCESSING LOSS

To process the traumatic loss of a loved one, the brain pushes everything out that it doesn't need. Unfortunately, that included my short-term memory. My brain on stress created many humorous moments to interrupt my grief. After visiting the Fallen Hero Family Center at Fort Carson I climbed into my GMC Jimmy, pushed the accelerator. Nothing. Dead. *Oh no, not car trouble.* My stress level escalated to stroke level. When I realized the key wasn't in the ignition, laughter plummeted my blood pressure back to normal.

Another time I stopped by Sam's Club for gas. I sidetracked myself and went into Sam's, but I couldn't remember the two items I needed, but managed to fill the basket with who knows what. As I drove into my driveway, I laughed. *I forgot to fill-up the gas tank or buy milk and bananas. How hard is it to forget milk and bananas?*

Another time, I handed a Fort Carson gate guard my ID after backing out of two gate lines, one labeled DoD registered cars only, to move to a shorter line. By this time four guards from three gates eyeballed me. *Kristoffer is dying right about now. Oh Mom.*

"Are you sure you want to give this to me, ma'am?"

"Yes, sir."

"Are you *sure?*"

"Yes," pointing to my Army-issued, get-on-base-without-a-bomb-detector-check, family survivor sticker bonded to my windshield.

The gatekeeper flashed my credit card. We laughed as I dug out my government-issued photo ID.

Before my first *real* Memorial Day, the Army strategically scheduled the unveiling of my son's name on the Special Operations wall of remembrance, the one I never wanted my son's name engraved on. I was happy to hear that my Ranger escort was the man who broke his leg and who Kristoffer replaced on the mission that took his life. I worried that he might feel false guilt and I wanted him to understand that God numbers our days.

Part of the weekend I learned more about Kristoffer's job as a JTAC. I wanted to put on the 35-pound vest Kristoffer wore, but it was too heavy. My Ranger escort dressed me in a tactical vest. I pushed it close to my heart and closed my eyes, trying to imagine how Kristoffer felt wearing his vest while performing his job. It gave me joy to pick up specialized equipment Kristoffer used and to take aim through the sights of guns light enough for me to handle. The weight of some guns and a bazooka surprised me. One Gold Star attendee snarked, "Well, it looks like you're having a good time." Yes. I was enjoying imagining my son's experiences.

While at Fort Bragg, someone mowed my knee-high grass that I'd intended to mow before I left. What a gift, mowed grass.

After returning home, I received an invitation to attend my first Special Forces military ball at Fort Carson. The commander gave me golden roses and asked me to stand in front of hundreds of soldiers and their spouses and announced, "We're your family now, Scoti." On Veteran's Day, Kristoffer's junior high invited me to their amazing Veteran's Day program where they honored his sacrifice. When the school principal asked, "How many have

parents, relatives or friends serving in the military?"
Almost every child in that auditorium stood.

MORE STARK REALIZATIONS

Kristoffer's death certificate arrived and I received another sobering shock.

Homicide.

No mother wants to read that word on her son's death certificate. And there it was. My son Kristoffer's death certificate read: homicide. No mother wants her child dead at the far-too-young-to- die-age of 29 years and 17 days. I shuttered at the un-checked box labeled 'suicide.'

Someone from Dover's morgue called to confirm if I really wanted the autopsy report and CD with pictures of Kristoffer's dead body that I'd requested. *Sure did.* When the package arrived, my doctor, Rob, interpreted the autopsy report, so I wouldn't draw wrong conclusions that would torture my heart. My doctor again confirmed that Kristoffer did not suffer.

I'd worried about all the alcohol I imagined Rangers consume and was relieved to hear that Kristoffer's liver was healthy. I handed Rob the autopsy CD to keep. If that autopsy CD stayed in my home, my curiosity would push me to open it and study the pictures.

Mourning the death of a loved one reminds me of an onion. Each layer that peels off stimulates tears, releasing the weight of mourning stinging the eye of the sorrowful soul. Life is so different without my son. Time is now divided between *before* and *after.*

I can't believe how *before* the unimportant upset me. And isn't that how so many Americans live their lives? Pursuing unimportant significance? Stepping on people, misrepresenting others to obtain unimportant importance. Getting stuck obsessing over unimportant compulsions? Screaming about spilled water that will dry?

One benefit of mourning? The lack of energy to swim against the flow of the unimportant. Being okay with letting go of the *shoulds*. Like one of those lazy river rides. Backside hanging in the water. Arms flopped over an inner tube. Head back, relaxed, facing the warm sun. Turning my heart toward the Son and allowing myself to drift and float in the current of mourning tugging at my heart.

The unfolding process of mourning is God's gift. If my mind had to absorb the full blunt reality of this loss on the first day, week or month, I'm convinced my brain would have exploded outside my skull. The best part of raw pain? How fresh and real God's Word is. How God speaks to my heart and comforts me through His Words written in Psalms.

Those *kick-me-in-the-gut* days, Memorial Day, July 4th and Veteran's Day, plus spoken and sung words, the Pledge of Allegiance and the *Star-Spangled Banner,* are no longer just another day or mumbled words. After *the news,* I was too angry to sing the *Star Spangled Banner.* Now I can't sing our national anthem or say the Pledge of Allegiance or say, "I'm Kristoffer's mom" without a catch in my throat or tearing up because my son died serving this country.

In the first few months after Kristoffer's death, I dreamed I was lost and had no way to return home. I phoned Kristoffer. "I'll come pick you up, Mom." In another dream, Kristoffer came to me. I felt joyful, delighted, excited to see him again. I asked Kristoffer a question. He began to answer. An abrupt awakening jerked me into instant consciousness—back to intense emotional pain.

After Sarah asked God to provide closure for her daughters, three-year-old Mikajsa described her daddy flying without legs (which unknown to her were blown off below the knees) in her room and playing with her. Mikajsa also told Sarah that Kristoffer also flew into 18-month-old Aalijah and Sarah's bedrooms. God answers our prayers in the most unexpected ways.

RESILIENCE MATTERS

I will never forget the sweet look of innocence on my son's face during our last conversation via Skype. After his 14th deployment, he was to transfer to Fort Benning to his new training job. I asked, "Will you still have to be deployed?

"Yes."

Not the answer I wanted to hear, but I was consoled by the fact that on his way to Fort Benning, he planned to stop at my home in Colorado and then at my mom's home in Mississippi. With anticipation and excitement, I could hardly wait to spend time with Kristoffer and visit his family in the South.

I did not want my son, my son's brother, my precious daughter-in-love's husband and my adorable granddaughters' father to die. Rather than a memorial display of his medals and flag display case on my buffet, I prefer him alive. I don't want his name engraved on a beautiful tombstone or obelisk.

I miss my son.

At first, some days I could barely manage breathing. My mind raced, consumed with thoughts of Kristoffer. I wanted my son back to hug, to touch, for his wife to embrace and for his daughters to know their dad who loved them with all his heart.

The emotional pain remains a constant. Knowing my son is in a better place does not exempt me from mourning and pain. I allow myself to ride capricious waves of grief. On some days I can push back the reality of Kristoffer's death. Other days the finality refuses to be ignored. *This can't be true. I don't want this to be true. Oh no, it's true.* Sometimes, the emotional pain overwhelms my physical strength. With immense effort, I urge myself forward. *Just take one step, one more step.*

Sometimes I can't distinguish between whether I'm starving, even when I've just eaten, or if it's the feeling of raw emotional pain burning inside my chest—a fire that chocolate or food cannot quench.

At the end of the second year of Kristoffer's death, I chose one word to live by. Every year I select a word to focus on, instead of making resolutions, which I never keep. My word for 2014?

Resilience. Knocked down, but not knocked out.

One key to enduring this painful reality? By turning to the Man of Sorrow, to *Adonai,* my Lord, Master, Owner and my Strong Tower. (Proverbs

18:10, Psalm 9:10, Psalm 20:1, 7). Kristoffer grew up a common boy from Colorado Springs and San Diego and died as the most deployed Special Operations Ranger in history.

Kristoffer spent a decade with the 2nd Ranger Battalion either preparing for war or in direct contact with the enemy in Iraq and Afghanistan. My son died so that Americans can sleep well at night. Jesus, a common boy from Nazareth, died so every person on earth can live every day with the assurance that heaven is both a reality and a possibility through Him.

Just as my heart suffered because my son died for our freedom, God's heart agonized when His Son died for every person's spiritual freedom. *El Yeshuw'ah,* The God of My Salvation and The Light of the World, sacrificed his life to save, deliver and move Kristoffer to eternal safety.

Many people spend their lives running away from difficulties or trying to sprint past them as fast as possible. My son bolted toward challenging, dangerous situations. Challenges aren't to be wished away. Just as soldiers are willing to die so Americans can be free, Jesus died on the cross to secure our spiritual freedom. Christ walked toward Jerusalem, toward the cross, toward deadly pain to bleed out and secure our eternal freedom from death.

The Army's incident report described my son's truncated body lying face down in a blast hole in the Afghan dust. All I wanted to do was to run to my son and save him. When tortuous mental images of my son bleeding out rip at my heart, I replace those pictures with God lifting my son out of that blast hole and into the reality of His eternal love, peace and life. When my mother's heart drowns in the valley of mourning and tears, my built-in homing instinct for the eternal longs for heaven—resurrection and reunion with my fallen hero, risen son.

Compared to heaven and all of eternity, the pain of grief on this earth lasts less than a nanosecond, a mere pinprick, a scar upon the heart. I look forward to the only scars in heaven—Jesus' scars. My pain, my scars, my tears will be no more. Only eternal joy and praising God alongside those I love. By the stripes torn in Christ's flesh by a barbed whip, we're healed, meaning healing comes through being united spiritually to God.

Many knew Kristoffer as a friend, a son, a brother, a husband, a warrior. Many know Jesus as a teacher, a prophet, a good person. I pray that you come to know Him as *God's Son, your Savior,* who longs to infuse you with hope and healing in a world filled with injustice and hurt.

Ravi Zacharias wrote in his book, *There is a Plan:*

"At the end of your life one of three things will happen to your heart: it will grow hard, it will be broken, or it will be tender. Nobody escapes. Your heart will become coarse and desensitized, be crushed under the weight of disappointment, or be tender by that which makes the heart of God tender as well. God's heart is a caring heart."

The Joint Fires Observer training center at Fort Sill was named Domeij Hall in honor of my son. At the ceremony, Kristoffer's two-year-old daughter, Aaliyah, looked at Kristoffer's picture etched on the marble memorial and said, "Hi, Daddy," and then her tiny hand patted his marbleized face. My daughter-in-love and I requested that John 15:13 be engraved on the memorial plaque: *"Greater love has no one than this, that one lay down his life for his friends,"* not only to remind every soldier walking through those doors of Kristoffer's sacrifice, but also, more importantly, the message of the cross: God longs for a relationship with you and to hear you say, "Hi, Daddy." He regards you personally as worth dying for, and that your life is worth the exchange of His own.

Etched on every tombstone are two dates that belong to God, the day God planned our birth and the date God knows we'll die. Between those two dates is just one simple line—the dash—that stands for the time that's yours and mine. My son packed an awful lot of living into his dash. Have you given serious thought to your dash, your future, your hope, your legacy?

Pain, sorrow, violence, suffering and goodbyes are the laws of earth. No more death, no more sorrow, no more crying, no more pain and joyful reunions are the laws of heaven. My son attended death's funeral. When the law of earth played my son's *Taps,* heaven played *Reveille*; Kristoffer's wake-up call to rise and live forever.

Just as I could not ignore the insistent knocks on my door the night I received *the news,* I cannot ignore what happened. I need *Et Yeshuw'ah,* The God of My Salvation (Isaiah 12:2), who is stronger and wiser than I, who in eternity will provide meaning to my *why.* Meanwhile, I live by God's promises, not man's explanations. Sorrow seasons my tears and my heart as I crawl, limp and dance toward heaven. Pain, loss and grief drives us to what really matters in this life—authentic relationship with a sovereign God and trusting *who God says He is*.

Even so, I still fly blind trying to navigate turbulent ups-and-downs of mourning. Unpredictable emotional loops, rolls and spirals send me crashing. I burn with longing for my son to still be alive. I've lost all power to reclaim before-my-son-died *normal* or to control after-death's sting. Sorrow's silent, salty language runs liquid down my cheeks, releasing my heartbreak to the God of all comfort. God counts, treasures and stores every costly sacred teardrop in His bottle. (Psalms 56:8)

KEEP MOVING

In year two, agony's oppressive foot firmly planted my spirit in the nether regions of grief. I feared losing the key to escape my spiral into a deep depression. I needed to make a change, so I decided to try CrossFit for 30 days.

After the first week, the trainer gave me his pep talk about how I needed to be motivated. I was honest. "Kristoffer's death shattered my motivation, my drive. Finishing anything drains me emotionally and physically. All I can commit to is the one-minute drive to CrossFit. I need you to push me."

"I can do that." And Josh did. I've transitioned from hating CrossFit, to a love-hate relationship, to wondering, *Am I crazy? Why am I killing myself?* to *I want an Army Ranger hard body.* I wish Kristoffer were here, because he'd sure be proud of me, even though I'll never be able to complete the Hero WOD (workout of the day) named in honor of him.

My CrossFit experience reminds me of my journey of mourning. During one difficult burpee spree between reps with barbell push presses, my tummy laid cemented to the floor. My nose inhaled the smell of the sweaty, rubber mat as I sucked oxygen into my burning lungs.

"Keep moving, Scoti."

I bent my leg at the knee and waved it back and forth. Pretty sure that's not the movement the trainer wanted. I managed to crawl to my knees, wobble up, push butt out and heels to floor to finish a brutal round of burpees and pushing barbells over, under, here, there and everywhere.

Even when I think I'm gaining strength, my body tells me otherwise. Some days just putting one foot in front of the other feels like I will shatter to pieces. I wear the same outfit three days in a row, three dishwasher loads of dirty dishes sit rinsed in the sink and clean laundry seems to breed in the family room, but I soldier on, pushing my limits.

"Do you not know? Have you not heard? The LORD is the everlasting God, the Creator of the ends of the earth. He will not grow tired or weary and his understanding no one can fathom. He gives strength to the weary and increases the power of the weak." *(Isaiah 40:28-29)*

Every year, holidays and Kristoffer's birthdate and death date continue to come and to go. With the help of the Lord, great friends, Gold Star moms and CrossFit I beat back mourning's depressive pall. Still wondering what that endorphin rush feels like, though.

After one brutal week at CrossFit, my body buzzed and I asked my trainer, "Will it always be this hard?"

"It will always be a challenge. We're working on increasing your workload capacity." Then I realize I'm doing twice as much as I was several weeks before. When a trainer writes a killer warm-up and workout on the board, I think: *I can't do that.* But raw grit pushes me through the WOD, one rep at a time and I collapse into sleep sound that night.

And that's how life and loss and grief and resilience operate—it will always challenge me to push forward—one rep at a time.

CALLED TO SERVE

Generals spoke glowing words about my son and commented how proud I must be of Kristoffer. Truth be told, I don't know who they are talking about. His ten years of service are a black hole. My son never talked about his job. And I'll be dead before I can access the Freedom of Information Act to know what part my son played.

Kristoffer told his wife, "I have stories to tell one day."

But that day never came.

Every Gold Star parent yearns to hear from their child's military friends. My heart hurts when any soldier suffers from their demons and survivor guilt, especially medics. I'm so grateful to the medics who did everything possible to save my son's life. However, God had other plans for Kristoffer.

A six feet five inches tall Ranger remarked, "I was afraid to contact you, a Gold Star mom," I laughed, because I think of every Ranger as a magnificent, fearless warrior. Our children's buddies know our fallen sons and daughters in a way that we will never know them. For me, it's important to understand who my son was and hear about the adventures my son experienced. I can't fully express how hearing from anyone who knew my son takes the sting out of the ever-persistent pain.

I am most comforted and content when I'm visiting my daughter-in-love, hugging or playing with my grandchildren or in the presence of Kristoffer's Ranger buddies—the closest links on earth to who my adult warrior son was.

The first month after Kristoffer was killed, I received dozens of cards from friends and strangers saying, "We'll never forget."

Yeah, right. You'll get on with your lives.

A mother's love never dies. We fear people will forget our children. Death leaves a heartache no one can heal. Love leaves a memory no one can steal. Hearing our children's Ranger buddies share their memories comforts our ever-mourning hearts that our fallen children will never be forgotten. No matter how small the memory, we love hearing stories about our children or receiving pictures, no matter how much time has passed.

Please don't be afraid of us.

My son died from visible wounds inflicted by an IED. Gold Star parents are not afraid to listen to your memories, your pain, your trauma. We grieve when others, who served with honor, succumb to death from invisible wounds of the soul. Gold Star parents pray for opportunities to encourage those struggling with their demons that wish them dead. We'd rather shoulder the pain with you.

On September 24, 2011, less than a month before Kristoffer was killed, he wrote these words on his Facebook page: "Then I heard the voice of the Lord, saying, 'Whom shall I send and who will go for us?' Then I said, 'Here am I. Send me!'—Isaiah 6:8. Thank you for all the love. If I don't get back to you anytime soon...sorry."

Kristoffer felt truly called by God to be a Ranger. Before a deployment, he'd often shoot me an email. *"I'm off to do the Lord's work."* I confess...Army Ranger never appeared on my top ten list of *called by God* occupations for my son.

How and where we live out our calling looks different for each person. I'm awed by how my son lived out his high calling. Fully aware of the risks, he wanted to make a difference and like a missionary, he was willing to lay down his life for his values, his family, his friends, even strangers. How many people can say they live from the heart with that kind of passion and integrity?

Those who fought alongside my son reveal the results of my prayers for God to fulfill *'a future and a hope'* (Jeremiah 29:11-13) that my son would become a faithful husband, father and friend. Rangers tell me about my son's example and commitment to his family and faithfulness to his wife. Before Kristoffer left on his final deployment, he told Sarah, "I love you and want to spend the rest of my life with you and I'll do whatever it takes."

On TDYs, Kristoffer lost respect for married men who walked from the bar to a hotel room with a one-night stand. When one Ranger wanted to quit his marriage, Kristoffer encouraged him, which helped to save it. Another Ranger told me that on one deployment, Kristoffer walked up to him on the plane that was waiting for takeoff, "We're two guys over the limit. Go home and spend the time with your family."

Kristoffer was invited to the White House to attend a Medal of Honor ceremony honoring Leroy Petry. Kristoffer said, "Thank you. I'd rather stay home with my family."

The national and international media quoted his commanders. *"Sergeant First Class Domeij was the prototypical special operations NCO—a technically and tactically competent Joint Terminal Attack Controller and veteran of a decade of deployments to both Iraq and Afghanistan and hundreds of combat missions. His ability to employ fire support platforms made him a game changer on the battlefield—an operator who in real terms had the value of an entire strike force on the battlefield,"* said Col. Mark W. Odom, commander of the 75th Ranger Regiment.

"Sergeant First Class Kris Domeij will be dearly missed by the men of 2nd Ranger Battalion He was one of those men who was known by all as much for his humor, enthusiasm and loyal friendship as he was for his unparalleled skill and bravery under fire," said Lt. Col. David Hodne, commander of 2nd Battalion, 75th Ranger Regiment.

"This was a Ranger you wanted at your side when the chips were down. He and his family are very much part of the fabric that defines 2nd Ranger Battalion. He is irreplaceable...in our formation...and in our hearts."

Other comments were also posted on Facebook.

"Kris Domeij, you set the standard for fire support in the Regiment and then exceeded that standard every time you hit the ground."

"You were truly a master of your craft, and I always felt better knowing you were with us anytime we were outside the wire. Thanks for everything you did, and everything you stood for."

"You were a man among men. *I* learned a lot from you every time we spoke, and those things that *I* learned from you *I* implemented regularly to teach my men."

"When *I* needed a few quals just before my second deployment, *I* couldn't get them through my own unit so Kris invited me on two training exercises with him. *I* took leave and just met up with him in Arizona and then again in Arkansas. He had never met me in his life, and *I* wasn't even in the Army. He didn't care, he did whatever he could to help as many people as he could. If a couple of Marines needed some specific training before they launched on their next deployment, and he could help, he was willing to do whatever it took. Long story short, he took me under his wing, invited my Marines & me out on a couple of exercises, and taught us stuff that saved our lives."

What meant the most to me when I learned of my son's death? When the

Chaplain told me he witnessed my son reading his Bible while deployed and when the Chaplain told those who attended his funeral, "Kristoffer had rock solid values."

Even though my world has changed and nothing will ever be the same, as I look back on my baby, the boy, the man, the warrior, Kristoffer now experiences the truths of these ancient and timeless texts in 1 Corinthians and 1 Peter 1:23-24: *"All people are like grass, and all their glory is like the flowers of the field; the grass withers and the flowers fall, but the word of the Lord endures forever."* Our life is but a temporary tent and if that tent is destroyed, we have a home in heaven. Kristoffer lived knowing that faith in the death and resurrection of Christ is *"to be absent from the body is to be present with the Lord."*

-SCOTI SPRINGFIELD DOMEIJ
PROUD 2/75 GOLD STAR MOTHER OF SFC KRISTOFFER DOMEIJ
KIA OCTOBER 22, 2011 ON HIS 14TH DEPLOYMENT

AUGUST 2011

"EXTORTION 17"

On the night of August 5th - 6, 2011 one of the worst tragedies in modern special operations history occurred. By this point in the war, the men who made up the special operations community were some of the most proficient and combat-hardened warriors the world had ever seen. Even so, the enemy always has a vote.

1st Platoon, Bravo Company, 2/75 was on a longer than normal deployment as the rest of the company was rotated to be on Team Merrill and they surged ahead with them. Their platoon had yet another raid mission in pursuit of a high value target in the Tangi Valley, which was in Wardak Province, on the night of August 5th. The mission was not easy, as the Rangers took contact not only during their movement to the target but also on the target. Despite the tough fight that left some wounded, the enemy combatants were no match for the Ranger platoon. They secured the target and were finishing up gathering anything of value for intelligence when it was suggested by the Joint Operations Center (JOC) back at the FOB to launch a platoon of SEALs from a Naval Special Mission Unit to chase down the three or four combatants that ran, or *squirted* from the target.

This was a notoriously bad area and the Ranger platoon sergeant responded that they did not want the aerial containment that was offered at that time. The decision was made to launch anyway. The platoon-sized element boarded a CH-47D Chinook, callsign *Extortion 17,* as no SOF air assets were available on that short of notice. As Extortion 17 moved into final approach of the target area at 0238 local time, the Rangers on the ground watched in horror as it took a direct hit from an RPG. The helicopter fell from the sky, killing all 38 on board. The call came over the radio that they had a helicopter down and the platoon stopped what they were doing to move to the crash site immediately. Because of the urgency of the situation, they had to leave the detainees they fought hard to capture behind.

The platoon moved as fast as possible, covering seven kilometers of the rugged terrain at a running pace, arriving in under an hour. They risked further danger by moving on roads that were known to have IEDs to arrive at the crash site as fast as they could, as they were receiving real time intelligence that the enemy was moving to the crash site to set up an ambush. Upon their arrival, they found a crash site still on fire. Some of those on board did not have their safety lines attached and were thrown from the helicopter, which scattered them away from the crash site, so the platoon's medical personnel went to them first to check for any signs of life. With no luck, they then began gathering the remains of the fallen and their sensitive items.

Similar to the Jessica Lynch rescue mission almost a decade prior, the Rangers on the ground decided to push as many guys as possible out on security to spare them from the gruesome task. Approximately six Rangers took on the lion's share of the work. They attempted to bring down two of the attached cultural support team (CST) members, but had to send them back as they quickly lost their composure at the site of it all. On top of that, the crashed aircraft experienced a secondary explosion after the Rangers arrived that sent shrapnel into two of the Ranger medics helping to gather the bodies. Despite their injuries, they kept working. Later in the day they had to deal with a *flash flood* from enemy fighters releasing dammed water into the irrigation canal running through the crash site in an attempt to separate the Ranger platoon, cutting them in half. Luckily, because of the sheer amount of water heading toward them, they heard it before it hit them and were moved out of the way before anyone was hurt. If that wasn't enough, there was also an afternoon lightning storm that was so intense it left some of their equipment inoperable and their platoon without aerial fire support.

Meanwhile, 3rd Platoon, Delta Company from 1/75 was alerted after coming off a mission of their own. They took a small break to get some sleep before they flew out to replace the other platoon, which would hold the site through the day. Once they awoke, they were told to prepare to stay out for a few days. They rode out and landed at the nearest HLZ, seven kilometers from the crash site and made their way in with an Air Force CSAR team in tow.

After arriving, the platoon from 2/75 had to make the seven-kilometer trek back to the HLZ, as that was the nearest place a helicopter could land in the rugged terrain. The men were exhausted, having walked to their objective the night before, fighting all night, running to the crash site, securing it through the day only to execute another long movement to exfil.

New to the scene, the platoon from 1/75 did what they could to disassemble the helicopter and prepare it to be moved. The last platoon evacuated the bodies and sensitive items on board, so now the only thing left was the large pieces of the aircraft spread out across three locations. They were out for three straight days, using demolitions as well as torches to cut the aircraft into moveable sections, and then loading them on to vehicles that the conventional Army unit that owned the battlespace brought in.

Despite the gruesome and sobering task, Rangers worked until the mission was accomplished. The third stanza of the Ranger Creed states that you will never fail your comrades, and that you will shoulder more than your fair share of the task, *whatever it may be,* one hundred percent and then some. The

Rangers of these two platoons more than lived the Creed in response to the Extortion 17 tragedy.

SEPTEMBER 2011

"GRENADE"

In July of 2011, I began my third combat deployment as a Ranger in 3rd Platoon, B Company, 2/75 as a tabbed SAW gunner. We would be extended this trip since it was our turn to be Team Merrill. This meant we would be extended by two months and would bounce around all over Afghanistan from FOB to FOB. The first place we headed was Kandahar, the only base in Afghanistan where the sewage pond is right in the middle of the base. You can imagine the smells. If you know anything about Afghanistan, you know that Kandahar and the surrounding provinces are littered with IEDs. It was pretty stressful to go out on missions there; we were scared shitless to step on one. At least I was. It's not exactly how I want to go out.

Being there in the summertime we experienced Ramadan. It's a month-long holiday where Muslims basically don't do anything. Not even eat, at least during the day. So, considering that they had no energy, the chance of guys running away on target was rare. Good for us; nobody wants to take off running after a guy with 60 to 80 pounds of gear on in the middle of July.

We busted our ass in Kandahar for a month, going out almost every night. Then we heard we would head north to Logar province to FOB Shank. The upside was it was a little cooler, the downside was most of our missions would be in the mountains. You can't land on the target all the time in the mountains like you can in the south, so there was a lot of walking.

FOB Shank could be a pretty stressful place. We took indirect fire once a week minimum and lived in tents surrounded by sand bags and mortar shelters. It was a pretty cool looking place, actually. I felt like I was at war there. I liked it there, but anything was better than Kandahar. The first few missions in Logar were good. We took contact two or three times and had successful missions. After two weeks of being in Logar, we went on another mission.

We landed at a small COP about five kilometers from the target and walked in. The walk sucked. We started out at the COP and then went through what seemed like an abandoned town, muddy fields, over at least six walls, across a river and through some more urban area and fields. When we finally reached the target compound, the walls were about 20 feet high and the gate proved difficult to get into. When we entered, the plan was for my squad and I to go right and the rest of the platoon and 3rd Squad would go left to one tiny room in the corner.

Well, that didn't happen. I got pushed left with Frank from 2nd Squad and Oskar from 3rd Squad. Plans sometimes don't work like you want them to. I was the number one man a small room up the stairs through an open door. I shined my laser through a window facing us and saw nothing, so continued. I came up the stairs, peeked in the room and saw a man sleeping and some messed up sheets next to him. *Either someone else is up and moving in here or they left before we arrived.* As I button-hooked the corner-fed room, a man got in my face and screamed like a girl, so I pushed him up against the wall and the team leader from 2nd Squad attempted to subdue him. This guy was oddly tough, ironic for the way he reacted a couple seconds earlier.

The squad leader from 3rd Squad had the guy locked down as we tried to cuff this one. He yelled, "Pipitt, switch me!" So we switched and I walked over to flex-cuff the other guy. As I put one zip-tie around his wrist there was a loud explosion that knocked me on my ass. Smoke filled the room along with the unrelenting smell of explosives.

We screamed for help over the radio for what seemed like much longer than it should have taken for the rest of the platoon to get to us. I felt like my entire body was on fire. My hands curled into fists without me having any control, my mouth went dry and I felt true panic. I watched Frank and Oskar lie there, helpless too, calling for help. I'll never forget the wave of emotions that hit me all at that moment. I was watching two of my brothers bleed out and there was nothing I could do. Something I will never forget is the hopelessness I felt in that moment. The thought of one of them dying there was unbearable. I give serious credit to any Ranger that has witnessed such things.

After a minute of screaming for help the rest of the platoon arrived. The other guy that I was in the process of flex-cuffing was still alive and sat in the corner next to me in a panic. My platoon sergeant came through the door and put ten to fifteen rounds into his face. Blood flew everywhere. Some of it got on my helmet, which I still have today sitting on my bookcase. For me, that was justice at its finest. By now, both medics were in the room working on us. I remember telling one of them to work on Oskar and Frank first because I knew I wasn't dying after my platoon sergeant looked me over made the call that I was fine. But the pain overcame me and I screamed for pain medication. I finally received an IV and was off to ketamine land.

The next thing I remember is waking up in the FOB Shank *hospital.* All the NCOs and PL were standing around me. One of my best friends was holding my hand, something else I will never forget. My PL handed me the phone and said call your mom and let her know you're ok. I called my girlfriend instead. I let her know, then called my mom, but my girlfriend had already told her so she was a wreck when she answered the phone. That wasn't something I needed at the time, but it was understandable. Everything from then on was a blur until I arrived in Germany and came to my senses. I do vaguely remember all the guys laughing at the hilarious things I said.

I ended up suffering multiple shrapnel wounds to both legs, left arm and both feet. I had compartment syndrome on my right lower leg, so a fasciotomy was performed on both sides to relieve the pressure, leaving two giant holes in my leg for 12 days before they were closed. If I told you this hasn't affected me mentally I would be lying. It has been a rough two years since. I have had the phrase PTSD shoved down my throat, and it has made me grow to hate the term. It's not a disorder. Obviously someone will be affected by combat and getting wounded in combat. All three of us were, but that's another story. I am fully recovered now with only minor pain here and there, but for the most part I am functional and I would go back to Afghanistan and wreak havoc again and again if I could. Oskar, Frank and I are all alive and well thanks to the men of 3-B and all attachments.

-KASEY PIPITT, 2/75

EPILOGUE

Y ou may have noticed this book ended rather abruptly and without much of a conclusion. That was very much on purpose, as the story is not over. Rangers are still going out on target, still fighting our nation's enemies and still being wounded or killed in action. At the time of this book's writing, four more Rangers have been killed in action: Sergeant Tanner Higgins, Sergeant Thomas MacPherson, Sergeant Patrick Hawkins and Specialist Cody Patterson. A career Ranger, Command Sergeant Major Martin R. Barreras was killed from wounds sustained in action while serving in the 1st Armored Division. Many more have been wounded, most notably on October 6, 2013 when B Company, 3/75 sustained nearly 30 wounded in action in a mass casualty event. Since 9/11, The Regiment has had 64 Rangers make the ultimate sacrifice, and another 672 wounded in action. Rangers have been awarded a Medal of Honor, a Distinguished Service Cross, 49 Silver Stars, 303 Bronze Star Medals for Valor and more than 600 Purple Hearts.

The men of the 75th Ranger Regiment rose to the occasion when their country needed them most. They have executed every mission they were assigned to the very highest standard, setting the bar for future generations. My hope is that every person who reads this book has an immense amount of respect for the sacrifice and contributions that Rangers and their enablers made in the War on Terror. It is cliché to say freedom is not free, but that statement speaks volumes. Blood, sweat and tears have been poured out on behalf of the American public; the men who shed these precious liquids have not asked for anything in return, except maybe to remember those who made the ultimate sacrifice.

Rangers will continue to energetically meet the enemies of our country on the field of battle, moving further, faster and fighting harder than any other soldier. Rest assured that no matter the challenge, Rangers will be there on behalf of the American people, taking the jobs nobody else can or will do.

Rangers Lead the Way!

A WORD ON TRANSITION

"Warriors gather together because they long to be with men who once acted their best; men who suffered and sacrificed, men who were stripped of their humanity men who were willing to die for one another."

CSM MARTIN R. BARRERAS

INSPIRED BY "THESE GOOD MEN" BY MICHAEL NORMAN

As you read this unparalleled collection of stories of Rangers in the War on Terror, you may have re-experienced some events of your own. This is common and totally normal. What's also completely normal is for a Ranger to squash feelings and emotions that arise deep within, sometimes using alcohol, a killer workout, or withdrawing so that externally no one can see he is affected. The problem will surface at some point and could result in disaster; the end of a relationship, a losing encounter with law enforcement, a lost job, or worse.

But there's a secret: Every Ranger feels the same way. Externally, we look hard as nails, that nothing bothers us, but when you unpeel the layers of our lives you'll find broken relationships, lost jobs, lost opportunities and more. Add to that a physical injury or wound that forces us to depart active duty and we start to feel the best thing we did in our life is now in the past. It doesn't have to be that way.

In 2010, a group of Ranger veterans formed Gallant Few, Inc., a 501(c)3 nonprofit with a priority focus on US Army Ranger veterans (and other veterans as resources permit). Our core belief is that a Ranger should never transition alone without another Ranger buddy close by. The Gallant Few Ranger network is nationwide and there is a Ranger in the network near you now. Please reach out to us.

Also, we need more Rangers (and veterans of all eras, branches of service and experience) that have already successfully transitioned to join us as mentors.

While we say we will "fight on to the Ranger objective though I be the lone survivor," the reality is active duty Rangers very rarely operate alone. You always have a Ranger buddy. Don't walk that transition patrol alone.

Join us: www.gallantfew.org

Email us: ranger@gallantfew.org

Call us, Office: 817-567-3293

KARL MONGER: 817-600-0514

1/75, 1990-1993

RANGER CLASS 14-83

"When this war comes to an end, most of you will return to the way of life which you fought so hard to return to, to pick up the threads of your civilian pursuits. You will bring back with you many nostalgic memories of your fighting days both bitter and pleasant. But above all, you will bring back with you many personal characteristics enriched by your experiences with the Rangers.

In whatever field or profession you may follow, I know you will continue as civilians with the same spirit and qualities you demonstrated as a Ranger. Your aggressiveness and initiative will be tempered to adjust to civilian life with little difficulty. In your hearts as in mine, you will always have that feeling...of being a Ranger always!"

COLONEL WILLIAM O. DARBY

We are Rangers for life. When we take off the uniform, we are not stripped of the prestige, honor and high esprit de corps of being a Ranger. The only change is the objective in which we find our next mission. Your Ranger Leadership is needed in the civilian world; to set the example for others to follow, to lead the way. It won't be easy, there will be extremely tough days, days when you're surrounded by many people yet feel totally alone. That is when you call your Ranger buddy, the one you can count on, the one that has been there for you through it all. We cannot fight on to the Ranger Objective alone, we will fail. It is time to ACT. It is time to be the leader you know you can be. Become the leader in your community and seek out other Rangers to link up with. Find ways to make a difference where you live. Find your Next Mission, find your purpose and continue to fulfill

Abrams Charter, using your Ranger Knowledge to educate and lead those around you.

If you are thinking of transitioning out of the military, talk to someone first; someone that has gone before you. Hear their stories and make an informed decision. Our mission at The Darby Project is to facilitate a successful transition for Army Rangers from active duty to a civilian life filled with Hope and Purpose. Reach out to us before you make your decision and we'll help guide you towards the right one. If you've already transitioned, we need you. Your story needs to be told so that other Rangers can hear it.

It Starts with YOU.
Want to take action?
Visit us:
www.darbyproject.org/signup

BRYCE MAHONEY
C. CO 3/75
RTLW

ACKNOWLEDGEMENTS

There's one thing the reader of this book should realize: this book wouldn't exist if not for the support and hard work of dozens of people who believed in it.

My wife Lauren, as usual, provided me with steadfast support and encouragement throughout this project, and many others. She listens to my frustrations, understands when I need to step away to gather myself, and shares with me the hope of accomplishing something truly special, even at the sacrifice of our family and relationship at times. I couldn't ask for a better friend and partner. She's one of the strongest women I know; I am lucky to have her in my life.

My parents, Marty Sr. and Marie Skovlund and Robert and Arleen Wall, have provided support and encouragement in so many ways. They understand the magnitude of this project, and have from the beginning, and making it possible for me to see it to completion when at times it seemed unfeasible. Their constant guidance and advice, even though I may not always show it, is a major factor in my motivation to see this through.

The contributors to this book made *Violence of Action* possible and without their stories you wouldn't hold it in your hands right now. They exposed themselves in a way few are willing and because of their courage they've made recording a historic time in Ranger history possible. Some of them are now working on books of their own and I encourage anyone reading this to keep a lookout for them.

If it were not for the men of C Company, 1ˢᵗ Ranger Battalion, I would not be the man I am today. From day one when I showed up as a young, new Ranger, they established a standard of excellence for which I continue to strive, and. I don't think any of them truly understand the impact they've had on me. As I worked through this book, I couldn't help but think of previous Ranger buddies, team leaders, squad leaders and platoon sergeants who might end up reading this. It was that thought that drove me through over ten rounds of editing, long nights of research, and the nearly unbearable weight of making sure this book was done correctly.

The 75ᵗʰ Ranger Regiments Public Affairs shop was truly exceptional in helping me complete this project without delay or worry of compromising the Regiment's mission. Tracy in particular went out of her way for this project, and I can't thank her enough for her help.

A lot of research and interviews with subject matter experts went into the making of this book. I won't name most of them by name—they know who they are—but I appreciate them taking the time to talk over periods of the Regiment's history with me and making sure I was telling our story as accurately as possible. I only served for a portion of the time this book covers, so having these Rangers as references makes all the difference in the world. Major Andrew Fisher and Master Sergeant Harold Montgomery put a lot of work into the section about Ranger Medics. They are legends in their own right, known for their work in the medical field, for the 75th Ranger Regiment specifically, but also for the military at large. Their contribution to this book underscores the Regiment's impact in advances in tactical trauma care. Their expertise speaks far more loudly than I could on my own.

This book went through several (more than ten) rounds of editing. Charlie Faint and his wonderful wife Lilla, Leo Jenkins, Matt Sanders, Jenna Evans, Scoti Domeij, Mike Wall and Jack Murphy took a significant amount of time out of their schedule to help perfect this book. Their efforts in both the content editing and copy-editing phase of this project truly made the difference in the pursuit of excellence for this book.

It's a thankless job, but I would be remiss if I did not mention Lorie DeWorken, who did the cover and interior design of the book. It's a detail that is often overlooked, but if it's not done right then it distracts from the words in the worst way. Her patience as well as understanding of what we needed was appreciated, and I would recommend her services to anyone else looking for top quality work on their book.

There have been a few organizations that played a large role in the book's development. Namely, SOFREP.com and shadowspear.com provided a lot of resources and guidance on this project. Both organizations have a crack staff that will bend over backwards to help fellow veterans out and I encourage anyone reading this book to check their work out as well. I would also like to mention Nick, Kerry, Jack, Dale and Gary for not only providing reviews for the book, but their honest feedback on what we had written and compiled. All five of these men have done amazing things both in the military and out and continue to support their fellow veterans in any way they can.

We had a few last-minute struggles with the completion of this book. One of which was regarding the foreword. Mat Best, the man who has brought more than a few smiles and laughs to the veteran community through his YouTube videos, stepped up big time. He is an excellent representative of the Ranger community, both during his time in uniform as well as his time since separating from the service. When choosing someone to write a foreword for a work such as this, we wanted someone who could accurately represent the men in this book. He more than fit the bill and we were thankful to have him aboard this project.

Finally, I would like to thank God. I am a man of faith and He has carried me through both the good and bad times. My prayers have been answered on many occasions and His comfort and guidance have made a significant impact in my life—and on this book.

GLOSSARY

11B	Alphanumeric designator for infantry in Military Occupational Specialty (MOS) code
160th SOAR	160th Special Operations Aviation Regiment. See SOAR
1SG	First Sergeant. The senior enlisted soldier in a company, and principle advisor to the company commander
A-10	The only jet-engine aircraft designed solely for close air support. Its primary weapon is a 30mm GAU-8 Avenger rotary cannon, which is the heaviest automatic cannon mounted on any aircraft
AA	Assembly Area. References the area that paratroopers meet at on the drop zone after an airborne operation
AAA	Anti-Aircraft Artillery
AAR	After Action Review. This is a debrief after every mission, to review what was supposed to happen, what actually happened, and what improvements can be made

Abrams Charter	Enacted when Gen. Creighton Abrams, then Chief of Staff of the Army, directed the reestablishment of the 75th Ranger Regiment. The Abrams Charter directs Rangers to share tactics, equipment, leadership and experience gained in Ranger Regiment with the rest of the Army to better the entire service
AC-130	A cargo aircraft outfitted with myriad weapons systems and sensors used primarily for special operations close air support of ground troops
ACOG	Advanced Combat Optical Gunsight
ACU	Army Combat Uniform
AFIP	Armed Forces Institute of Pathology. Conducts post-mortems on deceased service members
AFO	Advanced Force Operations. Refers to the early special operations teams that operated in Afghanistan
AG	Assistant Gunner
AO	Area of Operation(s)
APC	Armored Personnel Carrier
ARSOF	Army Special Operations Forces
AT	Anti-Tank
B-1	Air Force bomber aircraft, capable of supersonic flight carrying large payload
BAF	Boat Assault Force or Bagram Air Field. Boat assault force references an infil to an objective from a boat platform. Bagram Air Field is a hub of coalition activity not far from Kabul, Afghanistan's capital city
BP	Blocking Position. Elements that provide security around an objective so that enemy forces cannot get in or out
BDA	Battle Damage Assessment. Usually performed to confirm the results of an airstrike

BIAP	Baghdad International Airport
Birds	Term used to reference primarily helicopters, but also other air platforms
BUD/S	Basic Underwater Demolition / SEAL. US Navy SEALs' initial course famed for its staggering rate of attrition
C-130	Aircraft, primarily Air Force, used for transporting personnel and equipment, reconnaissance, close air support, etc…
CAS	Close Air Support. Airstrikes within close proximity of friendly forces requiring detailed integration between pilot and ground forces
CASEVAC	Casualty Evacuation. The movement of a patient from the point of injury or casualty collection point with no en route medical care or medical equipment on board
CBRN(E)	Chemical, Biological, Radioactive, Nuclear, (Explosive)
CCP	Casualty Collection Point
CCT	Combat Controller (Team). Air Force special operations member who holds FAA air traffic controller certification and is typically JTAC qualified. Vital in conducting austere airfield surveys and controlling close air support
CENTCOM	Central Command. The US' overarching military command in the Middle East, commanded by a three or four-star general
Chalk	A group of paratroopers or other soldiers that deploy from a single aircraft. The size of a chalk depends on what aircraft is being used
CLIF SHOT®	Energy gel high in glucose and sometimes caffeine for a quick boost
CLP	Cleaner, Lubricant, Protectant

CNX	Canceled
CO	Commanding Officer. Usually references a company commander
Combat Scroll	References the unit's deployment patch, worn on the right shoulder after a soldier has deployed. In the 75th Ranger Regiment it is called a Combat Scroll
Conex	ISO/shipping container
CONOP	Concept of the Operation. An abbreviated version of an Operations Order that is most often used by special operations because of the shortened planning process
CONUS	Continental United States
COP	Combat Outpost. A military presence that is smaller than a Forward Operating Base but larger than a patrol base
CP	Command Post
CPT	Captain. In the 75th Ranger Regiment, typically this rank will control a platoon or if a senior Captain, will control a company
CQB/CQC	Close Quarters Battle/ Close Quarters Combat
Cric	Cricothyrotomy (tracheotomy). A hole made in the neck to allow a compromised airway to function
Crye	Crye Precision®. Creators of Multi-Cam® camouflage pattern
CSAR	Combat Search and Rescue
DoD	Department of Defense
DZ	Drop Zone
EMT	Emergency Medical Technician
EOD	Explosive Ordnance Disposal

ETAC	Enlisted Terminal Attack Controller. Predecessor to the term JTAC. See JTAC
Exfil	The removal of an element from the objective, usually to return to base
F-15	Air Force multi-role fighter jet, larger, with greater payload
F-16	Air Force multi-role fighter jet, small, quick, lower payload
F3EAD	Find, Fix, Finish, Exploit, Analyze, and Disseminate. Targeting system built on close coordination between operations and intelligence functions, intended to drive friendly operations at a pace faster than the enemy can withstand
FARP	Forward Aerial Refueling Point
FMC	Final Manifest Call/Fully Mission Capable
FO	Forward Observer. In the 75th Ranger Regiment, may or may not be JTAC qualified depending on experience level. The FO controls air assets and conducts call for fire missions
FOB	Forward Operating Base. The most common military installation in the deployed environment
FRAGO	Fragmentary Order. References a change to the mission
FSO	Fire Support Officer
F(i)ST	Fire Support Team
GAF	Ground Assault Force. References an infil to an objective from a ground vehicle
Gerber®	Folding multi-tool typically containing knife, pliers, scissors and file
GFC	Ground Force Commander

GMV	Ground Mobility Vehicle. Special operations variant of a HMMWV
GP	General Purpose
GWoT	Global War on Terror(ism)
HAF	Helicopter Assault Force. References an infil to an objective from a helicopter
Halo	First person shooter multi-player video game
HEDP	High Explosive Dual Purpose. Variant of the High Explosive Anti-Tank warhead with a fragmentation sleeve, increasing its effectiveness against personnel
HHC	Headquarters and Headquarters Company. The command and support element in every battalion
Hilux	Toyota pickup truck, popular in the Middle East
HIMARS	High Mobility Artillery Rocket System. A U.S. light multiple rocket system mounted on a truck frame
HLZ	Helicopter Landing Zone
HMMWV	High-Mobility Multipurpose Wheeled Vehicle (Humvee)
HUMINT	Human Intelligence
Humvee	Slang for HMMWV or GMV
HVT	High Value Target
IED	Improvised Explosive Device
IMT	Individual Movement Technique. References the three to five second bounds that troops perform under fire
Infil	The movement of an element to the objective, whether by air, land, water, or a combination
IR	Infra-Red. References the lasers on Rangers' rifles that can only be seen with night vision devices

ISAF	International Security Assistance Force
ISR	Intelligence, Surveillance, Reconnaissance. Typically refers to aviation platforms that serve those functions
J-2	The intelligence directorate of a joint staff; intelligence staff section
JDAM	Joint Directed Attack Munition. References GPS-guided 'smart bombs'
J-LIST	Joint Lightweight Integrated Suit Technology. The full body suit that is worn for protection against chemical, biological, radioactive and nuclear threats
JMPI	Jumpmaster Personnel Inspection
JMAU	Joint Medical Augmentation Unit
JSOC	Joint Special Operations Command. An elite organization that is a sub-unified command of SOCOM and oversees the Special Mission Units
JTAC	Joint Terminal Attack Controller. A service member qualified to control airstrikes and call for fire missions
KIA	Killed in Action
LAW	Light Anti-tank Weapon
Layout	Pre or post-mission check to ensure one has all necessary items
LOA	Limit of Advance
LZ	Landing Zone
M-4	5.56mm rifle, common to US Military
MBITR	Multi Band Inter/Intra Team Radio. Common radio carried by most Rangers
MC-130	Air Force cargo plane providing infil, exfil and resupply to special operations personnel

MEDEVAC	The movement of a patient either from the point of injury, or a casualty collection point, to a medical facility
MEF	Marine Expeditionary Force
Merrell (®)	References hiking boot brand favored by many
Merrill	Name of Special Operations Task Force during 2010 and 2011
MICH	Modular Integrated Communications Helmet
Mid-rats	Midnight Rations. Refers to the meal that is served at midnight as lunch for those who work on a 'reverse' schedule
Mk-19	40mm belt-fed grenade launcher. 1500m effective range
Mk-46/48	Special operations variant of M-249 5.56mm squad assault weapon (SAW). Mk-48 is 7.62mm variant
MOLLE	Modular Lightweight Load-carrying Equipment. Pouch system issued to Rangers early in the GWoT
MPC	Multi-Purpose Canine
MRE	Meals, Ready to Eat. High calorie field rations given to troops
MWR	Morale, Welfare, and Recreation. Generally, MWR is the term used to reference the place service members can access the phone or internet to communicate with loved ones back home
NAI	Named Area of Interest. A building or area of expected or suspected enemy activity
Nalgene®	Rugged plastic water bottle
NCO	Non-Commissioned Officer
NLT	No Later Than
NOD/NVG	Night Optical Device, Night Vision Goggles

NSW	Naval Special Warfare. Encompasses Navy's special operations units
OCO	Overseas Contingency Operations
OCONUS	Outside the Continental United States
ODA	Operational Detachment Alpha. US Army Special Forces' basic unit. Typically comprised of 12 personnel. See SF
OP	Observation Point or short for 'Operation'
OPSEC	Operational Security. Information critical to operations that cannot be shared without serious effect to the outcome of the mission
PA	Physician's Assistant
Pandur	Six or eight-wheeled all-wheel-drive armored personnel carrier/vehicle
PCI	Pre-Combat Inspection
Peltor®	Communications headset which provides radio traffic, loud noise reduction and quiet noise amplification
PFC	Private First Class. A young soldier, typically a rifleman and relatively inexperienced
PJ	Air Force Pararescueman. Highly trained combat search and rescue (CSAR) personnel
PKM	7.62mm machine gun developed by Kalashnikov and propagated through Russian and Middle Easter countries
PL	Platoon Leader
PMCS	Preventative Maintenance Checks and Service
PMN	Russian-made anti-personnel mine
Ponzi Grenade	Russian-made anti-personnel hand grenade

PRC-117F/G	Portable radio capable of transmitting farther than MBITR, but is significantly larger and heavier
Pro-Mask	Gas mask issued to troops for use during threat of CBRN attack
PT	Physical Training
PUC	Person Under Control
PVS-14/15	Night Vision Goggles (NVGs). PVS-14 is monocular, PVS-15 is binocular
PX	Post Exchange. Department store on military installations
QRF	Quick Reaction Force
RBA	Ranger Body Armor
Recce	Short for reconnaissance
RFR	Ranger First Responder. References the minimum medical qualification all Rangers must be certified in annually
RFS	Release for Standards. Refers to the process that a Ranger is separated from the Regiment for sub-standard performance
RRC/RRD	Regimental Reconnaissance Detachment / Regimental
Reconnaissance CO	Both the same unit, but when the Regiment stood up the Regimental Special Troop Battalion, RRD became RRC
RTO	Radio-Telephone Operator. References the communications specialist in each element
RI	Ranger Instructor. Instructors in RIP and Ranger School
Rio Hato	A small town in Panama over which Rangers jumped during Operation Just Cause in 1989

RIP	Ranger Indoctrination Program. The 75th Ranger Regiment's three to four-week selection process until it was replaced with the eight-week Ranger Assessment and Selection Program (RASP)
Rip-Its	Knock-off energy drink, ubiquitous downrange
ROD	Remain Over Day. References a mission that extends past one period of darkness
ROE	Rules of Engagement. The rules that dictate what actions troops can take in combat
RPG	Rocket Propelled Grenade
RRD/RRC	Regimental Reconnaissance Detachment / Regimental Reconnaissance Company. Both the same unit, but when the Regiment stood up the Regimental Special Troop Battalion, RRD became RRC
RRF	Ranger Readiness Force. References the alert status of a Ranger unit
RTB	Return to Base
RTO	Radio Telephone Operator. Typically attached to the ground force commander's hip, he carries and mans the primary radio during actions on the objective
SAW	Squad Automatic Weapon
SBF	Support by Fire
SCAR	Special operations forces Combat Assault Rifle. Available in light (5.56mm) and heavy (7.62mm) variants
SEAL	Navy's elite special operations force, short for 'SEa, Air, Land'
SF	Special Forces. Refers specifically to the 1st Special Forces Regiment, an Army special operations unit. They are also commonly known as Green Berets, for their distinctive head gear

SFC	Sergeant First Class. Usually controls a platoon
SGT	Sergeant. Usually controls a three to four-man element
Skedco	A draggable rescue system for pulling or carrying immobilized casualties to safety
SMU	Special Missions Unit. Refers to units that fall solely under the Joint Special Operations Command. Commonly referred to as 'Tier One' units in the media
SOAR	Special Operations Aviation Regiment. References the 160th SOAR, which provides special operations aviation platforms for all SOF
SOCOM	Special Operations Command. Oversees all special operations units from all branches
SOF	Special Operations Forces
SOFA	Status of Forces Agreement. Cooperation between governments to allow military operations of one nation within another's borders
SOP	Standard Operating Procedure
SPC	Specialist. Usually a member of a fire team
Squirters	Term used for any enemy that runs from the objective
SSE/I	Sensitive Site Exploitation/Information. The search for intelligence after an objective has been cleared
SSG	Staff Sergeant. Usually controls a six to nine-man element.
Stryker	Armored troop-carrying vehicle that has wheels instead of tracks, commonly used for ground movement of combat forces
STT	Special Tactics Team. Comprised of Air Force CCT and occasionally PJ and TACP personnel. Responsible for most tasks related to managing air assets during an operation

TACP	Tactical Air Control Party. Air Force forward air controllers. Traditionally consist of two personnel, a Joint Terminal Attack Controller (JTAC) and an apprentice radio operator. Now often operate singly
TF	Task Force
ToT	Time on Target. The time that the element will arrive at the objective
TSAF	"This Shit Ain't Free" - a saying in the Ranger community, made popular by a 3/75 Ranger who started a company by the same name
TST	Time Sensitive Target. A target that comes up on short notice and must be acted upon quickly
USASOC	United States Army Special Operations Command. Refers to the branch that oversees all Army special operations units
XO	Executive Officer. The second in command in a military unit
WARNO	Warning Order. Preliminary notice of order or action soon to follow

THE RANGER CREED

Recognizing that I volunteered as a Ranger, fully knowing the hazards of my chosen profession, I will always endeavor to uphold the prestige, honor, and high esprit de corps of my Ranger Regiment.
Acknowledging the fact that a Ranger is a more elite soldier, who arrives at the cutting edge of battle by land, sea, or air, I accept the fact that as a Ranger, my country expects me to move further, faster, and fight harder than any other soldier.

Never shall I fail my comrades. I will always keep myself mentally alert, physically strong, and morally straight, and I will shoulder more than my share of the task, whatever it may be, one hundred percent and then some.

Gallantly will I show the world that I am a specially selected and well trained soldier. My courtesy to superior officers, neatness of dress, and care of equipment shall set the example for others to follow.
Energetically will I meet the enemies of my country. I shall defeat them on the field of battle for I am better trained and will fight with all my might.
Surrender is not a Ranger word. I will never leave a fallen comrade to fall into the hands of the enemy and under no circumstances will I ever embarrass my country.

Readily will I display the intestinal fortitude required to fight on to the Ranger objective and complete the mission, though I be the lone survivor.

RANGERS LEAD THE WAY!
-CSM NEAL R. GENTRY

ABOUT THE AUTHOR

Marty Skovlund, Jr. was born and raised in Huron, South Dakota, where he enlisted in the U.S. Army immediately after high school. His first assignment was to the 1st Battalion, 75th Ranger Regiment. While at 1/75, he served in a variety of roles and deployed to both Iraq and Afghanistan on multiple occasions. After his fifth deployment, he volunteered for recruiting duty and was assigned to the Syracuse Recruiting Battalion as a recruiting NCO. In 2012, he founded Blackside Concepts, LLC and separated from the Army after eight years of service in June 2013 to run his business full time. After three years, he sold his business to focus on his newfound goals as a writer and filmmaker. He is happily married with his wife of seven years, and is father to a beautiful little girl - their first. He currently resides in his hometown of Huron.

CPSIA information can be obtained
at www.ICGtesting.com
Printed in the USA
BVHW041741181118
533441BV00016B/271/P

9 780998 900506